D1275752

Mixed Media

Mixed Media, Second Edition, introduces readers to the tools necessary for making moral and ethical decisions regarding the use of mass media. The chapters in this text offer insights on:

- Similarities and differences among the ethical dilemmas faced by the mass media
- Common ground on which to evaluate media behavior
- Media obligations
- Professional ethics
- Ethical theory and its application to the modern media
- Considerations of truth and harm

New to the second edition is a focus on the three mass media industries most pervasive in today's society: the news media (journalism), advertising, and public relations, with individual chapters giving equal coverage to each. It includes an increased emphasis on "new media" and how ethics affect such concepts as social media, word-of-mouth marketing, and citizen journalism. Readers will come away with a greater appreciation for moral philosophy and theory as a foundation for decision making, and will develop a personal "yardstick" by which to measure their decisions.

This text has been developed for courses covering ethics in public relations, advertising, and journalism. Offering valuable lessons applicable to all forms of communication, Mixed Media serves as a critical starting point for understanding and developing answers to ethical questions. These lessons serve not only to better students' ability to make ethical decisions, but also to better the media professions as they become practitioners in the mass media industry.

Thomas Bivins is the John L. Hulteng Chair in Media Ethics in the School of Journalism and Communication at the University of Oregon where he is the head of the Graduate Certificate Program in Communication Ethics. He has worked in television and radio broadcasting, advertising, corporate public relations, and as a graphic designer and editorial cartoonist. He is the author of books on media ethics, public relations writing, publication design, advertising, and newsletter publication.

Mixed Media

Moral Distinctions in Advertising, Public Relations, and Journalism

Second Edition

Thomas Bivins

Routledge
Taylor & Francis Group

NEW YORK AND LONDON

First edition published 2004
by Lawrence Erlbaum Associates

This edition first published 2009
by Routledge
270 Madison Ave, New York, NY 10016

Simultaneously published in the UK
by Routledge
2 Park Square, Milton Park, Abingdon, Oxon OX14 4RN

Routledge is an imprint of the Taylor & Francis Group, an informa business

© 2004 Lawrence Erlbaum Associates
© 2009 Taylor & Francis

Typeset in Goudy by Prepress Projects Ltd, Perth, UK
Printed and bound in the United States of America on acid-free paper
by Sheridan Books, Inc.

Library of Congress Cataloging in Publication Data
Bivins, Thomas H. (Thomas Harvey), 1947–
Mixed media: moral distinctions in advertising, public relations, and journalism/Thomas Bivins. — 2nd ed.
p. cm.
Includes bibliographical references.
1. Mass media—Moral and ethical aspects. I. Title.
P94.B53 2009
175—dc22
2008048441

ISBN10: 0-8058-6321-4 (pbk)
ISBN10: 0-203-87488-9 (ebk)

ISBN13: 978-0-8058-6321-5 (pbk)
ISBN13: 978-0-203-87488-2 (ebk)

Our job is not to make up anybody's mind, but to open minds and to make the agony of decision making so intense you can only escape by thinking.

Fred Friendly

Contents

Preface

Media professionals spend a great deal of time talking about "doing the right thing." Why is it then that the consumers of mass media perennially find so much fault with the ethics of the disseminators of news, information, and entertainment? What has led the purveyors of mass communication to believe and act the way they do? Do they have a special obligation for ethical behavior that ordinary citizens do not; or do they, in fact, have a special waiver of the basic moral tenets that the rest of us must accept in order that we may have access to a "free marketplace of ideas"? These are the questions we must ask ourselves if we are to be moral agents of the mass media.

This book is designed to familiarize you with the tools needed to make moral decisions regarding the use of mass media, both as a consumer of the "products" of the media and as a potential working member of the media. You should realize from the outset that there are no "right" answers in this book—only answers that are "most appropriate" in certain situations. To whom they are the most appropriate is a major concern of this book. Many questions will be asked, and many answers will be discussed. Ultimately, it will be up to you to draw your own conclusions about the rightness of the answers you choose to accept. It is to be hoped that you will come away with a greater appreciation for the complexities of making a moral decision. At the very least, you will be forced to develop a personal yardstick by which to measure your decisions.

The Scope of this Book

This book has been written with three primary mass media industries in mind: the news media (journalism), advertising, and public relations. Although entertainment media, such as television and the movie industry, are certainly worth investigating, these three are the ones most likely to attract the future practitioners now learning their craft in the journalism and communication programs so prevalent in our colleges and universities today. The lessons learned concerning ethical behavior within these three industries are lessons that can be applied to any other form of communication, information-based or other.

In addition, much has already been written concerning the entertainment industries and their effect on our culture. And, certainly, volumes have been penned bemoaning the state of modern journalism. However, advertising and, especially, public relations are often given short shrift or—worse—compared with journalism, assuming that the moral dictates of the one will apply across the board to the others. That is rarely the case, and this book is designed to point out the differences that exist among these three practices in hopes that reasonable and specific guidelines can be developed by which they may be analyzed and, if need be, judged according to their specialized functions within our society. Ultimately, the dicta of truth and minimizing harm should apply to all mass media, but in differing doses and for decidedly different reasons.

The Structure of the Book

The only possibility of arriving at anything approaching a satisfactory response to our moral dilemmas lies not with rote answers to prepackaged questions, but with real sweat that comes only from real thinking. And real thinking can only happen if the thinkers understand as much how to think as what to think about.

The ethical dilemmas faced by the mass media are not unique to them alone; however, the appropriate responses to those dilemmas are often dictated by the position of importance the media hold in our society. The media are different enough from the rest of society to require a different set of ethical guidelines. And they are different enough from each other that no single set of standards suffices for all of them. They differ in a great many ways: Chief among these are their differing goals and loyalties. In Chapter 1, we look at their similarities and differences and discuss whether there is any common ground on which to evaluate media behavior.

The media are powerful but, like the rest of us, they do not operate in a vacuum. Because they are an integral part of our society, everything they do affects everything else. And, like the rest of us, they are obligated to a great many people by virtue of those effects. Many journalists will say that they are not obligated in any way except by their "natural" charge to serve the public interest. However, no media institution can ignore the potential harm it does by ill-considered or knee-jerk decisions. Obligation is at the heart of much that is presented in this book. Although our society strongly favors individual freedom, we also recognize that without community we are simply isolated and self-interested beings. Somewhere, a balance must be struck between individual autonomy and community interests. The news media have traditionally shown a mistrust of anything that smacks of subjectivity. They claim that their professional autonomy is impugned each time they are asked to care. On the other hand, both advertising and public relations are nothing if not subjective. They, however, are asked to care as much for their audiences as for their clients—a task that may be as difficult to carry out as that of the subjective journalist. To whom the media are obligated and why is discussed in Chapter 2, and frequently throughout the book. It is a central theme of this text.

If the media are professions, as some claim, then they must consider the consequences of their actions on all affected parties. This doesn't mean that they must cater to all interests. It means that they should at least recognize all interests. Professionals value autonomy, possibly above all else. Without the ability to make decisions free from outside pressure, the education and expertise of the professional would be wasted. However, part and parcel of being a professional is the charge to serve the public interest and to mitigate harm to those affected by any actions taken on behalf of a client or a "public good." Professional status brings with it a duty to honor professional standards; it does not imply a total disregard of personal ethics or societal norms. Professional ethics are discussed in Chapter 3.

A good portion of this book is devoted to exploring how ethical theories can be applied in modern-day moral decision making. Don't be afraid of these theories. After all, they represent merely the thoughts of those who would have us act "morally," or in the "right" way. It is clearly impossible to bring every relevant theory to bear in any single book; however, there are certain theorists who are repeatedly mentioned in leading texts on applied ethics in fields from business to medicine, law to mass media. You will find that they, like us, don't always agree with one another. You will also find that parts of their theories are debatable. That's the nature of theories. As Mark Twain said, "There's . . . [a] trouble about theories: there's always a hole in them somewheres . . . if you look close enough." Ethical theory and its application to the modern media is discussed in Chapter 4.

Chapter 5 outlines a method for ethical decision making based on the many questions dealt with in this book and on a thorough understanding of the theories presented here. This worksheet is an admission that there are multiple factors affecting moral decision making and myriad approaches to solving ethical dilemmas. It is also designed to lead you through the process in a way that encourages you, as a moral agent, to consider the full range of variables inevitably involved in moral decision making. Although this book was written for college students, a great many professionals have successfully used this checklist, including lawyers, doctors, nurses, accountants, clergy, and media practitioners of all kinds. It is placed here in the book because it demonstrates concretely how to use the theory discussed in the preceding chapter.

No media professional can justify lying. To tell the truth is the first (and some would say, the only) commandment of professional communicators. Certainly, it is as important to advertising and public relations as it is to journalism; however, the way in which the truth is revealed can be quite different and can offer special challenges to media professionals. Both truth and lying can hurt, and mitigating harm is one of the chief obligations of the media. Harm can be confined to a few or encompass millions. At the heart of any attempt to avoid harm is a responsibility to care about those whom we affect by our actions—care enough to honor their dignity and preserve both their integrity and ours. Ultimately, telling the truth and avoiding harm is what media ethics is all about. Virtually every dilemma faced by the media today boils down to either truth or harm, or both. We must recognize the different "truths" of the media professions in order that we may set realistic standards for this greatest of obligations. We must also care enough about our audience that the thought of harming them, even incidentally, will give us pause. And if we pause long enough, we may come up with a solution to our dilemmas that results in the least amount of harm being done to anyone. After all, the media exist to help, not to harm. The vital considerations of truth and harm are taken up in detail in Chapter 6.

Chapter 7 introduces public relations and advertising and begins a discussion of the ethical issues common to both practices, including First Amendment constraints, and the nature of persuasion and propaganda. Some additional, contemporary theories are also introduced dealing with the way consumers process messages, especially persuasive ones. Since persuasion is central to what both public relations and advertising do, it is important to understand it as fully as possible before dealing with the specifics of either profession.

Chapters 8, 9, and 10 tackle the complex ethical issues associated with public relations, advertising, and news journalism, respectively. It is here that the ethical details of issues specific to each of these media are fleshed out. Much of what is covered in these chapters deals with the current state of each of these industries; however, it would be a serious mistake to ignore the impact of modern technology on the future of the mass media. So, each chapter also deals with the uses and effects of "new media" on public relations, advertising, and news journalism, and the ethical considerations that are inherent in all forms of mass communication.

Chapter 10 begins with a discussion of the "big picture" issues encountered in news journalism: objectivity and bias. Aside from that difference, these three chapters follow roughly the same format. The relevant industry is defined and recent scholarly research delineating the broader ethical landscape is presented, followed by a discussion of the most common ethical issues in each area including examples of these issues and recommended solutions. These solutions are often developed through research devoted specifically to the issue being discussed.

Can It Work?

A great many decisions are made under deadline pressure, nearly all of them the result of experience. Let us add to that experience the ability to weigh the pros and cons of the ethical facets of our decisions. Certainly it is true that practice makes perfect and that the more we practice moral decision-making skills the more finely honed they will become. After all, the public doesn't necessarily fault the media for coming down on one side of an issue or the other as much as it faults them for doing so in a seemingly knee-jerk way, or for falling back on their First Amendment rights as the only justification for their actions. If we can simply prove to them that we thought about these dilemmas seriously before making an educated decision, we may actually gain some respect.

Ultimately, the lessons learned in each such process serve not only to better our ability to make decisions, but also to better our professions as we become more productive, and more ethical, members of the mass media.

Acknowledgements

This second edition is a significant revision of the original and is based on the thoughtful advice and help of a great many people. Chief among those are the reviewers and users of the book whose praise and criticism helped me in determining what has worked and what needed improvement: Jay Black, University of South Florida, St. Petersburg; Allison Harthcock, Butler University; and Lee Wilkins, University of Missouri. I owe them a great deal. The patient and kind people at Routledge/Taylor & Francis, including Kerry Breen and her predecessors at Lawrence Erlbaum, have been key players in the production of this book, and I thank them all. I especially thank the Senior Editor, Linda Bathgate, who has been with me since the very beginning of the first edition and has gently urged me every step of the way with encouraging emails and personal meetings at nearly every professional and academic conference I have attended for the past six or seven years. I owe her a dinner. I would also like to thank my friend and colleague Jane Marcellus for her insightful reading of several of my new chapters. Without her, I might have never found my real voice and been buried instead beneath the heap of information I had collected. And I want to thank my students, for whom I wrote the book in the first place. They have been boldly honest with both their praise and their complaints. I have responded as best I could. After all, they are and always will be my audience. Finally, although it has become clichéd to thank one's spouse, I would like to thank my wife Lonnie. She has encouraged me when I was discouraged, prodded me when I was procrastinating, and chided me when I refused to leave my computer for days on end. You can't please everybody, but she makes me believe that I've pleased her. I hope I have.

Chapter 1

What is Media Ethics?

Always do right. That will gratify some of the people, and astonish the rest.

(Mark Twain)

Ethics and the Act of Communication

Communication is basic to being human, and is essential for social interaction. But because communication plays a significant role in influencing others and because intent is so important as a motivation, the likelihood that ethical issues will arise as a result of communication is great indeed. The fact that media practitioners consciously choose specific means of communication in order to reach a desired end pretty much guarantees that issues of right and wrong will arise.[1]

Most of us accept that much media-originated speech is designed to influence, in one way or another, our attitudes and behaviors. We distinctly do not, however, accept that that speech will or should be allowed to force us into a particular attitude or behavior through such methods as deception, coercion, carelessness, or even laziness.

It is clear that the act of communication is inextricably bound up with the potential for ethically questionable practices. How mass media communicators unravel that knot is the subject of the rest of this book.

Ethics or Morals?

Would you feel worse if someone called you unethical or if someone called you immoral? Most of us react differently to these two words, but we can't quite pin down the reason why. Ethics has come to be recognized as the study of concepts such as *ought*, *should*, *duty*, and so on, whereas *moral* tends to be attached to activities that are either good or bad and the rules that we develop to cover those activities. Some prefer to think of morals as being culturally transmitted indicators of right and wrong whereas ethics is merely a way to determine what we ought to do. We tend to associate *immorality* with the Judeo-Christian concept of sin and, because of the long-standing Puritan heritage within our culture, sin is most often equated with evil. *Unethical*, on the other hand, has become a more acceptable term in our modern culture because it tends not to carry the connotation of *evil* doing; rather it is used most often to connote *wrong* doing (versus doing right). In a sense, to be ethical or unethical rather than moral or immoral seems to be a reflection of modernity and connotation rather than representative of any real differences in meaning. In fact, it wouldn't be improbable to suggest that the words *ethical* and *unethical* would more likely be heard (if at all) in newsrooms and media agencies than *moral* and *immoral*.

For our purposes, however, the terms will be used pretty much interchangeably, except when noted otherwise. In fact, the technical term for making ethical decisions is *moral decision making*, a term that will be used throughout this book.

The Media and Morality

Whether the media simply reflect our cultural morality or they directly influence that morality is a question of considerable debate and disagreement. Undeniably, the media influence our lives in myriad ways—some good, some not so good. We rely on them for information vital to our daily lives, including everything from hurricane alerts to the variety of products available for headache relief. They also sell us ideas and images we might not otherwise be exposed to were it not for the "mass" nature of the media. They can, and sometimes do, remind us of the joys of being human; but they just as often pander to our basest instincts.

The media reflect our lives in a number of ways as well. We see ourselves in newscasts, we wonder with commentators at the seeming increases in violence and other undesirable cultural trends, and we increasingly enjoy ever speedier and flashier entertainment. In fact, the debate over whether the media contribute to or merely reflect societal mores is really a false one. It is ridiculous to think that they don't do both. They do reflect what we are right now, sometimes distilled so much as to be simply a caricature, but reflective none the less. They also constantly test our reactions to change, and back off only when it becomes unprofitable for them not to do so. They may not innovate as much as many would like, but they do evolve, and so influence us in often subtle ways. Is this necessarily bad? No. All societies are organic in the sense that they are constantly changing. Modern mass media are both reflective of that change and effective agents of it.

Are the Media Prone to Ethical Dilemmas?

Truth be told, we are all probably prone to as many ethical dilemmas in our daily lives as most media people. Why, then, do we seem to attach so much importance to what the media do? The answer is varied and complex. First of all, the ethical dilemmas we face each day may not affect large numbers of people. Our decision to tell that "white" lie when our best friend confronts us with a new (and questionable) hair style affects only the two of us, at least initially.

But an editor's decision to run a questionable photo on the front page of the paper affects a great many people. An advertising executive's decision to run an ad symbolically demeaning women affects more than just the agency and the advertised product. Likewise, a public relations practitioner's decision to defend a political candidate's character when that character is clearly questionable certainly has ramifications far beyond the candidate himself and his personal life. These examples, and thousands like them, serve to point out the very public nature of media.

The media are not called "mass media" for nothing. Our individual daily actions don't, in Humphrey Bogart's famous words, "amount to a hill of beans" when compared with actions that affect the lives of millions. It is only logical, therefore, that the decisions the media make should come under closer scrutiny than our own. Additionally, there is some feeling that the media are playing a very different role from the one average citizens play in that they are acting to inform us on matters about which we would otherwise have little knowledge. In fact, the rationale used by nearly all forms of media (journalism, advertising, and public relations included) is that they are performing a public service by adding to the "marketplace" of information. However, that "public service" is certainly questionable given the amount of criticism leveled at all forms of media today. In fact, the notion that the media *should* perform a public service tends to set them apart from the rest of society and sets up an "us–them" attitude that is not totally without basis.

The Media Are Not Us

In other words, although the media, in some cases, represent us (as consumers of media) and in other cases represent others, in only the rarest of instances do they represent us directly. There is a school of thought that paints the news media, for instance, as the representative of the people, acting on their behalf in a "watchdog" function over government and other public agencies. However, that function is as much self-serving as not. We must never forget that the media also operate within a capitalistic system, not just a democratic one, and that we purchase the news as much as we purchase any other commodity. That relationship is, therefore, not totally one of representation—it is one also of exchange.

The democratic foundations of this country clearly indicate a place for the media. Many of the top thinkers of the eighteenth and nineteenth centuries held the role of the press to be a necessary component of a democratic system. Thomas Jefferson called the press "the best instrument for enlightening the mind of man." In his later life, however, even he spoke out against the abuses of the media of his day. The problem in understanding the place of the media in our democracy is that the media today are not constituted the same way that the media of our country's founders envisioned. By the twentieth century, the media had become imbued with all the trappings of modernity, and media scholars such as John Dewey and Walter Lippmann were starting to believe they no longer played an influential role in the democratic process. They had become, in the opinions of many, ineffective and self-serving, seeking only to entertain or impart their own opinions. The media had become estranged from the very society they were supposed to serve. Certainly, the media, especially the news media, changed as a result of such scrutiny in the early part of the twentieth century. Objectivity became the driving goal of journalism. Despite these changes, the media remain different from the people they serve, so different, in fact, that the average person doesn't really know what the media do—and, especially, how they make their decisions.

To realize that the media are not us is not necessarily to denigrate the media or their role in our society. It is simply to realize that the decisions the media make today are not always on our behalf (a subject that will be treated in more detail in Chapter 3). For example, when a local television news program airs a segment on a town meeting, it is, ostensibly, in the public interest. However, are the segments filled with entertainment also in the public interest? How much of the news is really there simply to attract our attention? How much is there to help us? When an advertising agency decides (with its client's approval) to run a series of ads depicting violence or using sexually charged visuals, is it in our best interest or in the interest of selling the product? Do public relations practitioners act on our behalf when they use "spin" to obfuscate the facts? The point is that the media are separate entities existing in a complex and competitive environment, and they can't always afford to act in our best interest. They must, of necessity, sometimes act in their own. What we would hope for, however, is that those instances would be limited to necessity and become not the rule but the exception.

Media Culture and the Clash of Priorities

When shiny new journalists, advertising executives, or public relations practitioners take their first jobs, they often do so with great expectations that they will be able to honor their personal ethical codes above all else. What a shock it is for them to discover that the industries in which they have chosen to work already have a pretty fair idea of how things should be done and have set their own "principles," which they expect will be used. This socialization is common to all media industries and even begins when many of these neophytes are still in school.

Ask a budding young journalist whether there are any circumstances under which the media should be censored (by others or even by themselves), and you will invariably receive an instantaneous and emphatic No! Similarly, ask an advertising major at any leading university whether there is a definition of "taste" that he or she would be willing to follow in creating ads for their clients, regardless of what the client wants. Guess what the answer will be?

A good example of how quickly socialization takes place was detailed by students from the School of Journalism & Communication at the University of Oregon recounting their experiences when thrust, suddenly, into the real world of crisis news gathering. A number of students were pressed into service by leading news organizations during the shootings at Thurston High School in Springfield, Oregon, in 1998. Their experiences make for an interesting case study in media socialization. Some simply accepted the roles they were assigned, adrenaline pumping. Others, having not yet shaken the thinking processes forced upon them by the routine of daily education, worried over the ethicality of their actions when asked, for example, to confront grieving parents for interviews mere hours after the deaths of their children.

We should not be surprised, then, that long-time media practitioners adhere, almost religiously, to principles and codes derived from "real world" experience rather than any "ivory tower" contemplation. For example, in a recent meeting of a student chapter of the Society of Professional Journalists (SPJ), a local news director was asked whether an incidence of undercover reporting by a local television news organization was deceptive and, thus, in violation of the ethical code of SPJ. The news director responded that such codes were made up by people who didn't understand the realities of real-life journalism. He was wrong, of course. The SPJ code was drafted by working journalists, the same as the major codes of both public relations and advertising were drafted by professionals in those areas. Unfortunately, this attitude pervades newsrooms and advertising and public relations agencies all across the country and is one of the chief obstacles to moral decision making.

In his book *Democracy Without Citizens*, Robert Entman says that the key to understanding modern journalism is to realize that it operates within the context of organizational structures and routines, and that these structures and routines provide for what he calls "news slant." In other words, the very way in which news is gathered and the routines of the process itself have had a detrimental effect on journalism. According to Entman, the media "are stymied on the demand side by the lack of public hunger for relevant information, and on the supply side by overreliance on elite services and the industrial imperatives of efficiency and profits."[2] The hunt for greater profit has led, in turn, to a need for efficiency, leading, finally, to a routine of dependency on whatever method of news gathering is easiest and fastest.

This media laziness, albeit not universal, is prevalent enough to be of concern. Although deadline pressure has always been a part of news gathering, the move toward greater efficiency is the direct result of economic pressure. The proliferation of magazine news programs on network television speaks directly to this approach. Hidden cameras, exposés, and other "investigative" techniques are very often the easiest methods of gathering some kinds of information (and certainly more attention-getting), and are often cheaper to produce and run than sitcoms and dramas, which are most often purchased from production companies.

When the priority of news gathering becomes to get the story fast, the temptation is great to shortcut not only the process but also any inclination to ponder troubling questions of ethicality. In short, the economic imperative may far out-weigh the moral imperative.

The Effects of Organizational Structure on Moral Decision Making

Pressures upon decision makers are not limited to economic factors. The roles we take on as media practitioners also imply a responsibility to perform certain functions associated with those roles. *Responsibility* could be defined as a *bundle of obligations associated with a job or function*. In other words, responsibility refers to more than just the primary function of a role; it refers to the multiple facets of that function. Reporters are responsible for covering newsworthy events, for example. As part of that responsibility, they are expected to present a fair and balanced account from an objective viewpoint. However, a more important ques-tion can be asked when assessing the ethical implications of roles associated with the media (or any occupation, for that matter): Does responsibility naturally equate with accountability? *Accountability* refers to *blaming or crediting someone for an action*—normally an action associated with a recognized responsibility.[3] The assumption, therefore, would be to hold a person who is responsible for an ac-tion accountable also for the results of that action. This position assumes that the responsible person is relatively autonomous, or free to make decisions as-sociated with his or her job without outside pressure or influence. And, under normal circumstances, we would hope that media practitioners—especially jour-nalists—would have that autonomy. However, the nature of "outside" influence has changed considerably over the past 25 years or so. Today, the most troubling influences in all forms of media can, and often do, come from the inside.

For example, can a major news organization that is overseen, or run directly, by an entertainment division make entirely autonomous decisions about its re-portage? As the three major network news operations (ABC, NBC, and CBS) can attest, the job of news becomes undeniably complex when the news divi-sion is subsumed by a large, non-news-oriented organization (Disney, General Electric, and Viacom, respectively). And when entertainment value is believed by non-news people to supersede news value (and those people are tacitly in charge), the groundwork is laid for a decision-making hierarchy that will gradu-ally dilute the authority of media practitioners to follow their own personal and professional directives.

Furthermore, the temptation to pass the buck on decisions of all types, includ-ing moral decisions, increases mightily as the organizational hierarchy becomes more complex. Increasingly, media are becoming big business. Newspapers are owned by conglomerates, public relations and advertising are often partners under the same ownership, and everywhere the entertainment function often overrides the information function. Decision making, likewise, is becoming at-tenuated with accountability spread thin throughout large and complex organi-zations. As pointed out earlier, the structure of the modern news organization, for example, plays a determining role in how news is gathered. In the same way, the structure of large organizations of any type tends to affect the way in which decisions are made.

Complex organizations tend toward decentralized decision making, which, in turn, calls for professionalized decision makers at every level.[4] The ideal would be for both the responsibility and the accountability of decision making to correlate. However, these same organizations lend themselves too readily to a dilution of accountability in decision making. Moral "buck passing" becomes the rule rather than the exception. It is too easy to blame others for decisions over which we have had minimal input or control. The public relations practitioner who is caught in a deception can, too easily, blame her client. An advertising executive can attempt to justify a tasteless ad as a client-based decision. Reporters can slough off blame for invasion of privacy on their editors. The softening of network news can be blamed on pressure from above. This failure to assume accountability for our actions because of "orders" from above is frequently referred to as the "Boorman defense," after the Nazi war criminal who uttered the now famous "I was only following orders." Although this label may seem to some to be extreme, the tendency toward moral buck passing will not lessen as long as organizational hierarchy encourages the dilution of responsibility and accountability.

As human beings, we seek accountability. We want to know who is responsible for certain actions and who is accountable for the consequences of those actions. The dilution of accountability now common to most large organizations (including media organizations) frustrates onlookers who can't determine who is to blame when something goes wrong. This confusion is exacerbated when factors other than media influence play a role in certain consequences. Consider the string of school shootings in 1998–1999. It was not uncommon to hear parents and others place much of the blame for what they considered "copycat" shootings on media coverage—and for all the shootings on media violence in general. The tendency to place blame is entirely normal; however, the degree of accuracy involved in assessing accountability is problematic at best.

Moral Excuses

Are there circumstances under which rational people will hold others not accountable for their actions, even though they are responsible? Most of us recognize a legitimate excuse when we hear one. There are several common "excuses" that we typically accept as valid when assessing blame. *Constraint*, for instance, refers to both physical imperatives and lack of alternatives. For example, if a person is coerced into doing something that he normally would not do, we tend not to blame him for that action. A bank clerk who is robbed at gunpoint is certainly responsible for the money in his till, but is not accountable for its loss. This is a physical constraint. The same would apply in a situation in which a person is constrained by lack of alternatives. For instance, a company is ordered to comply with new EPA regulations, but the technology needed to comply hasn't been fully developed yet. It cannot be held accountable for non-compliance until the technology is ready to go on line (as long as the company is attempting to comply in a timely fashion.).

We also tend to forgive in instances in which the outcome of an action could not reasonably have been predicted. An excellent example of this occurred in 1996 when *Newsweek* magazine decided to run a story on the US chief of naval operations Admiral Jeremy Michael (Mike) Boorda. It had come to the magazine's attention that the admiral was possibly wearing bronze Vs, signifying *valor*, on two of his 16 merit ribbons—an honor he had not technically earned. Although Boorda had been on combat duty aboard ship during the Vietnam War, he had not actually been in combat—a requirement for the attachment of the V to his ribbons. The admiral's office was contacted by *Newsweek* and an interview date was set. Shortly before the interview was to take place, Boorda committed suicide. Was the magazine in any way accountable for this tragedy? The newsworthiness of this story could certainly be questioned. Boorda had already discontinued wearing the ribbons several years before. What possible motive could *Newsweek* have for wanting to run a story this long after the fact? Even assuming for the moment that the story might have had some news value, we must still ask ourselves whether *Newsweek* could have reasonably expected that the subject of its story would commit suicide over the disclosure that he was assuming an honor he did not, in fact, earn? Probably not. Despite this aspect, however, we must still consider in what way the magazine contributed to the final outcome and question whether or not the harm could have been mitigated or avoided altogether. This is a subject we will take up in detail in Chapter 6.

Let us return briefly to the notion that accountability for moral decision making has become diluted in modern mass media organizations. If this is, in fact, even partly true, what is to become of our personal ethical standards once we become enveloped in the complexities of mass media structures and routines?

Can Personal Ethics Become Professional Ethics?

So far, we've been talking about the elements of modern media that make compromising personal principles highly likely; however, there are other principles not usually questioned by the media that also potentially compromise personal values—the importance of privacy, for instance. For journalists, personal views on the importance of privacy can potentially be overridden by a professional principle of providing the public with information useful to them. The obligations incurred by an individual assuming a professional role may, in fact, differ radically from personal obligations. For example, it may never be appropriate for a private individual to reveal secrets about someone that might result in that person's reputation being ruined, even if the information is true. Take that same private individual and make her a journalist whose job is to investigate the extramarital love affair of the President of the United States, and her actions might not only be deemed appropriate, they might prove to be necessary.

The point is that when we adopt a profession whose entire reason for being is to provide information, we may find the obligations of that job may, and generally do, supersede those of our personal lives. By letting our personal principles take first priority, we could be compromising our professional principles. The question then becomes: Which do we want most to be, a private citizen or a media professional? Although the two roles are not mutually exclusive, there is an awareness that one assumes the mantle of professionalism willingly, accepting that a muting of personal values is part of the payment for doing so.

This does not mean that we suddenly become immune to human suffering or deaf to pleas for civility or good taste. It simply means that professional values may, and often do, outweigh personal values. A good example, and one that will be dealt with in more detail in Chapter 6, has to do with harm. From a perspective of needing to mitigate harm that might be caused by our actions, we must decide how much harm we will allow before the option that would bring about that harm is no longer viable. The first two choices are easy: If more harm than benefit will occur because of our action, we should refrain from taking it. If more benefit than harm is likely to accrue, we should take the action. However, what are we to do when the harm and the benefits are equal? A personal principle might tell us to err on the side of caution and not take the action. But what about our professional obligations? What do they dictate? As a journalist, for instance, the decision about whether to run a story or not may depend on the amount of harm versus benefit that might transpire as a result. If the benefit outweighs the harm—publish. If the harm outweighs the benefit—don't publish. If harm and benefit appear to be equal—publish. Why? Because our default position as a professional journalist is to provide information unless there is a good reason not to. And although this may differ from our personal obligations, it should nonetheless be honored. After all, that is the path we have chosen to take.

To some degree personal and professional principles will certainly mesh. However, deference is usually, and possibly rightly, given to professional principles. After all, those principles ideally have been established for good reasons—reasons that go beyond satisfying personal values. The ultimate test of any principle, personal or professional, must be the efficacy of the resulting actions based on those principles—not just for the person acting (the moral agent), but for all those involved or affected by the action.

Media Similarities: The Common Threads

The media are alike in a number of ways. The most common connection is that they are all mass media—that is, they deliver their information to mass audiences and/or seek to inform or influence large audiences through mass distribution of messages. Aside from their "mass" nature, however, the media are similar in other ways as well.

From an ethical perspective, they all are obligated to moral claimants: those who have some stake in our decisions. They are affected by what we do or say. We will discuss the nature of this obligation to our moral claimants in detail in the next chapter. For now, we can assume that journalism, advertising, and public relations all have claimants to whom they are obligated, be they employers, clients, or various other constituencies. In fact, as will be discussed in Chapter 3, some pretense of obligation to the public interest is, at least tacitly, part of the assumed duties of all of these occupations.

The media under discussion here all profess a duty to truth telling. The ideal of truthful information is at the heart of all communication and is assumed as the normal default in our everyday exchanges with each other. Any mass medium without a basic obeisance to truth would fail to impress any of its constituents. This is not to say that all mass media treat truth the same way, or even define it the same way. It does indicate, however, the place of truth telling in our basic conception of communication. Truth will be discussed more fully in Chapter 6.

In addition to truth telling, the mass media share a duty of avoidance of harm toward their constituents. This is one of the most difficult areas to assess since each of the mass media, again, tend to define harm differently. However, to the extent that harm is an undesirable outcome of most legitimate mass communication, its avoidance is a shared desire among the media. It serves no purpose, for instance, for advertisers to intentionally harm their markets. When this does occur (as in cigarette advertising), we are quick to grasp the ethical implications. Harm will be discussed in more detail in Chapter 6.

Finally, the mass media also share a need for credibility, for without credibility their messages are less effective, even unbelievable (regardless of how truthful they may be). Credibility is closely tied to truth telling. Sources known for their veracity are more likely to be held as credible, and looked to for information in the future. Credibility can be damaged in a number of ways. News outlets can lose credibility by lack of accuracy or by seeming to be biased. Advertisers lose credibility by peddling false claims or by insensitivity to market tastes. Public relations practitioners lose credibility by not being open enough in their dealings with news media. And these are only a few examples of how credibility can be compromised. A mass medium without credibility is doomed to have its message ignored by its proposed target audience. Credibility also implies trust, a topic that will be taken up when we discuss the professional nature of the mass media in Chapter 3.

Ultimately, however, it's not by their similarities that we tend to distinguish among the media, but by their differences. It would be a false assumption to believe that we can judge the ethicality of any action taken in one form of media by the template used to judge another. To some degree, the similarities will help us reach a common ground from which we may then depart into an exploration of the differences. In order to successfully discuss media ethics, we must fully understand what sets the media apart, but we must not ignore the ways in which they are alike—despite protestations to the contrary.

Media Differences: A Coat of Many Colors

Whereas the media are set apart from society in some ways, they are also set apart from each other in ways that are often even more significant. For instance, although truth telling may be a primary value among all the media, how that value is constituted and how it is honored may be quite different. And, although the public is definitely a major stakeholder in any media activity, the ethical obligation to that public may be conceived of in very different ways by the different media. Perhaps the most instructional way to envision the key differences among the media is to investigate two important aspects: their goals and their loyalties.

Media Goals

What do the media hope to accomplish? The answer to that question points directly to the major differences among the media. The goals established by the various media are sometimes explicit, sometimes implicit. Increasingly, those goals include turning a profit (a goal we sometimes pretend is unique to today's world). Although profit is certainly an acceptable goal in a capitalist system, it should not be the only goal—especially given the expectations we place on our media in this country. Our expectations, to a large degree, also shape the goals of the media. However, all communication has in common a primary set of goals. Which of the set is used at any given time depends on the medium and the purpose to which the communication is being put. The most common of those goals are information dissemination, persuasion, and entertainment. Naturally, each of these approaches to communication can overlap the others and each can be used in support of the others. For example, an advertisement may be entirely informative; however, its ultimate goal may be to persuade. Entertainment may be used to introduce information or to make the persuasive process more palatable. In most public relations campaigns, for instance, informational communication usually precedes communication aimed at attitude or behavioral change. With this in mind, let's take a look at the most likely goals of each of the media in question.

Goals of the News Media

What would you imagine to be the primary goal of the news media? The received ideal, of course, is that the United States is based on the notion of popular rule. Public opinion (the basis of that rule) is to be expressed periodically through elections, and opinion, in turn, can best be cultivated by a free and vigorous press. Can we infer from this ideal, then, that the goal of the news media (or journalism in general) is to keep the electorate informed? If we still believe in the ideal of journalism, we must accept this as the primary goal. After all, doesn't the First Amendment guarantee the right to a free press? Although not explicitly stated in that amendment, the obligation of the media is generally understood to be as stated above—providing, first, information we need to fulfill our roles as citizens.

As we've come to expect, however, there is more than one goal involved here. The news media also give us what we *want*, which typically leads to a sort of dynamic tension between the two extremes. It is a given that in order to give us what we need, the media also often have to give us what we want. In the early part of this century, philosopher John Dewey envisioned a press that would combine insider information and popular appeal. He knew that giving us only what we needed would prove a useless endeavor. Striking that balance between the "medicine" and the "spoonful of sugar" needed to get it down may be modern journalism's greatest test. In the words of the communication scholar Richard Johannesen,

> The search is for an appropriate point between two undesirable extremes—the extreme of saying only what the audience desires and will approve and the extreme of complete lack of concern for and understanding of the audience.[5]

Clearly, then, the goal of the news media is to bring the public information that both informs and interests them. Let's leave it at that for the time being and move on to two other, vastly different, forms of media: advertising and public relations.

Goals of Advertising

The argument has been made, somewhat successfully, that both advertising and public relations, like the news media, provide important information to the public. Advertising, for instance, has long claimed that the information it provides is of vital interest to (and, in fact, is needed by) the public. This view has been supported by the Supreme Court, which held that the public's decisions regarding commercial purchases need to be "intelligent and well informed," clearly placing advertising communication into the category of *needed* information. Given this, what then would you suppose the goal of advertising would be?

Certainly one of the goals is to inform the public about the availability of and details about various products and services. But couldn't we also say that the ultimate goal of advertising is to sell something? Whereas the first goal seems to align nicely with that of the news media in that the information is designed to lead us to a knowledgeable decision, the second tends to strike us as indicating a decidedly vested interest. However, couldn't we say the same sort of thing about the news media? Isn't the combination of information and entertainment now so adroitly packaged by nearly every news outlet designed to "sell" us the news? Is this any different from advertising? The answer, of course, is yes. Even conceding that news may be packaged to sell, the "product" we end up with is still information we need (in the ideal sense, at least). The product we end up with in response to advertising is vastly different. The primary goal of advertising, then, is more likely to be to sell a product than to impart information. Like public relations, however, advertising may inform or entertain in order to persuade later.

Goals of Public Relations

Like the news media and advertising, one of the primary goals of public relations is to inform. The goal of information dissemination can be the sole purpose of communication, as when performed by a government public information officer or as published in those countless booklets from the government clearing house in Pueblo, Colorado. As mentioned earlier, public relations often begins with information, then moves to persuasion; however, depending on the overall goal of the campaign, public relations communication, like advertising, can begin directly with persuasion. And, like advertising, the information produced by public relations can also be viewed as contributing to the "marketplace of ideas." In fact, this is a point that needs to be made on behalf of both advertising and public relations. There is a school of thought that holds that public communication of any kind potentially contributes to public debate.

I. F. Stone, in *The Trial of Socrates*, traces the history of western democracy to the living democracy of the Greeks—specifically the Athenians—who valued open discourse above all else. In fact, the idea that human beings had intelligence sufficient to be reached by reasoned argument was so embedded in the Athenian culture that they designated a goddess of persuasion.[6] Stone suggests that such a divinity represented not only democracy, but also the ideal way to achieve it—persuasion through reasoned discourse. To many early Greek philosophers, *rhetoric* implied persuasion. So important was the ability to represent oneself in open debate, that an entire class of teachers of rhetoric evolved (sophists) whose purpose was to teach the methods of rhetorical persuasion to those unfortunate enough to not have been formally schooled in it.

If we trace the rise of modern democracy to those Greek roots, we can draw a parallel as well between persuasion as a cornerstone of the entire political system and the necessity for providing each citizen a voice in that system, regardless of the issue or political alignment. It could be said that the provision of such ability serves the public interest in the ideal way—by providing for a free, balanced, and open debate among democratic equals. In this sense, both advertising and public relations parallel the theory of journalism, which is based on the belief that the public good is being served through the free expression of its practice. The very notion of a free press relies on the understanding of how such a device fits into and contributes to the ideal of free speech, which is most often construed to mean a citizen's right of access to all sides of an issue.

Ultimately, however, public relations must admit to sharing with advertising the time-honored goal of persuasion through communication—a goal not in the least ignoble. But, it must also not succumb to the temptation to make more of its motives than they legitimately merit. Public relations is not journalism, and needn't have any pretense to the goals of that practice in order to become legitimate. Both it and advertising are justifiable professions in their own rights.

Media Loyalties

One of the major differences among the media is the issue of loyalty. Loyalty can be defined as "faithfulness" or "allegiance." Loyalty also implies that something is owed to that to which we are loyal. Loyalty can be contractual, as in advertising and public relations (at least in most cases), or it can be implied, as in the news media's obligation to their public. In either event, the sense of owing or being obligated is part and parcel of what being loyal means. Here is where we begin to see real differences among the media, for where our loyalty lies is generally where our best efforts are devoted.

Loyalty in the News Media

Once we concede that the implied goal of the news media is to inform us, it is easier to understand where their loyalties *should* lie. Clearly, there would be an obligation to their primary constituency (the public) to bring them information that both informs and interests them. (*Interests* in the sense that it is information the public *wants*.) Since we will be discussing claimants (ethical stakeholders) in detail in Chapter 2, it is sufficient here to say that the loyalties of the news media are necessarily split. As noted, the primary claimant here is the public; however, loyalty must also extend to stockholders, publishers, owners, and so on. Thus, the reality of economic viability will certainly intrude on loyalty to the public, but for our purposes here let us assume that, in an ideal sense, first loyalty goes to the public receiving the information. In fact, the value that most journalists place on autonomy (the ability to remain largely free from outside pressure) practically insures that they will consider the public as their number-one claimant.

Loyalty in Advertising and Public Relations

At this point, it should be coming clear that for many purposes advertising and public relations have a good deal in common and are, thus, separated from journalism in some important ways. Loyalty is one of the most important of those ways.

Both advertising and public relations are client-based occupations. That is, they serve clients rather than the general public. The degree to which the purpose of either advertising or public relations is advocacy rather than counseling will determine the priority of loyalties. An advocate usually acts as an agent of the client, performing some service on the client's behalf or representing the client's interests.

Advocates are expected to be subjective—that is the nature of advocacy. Subjectivity brings with it an implicit understanding that one's first allegiance is to the client. To the advocate falls the job of bringing skills of persuasion to bear through methods and on issues often predetermined by the client. Since they often have no hand in arriving at either the focus or the nature of their advocacy, the question arises whether they can be expected to consider the broader implications of their actions—a question we will take up shortly. At this point, suffice it to say that client loyalty generally supersedes loyalty to any third party for both advertising and public relations.

Forming Ethical Standards for the Mass Media

Can we arrive at shared standards for the mass media? Probably not. Shared standards are not possible if we look at the various mass media as having different goals and differing sets of obligations to their constituencies. Whether they are shared or not, ethical standards of any type will require a devotion to ethical action, and ethical action often comes into conflict with our instinct to act in our own self-interest. This tendency toward egoism is manifested at every level of our lives and reflected not only in our actions but also in our deep-seated sympathy for the tenets of self-interest. We innately understand the desire of our employer to turn a profit, or of our media conglomerate to expand, or of our client to want to sell her product. We understand in the same way that we justify our own decisions to move ahead in life. That is why it is important to understand ethical standards from at least three perspectives: the personal, the professional, and the societal. By understanding the ethical principles associated with each level, we are less likely to act self-interestedly. However, it would be erroneous to assume that these levels are interchangeable or that a decision made using personal ethical standards would automatically apply at the professional or societal levels or vice versa.

Most of us tend to act at each of these levels with no particular priority assigned to any one, forgetting that we are obligated differently at each level. These obligations can, and often do, conflict. However, since we tend to assimilate ethical principles at each of these levels, we cannot truly separate them—nor should we. Instead, we must learn to recognize when professional standards override personal standards, or when obligations to society outweigh obligations to our employers or to ourselves. In other words, we must learn how and when the standards of each level apply. We cannot, try as we may, divorce ourselves from any of these standards and obligations and exist only on one level. How our standards develop at each level has much to do with our values and ideals, for from these two sources come our principles—the basis for our ethical actions at every level.

Values, Ideals, and Principles

When we say that truth is of paramount importance to journalism, we are stating a professional value. When we talk about believing in the sanctity of life, we are expressing a personal value. When we tout journalistic objectivity, we are really talking about an ideal in the same way that being virtuous may be a personal ideal. When we say that we will not print the names of rape victims, we are talking about a principle based on the value of privacy. Likewise, a principle of not printing the names of alleged perpetrators could be based on the ideal of "innocent until proven guilty." Although the differences among these three concepts may seem at first to be small, there are some distinct definitional contrasts.

Values

The educator and ethicist Clifford Christians defines values as those things that "reflect our presuppositions about social life and human nature."[7] Values cover a broad range of possibilities, such as aesthetic values (something is harmonious or pleasing), professional values (innovation and promptness), logical values (consistency and competency), sociocultural values (thrift and hard work), and moral values (honesty and non-violence).

Values are also further defined by philosophers as being either instrumental or intrinsic. An *instrumental value* is one that leads to something of even more value. For example, money usually is seen has having instrumental value, because possessing it leads to other things of greater value, including (we suppose) happiness. Other values, such as happiness, are said to possess *intrinsic* value—they are sought after because they are ends in and of themselves, and don't necessarily lead to greater values. As journalists, for instance, we could value truth telling because it leads to an honest account of what's happening in the world, which leads to our fulfilling our goals as reporters, which leads to us being satisfied with ourselves, which leads to happiness for us. Conversely, we could simply value truth telling as an end, as did Immanuel Kant (whom we will talk more about in Chapter 4). However, we need not trace every value through to its intrinsic conclusion; rather, we should simply be aware that some values can be ranked as more important to us because they are ends to be sought in themselves and not means to other ends.

Ideals

Ideals, on the other hand, are a bit easier to define. Vincent Ryan Ruggiero defines an *ideal* as "a notion of excellence, a goal that is thought to bring about greater harmony to ourselves and to others."[8] For example, our culture respects ideals such as tolerance, compassion, loyalty, forgiveness, peace, justice, fairness, and respect for persons. In addition to these human ideals are institutional or organizational ideals, such as profit, efficiency, productivity, quality, and stability.

As Ruggiero noted, ideals often come into conflict with each other. In such cases, decisions become much harder to make. Ruggiero, like many other ethicists, simply suggests that we honor the higher ideal. Of course, the higher ideal may not be that easy to determine. For example, a choice to place the journalistic ideal of providing information an audience wants over the societal ideal of honoring privacy could result in a decision to run a story that may, in fact, violate someone's privacy.

Principles

Principles are those guidelines we derive from values and ideals and are precursors to codified rules. They are usually stated in positive (prescriptive) or negative (proscriptive) terms. For example, "Never corrupt the integrity of media channels" would be a principle derived from the professional value of truth telling in public relations. Or "Always maximize profit" might be derived from belief in the efficacy of the free-enterprise system.

The ideals, values, and principles of the media will differ according to the differing goals and loyalties of each. Of course, there will be some common ground. Truth telling is an ideal agreed upon by all mass media. On the other hand, objectivity would be an acceptable ideal for journalism all the time, but only in rare cases for advertising and public relations. Freedom of speech is not only an ideal, but also a value. We value freedom of speech, but attaining total freedom may be idealistic (or even unrealistic).

When we begin to establish principles, we are committing ourselves to a course of action based on our values and ideals. When we act ethically, we typically act on principle. Principle can serve as a guideline for ethical action. That is why principles often tend to become codified, as policies, codes, or laws. A newspaper's policy against publishing the names of rape victims is probably based on a belief in privacy for victims of violent crimes. The principle of that belief (value) is to withhold the name, or non-disclosure. In the same way, valuing human life can lead to a principle of non-violence. In both cases, action (or inaction) is the result of the principle and is derived from it in the same way that the principle is derived from the value or ideal.

Normative Principles in Applied Ethics[9]

The following principles are the ones most commonly appealed to in applied ethical discussions:

- *Personal benefit*: acknowledge the extent to which an action produces beneficial consequences for the individual in question.
- *Social benefit*: acknowledge the extent to which an action produces beneficial consequences for society.
- *Principle of benevolence*: help those in need.
- *Principle of paternalism*: assist others in pursuing their best interests when they cannot do so themselves.

- *Principle of harm:* do not harm others.
- *Principle of honesty:* do not deceive others.
- *Principle of lawfulness:* do not violate the law.
- *Principle of autonomy:* acknowledge a person's freedom over his/her actions or physical body.
- *Principle of justice:* acknowledge a person's right to due process, fair compensation for harm done, and fair distribution of benefits.
- *Rights:* acknowledge a person's rights to life, information, privacy, free expression, and safety.

These principles represent a spectrum of traditional normative ethical principles and are derived from both consequentialist and duty-based approaches (see Chapter 4). The first two principles, personal benefit and social benefit, are consequentialist since they appeal to the consequences of an action as it affects the individual or society. The remaining principles are duty-based. The principles of benevolence, paternalism, harm, honesty, and lawfulness are based on duties (obligations) we have toward others. The principles of autonomy, justice, and the various rights are based on moral rights.

Policies

Policies, a step removed from codes, set principles into standards that we can then use to guide our actions. Policy standards are not intractable; rather they serve as indicators of our values and principles. As such, they are open to scrutiny and question, and even change as our values and principles may also change. Policies, even ethical policies, must be amenable to change in order to remain applicable to an often-changing environment. The key is to use a policy standard as a default position, subject to evaluation as warranted but acceptable at face value in most cases. Thus, deciding to reveal the name of a rape victim would have to be justified on grounds that superseded a newspaper's standard of nondisclosure based on its belief in the privacy of crime victims. Those grounds might include the victim's desire to be heard publicly combined with the paper's desire to put a real face to a crime statistic, for instance.

Keep in mind that policies are usually developed, not for entire industries, but for individual entities within those industries—newspapers, television news rooms, corporate public relations departments, advertising agencies, and so on. Industries and professions tend to codify policies into codes, the next step up the ladder of formalizing our ethical values. (See Figure 1.1.)

Professional Codes and the Law

Everyone knows that being legal doesn't necessarily mean being ethical. All media, at one time or another, have used the "It's not illegal so it must be all right" dodge. And, in truth, legality certainly plays an important part in ethicality. The

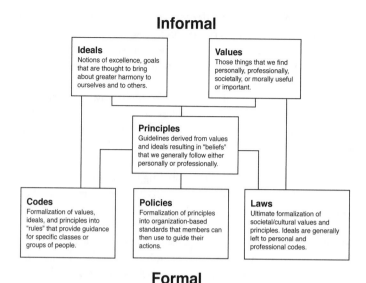

Figure 1.1 Construction of moral guidelines.

law, however, can only serve to prohibit the most obvious violations of societal standards. Its basic function is to codify the customs, ideals, beliefs, and moral values of a society. It is unreasonable to expect the law either to establish moral standards or to cover the vast array of human conduct. So whereas it may be legal to use sex to sell a product, for example, it may not be entirely ethical. That's where professional codes come in.

Professional codes tend to establish a general goal or ideal, or define the ideal practitioner, and generally indicate how to attain that goal or become that practitioner. Additionally, codes usually indicate to whom the practitioner is obligated and how. Because codes are typically occupation-specific, there tend to be as many different codes as there are professions, each with its own set of highly specialized prescriptions and proscriptions. However, there seems to be no set agreement as to the value of professional codes, a topic we will take up in more detail in Chapter 3. For now, suffice it to say that codes are the logical next step in the progression from identifying values, to developing principles, to setting standards, to creating policies. After codes would come the law, and, as we have seen, the law doesn't usually deal with moral matters.

Can the Media be Ethical?

The real question is: Do the media want to be ethical? The problem, as we shall see, is that the dictates of the various media professions often impose a "way of doing things" that clashes dramatically with societal norms. The routine of media work, and the accepted standards that rapidly socialize neophytes into the media occupations, frequently serve to blunt personal or societal principles. The accepted decision-making norm for most media is situational—every determination is made on a case-by-case basis, rendering consistency practically moot. The result is that the reputation of the media (in all its forms) has increasingly suffered in the eyes of the public. Every time a journalist invades a grieving family's privacy, the reputation of the entire profession suffers. Each deceptive or misleading advertisement is a black mark against all of advertising. And every public relations "dodge" used to avoid bad press results in achieving just that.

The single greatest roadblock preventing the media from ever conceding to constraint (even self-constraint) is their abiding belief in their "right" to do anything they want free from outside interference. However, rights are best served when tempered by obligation. As we shall see, the media are as obligated as any other entity by virtue of the effects they have on others. The web of obligation woven by every action having moral consequences is far-reaching and unavoidable. Those wishing to live without obligation to others would do well to heed the warning of the seventeenth-century philosopher Thomas Hobbes, who proposed that human beings without a sense of obligation to each other (in the form of a "social contract") would be but "solitary, poor, nasty, [and] brutish" creatures. In the words of the philosopher Henry Rosemont, Jr., "[The] manner in which we interact with others . . . will clearly have a moral dimension infusing all, not just some, of our conduct." That moral dimension would demand conduct effected with reciprocity, and governed by civility, respect, and affection for others.[10]

The modern mass media exist in an increasingly interrelated world, one in which every action has the potential to affect increasingly broader constituencies. We have only to look at the events of September 11 and the subsequent wars in Afghanistan and Iraq to understand how profoundly 24-hour news services and satellite delivery systems can affect global interaction. The key to moral decision making is to understand the interrelationships inherent in the actions of the mass media, and to consider the potential outcome of those actions from a perspective infused with care for others and a sense of obligation to serve rather than to prevail.

Chapter 2

Moral Claimants, Obligation, and Social Responsibility

It seems to me that a man should secure the well done, faithful servant, of his own conscience first and foremost, and let all other loyalties go.

(Mark Twain)

Whenever we make moral decisions, we affect other people. In fact, anyone who is affected by our decisions or has some effect on us could be considered a stakeholder—or, in the language of ethics, a moral claimant. This claimant could be our reading or viewing publics, the people who pay our salaries, our families, friends, those we are reporting on, their families, our fellow professionals, or virtually anyone. The fact that the media seriously affect so many complicates moral decisions, because we must consider all those affected or be found lacking by those whose moral claims we do not consider.

As mentioned in Chapter 1, our daily decisions as private individuals don't usually affect that many people, but the influence of even those private decisions may have repercussions far beyond our immediate circle. Imagine, then, the impact the media have on vast numbers of people every day. If we are to act as responsible media practitioners, we must consider all of those people every time we make a decision affecting them. In order to accomplish that, we must first decide exactly who those people are and what likely effect we will have on them. For all media there are *four primary claimant groups:*[1]

- our clients/customers;
- the organization for which we work;
- the profession of which we are a part;
- and society as a whole.

Naturally, the order in which we address these groups will depend on a number of variables, including:

- the media job we hold (in journalism, advertising, or public relations);
- the environment in which we are having to make a moral decision (political, economic, and social factors included);
- the nature of the decision itself;
- and the constraints we feel as a result of these other variables.

The danger is that because of these constraints, we are more likely to honor our obligations to those who most affect us rather than the other way around. For example, because of our reliance on clients (who provide our operating capital) in public relations and advertising, the tendency is to consider them our primary claimants, sometimes neglecting those whom we affect directly with our messages—our target publics or audiences. That's why it's important to develop an organized method of identifying moral claimants. If we understand our *functional* relationships with these various constituencies, we can then begin to sort out our *ethical* obligations to them.

Considering the consequences of our actions is one of the primary ways in which we define our relationships to others. We tend to avoid actions that result in negative consequences for others, and to promote actions that bear favorable consequences. An advertising agency, for example, promotes its client's interests because the consequence of not doing that would be the loss of the client. In other words, the client has potentially greater effect on the ad agency than vice versa. Likewise, the agency has a potentially greater effect on its target audiences (consumers) than the other way around—at least under normal conditions. And what about the advertising industry in general? Don't the actions of each agency affect the whole of the industry for better or worse? The same applies to news outlets. The mistake of one network television news anchor reflects not only on her, but on her network and on broadcast journalism as a whole. In other words, we are linked to all our stakeholders (constituents, publics, markets, audiences, etc.) by the effects our actions have on them and by the effects they have on us.

Relationships among Media and their Claimants

Since the various media and their constituents are interrelated (through effects), relationships among these parties become extremely important. How they affect each other is often a result of the level of dependency among the various parties. There are several identifiable relationships among parties based on level of dependency.[2]

- Those among parties that are *symmetrically independent*. That is, the parties are independent enough that each could survive the loss of the other. This sort of relationship allows for extreme flexibility, yet may allow hedging in the areas of obligation and duty since loss of, say, Party B is not crucial to Party A's survival and vice versa. For example a printing facility that runs the local weekly on its presses is dependent on the newspaper for part of its business. Likewise, the paper is dependent on the printer. However, both the printer and the paper could survive without each other if necessary. The printer will take on other clients and the paper will find another printer.
- Those among parties that are *asymmetrically dependent* on each other. This implies that although Party B may be dependent on Party A for survival, Party A may not be dependent on Party B. This allows for some leveraging

ability and potential coercion on the part of Party A as well as hedging in the areas of obligation and duty. For example, in order to save money, a company may cut employee salaries (or not raise them), increase work demands, or otherwise mistreat employees who may be completely reliant on the company for a job. This would be "hedging" on the company's obligation to its employees.

- Those in which the parties are so *interdependent* that neither can survive without the other. Two or more parties engaged in this type of coexistence must reach mutual understanding and compromise in order to survive. The relationship between the entertainment "news" industry and the celebrities that they cover is this type of association. Neither the industry nor the "stars" it covers can survive without each other. Some level of compromise must be reached in order for them to survive. This causes an ongoing tension between the parties that is managed only by constant adjustment in the relationship in order to maintain balance.

It is important to note that these categories may not apply to a given relationship among parties all the time, and can, in fact, be situational. For instance, a company may be in the power position with its employees most of the time, but a strike by union employees may neutralize that position, at least for a time.

Strong and Weak Claims

We tend to sort claimants by their relationship to us, and we tend to base our obligations on how *functionally* reliant we are on them, not the other way around. For example:

- *We are typically more obligated to those upon which we depend for major support.* For example, a television station depends on its owner for startup capital, without which it could not survive. In most cases the owner has the power position over major decisions the station may make. The owner has a stronger functional claim on the actions of the station.
- *We are typically more obligated to those with whom we are mutually dependent.* For example, the television station is dependent on its advertisers, without whom it could not survive. At the same time the advertisers are dependent on the station as a primary media outlet, which they need to help ensure their survival. They have strong functional claims on each other's actions.
- *We are typically less obligated to those that depend on us for major support.* For example, the non-profit community (social service agencies, charities, etc.) may use the local television station as an outlet for announcements and for news coverage; however, the station may choose what to run and what not to run. The agencies' functional claims are, thus, weaker.
- *We are typically less obligated to those that are totally independent from us and from whom we are totally independent.* For example, television stations in a given

area do not rely particularly on each other and, in fact, actively compete for the same advertisers and audiences. Their functional claims on each other are weaker.

In this ranking, the notion of claims is based on the necessity to maintain certain relationships over others. It is entirely *functional*. For instance, as a PR firm it may be more functionally important to maintain a good relationship with clients than with their target audience. That's because the claimants are defined based only on their functional relationship to the organization and how dependent they are on us versus how dependent we are on them. Thus, any ranking will be made purely on an *amoral* basis (no ethical values are applied). The nature of functional obligations is that they carry no *moral* weight.

But, from an ethical perspective, this just doesn't seem right. From an ethical perspective, it would seem that the party with the most power in a relationship is more morally obligated, if for no other reason than it has most of the power and therefore more potential to harm the weaker party. Although the weaker party is certainly obligated (perhaps simply to hold up its end of a contract), its position as the dependent party puts it at a natural disadvantage and somewhat at the mercy of the more powerful party.

Thus, a simple rule might be, *those with the greater power in a relationship are more morally obligated.* And although there are many subtle and varying levels of power within any relationship, the parties involved usually recognize when they have the upper hand and when they do not.

If we substitute *moral* obligation for *functional* obligation, the question then becomes: Does an obligation to a stronger claimant outweigh an obligation to a weaker claimant simply because of the functional nature of the relationship? This goes to the heart of obligation as an ethical construct and highlights the tension between obligation to stronger claimants (such as owners of media outlets or clients of advertising agencies) and obligations to weaker third parties (such as those on the receiving end of our messages). For instance, does the obligation to turn a profit at an advertising agency absolve the agency of an obligation to be truthful to their target audiences? Functionally, they may be better off honoring client interests, but are they better off morally?

Ethical Applications

Each decision with ethical implications brings with it certain obligations. This is the point at which we must begin to balance those obligations among competing claims, and at which need to consider the broader scope of *moral* obligation. To more completely discharge our obligations to the array of moral claimants that we face at every decision point, we must also consider consequences. As noted earlier, the effects of our actions on others are the main reason we recognize obligation in the first place. This fits nicely with the concept of identifying moral claimants by our effect on them and/or their effect on us. However, we must recognize both our functional relationships and our ethical obligations. For instance, although we may be able to identify an asymmetrical relationship in the form of a special interest group, this only tells us that we must deal with that group through some functional, non-moral activity. It does not indicate our ethical obligation.

The Nature of Obligation

Obligation usually implies a bond, either legal, social, or moral—an owing of something to someone or something. That obligation exists whether we choose to recognize it or not. Obligation is a natural concomitant of living within a society. Because of our social interactions, we incur obligation, and we tend to recognize that we have done so.

The term "obligation" is roughly synonymous with the term "duty," as used by a number of philosophers. The general assumption about moral duties is that we have them. These duties are not merely those that we create through such actions as making promises or incurring debt. We also have "natural" duties to others "simply because they are people who could be helped or harmed by our actions."[3] We also are obligated merely by being members of human society. One is obligated at the personal, familial, occupational, and societal levels—each representing differing intensities of obligation and differing levels of formality. The educator and ethicist Louis Day reminds us that "our moral calculations affect other humans, regardless of whether these individuals are known personally to us or are members of that amorphous mass known as the public."[4] The philosopher T. M. Scanlon suggests that "what we owe to others" is determined, to a great degree, by what they can justifiably expect of us.[5] In other words, we must treat others as they expect to be treated—a version of the Golden Rule.

Obligations arise not only from general social relationships but also from relationships described by our roles and functions in life, including our jobs. Thus, we are obligated explicitly and implicitly in our relationships with others we come in contact with through our daily work. In the view of philosopher Bernard Gert, duties are primarily connected with jobs, offices, positions, and the like.[6] Duties are both voluntarily incurred and forced (as the duty to obey the law). "Do your duty," in the sense of natural obligation, is one of the key rules set down by Gert. However, he emphatically points out that doing your duty is not synonymous with simply doing what you are paid to do. "One's job involves duties only to the extent that the job does not require one to kill his innocent victim, though he may have been paid a sizable sum to do that. One cannot have a duty to unjustifiably violate a moral rule."[7]

Ross's Moral Duties

Moral philosopher William David Ross defined six areas he believed all human beings would recognize, in one form or another, as being morally binding.[8] He referred to these obligations as *prima facie duties*, which means that they should be considered binding, all other factors being equal—in other words, if no other duty or complication interferes with the consideration of the obligation in question. Ross believed that we would recognize these duties because we are human beings, and as such we are inclined to live in social structures held together in part by obligation. Ross's six categories of obligation are as follows:

- Duties of fidelity: If you promise (explicitly or implicitly) to perform some act or to abstain from performing some act, then you are obliged to perform that act or to abstain from performing that act. For instance, most relationships, professional and personal, assume a duty to tell the truth, or at least not to lie. Duties of fidelity would also include remaining faithful to contracts, explicit or implicit, and keeping promises. This category also includes duties of reparation; that is, if you perform a wrong action with respect to another person, you are obliged to undo the wrong.

- Duties of gratitude: If any person performs some service (favor) for you, then you have some obligation to the person who performed the favor. This would apply both to relationships between friends and to relationships between employer and employee. For example, if your employer treats you in an exceptionally favorable manner, above that normally expected in an employee–employer relationship, your obligation would deepen to honor your employer's wishes beyond the duty of fidelity.

- Duties of justice: If any person merits a distribution of something (typically something that will result in pleasure, happiness, or satisfaction), and you can bring that distribution about (or prevent an unmerited distribution), then you are obliged to distribute what is merited (or prevent/withhold what is not merited). In practice, this can often mean giving greater consideration to the claims of those who deserve it rather than to those who demand it, regardless of their position or power.

- Duties of beneficence: If you can make some person better with respect to their state of existence, then you are obliged to do so. An example of this would be corporate philanthropy or the pro bono work of professionals. In a decision-making situation, this duty may oblige you to act when non-action is preferred or recommended by others.

- Duties of self-improvement: If you can make yourself better with respect to your state of existence, then you are obliged to do so. This can cover anything from preserving your own integrity to taking advantage of a favorable situation for self-improvement.

- Duties of non-injury: If you are in a position to avoid hurting someone, then you are obliged to do so. This contrasts with the duty of beneficence. Although not injuring others incidentally means doing them good, Ross interprets the avoidance of injuring others as a more pressing duty than beneficence. This may, in fact, be the most important of Ross's duties, since it implies that the possibility of injury to any claimant to whom you are obligated must be assigned some weight. However, this very often results in a form of cost–benefit or risk–benefit analysis, which is counter to the underlying premise of duty-based theory: that rules can, and should, be moral in and of themselves, and not based on considerations of outcome.

Naturally, all of the six obligations listed by Ross may be applicable in any potential relationship among parties; however, it is more likely, given the direction of consequences, that more of them will come into play with those who are asymmetrically related—those with weaker functional claims on us. Given that there is typically an imbalance in obligation in favor of stronger claimants (e.g., owners, employers, and clients), we need to be particularly careful to offset this tendency by honoring all obligations, especially those to weaker parties.

The key is to remember that we are tied to our stakeholders by more than just economic or political linkages. We are tied to them socially, and social links imply obligation. We must always ask not only to whom we are linked, but also in what way we are linked, observing both functional and ethical ties. We may, after determining our obligations, ignore them. But we cannot avoid the likelihood that others recognize these same obligations and are very likely to hold us accountable when we do not honor them. As you might imagine, however, not everyone agrees that the media have any obligation at all toward their claimants.

The Libertarian Approach

When we hear the word "libertarian," we often conjure up an image of gun-toting cadres of non-conformists holed up in some remote region of the country awaiting the inevitable government attack. What we don't usually think of is the modern media. In a sense, the United States was founded on the concept of libertarianism. Roughly speaking, libertarianism holds that freedom should be unbounded; there should be no restrictions on an individual's freedom to do what he or she pleases. If we remember how the United States was founded—as a reaction to tyrannous authority—we can better understand the libertarian position.

Modern journalism maintains a very strong flavor of libertarianism in its refusal to bow to outside pressure, especially governmental pressure. The First Amendment of the Constitution literally guarantees this freedom. Journalists are free to report on anything they deem important to their constituencies. In many states, they are even free from prosecution if they choose to withhold the names of sources. In fact, some would say that journalists are and should be free from any obligation save that of providing the news; for by providing the news, they are serving the public interest—and that is responsibility enough.

This thinking is a reflection of the "invisible hand" theory of Adam Smith, who pointed out that the duty of a capitalistic endeavor was to make a profit and remain viable, for by doing so the rest of society was duly served. Modern conservative economists echo this sentiment when they state that the job of business is not only to survive but also to do well. A business that thrives will employ more workers, provide more products and services, and strengthen the overall economy in the process. If business is left alone, free from government intervention, either it will thrive or it will not—but it will do so in a marketplace immune from restrictions.[9]

It is not difficult to understand why the modern press grew from this libertarian model. After all, the job of journalism is journalism. The modern journalist gathers the news and reports it with as much objectivity as can be mustered. In fact, objectivity is the mainstay of a libertarian press. If reporting is truly free from bias, then no one can justifiably intervene in its process. And although objectivity is recognized today as an ideal rather than an absolute goal, the belief that the press should not owe allegiance to anyone or anything but itself is a very powerful one. After all, allegiance implies obligation, and obligation implies reciprocity. A press encumbered by debt is not, by definition, a free press. An interesting question arises, however, whether the press discharges its only obligation to the public it serves by simply providing them with a balanced account of the day's news.

The Social Responsibility Approach

The idea of social responsibility developed originally as a means of indicting American business, whose sense of obligation to the public was decidedly lacking in the early part of the twentieth century. With the increasing realization that everything that business does affects huge numbers of people came a concomitant call for greater accountability. In the social responsibility model, organizations (even media organizations) are seen as operating at the behest of the public; thus, their rights are really privileges—and privileges come only at the expense of reciprocation in the form of agreed-upon responsibilities. This is a clear recognition of the interdependency between the media and their constituencies.

James Grunig cites three categories of responsibility that he suggests are recognized as binding to some degree on all organizations. At the very least, an organization should perform its basic task (gathering and disseminating the news, for example). Beyond that, it should take care of any potential consequences of its primary task, such as cleaning up pollution it has caused, or being a good employer, or responding to complaints. Finally, organizations may move into the area of general societal concerns such as literacy, disease prevention, hunger, and so on.[10] Grunig proposes that the first two categories of responsibility are naturally binding on all organizations. Anything less would be unacceptable to most of society. The third category, however, is more difficult to measure for effectiveness; and although organizations would certainly be encouraged to take on larger societal issues, most citizens wouldn't fault them if they did not. But how does this apply to the media?

In 1942, the role of the press in our society was formally recognized as one including both rights and responsibilities. In that year, a commission was established, originally by Henry R. Luce of *Time* and later by the *Encyclopedia Britannica*, to assess the state of journalism. Robert Hutchins, chancellor of the University of Chicago, was appointed head of the commission composed of 13 members from industry and education. The Hutchins Commission of Freedom of the Press studied the sticky question of a "free and responsible press" and presented its report in 1947. In its report, the Commission stressed that the media should not only do their job of informing the citizenry, but also involve themselves in the well-being of society as a whole.

Since that time, it has been assumed that a certain level of responsibility is owed to society by the news media; but exactly to what degree are the media expected to give up their traditional autonomy in order to serve the public interest (or cater to its wants and needs)? There is a constant tension in journalism between giving the public what they need as active citizens and what they want, often just out of curiosity. The decline in the public desire for so-called "hard news" in favor of "soft news" (often entertainment-oriented) and the news media's response of softening the news overall may be an indication of how strong the economic imperative impinges on the concept of social responsibility. The current trend in *user-created content* is another indication that the media are attempting to give the public what they want, even if involves the public creating its own news. This will be covered in much more detail in Chapter 10.

Further indications of media responsibility have surfaced in the concept of civic or public journalism—a model in which the news media become actively involved in the well-being of the community in which they operate. The social historian Christopher Lasch argued that the press today has abdicated its role as a proper forum for public debate by subscribing to the notions that information alone is the proper product of the media. In Lasch's words, "What democracy requires is public debate, not information." He decried the decline of the partisan press of the nineteenth century and proposed that "the rise of a new type of journalism professing rigorous standards of objectivity do[es] not assure a steady supply of usable information."

> Unless information is generated by sustained public debate, most of it will be irrelevant at best, misleading and manipulative at worst.[11]

The journalist and educator Jay Rosen also finds objectivity outmoded as a concept and unworkable as an ideal. Rosen believes that "journalism should be involved in re-engaging people in public life." According to him, public journalism "recognizes the overriding importance of improving public life."

> In the next few years, it will be critical for people in journalism to declare an end to their neutrality on certain questions. For example, whether people participate or not, whether we have genuine debate in this country, whether

the political system works, whether public life draws the attention of citizens, whether political leaders earn our respect.[12]

These questions, he proposes, can best be answered by a press that is not afraid to take sides. Others argue that a partisan press, a press that loses its objectivity, will be incapable of giving us information that we can trust is balanced enough to allow us to make up our own minds, therefore limiting our autonomy as decision makers.

Thus, the arguments in favor of a press free from outside control are likewise strong. By permitting, or expecting, a less than objective account, consumers of news increase their own burden of gathering the facts for themselves. This dilemma is what prompted Walter Lippmann, in the 1920s, to call for an objective press in the first place. The question then becomes: What level of responsibility can the media accept before they lose the autonomy they need to remain fair and balanced? Obligation implies outside pressure, and we have already seen that the disparate media are obligated by the very nature of their jobs. And although the press may be obligated increasingly toward promoting the public welfare, there is a danger that such leanings may result in the news media becoming more like their cousins in advertising and public relations—professions in which bias is expected. Like journalism, advertising and public relations also value autonomy, but bridle to a lesser degree at outside influence—especially if that influence is wielded by those controlling the purse strings. However, as we see in the next chapter, the nature of professionalism works against the most egregious infringements on social responsibility for all of the media, including advertising and public relations, through the ideal of serving the public interest.

What Does it All Mean?

By understanding that the media are linked relationally to their constituents both functionally and morally, we can begin to understand the often complex interrelationships among the various media and the economic, political, and social environment in which they exist. Successfully functioning organizations, including the media, recognize that they must contribute to society as a whole, not just to their own well-being. To do so, they must recognize not only the people who have some claim on their actions, but also the nature of these claims, and ultimately how they are obligated to these people—functionally and morally.

The media are obligated to a vast array of claimants and must discharge those obligations satisfactorily in order to act ethically. And although obligations may differ among the various media, commonalties do exist in such areas as truth telling and prohibitions against harm—topics we visit in detail in Chapter 6. As we see in the next chapter, the type of relationship that exists between a profession and those it serves dictates, to a very great extent, the level of ethicality that can be expected of that profession.

Chapter 3

The Media and Professionalism

The most permanent lessons in morals are those which come, not of book teaching, but of experience.

(Mark Twain)

The question of professionalism in media looms large within the overall landscape of ethical behavior. Professions are supposed to have strong ethical standards that, in some ways, set them apart from other occupations. At the same time, because these standards set them apart, the potential for deviation from societal norms is much greater. For example (assuming for the time being that journalism is a profession), a journalist is typically more obliged to gather a story than to become a part of it. That is how most journalists justify not interfering in a story—to come to someone's aid, for instance. In fact, the long-held standard of non-interference is a mainstay in modern journalism, for without it, a journalist may lose his objectivity. However, professions carry with them much baggage. Licensing, restrictions on membership, codes of conduct, prescriptions for proper actions, all tend to put off working journalists. Thus, most journalists shy away from the notion of their occupation becoming a full profession. On the other hand, public relations has historically embraced the trappings of professionalism seeking to gain the respectability normally associated with other professions, such as law and medicine. Why the difference? In fact, why would any occupation want to become or not become a profession?

Before we begin to explore whether or not the various media are or should be professions, we must define—as much as possible—what a profession is. Perhaps the best way to tackle that question is to describe the characteristics common to most professions. The ethicist Michael Bayles sets down three central features and three secondary features that tend to be present in most professions.[1]

Central Features

- Extensive training is usually required to practice within a profession. Most professions have academic degrees associated with them (law, medicine, engineering, nursing, and so on).

- The training involves a significant intellectual component. Whereas occupations in general usually involve physical training, the professions also require intellectual training, which is usually predominant. This is especially important in the counseling professions such as law and medicine (and, perhaps, public relations). This provision of advice rather than "things" is a secondary characteristic of most professions.
- The result of the training is an ability that provides an important service to society. Most of the "traditional" professions provide services vital to the organized function of society (law, medicine, engineering, teaching). These services are necessary not only because they contribute to society in general, but also because not everyone in society is either willing or able to provide these services for themselves.

Secondary Features

- Another common feature among professions is credentialing. Most professions have some method of certifying or licensing their members. Lawyers are admitted to the bar, physicians are granted licenses, as are architects, engineers, and dentists. Not all professions are licensed, however. College teachers are granted advanced degrees but need not be licensed in any other way. Not all accountants are CPAs. However, what sets professions apart from other occupations are their credentials—usually a college degree, and in some cases, an advanced college degree. This type of credentialing refers back to the aspect of extensive training.
- A professional organization is also a common feature of most professions. These organizations usually strive to advance the goals of the profession and promote the economic well-being of their members. However, the advancement of professional goals generally takes precedence over economic considerations. This is what sets professional organizations apart from trade unions, for instance.
- Finally, and very importantly, most professions stress autonomy among their members. Being able to perform work free from interference (especially from those with less expertise) is vital to being a successful professional. After all, most professionals are hired exactly because their expertise is needed. However, as Bayles points out, exactly how far that autonomy should extend is still an open question, and one that will be addressed in detail below.

Are the Media Professions?

Bayles specifically mentions journalism as being one of those fields having an "equivocal status" as a profession in that it is "still quite open to people with training in other areas."[2] Many prominent journalists did not go to school in journalism. Many were educated in the liberal arts. Increasingly, however, those entering the media fields are graduating college with degrees in journalism or specific areas of communication media. This influx of workers with intellectual training as well as practical training in the media fields may tend to professionalize the practices even further.

It is also important to distinguish between an occupation's being a profession and undergoing professionalization. Becoming professionalized involves developing standards of performance and some training in them.[3] As occupations move further toward professionalization, they may also develop organizations to represent them, core bodies of knowledge to intellectualize the field, and methods of credentialing to maintain standards of performance. Although among the media fields only public relations freely admits to wanting to become a profession, both advertising and journalism contain elements of professions.

All three media occupations have relatively *strong support organizations*—in some cases, several. For example, public relations has both the Public Relations Society of America (PRSA) and the International Association of Business Communicators (IABC), with PRSA being the largest professional organization in the United States. Among the most influential of advertising professional organizations is the American Advertising Federation. The two largest organizations for print journalists are the Society for Professional Journalists (SPJ) and the American Society of Newspaper Editors (ASNE), and for broadcast journalism, the Radio-Television News Directors Association (RTNDA) is one of the largest. Other organizations exist for specialized areas of journalism. For example, the American Association of Magazine Editors (ASME) yearly announces awards for outstanding and ethical magazine journalism and holds a watchdog function over unethical (especially advertising) practices among magazines.

An *established intellectual tradition* coupled with a strong professional organization is a clear indicator of increasing professionalization among the media. With media internships on the rise, the *practical and technical aspects* of professionalism are included in the mix. On the final two criteria, *credentialing* and *public service*, there is still a great deal of disagreement. For example, neither licensing nor certification is required of any person working in the media. Exceptions would be trade associations and some affiliation (often, union membership) or certification for specialized technical work such as cinematography, directing, acting, and various other occupations associated primarily with the entertainment media. But for the "professions" of journalism, advertising, and public relations, there is no licensing.

In journalism, especially, the mere mention of licensing raises hackles. Licensing would indicate control, and journalists will abide no control over their jobs. In fact, the feeling of autonomy is so strong among journalists as to forestall any attempt at licensing or even credentialing (despite the increase in college graduates entering the field fully credentialed—at least intellectually). Journalism maintains a strong libertarian stance, even today. Although many journalists will admit to having a professional association (SPJ) and a code of ethics (either SPJ's or their own media outlet's), they generally stop short of claiming that they belong to a profession.

Most advertisers, on the other hand, are more ambivalent about the notion of their business becoming a profession. Remember, advertising is different enough from journalism to require an entirely different communication model (information/persuasion versus pure information). In addition, most advertising performs an "agency" function. That is, advertisers work for clients who make the ultimate decisions concerning their products and how they are marketed. In other ways, however, advertising meets many of the criteria for becoming a profession. It has a fairly large professional organization that represents the field and a code of ethics. College degrees are offered in the study and practice of advertising, which requires that it have a learnable intellectual component. However, advertisers are not licensed, nor is it clear that they have the same level of autonomy associated with other professions or that they provide an indispensable service to society in the way law and medicine do.

Public relations has been striving for sixty years to gain acceptance as a profession. The founding of the Public Relations Society of America (PRSA) in 1948 presaged the steady rise of public relations from an occupation to a near-profession. Although members of PRSA are not licensed, they are (voluntarily) accredited through a process similar to licensing. This accreditation, however, does not carry the weight of licensing. For example, a PRSA member who loses his accreditation may still practice public relations—unlike a physician who loses her license or an attorney who is disbarred. So, although public relations has most of the trappings of a profession, it is still struggling to develop and maintain enforceable standards in the same way as law and medicine. Of course, this does not mean that public relations is not a profession. We will return to that question at the end of this chapter.

Finally, among the three media industries we are concerned with here, there are several other distinctions associated with professionalism that affect their ethical positions. First, professionals may be either self-employed or employees of a larger organization. Most journalists, for instance, are employees, whereas many public relations practitioners are self-employed consultants. Advertisers are most often employees in an agency, as are many public relations people. Because self-employed individuals encounter different challenges from employees, we can expect that ethical considerations will differ as well. For instance, self-employed consultants (as in public relations) must deal with the ethics of client acquisition and conflict of interest. Employed professionals, on the other hand, may have to deal more often with reconciling their professional ethics with the bottom-line mentality of their employer.[4]

Another distinction is between those professionals who have individuals as clients and those that have larger entities as clients. A journalist's "clientele" is large and amorphous. A public relations practitioner may serve individuals, groups, or organizations. So may advertisers. Obviously, there is a great deal of variation, and each of the media professions may serve, alternately, individuals and groups/organizations—and be ethically obligated to each in different ways.

Service to Society

One of the key features that differentiates a profession from an occupation is service to society as a whole. Certainly, it can be said that both law and medicine provide this service, but so also do professions such as engineering, dentistry, nursing, accounting, teaching, and many others. The question of service to the public or in the public interest is one that has concerned nearly all professions at one time or another. Answers have ranged from the ideological to the practical, and have taken the form of everything from token articles in codes of ethics to complete programs designed to carry out what many consider to be the premier obligation of a profession. The question is: How real is the discharge of this obligation?

Some have called this service orientation an ideology that maintains that "professionals adhere to the ideal of service to all of humanity . . . They serve anyone in need regardless of monetary reward or the status of the client."[5] This service orientation has become the keystone among *professional values*, those commonly held beliefs that serve to cement individual practitioners into a single profession. And, although serving the public interest is not necessarily a criterion used to define professionalism, it is one of the most often cited values of professionalism.

According to the ethicist Michael Bayles, professionals in our society are at the top in prestige, wealth, and power, and because they frequently make decisions that affect others,

> The granting [by society] of a license and privilege in effect creates a trust for professionals to ensure that these activities are performed in a manner that preserves and promotes values in society.[6]

The professions themselves often attempt to justify the respect with which society holds them and the level of support they in turn command from society by frequently citing the public service aspects of their roles.

> The animating purpose of a profession is to contribute maximally and efficiently to human welfare . . . The same purpose (together with great interest in the work itself) is the motive of the true professional, not desire for compensation . . . [T]he professionals' aim is to serve mankind and they are expected to affirm ("profess") this by accepting their professions' codes of ethics.[7]

How Can Professions Serve the Public Interest?

There are some basic ways in which most professions attempt to serve the public interest. *First, a profession may serve the public interest in a general sense by simply "being there."* This postulation is somewhat reminiscent of Adam Smith's invisible hand, whereby the effective functioning of a capitalistic economy ultimately serves all of society through discharge of its normal duties to maximize profits. However, whereas a successfully functioning economy may benefit as the result of a goal-oriented drive to maximize profits, professionals are generally assumed to be guided by an ethical imperative of service to the client—making the "hand" more visible, but nonetheless operative. Medicine and the law fall under this heading. Merely by being available to the public, they serve the public welfare. Availability, of course, has led to serious debates over such topics as national health care and equal legal representation. However, for our purposes, a profession such as journalism ideally serves the public interest by providing citizens with the information necessary to participate in a democratic society. In the United States, access to information is deemed as important as access to health or legal representation. Thus, as with medicine and law, journalism serves the public interest in this general sense—simply by doing its job. As might be expected, however, not everyone agrees with that proposition.

The Public Journalism Debate

As noted in Chapter 2, the historian Christopher Lasch has argued that the press today has abdicated its role of a proper forum for public debate by subscribing to the notion that information alone is the proper product of the media. In Lasch's words, "What democracy requires is public debate, not information." "Unless information is generated by sustained public debate, most of it will be irrelevant at best, misleading and manipulative at worst."[8] Lasch's warnings have not gone unheeded. The rise of what has been dubbed "public journalism" is a direct response to the idea that journalism itself must become an agent of change in a world crying out for direction. The idea of public journalism is communitarian in nature.

Communitarianism demands involvement in the community in which one resides—a general focus on the community rather than the individual. It decries the notion that anyone can be detached and objective in the face of community obligation. This would include journalists as well as other occupations operating within a given community. For example, a newspaper practicing public journalism might spend more time studying problems facing the community, open a forum for debate within its pages, and even go so far as to recommend solutions (or, at least, side with some suggestions over others). At the root of this movement is the suspicion that objectivity is simply an unrealizable, perhaps even counterproductive, ideal, and that journalists might as well admit it and move on.

Not surprisingly, many traditional journalists warn that involvement at this level would erode the trust that the people have in the objectivity of journalists. Where else, they ask, can these people turn for unbiased coverage of the day's events? Without that objectivity, journalism becomes merely another opinionated voice. Others counter that it is possible to do both—to have objective reporting on some issues while taking sides on others. What is clear is that simply doing one's job does not necessarily absolve one of all obligations towards others. Journalistic endeavors that ignore the concerns of the community may not survive in today's competitive media environment—a point not lost on most local news operations. Thus, the debate over public journalism, exactly what it constitutes, and whether it can coexist with the more traditional form of objective journalism will certainly continue for quite some time.

Pro Bono Work

A second way in which the public interest may be served is through *pro bono* work. This approach to satisfying the public interest debt of a profession is clearly outside the realm of journalism, for although journalism may (and often does) point out the ills of society, it rarely becomes involved in solving them (part of the public journalism debate). Thus, pro bono work is most commonly associated with the consulting professions. Pro bono literally means "for good," and is supposed to be work carried out by professionals in the public interest. We often hear of attorneys and physicians taking on pro bono cases, usually those who cannot pay for their services. (That is why pro bono work is often thought of as being free of charge.) In fact, many in public relations and advertising also take on pro bono clients, often social service agencies or political causes viewed by most as being public-minded. However, Michael Bayles argues that such endeavors as lobbying and public interest activity do not completely fulfill the responsibility a profession has to act in the public interest, because the individual professionals are not serving the *public* interest, they are merely serving a *particular* interest—something that they are *personally* interested in. Thus, the public interest cannot be served by professionals working on behalf of any such singular interest or client, even if that client is a social service agency.[9]

The reason is that professionals (especially those acting as agents) typically assume the role of advocate. This implies that the professional, under these circumstances, must remain an interested party, and as long as she favors one side of an issue or another, she cannot serve the public interest. For example, a public relations professional assuming pro bono work on behalf of a pro-choice interest group is really acting on behalf of the client—no matter how much that client may believe its actions are in the public interest. In the same way, public relations professionals working on behalf of a pro-life group espouse their client's position. Both sides certainly are serving an interest, but neither can be said to be serving the *public* interest.

One way the advertising industry has managed profession-wide pro bono work is through the Advertising Council. Founded during World War II, the Advertising Council was composed of volunteer ad agencies from around the country that dedicated their time and resources, free of charge, to promote national causes such as the sale of War Bonds and American Red Cross blood drives. Since that time, the Ad Council has continued to work on behalf of non-profit organizations by providing them with reduced-rate advertising services through its volunteer member agencies. Among its long-standing clients are the United Way and the forest fire prevention campaign featuring Smokey the Bear. Another similar example is the American Civil Liberties Union (ACLU), which historically takes on cases that involve Constitutional Amendments (particularly, the First Amendment). They represent, in a way, the urge of the legal profession towards pro bono work, and they take on cases regardless of public image. For example, they have represented both jailed journalists and the Ku Klux Klan. In this sense, the ACLU is acting not out of a personal like or dislike for the cause or the client, but out of a belief that *any* party deserves the protection afforded by the First Amendment.

What is clear is that the public interest must be served in order for any of the media industries to become true professions. Whether these practices can or even want to become professions is the subject of much debate, some discussed already. However, the inevitable obligations between the media practices and those they affect cannot be ignored, and one of the strengths of professionalism is that these relationships are carefully drawn and the obligations clearly defined. Let us turn, then, to a different approach to defining the relationship between the media practices and their moral claimants—one based on the *professional ethics model*.

The Professional–Client Relationship

Much is often made of the distinction among advertising, public relations, and journalism. Advertising is most often viewed as an agency-based practice with advocacy on behalf of a client as its primary goal; public relations as a consulting practice, also with advocacy of a client as its goal; and journalism as a slightly paternalistic practice (in that it sets the news agenda) with the public interest at heart. Of course, each of these views is both partly correct and partly incorrect. One of the key elements of a profession is that it serves a client or customer. Physicians and dentists have patients, lawyers have clients, as do advertising and public relations. Teachers have students (increasingly thought of as customers). But the distinction between a client and a customer is a subtle and important one.

Client or Customer?

A client is someone to whom you are usually contractually obligated. A customer is someone who utilizes your services or uses your product but to whom you are not usually contractually obligated (in a legal sense). It could be fairly stated that both advertising and public relations are client-based occupations, whereas journalism is customer-based. However, because of the special place of journalism in our society and the fact that its "product" is the only one protected by the Constitution, the "customers" of journalism must also be considered differently. In fact, journalists are obligated to their public in some of the same ways that teachers are obligated to their students and physicians are obligated to their patients (not just as customers, but as clients). Of course, a journalist's customers expect a good product at a fair price, but they also expect that a certain level of expertise drives the manufacture of that product, including a service orientation not necessarily present in other customer-based occupations. In other words, they expect journalists to be devoted to the dissemination of news in ways they don't expect their grocery clerks to be dedicated to their jobs or taxi drivers to theirs. In the case of journalism, both the provider and the customer have heightened expectations based, in large part, on the understood importance of the "press" in the United States. Thus, the beneficiaries of the journalistic "product" are not simply customers; they are, in fact, clients.

It could be fairly argued, then, that the press does have a client, someone to whom they are contractually obligated. As the journalist and ethicist James W. Carey has said, "Insofar as journalism has a client, the client is the public."[10] Since the First Amendment of the Constitution is so often cited as a media directive, and the "public's right to know" a well-worn euphemism for the media's implied imperative to publish, we might call that relationship between the media and the American public a contractual one. With this construct in mind, let us consider the roles of journalism, advertising, and public relations and how they might deal with their relationships to their constituent publics (or clients) from a professional perspective.

Client–Professional Decision-making Models

One of the key ethical concerns of the professional–client relationship is that of balance. Who makes what decisions and for what reasons? The division of responsibility and accountability for decision making is what drives most professional–client relationships. Most models of this relationship fall into three categories: the client has most decision-making authority; the professional has most decision-making authority; the professional and client are equals.[11] However, most professional models exist along a continuum with various degrees of professional–client involvement (see Figure 3.1). It is rare to find a relationship that is wholly client-controlled or one that is entirely controlled by the professional.

Journalism and the Paternalistic Model

Journalism has evolved with more than a touch of *paternalism* in its character. According to Michael Bayles "A person's conduct is paternalistic to the extent his or her reasons are to do something to or on behalf of another person for that person's well-being."[12] Journalists have long held that they provide their constituency not only with what it wants, but also with what it needs; and that determination is generally made by the media themselves. Arguments in support of paternalism make much of the clients' inability or unwillingness to decide for

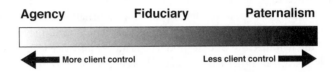

Figure 3.1 Professional-client relationship models. Professional–client relationship models lie along a continuum from that representing the most client control (agency) to that representing the least client control (paternalism). The fiduciary model represents a more evenly divided relationship, with a slight edge going to the professional. That edge is mitigated, however, by the necessity to foster and maintain the trust of the client.

themselves. For example, an extremely diligent person might be able to gather and digest enough of what is happening in the world each day to satisfy his curiosity. However, not many of us wish to spend our time doing so. We trust the media to do that for us. We accept the order in which news is selectively presented to us. We assume that the "top story" is the most newsworthy of the day. We expect that the news will be accurate and balanced. And we do all this because we believe that professional journalists are good at deciding what is news and what is not. At least, that is the tacit understanding. Every time a news director decides what story to run first in the local nightly television news cast, she is acting paternalistically. After all, she has been trained to decide such things, and has the best interest of the client (her viewers) in mind. The question is: Can the media (especially journalism) provide us with both what we need and what we want?

That balance between serving the public interest by providing them with what they need to become knowledgeable citizens of a working democracy and entertaining them with what they want is a delicate one. Every day, journalists walk this tightrope. Not wanting to appear too paternalistic (and in order to serve very real economic interests), they provide the public with what it wants—whether that is Michael Jackson trial coverage, endlessly repeated announcements on the whereabouts of Britney Spears, or nightly updates on Lindsay Lohan's state of rehabilitation. In short, journalists tend to be paternalistic a great deal of the time; however, by allowing their audience to dictate much of what they disseminate, they are also tilting toward more "client" control.

Not everyone sees this as negative. Some journalists view audience involvement in programming decisions as more democratic and far less paternalistic than otherwise. And although autonomy has traditionally been a keystone of journalistic practice in this country, true independence is clearly waning—if it ever really existed. So, whereas journalism tends to operate under a paternalistic model, making most of the decisions concerning what to cover, the desires of its constituent public (client) cannot be ignored. The question remains, however, how successful such an arrangement is as a professional model of decision making.

Advocacy and Agency

Both advertising and public relations can be said to be advocacy-oriented practices. To *advocate* is to take up the cause of another and to work on that other's behalf to promote that cause. Attorneys become advocates for client causes, "zealously" representing their interests.[13] Part of the assumption of advocacy is that the advocate takes up his client's cause fully, without regard to his own feelings. An advocate uses his expertise to advance a client's cause. Although counseling the client on the most effective course of action may certainly be a part of advocacy, most advocates proceed pretty much at the client's behest. Thus, advocacy fits well into what is known as the "agency" model of professional–client relationship.

Under the *agency model*, a professional acts most often under the direction of the client. Advertisers, for instance, may put together elaborate campaigns to serve their client's interests; however, the client picks the agency, determines the product to be marketed, and decides whether or not to use the ideas generated by the agency. Public relations agencies (or firms, as they are more commonly known) work pretty much in the same fashion. The agency model most clearly exemplifies what has been called the "ideology of advocacy." This ideology assumes two principles of conduct: (1) that a professional is neutral or detached from the client's purposes, and (2) that the professional is an aggressive partisan of the client working to advance the client's ends.[14] Such a construct allows the professional to absolve herself of moral responsibility for the client's ethical shortcomings. Obviously, this ideology would work well for professions such as the law in which even unpopular causes would sometimes need to be defended. Without such an ideology, these causes might go unrepresented. But what about other professions such as advertising and public relations?

There are several reasons why the agency model is not suitable for most professions, including the media.

- First, as we have discussed in Chapters 1 and 2, media professionals are variously obligated. These obligations cannot be discharged properly if all decisions are left to the client. Despite the commonly voiced belief that the primary loyalty of advertisers and public relations practitioners is to the client, we know that serious moral concerns can arise from ignoring third parties.
- Second, the agency model seriously decreases professional autonomy. Most professionals would object strenuously to abdicating their decision-making authority.
- Finally, professionals may accept or reject clients who do not meet their moral standards. According to ethicist Michael Bayles, "Professionals must . . . be ethically free and responsible persons."[15]

On the second point, the dilution of decision-making authority is more common in larger organizations in which practitioners most often serve as employees rather than true professionals. However, even this reduction in autonomy does not reduce a media practitioner's responsibility to act ethically—it only makes the lines of responsibility less clear. Less autonomous practitioners must also determine the ethicality of their actions; even though the major difference between them and their more independent counterparts, the degree of autonomy, may inhibit the degree to which the practitioner may object to actions he or she determines are less than ethical. Obviously, the independent counselor may advise, and thereby object, from a much stronger position than his counterparts subsumed either within an organization or an agency.

The Fiduciary Model

If paternalism represents the most professional control and agency represents the most client control, what then is an acceptable middle ground? Some have suggested the *fiduciary* model, under which both parties are responsible for decision making and their judgments are given equal consideration. The professional is recognized for her expertise and training (both intellectual and practical), whereas the client is recognized as the driving force behind the professional's activities. Under this construct, a consulting professional (such as an advertising or public relations practitioner) would take the client's problem, canvass all possible solutions, present the most viable options along with costs/benefits of each, and make a recommendation based on professional expertise. Once the client makes the ultimate decision which path to pursue, then the professional must work diligently on the client's behalf to carry out the chosen course of action.

Whereas this model has immediate implications for advertising and public relations, its application to journalism requires more explanation. Although journalism is certainly not a consulting profession, it does provide a valuable service to its primary public—its readers, viewers, listeners. The journalist is recognized for his expertise and training and the public is recognized as the reason for journalism to exist in the first place (that is, the driving force). The ideal of journalism would demand that the "press" present as complete a picture of the day's important events as possible to its audience. And the implied reason for this presentation of events? To provide the people with the information they need to make educated decisions concerning the environment in which they live and work. They make their decisions based on the provision of this information, much in the same way that a client makes a decision based on the information provided by a consulting professional such as an advertising or public relations professional.

This model allows clients as much freedom to determine how their lives are affected as is reasonably warranted on the basis of their ability to make decisions. However, the parties must recognize from the outset that there is a difference between them: The professional is usually at an advantage because she has a better grasp of how to handle certain situations. If this were not the case, the client would do the work for himself. Thus, the weaker party (client) depends upon the stronger party (professional) and so must trust the stronger party. According to Bayles, the professional has a special obligation to the client to ensure that the trust and reliance are justified. This obligation of trust is vital to all the media professions.

Trust and the Professional–Client Relationship

At the heart of the fiduciary model is the obligation of trust. Clients must feel that they can trust the professional who is acting, supposedly, in their best interest. As mentioned before, we typically relinquish various decision-making powers to others on a regular basis. We don't want to worry about traffic patterns, the timing of intersection signals, disposing of our own garbage, and the myriad other tasks performed by others on our behalf. We *trust* that these jobs are being done competently. However, we don't want to give over all our decision-making authority either. It is clear that professionals must engender trust in their constituencies in order to be allowed the autonomy they need to act on their educated judgments; and those judgments are what, in turn, perpetuate that trust. As the journalist and ethicist Joann Byrd has said concerning journalism, "[The public's] trust is a gift. And we earn it by being forthright about our reasoning."[16]

Clients trust professionals to do what they are supposed to do. What they are supposed to do is defined both by the client and the professional. For example, contracts between public relations and advertising professionals and their clients stipulate what each will provide. On the other hand, the expectations between the press and the American people have been fairly commonly held over the years. And although those expectations may be, and probably are, changing, their implication is usually clear. Some of these expectations include:

- For consulting professionals, *to use professional expertise to analyze the problem.* In the case of journalism this means using journalistic training to decide what is news, how to gather it, how to organize it in a meaningful way, and how to present it in a timely manner.
- *To formulate alternative plans or courses of action and determine their probable consequences.* Journalists are supposed to present a balanced picture, giving as many points of view as is relevant in order that their constituents may make informed decisions.
- *To make recommendations, or carry out certain activities on behalf of the client.* In the case of journalism, this last expectation depends on how far along the road to public journalism the particular outlet has moved. To a traditional, libertarian journalist, making a recommendation (outside the editorial pages) would be a literal sin. To a communitarian journalist, it would be an obligation.

In order to engender the trust needed for a successful fiduciary relationship, professionals generally must fulfill seven obligations to their clients.[17]

Honesty

The client always expects that the professional will be honest with him. This would extend to others as well, since not being honest with others would necessarily reflect on the client as well. Being honest with clients might include recommending options that are legitimately in the client's best interest, not just the professional's (by providing for more work for the professional instead of leading to an immediate and successful conclusion for the client, for example). Honesty would also include not stealing from a client (by padding bills or providing unneeded services, for instance).

For the professional journalist, honesty is an obvious obligation and requires that all information be truthful, complete, and balanced. However, it could also mean not using deceptive news-gathering techniques, or not obscuring the line between entertainment and news on a television magazine program.

Candor

Candor refers more to truthful disclosure than to honesty. A professional could be dishonest yet open about it. In other words, a person can tell the truth about being dishonest. Some believe that candor is at the heart of the professional–client relationship, at least for consulting professions. In those professions, including advertising and public relations, the client must be able to trust the professional to consult her and respect her informed judgment in all-important decisions. A client enters the relationship to receive information from the professional. If the professional withholds information he has reason to believe would influence his client's judgment, he alters the agreement (i.e., he manipulates the client's information so that her judgments conform to his own, paternalistic, model). Remember, we are not talking about disclosure to possible constituents other than the client here.

For journalists, candor might best be exemplified by a felt obligation to be as complete as possible in covering news stories. A lack of completeness can result in misrepresentation or misinformation, a cardinal sin among professional journalists. In addition, conflict of interest disclosure is becoming more commonplace in journalistic circles. And, with the rise in the digital manipulation of photographs appearing in both news and entertainment media, many are calling for increased emphasis on disclosure, stating clearly which photos have been digitally altered and why.

Competence

The most crucial characteristic of a professional is her ability to do what she claims she is capable of doing. It is unethical for professionals to hold themselves out to do or accept work they are not competent to handle; and, in fact, most professional codes require that professionals undertake only that work they are competent to perform and to continue learning in order to keep abreast of the field. This seems simple enough, especially for the consulting professions. An advertiser or public relations person should never claim to be able to provide a service he or she cannot provide; however, it is not that uncommon to hear of agencies of both types over-promising on capabilities or potential results. In the areas of advertising and public relations, agencies may be full-service (providing all the major types of service) or specialized (providing one or only a few types of service). To be the latter and to claim to be the former is to make a false claim concerning competence.

Strangely, competency in journalism is often assumed by the public. Many people outside journalism simply don't understand how it works or what it takes to be a journalist. Because journalism has traditionally been an "equivocal" profession—those without training specifically in the field may still practice in it—the level of expertise involved in performing the tasks of the profession is often misunderstood. The result is that many in the media audience fail to comprehend the difference between the competent and the incompetent journalist, thereby supposing an inferior product is reflective of the abilities of the entire profession; or worse yet, supposing that an inferior product is equal to an excellent one. Although the same is true in public relations and advertising, the effect in journalism is more damning because of the higher expectations for the profession.

Diligence—or Zeal

Although diligence is closely related to competence, it is not the same thing. One can be competent but not diligent. *Diligence* refers to pursuing a client's interest with vigor and intensity. Too often, professionals let important items slide—either through laziness or through work pressures. A client realizes that a professional may have other clients, but that does not absolve him of serving her interests with diligence. Whereas this is an expected obligation of most consulting professions, its place in journalism is not as strong. Certainly journalists must be diligent in their pursuit of important news; however, their audience is less likely to feel neglected if they don't pursue every story, only if they fail to cover the "big" stories. Diligence in journalism might also refer to the completeness of stories since an incomplete story may be misleading.

Loyalty

Loyalty is probably one of the most important differences among the media professions. *Loyalty* here refers only to that owed to the interests the professional is hired to serve, not to the client in all its dealings outside this relationship. And there are limits to this obligation. The biggest problem associated with loyalty is determining the boundaries between a professional's loyalty to a client and other responsibilities. For example, third-party obligations, as we defined them in Chapter 2, certainly affect the degree of loyalty owed a client. In addition, clients may expect only a loyalty that does not violate a professional's other responsibilities. For instance, a client can't expect a professional to commit illegal acts on his behalf.

Journalists also have divided loyalties. As discussed earlier, they are obligated to provide information that is both useful and interesting to their audience; however, they must also turn a profit for their owners, and follow the dictates of their professions and their own consciences. For a journalist, though, fidelity to the ideal of news gathering, what its ultimate purpose is and whom it ultimately serves, is the highest order of loyalty.

Fairness

Fairness in journalism will be discussed in some detail in a later chapter; however, the concept of fairness is part and parcel of all professions. For the consulting professions, *fairness* can refer to equality of service given to various clients. For example, ignoring one client in order to favor another, higher paying, client is patently unfair. Fairness also refers to how clients are chosen by professionals (including serving clients regardless of race, religion, ethnic origin, or gender).

Discretion

Discretion usually refers to confidentiality. Underlying discretion is privacy, the control of information about oneself that others have. Consulting professionals generally maintain client confidentiality, and, in fact, confidentiality clauses in professional codes are among the most common. The importance of discretion to professions such as advertising and public relations is obvious. Many of the clients of these professions are in competitive businesses. Their business strategies, including their advertising and public relations plans, are as important as state secrets are to national governments.

For journalists, confidentiality usually refers to that promised to sources in return for information. Sources would generally be considered as third-party claimants rather than clients, in the purest sense. However, the concept of source confidentiality is so strong a journalistic ethic that laws have been enacted to recognize it; and journalists not protected by such laws have sometimes gone to jail to defend source confidentiality.

Can the Fiduciary Model Work?

If we consider the media to be professions, consulting or otherwise, then they need to operate from within a model that brings out the best they have to offer, and that encourages ethical consideration of their primary constituency. The fiduciary model does that. For advertising and public relations professionals, this model provides for a way to discharge professional obligations while retaining as much autonomy as possible in decision making. Autonomy allows the consulting professional to adhere more closely to professional standards of conduct. In addition, the element of trust, so vital to this approach, has to be developed and maintained through the pursuit and practice of ethical behavior on the part of the professional toward the client.

For the journalist, this model provides a framework for understanding the obligations inherent in the relationship between the profession and its client—the consumer of news. These consumers must also trust the journalist, in the same way that advertising and public relations clients trust professional ad and PR people. The provision of good advertising and public relations enables clients to be more effective in their pursuits. In the same way, the provision of important information and news to millions of people every day enables them to better understand their lives and their place in the greater society of which they are a part. Without this information, they are far less likely to contribute effectively to society or to themselves. The "client" of journalism *trusts* the media professional to do the job right. The fiduciary model *requires* that it be done right. If the media professions consider their roles from the perspective of this model, they are far more likely to realize their ethical obligations, both to clients and to others.

Codes

One of the strongest reasons for belonging to a profession is that certain behaviors, peculiar to that occupation, are spelled out and either encouraged or discouraged by its code. For many, a formal code of ethics provides a first line of defense against proposed unethical actions. It is a reference point for the profession as a whole and a sounding board against which to test options for action. The ethicist Richard Johannesen states, "For some people, formal codes are a necessary mark of a true profession. For others, codes are worthless exercises in vagueness, irrelevance, and slick public relations."[18]

The media ethicist Philip Meyer, for example, suggests that the main benefit of codes lies in the work of "articulating a professional group's values," which, in turn, forces it to think about those values. Not only is the thinking of the members of the profession clarified through this analysis and articulation, but also the group's standards are clarified for outsiders. However, there is some question how valuable codes actually are. As Meyer has stated, "Written codes are often criticized for being of little help in making decisions. The values they list are obvious values, the behaviors enjoined are clearly bad behaviors." Speaking specifically of journalism codes, Meyer calls them "lacking in muscle," and "full of glittering generalities."[19]

Can codes be useful? Is there a way to codify professional values and principles that will result in useful guidelines for real-life practitioners? Johannesen thinks so. He argues that, despite the many problems pointed out concerning professional codes, "many of these objections might be lessened or removed."[20] He offers the following list of how professional codes function as useful guidelines for practitioners.

1 Codes can educate new persons in a profession or business by acquainting them with guidelines for ethical responsibility based on the experience of predecessors and by sensitizing them to ethical problems specific to their field.
2 Codes can narrow the problematic areas with which a person has to struggle.
3 The very process of developing the formal code can be a healthy one that forces participants to reflect on their goal, on means allowable to achieve those, and on their obligations to all claimants.
4 An effective and voluntary code may minimize the need for cumbersome and intrusive governmental regulations.
5 Code provisions can be cited as justification for saying no to a communication practice requested by peers or employers.
6 Codes provide an argumentative function. They can serve as a starting point to stimulate professional and public scrutiny of and debate over major ethical quandaries in a field.
   There is a range of argumentative claims that critics or defenders of a communication practice might use to assess ethicality in light of a code. It could be argued that a particular practice:

   • clearly is contrary to a precise, relevant, well-justified code;
   • is ethically suspect even though it falls outside the boundaries of any established code;
   • is ethical because the code invoked is irrelevant or inappropriate; is unethical because, although the strict letter of the code was honored, the spirit of the code was violated;
   • is ethical because key terms of the code are too vague and ambiguous for precise or meaningful application;
   • is ethically justified because one applicable code is superseded by another relevant code, or because higher values take precedence over the formal code;
   • is ethical because the facts of the situation, including intent and context, are unclear; and
   • should be judged primarily by legal statues rather than by an ethical code.

7 Codes should be seen has having a function not just of serving as rules of behavior, but primarily as establishing expectations for character. In other words, codes reflect a wide range of character traits necessary for someone to be a professional.[21]

Johannesen also cites 11 guidelines gleaned from a close reading of several scholars who have also studied codes of ethics.

1   The code should clearly differentiate between ideal goals and minimum conditions. *Ideal goals* are to be striven for but not necessarily always attained. *Minimum conditions* must be met in order for a practitioner to be considered ethical.
2   Neither heroic virtue nor extreme sacrifice should be expected by the code. Codes should be written for ordinary persons functioning under ordinary conditions.
3   Language should be clear and specific, free from ambiguity. Key terms should be defined, by analogy if necessary.
4   Provisions of the code should be logically coherent. The order and priority of the provisions should be clear, especially as regards the order in which obligations should be honored among the various claimants.
5   The code should protect the general public interest and that of all claimants with a stake in the decisions of the professional following the code. The code should make it clear that the profession should never profit at the expense of the public interest.
6   Provisions should go beyond the obvious ethical violations to focus on the potential problems that are unique to the profession for which the code is devised. For example, a public relations code might accentuate the potential for conflict between the client's interest and the public's.
7   A code should make provision for growth and revision—in fact, encourage it. No code should be seen as "carved in stone."
8   The code should make clear which of its admonitions refer to individual action and which to the profession as a whole.
9   The code should declare the moral bases on which it is founded. Most media codes, for example, cite truth as their guiding principle.
10   As many members as possible should participate in the formulation of the code, from every level within the profession.
11   The code must be enforceable and enforced. A code without "teeth" is a weak or even useless code.[22]

Finally, Johannesen points to two of the most important functions of codes. The first, and not always the most obvious, is a code's argumentative function. Codes can serve as touchstones for debate, providing the public with a reference point from which to criticize a profession's actions. A code can also serve as a defense against being asked to do something that goes against its provisions, or be used to develop policy, or serve as an ethical focus for an organization or profession.[23]

The second important function of a code is to depict the ideal character of the professional for whom the code is written. In the words of Karen Lebacqz, author of *Professional Ethics*, a "professional is called not simply to *do* something but to *be* something."[24] This goes beyond the common view of a code as simply a set of guidelines for professionals to follow. It speaks directly to character, an issue we will take up later in some detail.

How to Construct a Code of Ethics

Constructing a code of ethics is not an easy job, but it can be educational and, ultimately, useful. Following are two sets of guidelines gleaned from experts on the topic.

In an article written for the Center for the Study of Ethics in the Professions, Andrew Olsen provides some preliminary suggestions for developing a code of ethics for professional associations.[25]

1   A helpful way to start any project of significant size is with a *statement of purpose*. Begin writing a code of ethics by asking yourself and members of your organization, "Why does my (our) organization want to develop a code of ethics?" Generally speaking, it seems that codes of ethics with a clearly defined purpose are more clearly stated and better organized.

Many codes make effective use of defining a purpose by beginning the document with a *preamble* or a *statement of intent*. The *preamble* sets the tone of the document and outlines both the purpose of the organization and the purpose of the code. The *statement of intent* fulfills a similar purpose, but it focuses more on the purpose of the code and less on the purpose of the organization than does a *preamble*. Both are good ways to set the tone of the code and to establish a feel of cohesion within the group that is essential to the proper functioning of a code.

2   To assure that a code of ethics functions properly, the group or a representative body of the group must formulate it. Writing a properly functioning code of ethics is a collective task. Without a reasonable amount of group consensus concerning morally permissible standards of conduct relevant to the group, the code finds its home scribbled on a sheet of paper rather than in the actions and decisions of members of the group.

3   To counter the argument that codes of ethics are merely well-meaning statements on a rarely seen, and even less frequently and effectively implemented, document, a code of ethics must truly reflect the virtues of the group. Through a process of achieving consensus, writing a code of ethics becomes an excellent group-defining task. Consequently, a well-defined membership in the group, an outcome of devising and publicizing a code, aids in the functioning of the code. Through identification as a member of the group, a member's sense of duty to other members of the group and to the group's collective agreements expressed in the code is strengthened. As a result, the effectiveness of the code of ethics is also strengthened.

4   Here are some questions one might consider when deciding what should be included in the code:

- Who are the persons or groups of persons affected by your organization or the members of your organization, and how are they prioritized?
- What are your organization's main areas of action?
- What unethical decisions and actions would your organization like to prevent, and how could they be prevented?
- What type of ethical problems are members of your organization most likely to encounter?
- How can conflicting principles be resolved?

5   After your organization has answered these questions and formulated what needs to be included in the organization's code of ethics, the next step is to decide how to organize the code.

6   Just as principles within a code differ from group to group, so too, methods of organization differ from group to group. Factors that may affect how a group organizes its code could include such aspects as length of the code, how statements for inclusion in the code were formulated, and with what form of organization members of your group are most familiar. For example, if there is a small amount of information to be included in the code, then a simple ordered list may be the most appropriate method of organization. On the other hand, if there is a large amount of information to be included in the code, then more structured methods of organization may be most appropriate. For instance, if relationships were a major consideration in the formulation of statements, then it seems most appropriate to organize the code according to relationships. However, if relationships were not a major consideration but principles were a major consideration, then it seems most appropriate to organize the code according to principles and guidelines for the principles. The concept is rather simple, but it is mentioned here because its importance outweighs its simplicity.

7   Most codes can be placed into one of three commonly occurring categories.

- The codes in the first category, *brief codes*, have a small list of statements that rarely have much structure at all. However, even a small list of statements can provide guidance to members of a group if consideration is given to how the list can be prioritized.
- Other groups use the descending form: *Preamble/Statement of Intent, Fundamental Principles, Fundamental Canons,* and *Guidelines for the Principles and Canons.* This form centers on each principle individually and applies the principle to many relationships that members of the group may encounter.
- In contrast, another common form of organization of well-developed codes is one that highlights relationships between the group or member(s) of the group and other groups of society such as the public, clients, or employers. Such methods of organization often divide the

code into sections that begin with such headings as *Relations/Obligations to the . . .* followed by a list of standards and guiding statements relevant to the relationship.

8   A code of ethics is a means of uniquely expressing a group's collective commitment to a specific set of standards of conduct while offering guidance in how to best follow those codes. As such, authors of a code of ethics should explore methods of organizing a code and use of language in the code that will be well received by the codes' intended participants.

9   In addition, if one's group closely identifies itself and its work with the people involved, then a code of ethics that follows the relationship model above may be most appropriate. However, if one's group more closely identifies itself and its work with concepts and principles of the occupation, then a code of ethics that follows the descending principles model may be most appropriate. In either case, the code should both state the principles and offer guidance in how the principles should be followed. Giving guidance encourages participants in the code to develop and practice moral reasoning based on the collectively agreed-upon principles of the group enumerated in the code.

10   When writing a code of ethics, the code's authors must compose the code with a finely tuned attention to balance. A good code is written with the awareness that the code will be used in a variety of different situations, and each situation will prompt those involved to refer to the code for specific guidance. This presents an interesting challenge to the code's authors, who must write the code with enough information to be of use in the specifics of a situation while remaining general enough to be used for a wide variety of situations.

It is most likely this challenge that has prompted many authors to extend their code of ethics with sections entitled *Suggested Guidelines for use with the Fundamental Canons of Ethics, Standards of Practice,* or *Rules and Procedures.* In such sections, the authors attempt to foresee situations one might encounter that call for ethical considerations. Within these sections, the authors describe how one should interpret the principles of the code of ethics pertaining to one's specific situation. In many instances these guidelines will attempt to provide guidance on how to resolve conflicting principles. It is likely that these additional sections will add some time and effort to the writing process. However, much of what will be included in an additional "guidelines" section should surface in the initial brainstorming and writing process.

Considerations for Writing a Code of Ethics[26]

Chris MacDonald, who teaches philosophy at Saint Mary's University in Halifax, Nova Scotia, provides us with another take on constructing a code for individual organizations.

Most major corporations, and many smaller companies, now have Codes of Ethics, along with a range of other, issue-specific ethics documents. Such a document embodies the ethical commitments of your organization; it tells the world who you are, what you stand for, and what to expect when conducting business with you. The content of a Code, and the process for writing it, can vary quite a lot, but here are some of the standard issues to consider.

1 *Tailor-make your code.* Ideally, a Code of Ethics should be custom-made for your organization. Ask yourself, what makes your Code specific to your organization? Is there anything that differentiates it from similar documents devised other firms in your field, or in other fields? If not, what makes it your Code, other than the fact that your logo is at the top?

2 *Get employees involved.* The people who will be guided by the code should be actively involved in writing it. If your organization is too large to get everyone involved, consider selecting representatives from various departments or various business units. The document is bound to be more meaningful, and find higher levels of acceptance, if employees are part of the process.

3 *Consult key stakeholders.* It's a good idea to consult key stakeholders—including, for example, customers, suppliers, and local community groups—on what they think should be in your Code. This will help reveal what important external constituencies see as your key obligations, and will help make sure that the Code you write deals with the full range of issues that might confront your organization.

4 *Outsource the job only carefully.* Hiring a consultant to help write your code can be useful—but don't let them take over. A consultant can bring a wealth of knowledge and experience, and can help you avoid a whole range of pitfalls, from lack of clarity through to the inclusion of too little—or too much—detail. But at the end of the day, this Code is still yours; it should reflect your organization's values, principles, and aspirations.

5 *Seek out good examples.* If you're writing your own code, begin by looking at relevant examples. There are lots of good Codes out there (a quick internet search can be very revealing.) A code that is simply copied from another organization is unlikely to provide either effective guidance or inspiration—but there's also no point in reinventing the wheel.

6 *Be clear about scope.* Your Code should make clear who within your organization will be governed by it. Does it cover everyone from the mailroom through to the boardroom? Only senior managers? Who has to sign off on it? Keep in mind that lower-level employees may not take very seriously a document that senior managers either aren't bound by, or take lightly.

7   *Be specific about implementation.* How will the Code be implemented? Once it's written, will it gather dust, or will it influence policy and practice? What procedures are in place to make sure that writing a Code is more than just organizational navel-gazing? An effective implementation scheme (perhaps as an appendix to the Code) will explain to all concerned how the values embodied in your Code will be put into practice.

8   *Plan for education.* A key aspect of implementation has to be employee training and education. How will employees be educated about the Code? A Code can only be effective if your employees know about it. Will new employees receive training regarding the Code's requirements? Will current employees receive refresher courses? Especially for large organizations, the steps required to train employees on the requirements of a Code deserve special attention.

9   *Be clear about enforcement.* How, if at all, will the Code be enforced? Are there specific penalties for violating the Code, or is the Code merely there to provide guidance? Who will decide when an employee has violated the Code—will that be up to the employees' immediate supervisor, or will that be the exclusive domain of senior managers?

10   *Specify a sunset date.* When will the code be reviewed and updated? Times change, and new issues come to light, so consider specifying a date for revising and refreshing your Code.

Profession versus Professionalism: If It Walks like a Duck . . .

Do the media need to be professions? Maybe not, but there are certainly benefits that can be derived from acting like professionals. As already mentioned, professionals garner more respect that other occupations. They are often paid more and have a higher level of prestige within our society. Despite the common jokes about doctors and lawyers, they are still held in rather high esteem by the rest of us. To be a professional, in this sense, is to have entrée into that realm. In addition to the prestige associated with professionalism is the more important concern of how professionals are supposed to act. Professionals are assumed to be held to a higher set of standards than other occupations; and although we certainly find much fault with the professions, it is probably because of this increased expectation that we do so. Being a professional assumes a level of ethicality beyond that of societal norms—certainly different, but also enhanced.

As we have seen, the media "professions" all have professional societies, codes of ethics, intellectual bodies of knowledge, some degree of credentialing, and a prescribed level of practical expertise in their fields. They also bear the obligation of service in the public interest. The discharge of this service may be in some doubt (both in the ideal and the execution), but the expectation is still there. Ironically, in journalism, the least willing to be viewed as a profession, we find the strongest evidence for the performance of public service.

In short, the media may garner the benefits of professionalism by merely acting as if they were professions. However, this façade has its price. In order to be considered professional, we must act professionally, and that means observing the dictates of professional behavior—including its ethical imperatives. The payoff is that the media gain a modicum of respect that other occupations do not have. And it's not that the "public" doesn't recognize professional activity when it sees it. Paparazzi don't strike many of us as "professional" photographers in the way that photojournalists do. Neither do tabloid reporters compare favorably with those who work for the *New York Times*, or the *Washington Post*. The difference is professionalism, and professionalism implies a higher standard of behavior. We cannot have the one without the other.

Chapter 4

Theoretical Approaches to Ethics

There's [a] trouble about theories: there's always a hole in them somewheres, ... if you look close enough.

(Mark Twain)

Can understanding ethical theory help us make better moral decisions? Yes, it can. Each of us makes these kinds of decisions anyway, based usually on what we feel is right. That "feeling" isn't really just emotional or intuitive. It's a culturally transmitted as well as a learned response to certain conditions we recognize as having ethical elements in them. Our responses to moral dilemmas are based on what we have learned from our culture, our families, our education, and our society. It might surprise you to know that many of the norms that we glean from these sources are the results of serious moral theorizing.

Ethical theory, which comes from the study of moral philosophy, is simply an organized way of approaching ethical decision making. A theory is a method of explaining something we observe in our lives, the formulation of which will then allow us to predict such events in the future and more easily deal with them. For example, management theories show us different approaches to managing organizations, employees, and business environments. They help managers better understand the variables involved in running an organization and show them how to best cope with them. And, as we saw in Chapter 2, systems theory can be used to describe the relationships among media organizations and the stakeholders who make up their relevant environments. These types of theories are simply models of reality, thus they are best tested in the real world to see if they work. The same is true of moral theory. Whereas a great deal of moral theory is so complex and esoteric as to be practically useless to most of us, the specific field of applied ethical theory is designed to be used in the real world. That's the theory we're going to discuss here.

Why Can't We All Be Right? The Dilemma of Relativism

Before we get started on our exploration of ethical theory, we must first answer a very big question: Do we have the right to sit in judgment on other people?

This question is very much at the heart of a major moral dilemma today—the dilemma of relativism.

Essentially, there are three types of claims one can make regarding beliefs: subjective, intersubjective, and objective claims.

- A claim or judgment is *subjective* if its truth depends on whether or not it conforms to the tastes, attitudes, and beliefs of the claimer (the person making the claim). For example, to say that you like chocolate ice-cream with potato chips on top is a matter of taste.
- A claim or judgment is *intersubjective* if its truth depends on whether or not it conforms to the beliefs, attitudes, and conventions of the group to which the claimer belongs. For example, to say that it's rude to eat with your fingers is generally a matter of culture and custom—something widely recognized as either permissible or not within a particular society.
- A claim or judgment is *objective* if its truth does *not* depend on whether it conforms to the beliefs or attitudes of any group or individual. These are often claims of provable fact, such as "The earth is round," or "Water boils at 100 degrees Celsius."[1]

Relativism

Relativism in general asserts that standards are relative to something else: who you are, the society in which you live, or your cultural predisposition. For example, we can claim that we cannot judge what another society is doing (or a member of that society) since they are governed by the rules of their society, not ours. This is called *cultural relativism*. Cultural relativism suggests that there are no independent standards by which to judge correct or incorrect actions because all such standards are group- or culture-bound.

Ethical relativism is the view that all moral claims are intersubjective. Since different societies have different moral codes, there can be no objective standard separate from society by which to judge these codes. All moral standards are, thus, intersubjective. This means that the moral code of our own society has no special status either (except to govern internally). Therefore, we have no authority by which to judge the conduct of people in other societies. What we need, instead, is to become more tolerant of the practices of other cultures. If we were to take cultural and ethical relativism seriously, no action deemed acceptable by a given society could be called morally wrong. No society could claim that its conduct was morally superior to another. In fact, the only actions we could decide on would be those of our own society.

Subjectivism

At the individual level, relativism becomes what is known as ethical subjectivism. *Ethical subjectivism* is the idea that our moral opinions are based on our feelings, and nothing more. There is no right or wrong, only expressions of our feelings. Therefore, we can't judge another individual's actions or beliefs as being wrong or right since they are merely based on opinion and nothing else. Here's the kind of argument ethical subjectivism boils down to:

- "Using sex to sell products is morally acceptable." This simply means I approve of it, nothing more.
- "Using sex to sell products is morally unacceptable." This simply means I disapprove of it, nothing more.

Using sex to sell products is neither wrong nor right. The practice is simply a choice based on opinion. The guiding principle of subjectivism is based on the perennial demand, "Show me the rule."

Like relativism, subjectivism assumes that there are no objective truths. Thus, there are no such things as moral "facts," only our attitudes about morality. If there is no objective truth in morality, if right and wrong are only matters of opinion, and if opinions vary from culture to culture (and from group to group), how are we to decide whether an action is right or wrong? Does it follow that just because people and cultures disagree that there is no objective truth?

The Test of Reason

According to the philosopher James Rachels, the problem with the basic argument of both relativism and subjectivism is that it assumes only two possibilities: (1) There *are* moral facts in the same way that there are scientific facts; or (2) our "values" are nothing more than the expression of our subjective feelings—in other words, there are no moral facts. This argument overlooks a crucial third possibility, however: Moral truths are truths of reason. That is, a moral judgment is true if it is backed by better reasons than the alternatives.[2] Think of accepting ethical subjectivism as an excuse. We don't usually allow people to do things simply because they "feel" they're right. We want reasons.

What we have done instead is to develop theories of rightness and obligation based on the notion of reason. For example, each person ought to do whatever will best promote his or her own interests (*Ethical Egoism*). Or we ought to do whatever will promote the greatest happiness for the greatest number (*Utilitarianism*). Or our duty is to follow rules that we could consistently will to be universal laws—that is, rules that we would be willing to have followed by all people in all circumstances (the *Categorical Imperative*).

Although we may still pay a certain amount of lip service to relativism, we tend to want order in our lives. And order typically comes from rules and guidelines, not from allowing everyone to do what they want simply because it feels right. In addition, we realize that there are some things that are not morally acceptable, despite being endorsed by an entire society. Nazi Germany's legally sanctioned and systematic extermination of the Jews during World War II was most certainly immoral. Today, "ethnic cleansing" evokes the same sense of moral outrage in most of us. What relativism *has* accomplished is to force us to be more tolerant of differences among cultures and between individuals. It should not cause us to overlook unethical or immoral actions.

Why We Reason the Way We Do

Every time a journalist refers to the public's right to know as a reason for violating someone's privacy, she is using a *utilitarian* argument. When the same journalist points out that her paper has an absolute rule forbidding the printing of a rape victim's name, she is using a *Kantian* appeal. When a public relations practitioner says that upholding his professional integrity is more important than making money doing something he feels is unethical, he is defending his *virtue*. And when an advertiser says that he is using sex to sell a product because that's what works best, he is using *ethical relativism*. The point is that we all rely on ethical theory every day—we just don't realize it. The benefit in realizing it is that we can then begin to make more consistent decisions by having a better understanding of why we are acting the way we are.

As already pointed out, the way in which we respond to ethical dilemmas isn't entirely something we were born with. Although some of the most recent evidence does suggest that, as human beings, we might be genetically disposed to act in certain ways, these studies don't absolve us of the responsibility to try to be better than our genes dictate.[3] Other research seems to show that whether we're male or female may also predispose us to think and act in certain ways—cultural factors aside.[4] However, assuming for the moment that we just might be slaves to our genes, we are also products of our upbringing, our cultures, and our educational backgrounds. And we each live in a society that has its own set of social and moral norms. Add to that the fact that human beings are born with the ability to reason, and you have the basis for much of ethical theory. Together, these are the elements that have the greatest effect on the way we make moral decisions, and they are what we're going to discuss here.

Since what we are considering in this book are basically the media of the West—specifically, the United States—we will focus here on the ethical theories that have had the most influence on U.S. culture and on U.S. media. Those theories are primarily the ones born during the Enlightenment period in Europe and the United States—a period that ran roughly from the sixteenth to the nineteenth century. It is no coincidence that the United States was founded on Enlightenment philosophy, especially since most of the founders of this country not only were quite familiar with that philosophy but were also contributors to it. The Enlightenment was also known as the "Age of Reason," because the great thinkers of that time were becoming less attached to religious explanations for life and all its complications and more inclined to scientific accounts. And science, unlike religion, is based on the human faculty of reason, not on faith.

However, we will not slight the critics of Enlightenment theory, many of whom are feminist authors who hold that these theories have resulted in a society, and a media, that is contentious and competitive because of our philosophical heritage. And, in support of such concepts as communitarianism and some feminist concerns, we will make occasional forays into philosophies such as Confucianism, a societal construct based on interdependence rather than independence. Let us begin, then, with a look at a basic question affecting the activities of human beings: why they band together.

Social Contract Theory

One of the longest-standing Enlightenment concepts is that of the *social contract*. Dating back to Plato and Aristotle and espoused by a number of European philosophers (most notably Thomas Hobbes and John Locke), social contract theory is an attempt to explain why humans prefer an organized and communal state to one of total individualism and independence. Many of today's disagreements over whether journalism should be objective or subjective in its relationship with its audience stem from the argument over individualism versus communalism. How much allegiance do we owe the state? How community-conscious should a newspaper or television station be? Are the media active participants in community affairs or objective outsiders? These are all questions that have been discussed in different ways for thousands of years, but they still have relevance for us today—especially in how we regard the media and their place in society.

You'll recall from Chapter 2 that the media are variously obligated to their constituencies. One of the most important, and most often occurring, obligations is that of fidelity. Fidelity often suggests a contractual obligation, either explicit or implicit. For example, journalists are obligated by fidelity to their audiences; an implied contract exists whereby the journalist is responsible for providing useful and interesting news to his readers, viewers, or listeners. In the same way, advertising and public relations practitioners are obligated to their clients, with third-party obligations discharged through other duties such as non-injury and justice. This latter type of obligation is often referred to as social responsibility. It could be said that all media are, then, socially obligated.

The idea of social obligation has its roots in the social contract, which basically proposes that government is responsible to its citizens, who, in turn, lend it legitimacy by their willingness to obey society's rules.

As we have seen, some functions in society are also naturally obligated to society as a whole—especially the professional roles. And although the original idea of social contract had to do with the relationship between a government and the citizens it represents, it is entirely logical to extrapolate this sort of obligation between the media and their constituents. Let us look, then, at some of the philosophers who have considered the social contract and what these theorists have suggested is the proper relationship between citizens and their government.

Plato

As far back as the ancient Greeks, western philosophy has been concerned with the relationship of individuals to society. Two of the most important of the Greek philosophers, Plato and Aristotle, both gave a great deal of thought to the proper role of society and politics in the lives of human beings. In one of history's greatest works, the *Republic*, Plato (427–347 BCE) pictured a society in which the educated elite would rule, governing by reason and rejecting the emotional entanglements of life—such as the arts. Plato also envisioned a society in which individualism would be sublimated by an overriding obligation to serve society first. The primary reason Plato believed so strongly that only the educated should rule was that he doubted the abilities of the *hoi polloi* (a Greek expression referring to the uncultured mob, or the common people). He thought these people simply didn't have a clue about the reality of life around them.

In what is known as "the parable of the cave," Plato likens the existence of most human beings to that of slaves living in a darkened cave. These slaves are chained facing a large wall. Behind them, and unknown to them, a large fire is burning. Between that fire and the chained slaves are people, perpetually moving about, their shadows thrown upon the wall that the slaves must face. To the slaves, forever bound in place, these shadows and the sounds they hear coming from the moving figures are all there is of reality. It is this reality that the slaves talk and think about, since it is all they know. In order to break the bonds of this "reality," a person would have to free himself from his chains, turn around, and face the fire and the people moving to and fro in front of it. However, such an experience would probably be so frightening that it would result in the slave wishing to return to his original reality. And if the slave were forced to go to the surface, outside the cave, the experience of the blinding sunlight and vast panorama of this new reality would be nearly overwhelming. Even supposing that the slave became used to the reality of the world, he would never be able to explain it to his fellow slaves if he returned to the darkness of the cave, because their frame of reference wouldn't include these possibilities.

Plato believed most people were enslaved in their own bodies, not able to comprehend the reality beyond their humanity. A more modern interpretation, however, might indicate that we are still prisoners of our own illusions—illusions proffered in large part by the media. In fact, it was this very point that was the focus of much of the criticism of the media early in the twentieth century. For example, the social philosopher and media critic Walter Lippmann referred to the reality painted by an opinionated media as "the pictures in people's heads," alluding directly to Plato's writings.[5] Today, we have only to look at the phenomenon of the recent rash of "reality TV" shows to recognize how readily people will incorporate fiction into their daily lives. What transpired on *Survivor* each week invariably became the major topic of conversation around the water cooler until the following week's show. And, despite the appellation "reality," the shows are decidedly a sort of forced non-fiction at best.

Thus, the "parable of the cave" has far-reaching implications for those of us today who base most of what we know about the world beyond our walls on what the media tell us. Plato may have been right to assume that most people will be satisfied with the shadows on the wall, given how difficult it may be to accept the "real" world. Certainly, this story carries an important moral not only for journalism, but also especially for advertising and public relations, whose primary role frequently is to cast those shadows.

A Platonic view of the place of the media in our society was held (at least for a while) by Lippmann. In some of his earlier works, he proposed that information be controlled by an intelligent elite who would then pass it along to the media to be further interpreted for the people (not unlike Plato's concept of the perfect republic). All information disseminated this way would be completely objective and free of opinion. Although this particular "utopia" never came to pass, Lippmann is largely responsible for the idealized view of objectivity held by the press today. Thus, a Platonic view of the media would also place objective truth above all else, and allegiance to society above individualism. In other words, social responsibility would probably be placed ahead of press freedom.[6] In addition, we would probably find that the entertainment media would be rejected outright as not contributing positively to society, a view becoming a bit more prevalent these days.

Aristotle

Plato's student, Aristotle (384–322 BCE), continued the Greek interest in the social nature of human beings; however, where Plato focused on the group, Aristotle accentuated the individual. In his *Politics*, Aristotle suggested that the true aim of government was to aid its citizens in the realization of the good life. He stressed the seeming need for human beings to live in societies in order to become self-fulfilled—something they could not do in isolation. Aristotle believed that man is by nature a political animal, and it is the job of the state to make the acquisition of the good life a reality. He placed a heavy stress on the individual; however, he also noted that both the individual and society must work together toward the same ends. Obviously, his political ideal was a democracy that allows—even requires—personal involvement. And, unlike Plato, Aristotle championed the arts, especially poetic tragedy, because he believed that a message embedded within a creative context would have much more impact and staying power. And although he stopped short of describing a social contract between government and the people, he did shape the belief in a strong and cooperative society. We will visit Aristotle again when we look at virtue ethics later in this chapter.

An Aristotelian view of the press would probably emphasize its role in helping individuals fulfill their potential. According to this view, the best way for that to happen would be to keep the citizens informed enough to participate intelligently in the process of democracy. Sound familiar? It's not a coincidence that the modern American press is founded on the principal of informing the people. Aristotle would probably also emphasize the rights of the individual over those of the community, thus press freedoms over press responsibility (at least beyond its basic responsibility to inform). He would also probably favor the creative aspects of advertising, since messages creatively expressed are often those with the most impact (a fact that advertisers know well).

Thomas Hobbes

It wasn't until the Enlightenment that thinkers would revisit the relationship between the state and its citizens with such scrutiny. Thomas Hobbes (1588–1679) lived through some of the most turbulent periods of English history. He was born during the reign of Elizabeth I and lived to see the English Civil War brought to a conclusion. Hobbes was among the first of the Enlightenment philosophers to picture the universe as completely material and doubted that either heaven or God could be proved to exist outside the real world. Following the ideas of his day, Hobbes was one of the first to present the human being as a machine with all its parts working together to exist in the material world. In fact, the material world itself was machine-like in its workings, or, as he referred to it, "matter in motion." This mechanistic view of both human beings and the universe they inhabit heavily influenced his concept of how societies and governments were formed.

Hobbes believed that without society human beings would be living in a constant state of violent conflict over scarce resources—"a war of every man against every man." In his best-known book, *Leviathan*, he paints a dire picture of people without government in which individuals live a life in the shadow of violent death, "solitary, poor, nasty, brutish, and short." His solution to this "state of nature" was the *social contract*.

Under this social contract, human beings would band together in a state of cooperation in which labor would be divided, and the amount of essential goods would increase and be equitably distributed. In order for this arrangement to work, there had to be a guarantee that people would not harm one another—they had to be free from fear of attack, theft, or treachery. And, they had to be able to rely on each other to keep their agreements. But Hobbes was not a "the glass is half-full" sort of person. He believed that although people would band together for self-protection and to better their chances of survival, they would not remain faithful to the contract very long without being forced. Why? Because people, even those living together in a social contract, are still self-interested. Ideally, people will cooperate because they know that their interests are affected not only by what they do but by what other people do as well. In other words, if everyone pursued his or her own self-interests then they would all be worse off than if they worked together. However, Hobbes realized that, even by using reason, people would still come to the conclusion that being self- interested would be the best individual course to take.

This is how Hobbes reasoned it out. In living together with other people, you could adopt either of two strategies: You could pursue your own self-interests exclusively, or you could be concerned with other people's welfare as well as your own. Given these two possible strategies, there are four options.

- You could be self-interested while other people are generous, in which case you are getting a free ride.
- Others could be self-interested while you are generous, in which case you're a sucker.
- Everyone could be self-interested, in which case we'd all be back in a state of nature squabbling over scarce resources.
- Everyone could be generous—the ideal state of affairs.[7]

Given these choices, what would a rational person do? Hobbes suggested that anyone with half a brain would choose the first option. The dilemma, however, is that if everyone chooses option 1, then we're back to option 3—and that is unacceptable. The answer is mutual cooperation overseen by a strong government. People must agree to the establishment of rules to govern their relations with one another and to the formation of an agency (the government) with the power to enforce those rules. Hobbes held that such a government must have more power than any individual or any group in order to effectuate control over violations of the social contract. And, people would have only so much liberty as they would allow to others. Hobbes, thus, made allowances for an individual or a group to govern (a sovereign or a legislature), as long as governance is for the good of all, not the governing body. However, above all else, Thomas Hobbes believed that government—any government—was better than social chaos.

John Locke

John Locke (1632–1704) was a well-educated Englishman who, in addition to being a medical doctor, was profoundly interested in politics. His interest led him to become intimately involved with some of the most influential politicians and rulers of his time. His interest and familiarity with the "new" thinking in science and philosophy led him to write a number of political and philosophical works throughout his lifetime.

Locke was among those who proposed that human beings band together and form governments in order to better manage their affairs. Without society, Locke believed, people would simply exist in a state of nature, as self-interested individuals—though not as "brutish" as Hobbes depicted. Only by becoming a society of free individuals deciding their fates together would they reach their full potential as reasoning human beings (a bit Aristotelian). Like most of the other Enlightenment philosophers, Locke believed that human beings were endowed with the ability to reason, and that this is what set them apart from other creatures. And, as reasoning beings, they would not bear a government that did not respect their rights. Locke believed that sovereignty ultimately remained with the people, no matter what form the government took. In fact he proposed that the protection of the rights of the people (life, liberty, and property) was the sole legitimate purpose of government.

John Locke was among the first to suggest that if that trust were ever violated, it would become the moral obligation of the people to overthrow the government and replace it with one that worked properly. Locke was also a man who "walked the talk." During the Glorious Revolution of 1688, he was directly involved in helping place William of Orange on the English throne after James II had, with some reluctance, left it vacant. We can see in John Locke the roots of the movement that eventually led to the founding of the United States and the philosophical championing of the individual over the group.

On the other hand, Hobbes would probably propose a press that was responsible directly to government as a tool for control of the people (perhaps as a propaganda arm)—a form of forced social responsibility. And, in fact, the press of Hobbes's day was strongly controlled by the government. To Hobbes, the role of the press would not be to further either individual goals or societal goals, but goals established by society and legislated by the government.

Of the two, Locke's insistence on the preservation of individual freedom would play best with today's media. His vision of the social contract would place a heavy emphasis on protecting the people against government affronts to their individual freedoms—in other words, a completely free press. From a journalistic perspective, it is clear that we owe much more to Locke than to Hobbes for the conception of our modern press; however, the true value of what Hobbes and Locke had to offer lay in their theories of social contract. The idea that people would come together in consort in order to derive a better life for the conglomerate is part and parcel of America's ideology. Although we owe much more of our societal philosophy to Locke, Hobbes' image of the self-interested individual sublimating his own welfare for the greater good (even if that acquiescence is forced) is a persistent one in our society. In fact, the concept of the greater good, if not born from, at least was strengthened by the writings of all the social contractarians.

In short, the concept of the social contract is so ingrained in our social consciousness that we take it for granted that the government and its citizens are mutually obligated. An extension of that relationship is the role of the press in American society, and, by further extension, the roles of all media. Remember that Aristotle conceived of communication not as only pure information, but also as entertainment; and to the Greeks, especially, persuasion was a noble endeavor. Whereas the Enlightenment philosophers assumed the efficacy of rational argumentation and debate, the Greeks held it as essential to a working democracy. Any social contract has to recognize the place of such tactics in furthering the discourse so vital to a society's political well-being.

The Argument over Means and Ends

One of the longest running arguments in ethical theory has been that of whether means or ends should decide what is moral. Some philosophers have contested that a moral act is one that uses ethical means without consideration of the consequences, or ends. Others hold that the consequences of an act are what count. Good consequences are the result of right action. In other words, the means are ethical only if the results are good. The camps have been strongly allied with some of the greatest philosophical minds of the ages, and their arguments have been continued right up until the present day. These two points of view are usually called either *teleological* (having to do with consequences) or *deontological* (having to do with rules or duties). To simplify matters, we'll refer to these as *consequential* theories and *non-consequential* theories.

Non-consequential Ethical Theories

Every time you reference a law, a rule, a code, or a guideline, you are using non-consequential ethical theory to bolster your position. Likewise, if you are acting out of a sense of duty or obligation, you are using non-consequential logic. The idea behind *non-consequentialism* is that the action itself should be the focus of decision making, not necessarily the outcome of the action. Some actions are simply right or wrong by nature; and, as human beings, we intuitively understand this.

The earliest form of non-consequential ethics came from religion. The Judeo-Christian Ten Commandments are a good example of a rules-based approach to morality. If you keep the commandments, you are moral. If you break the commandments, you are immoral. This is pretty simple reasoning and is, therefore, very appealing to many people. In fact, the strong appeal of non-consequential ethics is that there is something concrete to base your decisions on. You don't have to dig any deeper than the rule that governs this particular action to find your answer. If your newspaper has a policy against running rape victims' names, then you simply don't run their names—no questions asked. If your professional code of ethics says always tell the truth, then you don't have to mull over whether you should lie or not. These guidelines are sometimes referred to as *conjunctive rules*, and specify a minimal cutoff point for a decision.[8] An example of an ethical conjunctive rule might be admonition in the Society of Professional Journalists' code never to distort the content of news photos or video. Application of such a guideline would clearly invalidate an option of "doctoring" a photo to remove an unwanted or distracting image.

Most laws, codes, policies, and regulations are the result of non-consequential ethical thinking: generally the result of people coming together to make guidelines by which to govern their own actions. The process itself is a major triumph of the Enlightenment and a direct result of the social contract ideas of many of the theorists already discussed. Exactly how these rules of conduct are derived, however, has been often debated. Let us look, then, at some of the more important contributors to this line of thought.

Immanuel Kant

Immanuel Kant (1724–1804) was born and lived his entire life in what was then known as Prussia. By all accounts, he was a quiet intellectual whose studious life ran like clockwork, day after day, and year after year. Despite his reserved lifestyle, Kant was a popular figure in his hometown of Königsberg, in eastern Prussia, and he became world-famous in his own lifetime.

In a period of just under ten years at the end of the eighteenth century, Immanuel Kant produced some of the most influential philosophical work of his or any other time. Through various volumes covering a huge array of topics, he developed a systematic view of the universe such as had not been seen since the time of the Greeks. Along with his other achievements, Kant also created an ethical system based solely on the human ability to reason and the belief that all moral actions were the result of virtuous intent.

Good Will

Kant held that nothing was good in itself except *good will*. In other words, no action, in and of itself, was either wrong or right. Only the motive of the actor lent the action its morality. If a person acted out of a vested interest (because of a possible consequence) then the act was non-moral—it had no moral implications whatsoever. But, if a person acted because she thought she was doing the right thing, then she was acting out of good will and the act was a moral act.

In Kant's view, actions have true moral worth only when they spring from recognition of a duty and a choice to discharge it. For example, using Kantian logic, an advertiser who avoided untruthful advertising because he was afraid of getting caught and fined would not necessarily be acting morally. However, if the advertiser recognized a duty to his constituents to tell the truth, and that is the reason he didn't lie, then the act would be a moral act.

Kant defined *good will* as the uniquely human capacity to act according to one's principles, not out of an expectation of potential consequences. In fact, Kant had learned through the writings of the Italian philosopher and royal counselor Niccolò Machiavelli that basing decisions solely on likely consequences could excuse any action, even the most abhorrent. In his famous treatise, *The Prince*, Machiavelli had proposed that any action taken by a monarch should be based on an assessment of the best outcome for the monarch himself. Under this guideline (which is also known as *egoism*), actions such as murder could be excused if they are in the best interest of the person making the decision.

Like other Enlightenment theorists, Kant believed that human beings were endowed with the ability to reason, and reasoning would logically lead to an understanding of how to construct moral rules to live by. Rational beings would, then, logically abide by the rules they set for themselves. In this, he was in accord with the social contractarians. Rules arrived at in this manner would also become morally obligatory, and Kant saw obligation (or duty) as the overriding determinant of morality. He believed that we would recognize our duty when we saw it because we could reason, and reason would lead us logically to recognition.

For Kant, there were two obvious types of duties: perfect duties and imperfect duties. *Perfect duties* were those that we must always observe; however, he framed these as proscriptions, or negative obligations. For example, "Never lie," or "Never kill." We must always refrain from these actions, no matter what. *Imperfect duties* were those that we must observe only on some occasions. These were framed as positive obligations, or prescriptions—such as: "Give to charity." He realized that some duties, such as "give to charity," could be observed only by those capable of doing so, whereas others, such as "don't kill," should, and could, be observed by everyone. Of course, he knew that rational beings would recognize when a duty was completely binding and when it was not. In this, Kant was an intuitionist, believing that human beings naturally knew right from wrong. The question remains, however, exactly how we should come up with the rules by which to live a moral life.

The Categorical Imperative

"We should act in such a way that we could wish the maxim of our action to become a universal law." That's the way Kant believed we would be able to develop rules of order, or duties. *Maxim*, in this sense, means the principle on which the action was based—the type of principle that people formulate in determining their conduct. So, if a person won't lie out of principle, he should be willing to apply that principle as a law, universally. Under the *Categorical Imperative*, we would only act in ways that we would want everyone else to act, all the time. Thus, if we wished everyone to lie all the time, then it would be permissible for us to lie. We could murder with impunity only if we would allow others to do so. However, Kant proposed that the proper use of the Categorical Imperative would have us act in a prescribed way regardless of whether we would wish to be treated that way ourselves. Kant reasoned that rational beings wouldn't tolerate a state of existence in which everyone could lie or kill without compunction. And, of course, that's true. How could we live in a society in which we would expect a lie for every question we asked, or one in which murder were the rule rather than the exception? Kant knew that social order could only come from rules formulated by all and obeyed by all. In fact, a key component of his Imperative is that those who legislate the laws are also bound by them.

Kant, writing as he did at the end of the eighteenth century, was probably heartened by the birth of democracy as a potentially viable form of government. In fact, his idea of a moral community was very much akin to the concepts of democracy given voice by the movers and shakers of the American and French revolutions (although he probably disagreed with the methods of both, since he viewed political change as most properly evolutionary, not revolutionary). If we look at his Categorical Imperative as a method of achieving a political state that promotes individual autonomy along with the general good, we can better understand the importance of his method. For example, using the Categorical Imperative, we begin by considering the formulation of laws that will be binding on all citizens all the time, with no exceptions. These laws will not only benefit individuals, but also the state as a whole—or the public good. These laws would also be binding on those whose responsibility it is to legislate and enforce them, because they are categorical. And these laws would respect the citizens of the state and their individual rights as human beings.[9]

This recognition of the inherent worth of human beings is a key feature of Kant's Categorical Imperative. As part of his method for recognizing moral duties, Kant insisted that we always act so as to treat others as ends in themselves and never completely as means to an end. In other words, we are not to use other people or treat them merely as objects. He rationalized that all human beings were owed a minimum of respect simply because they were human beings and capable of reason—in the same way as other natural rights philosophers believed that we are all born with "certain unalienable rights." For Kant, we all had the right to basic respect as human beings. Only if we demonstrated that we did not deserve to be respected would we relinquish that right. In other words, every person's autonomy would be respected except in cases in which the exercise of that autonomy conflicted with the public good (as represented by the laws of the state). So, we can see that Kant's method of arriving at moral rules allows not only individuals to construct moral guidelines for themselves, but it also permits whole communities to formulate laws for the governance of an entire political system under which individual rights are also clearly recognized.

Non-consequential Theory in Modern Practice

Kant's theory is still much debated today, mostly because of his seemingly absolutist stance on perfect duties. For example, there appears to be no clear reason why prohibitions against some acts should hold without exception. Is it never permissible to lie? What if the lie is to save another person from harm? Likewise, could we ever be justified in killing another person? How about in defense of one's family? These are important questions over which Kant clearly struggled. On the question of conflicting duties, for instance, Kant, much like other intuitionists, insisted that we would recognize which was the "true" moral duty and act according to our reason. This smacks a bit of the rationale given in this century by a Kantian scholar already covered in Chapter 2. William David Ross, whose six obligations were discussed as a means of identifying moral claimants, also held that rational human beings would be able to decide for themselves which of these duties were paramount in any given situation. The reasoning here is that the very struggle involved in determining the priority of duties is instructional in itself and will ultimately lead to more thoughtful decisions.

The fact that all of the media professions have codes of ethics, and that nearly all media outlets (journalistic, advertising, and public relations) have their own, individual, codes as well, speaks to the Kantian desire to make and follow moral rules. And these rules are almost always made with no exceptions in mind. When an earlier version of the PRSA code stated in Article 5 that "a member shall not knowingly disseminate false or misleading information," it means "no member—ever." Not surprisingly, most rules are like that.

Kantian guidelines continue to proliferate in every newsroom and media agency. They vary from the overly complex to the exquisitely simple. The former *Washington Post* ombudsman, Joann Byrd, has developed what she calls her "Four-Minute Ethics Guide." Her decidedly Kantian rules are:

- Do not kill.
- Do not cause avoidable harm.
- Act justly (meaning: Give people what they are due, treat them fairly).
- Help those in immediate need.
- Keep promises.
- Respect persons (as in: Appreciate their dignity and privacy and autonomy).
- Do not lie.

To these, Byrd adds the "only two principles of journalism [that] can be weighed on the same scale with the rules that guide the human race. They are: Inform the public and Serve the public interest."[10]

Another aspect of Kantian ethics apparent today is that of personal integrity. Kant's emphasis on individual autonomy and respect for persons as ends in themselves leads us to respect individual integrity as well. It also insists on our practicing individual integrity in recognition of our duties as moral agents. The legal scholar Stephen Carter, in his book *Integrity*, says that the practice of integrity today has three requirements.[11]

- First, a person must discern the difference between right and wrong. Of course, Kant believed that, as reasoning human beings, we were capable of doing just that. According to Carter, this first criterion "captures the idea of integrity as requiring a degree of moral reflectiveness."
- Second, a person must act on what she has discerned, even at personal cost. This brings in the ideal of an integral person as steadfast, which includes the sense of keeping commitments. You'll recall that the key to Kant's morality was good will—acting out of a sense of duty.
- Finally, Carter states that a person must be willing to say openly that she is acting out of an understanding of right and wrong, "which reminds us that a person of integrity is unashamed of doing the right thing."

Thus, on the view of both Kant and his successors, the moral person is the one who is willing to formulate rules that will then become binding on both her and on everyone else in her society. Then, that person must act out of recognition of those rules and out of respect for the integrity of others as well as her own. We can clearly see the influence Kant has had on modern ethical thought as well as its potential implications for the media. However, the question that must concern us now is whether simply following the rules, no matter how logically arrived at, is the only way we can conceive of moral action. Is it not possible that the probable outcome of our actions should also be considered?

Consequential Ethical Theories

Although rules of morality may seem to be the most common approach used, both historically and currently, such is not the case. If you think about it, even rules must be arrived at by considering the consequences of actions. For example, by proposing that public relations practitioners not lie to the media we are also asking, in effect: Why not? And when we ask why not, we're considering consequences. As already mentioned, consequentialism has acquired something of a bad reputation, at least in the Machiavellian form (egoism). However, no one today would seriously propose that we make moral decisions *without* considering the potential consequences of our actions. In order to better understand the nature of consequential ethical thought, we need to explore its most common forms.

First of all, all consequential theories contend that the moral rightness of an action can be determined by looking at its consequences. If the consequences are good, the act is right. If the consequences are bad, the act is wrong. What is right is determined by considering the ratio of good to evil that the action produces. The right act is the one that produces, or is intended to produce, the greatest ratio of good to evil of any alternative being considered. The two consequential theories we're going to discuss here are *egoism* and *utilitarianism*.

Egoism

Egoism contends that an act is moral when it promotes an individual's best long-term interests. If an action produces, or is intended to produce, a greater ratio of good to evil for the individual *in the long run* than any other alternative, then it is the right action to perform. Remember Machiavelli? He basically proposed that a monarch should do anything in his power to improve his position and to gain more power. Any act was justified if it aided the acquisition and maintenance of power, for a good ruler sometimes had to be ruthless if his people were to derive any benefit from his being in charge.

Also recall that Thomas Hobbes saw human beings as essentially egoistic (self-interested), and this is why a strong government was a necessary component of his social contract. Unless forced to do otherwise, he believed, most people would simply look out for themselves. Although the other social contractarians, such as Locke, took a slightly less callous view of the self-interested nature of people, they still recognized that the temptation existed. In fact, all moral decisions contain an element of egoism. When a reporter writes a story about a social problem, he certainly hopes that some good will come of it. He probably also hopes that some good will come to him as well—recognition, a promotion, a Pulitzer Prize. And there is nothing inherently wrong with self-interest, as long as it doesn't become the overriding reason for making a decision.

Not only people are egoistic. Organizations can act egoistically, as can entire nations (typically called chauvinism or jingoism). It wasn't that long ago that the infamous line, "what's good for General Motors is good for the nation," was uttered. When a local television news outlet withholds a story critical of a local car dealer because car dealerships are its main source of advertising income, it is acting egoistically. When an advertising agency runs a campaign for a big-name liquor brand directed at a minority with a known predisposition for alcoholism, it is acting egoistically. When a public relations firm decides to drop a controversial client because it is worried about its reputation, it is acting egoistically. This is not to say that these are unethical decisions; however, if self-interest is the sole motivating factor, they may well be.

There are some misconceptions concerning egoism that give it a worse reputation than it deserves. For example, egoists don't necessarily do anything they want. An egoist might undergo unpleasant or even painful experiences as long as the long-term outcome is positive. It is also not true that egoists are bereft of such traits as honesty, generosity, and self-sacrifice. Egoists can possess all of these traits, as long as they advance long-term self-interest. For example, an egoistic CEO might be willing to admit to wrongdoing in the short term if the net gain were a better reputation in the long run. In fact, it is not uncommon to hear public relations counselors phrase advise in egoistic rather than moralistic terms to their clients. You'd be much more likely to hear, "I think that course of action will damage our potential sales in the minority markets," than, "I don't think that's the ethical thing to do."

Of course, the most obvious weaknesses of egoism have been pointed out by numerous theorists, including some we've already discussed. First of all, egoism ignores blatant wrongs—actions that, in and of themselves, are morally unacceptable. That is why Machiavelli has such a bad reputation for recommending egoism as a legitimate form of moral decision making. Murdering your rivals just doesn't seem very democratic. We also recognize that egoism cannot be used successfully by everyone at the same time. If all people were egoists exclusively, we would probably end up back in Hobbes' "state of nature." We have seen for ourselves how, in unsettled times, whole societies become egoistic to the extent that they are willing to wipe out other cultures different from themselves. In short, there is simply no way to resolve conflicts of egoistic interests. All egoists are compelled to look out for themselves unless forced to do otherwise. Obviously, the interests of others must be considered as well as the likely consequences of our actions on these other parties. That's where utilitarianism comes in.

Utilitarianism

Although it was not entirely his idea, the credit for utilitarian philosophy is usually given to Jeremy Bentham (1748–1832). Bentham was something of a radical reformer in his lifetime, pursuing such causes as prison reform, public education, censorship, and government corruption. At the base of all of his activities lay a single guiding philosophy: The rightness or wrongness of any action can be judged entirely in terms of its consequences. Motives are, thus, irrelevant—completely the opposite of Kantian theory. Good consequences give pleasure whereas bad consequences result in pain. (This became known as the "pleasure–pain principle.") His idea was that the right course of action was the one that promoted the greatest pleasure or minimized the most pain. He called this philosophy *utilitarianism*, because it promoted an action based on its utility, or usefulness.

On the down side, Bentham is also largely responsible for developing utilitarianism into a coldly objective and formulaic method for making decisions. He was convinced, for instance, that pleasure and pain could be arithmetically calculated, and that the more objective the decision maker, the fairer the outcome. Under his conception of utilitarianism, there was no room for emotion or for the individual. Only the greater good was important.

Bentham continued to crusade for utilitarianism his entire life, bringing about numerous reforms in Great Britain. His philosophy was furthered by his disciple James Mill, who is largely credited with bringing Bentham's works to the forefront of British politics in the early part of the nineteenth century. Government and social agencies in Britain, even today, are heavily influenced by the utilitarian notion of the greater good and the welfare of all of society as having precedence over that of the individual.

John Stuart Mill

James Mill is probably best known, however, as the father of John Stuart Mill (1806–1873). The result of John Stuart Mill's work has been a utilitarian philosophy much more amenable to the individual and less rigid in its attention to the majority's happiness, and in one of his greatest works, *On Liberty* (1859), he asserted once and for all the rights of the individual. In addition to his more famous work, Mill is also credited with bringing the rights of women to the forefront in a series of works co-authored with his wife, Harriet Taylor, culminating with *The Subjection of Women* (1869). In it, Mill and Taylor (and after Taylor's death, her daughter, Helen) argued forcefully for sexual equality, a subject that had been largely ignored since ancient times (except, of course, by women, most especially philosophers such as Mary Wollstonecraft who wrote vehemently about women's rights in the eighteenth century).[12]

Modern Utilitarianism

Utilitarianism today has lost much of the mathematical machinery that Bentham developed in order to weigh good and evil against each other. In fact, today we tend to be suspicious of decision-making methods that use calculation as a basis. Think of the negative connotation of the word "calculating." How about the business practice of cost–benefit analysis—reducing everything to numbers (typically monetary)? Modern utilitarianism simply asserts that we should always act to produce the greatest ratio of good to evil for everyone concerned with our decision. Ideally, that would include all of the moral claimants affected by our decision. In this way, utilitarianism pays strict attention to third-party interests, thus not allowing client loyalty (for example) to override the best interests of others. In fact, one of the primary benefits of using utilitarianism is that it recognizes the four primary claimant groups: clients/customers, organization, profession, and society.

We can easily see the attractiveness of utilitarianism as a decision-making tool for the media. Every time a journalist argues that publishing a story benefits his readers more than it harms the subject of the story, he is using utilitarian logic. The common claim that the practice of advertising adds to the "marketplace of ideas" is also a utilitarian argument. In fact, making a moral decision without considering the likely outcome of the action on the various claimants would strike most of us as decidedly errant. One of the problems with utilitarianism, however, is that it causes us to have to make decisions on a case-by-case basis. Every decision requires that we stop and consider how our actions will affect everyone on our list. Then, we must balance the potential good against the possible harm caused by our action. If the good outweighs the harm—for the most people—then we go with the decision. Wouldn't following rule be a lot easier?

Act and Rule Utilitarianism

In fact, utilitarians have had similar problems with their own philosophy. That's why there are two basic forms of utilitarianism. *Act utilitarianism*, which is what we've been talking about so far, states that the right *act* is the one that produces the greatest ratio of good to evil for all concerned, and is used on a case-by-case basis. On the other hand, *rule utilitarianism* states that ethical actions and judgments can be based on *rules* that promote the greatest ratio of good to evil for all concerned.

For example, a reporter working under the act utilitarian guideline could write a completely fictitious story about a ghetto child hooked on drugs and how his life is a microcosm of the tragedy of our inner cities. The publication of this story could win the paper accolades and the reporter a major prize and a glowing reputation. It could also prompt intense public concern, and stimulate legislative activity to help correct the inequalities suffered by people living in the inner cities of this country. Under act utilitarianism, the publication of this fictitious story could be justified because it serves the greater good via recognition of the problem and probable social reform. However, is lying ever acceptable in journalism? Almost everyone would agree that it is not. How, then, can a utilitarian justify *not* writing the story?

Rule utilitarians believe that not every decision calls for a balancing of good over evil. They hold that some types of decisions can be made in advance, because the logical right choice can generally be said to be in the best interest of all concerned. For example, if we assume that lying, in any form, irrevocably damages the reputation of journalism, and that that damage is definitely counter to the greater good, then we can make a rule that says, "Never lie in journalism." The idea is that the greater good is nearly always promoted by following this rule. Any exceptions can be resolved using act utilitarian methods.

Weaknesses of Utilitarianism

The benefits of using utilitarianism as a decision-making tool are that it forces us to consider everyone concerned with our actions, and that it directs us to pick the alternative that generates the greatest good for the greatest number of people—a very democratic concept. In fact, that is exactly what makes a democracy work—majority rule. The majority choice is the one that is put into effect because the majority, by default, is the greatest number of people.

The problem, of course, is that the majority may not deserve the greatest good, a point made very clear at the beginning of the nineteenth century by a visiting Frenchman named Alexis de Tocqueville. Tocqueville had come to America to study its new form of government for himself, and ended up writing one of the most probing investigations of democracy ever produced, before or since. One of his most cogent insights was that the focus of majority rule under a democratic form of government might well lead to what he termed "the tyranny of the majority"—a point not wasted on anyone who has ever lost an election.[13] And, in fact, under utilitarianism, the minority basically loses out. Only by balancing utilitarianism with the theory of justice can we account for the often-neglected minority interest. The theory of *distributive justice* basically asserts that those who deserve something should get it, whereas those who are not deserving should not. Thus, a deserving minority might benefit from an action over an undeserving majority—a concept that runs decidedly counter to the purest form of utilitarian theory. In this country, however, we have variously recognized this shortcoming of utilitarianism by enacting laws to help mitigate the effect of the tyranny of the majority. Affirmative actions laws are a good example of the theory of distributive justice used as a counter to the "greater good" approach.

This potential conflict was not lost on John Stuart Mill, who, in his treatise on utilitarianism, dealt with the connection between justice and utility. Mill admits that certain examples of justice and injustice merit a higher consideration than the mere meting out of pleasure. For example, he agrees that we:

- Should not deprive anyone of his or her personal liberty, property, or any other thing that belongs to him or her by law. In other words, do not violate a person's legal rights.
- Should not take or withhold from anyone that to which they have a moral right. This is especially important if a bad law has resulted in someone either being deprived of their rights or having been given rights they do not deserve. The fact that these rights are conferred by law makes them legal rights; however, the fact that the law may have deprived someone of rights that they deserve makes those rights (prohibited by the law) moral rights. Think, here, of the segregation laws prior to the 1960s.
- Should give to those who are deserving, and withhold from those who are not deserving (the notion of distributive justice).
- Should keep promises that we have entered into voluntarily.
- Should not show partiality in circumstances in which impartiality is considered appropriate.

Mill warns us that a blind devotion to the greater good should be tempered first by these considerations.

The final indictment against utilitarianism is that it, like egoism, ignores blatant wrongs. Theoretically, utilitarianism could be, and has been, used to justify everything from segregation to genocide. The point is that neither non-consequential nor consequential theories are totally satisfactory as decision-making tools. Most modern philosophers have merged the two into acceptable hybrid systems that seem to accentuate the positives while attempting to eliminate the negatives. Now, however, let's turn to a totally different approach to ethical decision making—one that deals neither with the act nor the consequences, but with the character of the moral agent.

Virtue Ethics

Virtue ethics, or character ethics, has been around easily as long as both consequential and non-consequential theories; however, the Enlightenment pretty much guaranteed that an emphasis on duty, obligation, and the greater good would dominate Western ethical thought. It is only recently that the study of virtue ethics has elicited new interest. It is surprising, therefore, to find that the study of virtue as an ethical construct is at least as old as the ancient Greeks.

History of Virtue Ethics

The Greek philosophers (especially Plato and Aristotle) chose not to ask: What is the right thing to do? Instead, they asked: What traits of character make one a good person? They called these traits virtues and defined them as actions that, if practiced habitually, would ultimately result in a good character. In other words, virtues are needed for human beings to conduct their lives well. Virtues can be acquired, learned, and cultivated by the diligent person. Plato concentrated on what he called the "Four Cardinal Virtues": temperance, justice, courage, and wisdom. In Judeo-Christian cultures, desirable virtues might include these four plus gentleness, fairness, generosity, and truthfulness.[14] In fact, in early Christian theology the four cardinal virtues of Plato were combined with the three, often-cited virtues of faith, hope, and charity in order to act as a balance for the seven deadly sins. (As we all probably know—perhaps personally—these are lust, gluttony, greed, sloth, wrath, envy, and pride.) Of course, many lists are possible. James Rachels, in his book *The Elements of Moral Philosophy*, lists the following as a few of the possibilities:[15]

- benevolence;
- civility;
- compassion;
- conscientiousness;
- courage;
- courteousness;
- dependability;
- fairness;
- friendliness;
- generosity;
- honesty;
- industriousness;
- justice;
- loyalty;
- moderation;
- reasonableness;
- self-confidence;
- self-control;
- self-discipline;
- self-reliance;
- tactfulness;
- thoughtfulness;
- tolerance.

Aristotle, Plato's student, took a different approach to defining exactly what constituted a virtue. Aristotle held that a "Moral virtue is a mean between two extremes, the one involving excess and the other deficiency."[16] Aristotle dubbed this concept "the Golden Mean," and called for moderation in all things as the road to a virtuous character. For example, the middle ground between cowardice and foolhardiness would be courage. The mean between shamelessness and bashfulness is modesty; and between stinginess and wastefulness lies generosity.

According to Stanley Cunningham, however, Aristotle didn't intend that we should begin with the extremes and then identify the mean. This would tend to lead us into mediocrity rather than excellence. Instead, he believed that a person of moral maturity (one who had learned the habits of good character and subsequently gained the acuity of moral reasoning) would naturally seek the action that would further excellent moral character—an action that would logically lie somewhere between two extremes—one excessive, the other deficient. As Cunningham suggests,

> that same quality of goodness in the things we do is ultimately grounded in our perception or judgment about what is the right thing to do . . . It is the informed choice of a morally developed person whose cognitive apparatus and emotional status are in good working order.[17]

Aristotle also held that the process of reasoning that would lead to the moral mean was dependent on the individual and on the circumstance. The moral mean would, thus, be different for each person—no one, absolute mean would suffice.

> [E]verybody who understands his business avoids alike excess and deficiency; he seeks and chooses the mean, not the absolute mean, but the mean considered relatively to ourselves.[18]

And he was much in favor of teaching the young to develop the habit of moral reasoning so that, when they were adults, they would naturally gravitate toward the moral mean in any given situation.

> Arguments and teaching surely do not influence everyone, but the soul of the student needs to have been prepared by habits for enjoying and hating finely, like ground that is to nourish seed.[19]

Ultimately, the moral mean can be discovered only by the application of both learned theory and personal perception (the practical application of our natural senses to a situation).

Thus, Aristotle's model of the Golden Mean is not a simple, arithmetical calculation of an average action. Rather, it is the result of acquired character, a moral maturity, and an ability to perceive a situation accurately as it pertains to the individual involved. He would say that any person of moral maturity with an understanding of what is right and what is wrong would view the situation through the lens of his personal experience and naturally choose the moral mean. As every situation differs, every moral mean will likewise differ.

For example, an editor deciding on a privacy issue might decide to "soften" a story to avoid inflicting undue harm on the story's subject; however, this decision would not be based on first deciding on the extremes (for instance, publishing and injuring the subject of the story, or not publishing and depriving the public of information it needs). In other words, the decision is not a compromise between the two extremes. Rather it is based on the knowledge and experience of the editor, his vision of the place of journalism within society, the obligations inherent in that charge, and the myriad other factors that make up the whole of the issue. The decision is, thus, a choice to do the right thing under the circumstances, but based on a well-developed character, honed in the practice of journalism and tempered by both personal and societal morality.

Both Plato and Aristotle believed that a good character would result in good actions; and virtues, in turn, were cultivated by the practice of good actions—so the logic is somewhat circular. Regardless, the message is clear: A person's character dictates whether that person will conduct himself morally or immorally. A person possessing the virtue of honesty is not very likely to lie, since telling the truth is habitual with that person. A virtuous person is, therefore, a person of continuity—a person for whom moral action is based on a good character, not on consequences or rules. This sort of person will be consistent in her judgments because her character dictates it. You'll recall that the legal scholar Stephen Carter called for more integrity in moral decision making, and was cited earlier as an example of Kantian thinking. Carter could also be said to be a virtue ethicist in that he views integrity as an essential and desirable character trait—a virtue.

Virtue Ethics in Modern Practice

The real value of virtue ethics is that it places the onus of right action directly on the person making the decision. A person of strong character developed through habitual right action will make the right decisions, most of the time. A person of weak character will not. But how does this work out for those in the media? First, we must ask ourselves what we would consider virtues in the various media professions. For example, a list of virtues for journalists would probably include truthfulness, tenaciousness, fairness, and self-reliance. Certainly, there are others, but you get the idea. For public relations: truthfulness, loyalty, trustworthiness, honesty, diligence, and discretion. How about advertising? Certainly advertisers would cite truthfulness in common with the other media professions; but also loyalty, diligence, honesty, and tactfulness.

You may have noticed that these virtues all have one thing in common—they contribute to the effectiveness of the practice for which they are considered virtues. But what about other virtues not normally associated with these media roles? Why not consider compassion a journalistic virtue? Or civility, or friendliness? What's wrong with adding fairness, justice, and moderation to the lists for advertising and public relations? The answer, of course, is that these virtues might sometimes interfere with the functions of the media in ways the others would not. However, it is easy to see why so many outside the media often view them as unfeeling and egoistic when the very virtues we would most associate with being a good *person* are those that might hobble the media in the performance of their jobs as *professionals*. Nonetheless, it is hard to imagine a media practitioner of good character opting to override that character simply in order to get a story or keep a client. As Aristotle suggested, a person of good character will gravitate toward the moral mean. If he does not, can we truly say he is virtuous?

Finally, character can tell us something valuable about a person. For instance, one of the most often voiced opinions during the Monica Lewinsky–Bill Clinton scandal that lasted nearly a year was that it was a "character issue." Others countered that a person's private life (even a president's) shouldn't be anybody's business but his own. In fact, this is the most often-cited journalistic guideline when deciding on invasion of privacy issues. Typically, if a public official's private life doesn't interfere with the public performance of his or her duties, then invading that person's privacy is not called for. However, we might ask ourselves: What does this lapse in a person's *private* morals say about his or her *public* morals? According to virtue ethics, an inherently honest person would not lie under most circumstances. Logically, then, a person who does lie (especially habitually) could be viewed as a person of less than sterling character—at least as far as the virtue of honesty is concerned. It may be that, as the Greeks believed, a person cannot be publicly virtuous and privately not virtuous. As we have noted, the idea of a "split personality" being desirable in a leader is a particularly Machiavellian concept.

Weaknesses in Virtue Ethics

Are there weaknesses in virtue ethics? Of course. First of all, since the emphasis is on character and not on action, there is no easy way to determine a right action from a wrong one. Virtue ethicists simply insist that a virtuous character will result in virtuous actions. Also, there is no way to resolve conflicts of virtues. For example, should honesty supersede kindness (should I or should I not tell my roommate that her newly dyed green hair is nauseating)?

Nonetheless, we cannot ignore the idea behind virtue ethics if we are to make good decisions. We must consider the character of those with whom we must deal as well as our own character every time we make a moral decision. Some say that inconsistency is the hobgoblin of moral decision making. Having a virtuous character helps exorcise that particular spirit.

The Ethic of Care

We have seen that respect for other people is at the heart of a number of philosophies—most notably, Immanuel Kant's. In this sense, *respect* refers to a feeling of deference toward someone and a willingness to show consideration or appreciation to them. Respect itself is related to a number of other concepts including sympathy, the ability to empathize with others, compassion, and caring for others. These words are all closely related and often interchangeable. *Sympathy*, for example, refers to the act or power of sharing the feelings of another whereas *empathy* means to identify with and understand another's situation, feelings, and motives. Compassion and caring are likewise closely related. *Compassion* refers to a deep awareness of the suffering of another coupled with the wish to relieve it. *Caring* means to feel and exhibit concern for others, and can include empathy. No one would disagree that these are major determinants of moral action; however, to what degree they can or should be incorporated into a system of media ethics is debatable.

We have seen that professional obligations to truth telling, dissemination of important information to the public, loyalty to legitimate client interests, and other such duties may potentially clash with personal convictions of compassion and care for others. And, we have considered whether personal ethics can or should override professional ethics in circumstances in which the role of professional is operational. To some extent, these considerations and assumptions are based on the degree of importance attached to certain professional undertakings. We assume that some harm is a necessary by-product of many media activities, and that our primary responsibility is to do our jobs while mitigating as much harm as we can. However, is it possible, or even conceivable, that we could carry out our functions as media practitioners while working under a model in which the default would be "no harm to anyone"?

In her seminal work, *In a Different Voice*, developmental psychologist Carol Gilligan proposes what she calls an "ethic of care." According to Gilligan, most of our moral concepts have developed from a particularly male perspective. The major approach to moral philosophy over the past several hundred years has been what might be called an "ethic of justice," which is deeply rooted in a desire for individual autonomy and independence. The focus of this "ethic" is the balancing of competing interests among individuals. It is easy to see this model at work in the philosophies of Hobbes, Locke, Kant, and scores of other Enlightenment thinkers. In fact, individualism and sanctioned competition are at the heart of the American system of government and economics. And, although Gilligan doesn't necessarily take umbrage with this result, she does point out the troubling consequences of an ethic of justice untempered by an "ethic of care."[20] The formality of such concepts as duty and justice often results in objectification of human beings, or, at least, a distancing of the parties involved in and affected by moral decision making. Caring, on the other hand, requires a closer relationship between parties and recognition of the other as a subjective being.

Gilligan proposes that the female moral voice is characterized by caring. It considers the needs of both the self and of others, and is not just interested in the survival of the self. There is also more to this approach than simply the avoidance of harm. Ideally, no one should be hurt in interchanges among human beings. Although not dismissing the importance of justice and fairness, Gilligan points out that moral decisions should also make allowances for differences in needs. In other words, *need may dictate an obligation to care*. However, the feminist author Joan Tronto points out that a more appropriate term for obligation would be responsibility. She holds that *obligation* implies formal relationships and agreements, and refers to explicit promises and duties. *Responsibility* allows that we may have played a part in bringing about the circumstances that give rise to the need being expressed. In addition, responsibility requires that we ask ourselves if we are the best suited to give the care requested.[21]

Unlike Kant's imperfect duties, which were to be followed only if nothing else prohibited the action, the ethic of care requires, at minimum, that need be recognized as an important component of human interaction. Gilligan, and others using her approach as a basis for their own systems of care, point out that although an ethic of care may be a predominantly female construction, it is not limited to the female perspective and can (and should) be used by male and female alike.

Based on an "obligation to care," this approach would have us view ourselves as part of a network of individuals whose needs (when they become clear) create a duty in us to respond. In responding, we must pay attention to the details of the need and to the outcome of our response on others potentially affected by our actions.[22] This does not mean that every need requires a response. The seriousness of the need, the likely benefit derived from our response, our ability to respond to this particular need, and the competing needs of others in our network must also be weighed. Like most ethical decisions, responding to need requires a weighing of interests; however, relating to the need on an emotional level is a vital consideration absent from many other such formulas.

Individual autonomy, a mainstay of most Enlightenment philosophy, is not entirely absent from the concept of care. Julia Wood, in *Who Cares? Women, Care, and Culture*, suggests that a flexible sense of autonomy would allow us to value both the needs and interests of others while not neglecting our own needs. This flexibility would recognize the primary qualities our culture seems to value in care givers: *partiality* (the ability to focus with feeling on the needs of others), *empathy* (having insight into others' needs), and *willingness to serve others*. Woods proposes a concept of *dynamic autonomy* that involves an awareness of our individuality coupled with an ability to choose when to accentuate our own desires and points of view and when to emphasize and cooperate with those of others.[23]

Confucian philosophy agrees with much of the ethic of care, and disagrees with Western liberal thought that individual autonomy is the most important consideration of human interaction. For a Confucian, human interaction is an indispensable part of life—an essential component necessary to achieving self-realization. As the Confucian philosopher Henry Rosemont, Jr., states, "It is not merely that we are obliged, of necessity, to interact with others, we must care about them as well." Confucians are defined by their interactions with others. They are not autonomous; rather, they are "relational," leading morally integrated lives in a human community. As Confucius points out, "[I]f I am not to be a person in the midst of others, what am I to be?"[24]

Can the Media Care?

The question remains whether the media can consider an ethic of care as a realistic component of their moral curriculum. As we've seen, the media, especially journalists, value autonomy above almost all else. Caring and care giving imply a subjective viewpoint. We have also seen that the notion of objectivity itself can be viewed as a flawed concept. For example, the feminist theorist Linda Steiner holds that a "feminist ethic challenges the treatment of mass media subjects as objects—challenges the objectification of both mass media sources as well as their audiences. 'The goal would be to respect others' dignity and integrity, to make the process more collaborative and egalitarian, less authoritarian and coercive.' "[25]

Not only feminist authors but also many others point out that honoring the ideal of objectivity establishes an us–them relationship between the media and virtually everyone else. Whereas journalism seems to be the focus of much of the public's concern over the caring versus harm debate, advertising and public relations are merely assumed to be logically without care for anyone except the client. This difference in public attitude stems as much from a misunderstanding of the nature of the information media versus the persuasive media as it does from any lack of expectation that the latter will ever change. As we shall see, all of the media currently have in place ethical models that reflect, to some degree, a consideration of care.

Public Journalism Again

Part of the response to a distancing of the media from both their sources and their publics has been *public journalism*, an approach that considers the news media as both responsible and responsive to the community. As we discussed in Chapter 3, a news outlet practicing public journalism would be community-oriented by design. In fact, we are seeing more of this reflected both in the type of coverage and in the ambience of local television news. Although many bemoan the smiling faces and happy talk of much of this type of broadcasting, the approach is decidedly community-centered. Even local newspapers are experimenting with community-oriented approaches, such as the creation of voter forums during elections and web sites that invite reader involvement in deciding the content of news.

Whereas some worry that any public involvement in deciding what is "news" is dangerous, others point out that the economic necessity of providing consumers with what they want as much as with what they need is already a move in that direction. Quoted in Louis Day's *Ethics in Media Communications*, ABC's Ted Koppel apparently sees the fact that business decisions drive news decisions as a virtue, "because it gives the public a significant voice in shaping the news agenda. In short, the application of marketing principles to journalism has helped to 'democratize' the profession."[26] Although the economic necessity of giving the public what they want may be driving some movement toward a more participatory form of journalism, we cannot place a moral value on such motives since the intent, as Kant would say, is not to do good but to remain economically viable. On the other hand, the move toward public journalism is, by and large, an authentic attempt to bring the news media and the public closer together—clearly indicating a change in the level of care with which the media may be dealing with their constituents.

Persuasive Models and Care

Although journalism may be reluctant to inject an ethic of care into its discipline, public relations has a long history of trying to show that it's doing just that. And, although many would argue that public relations is biased by nature in favor of the client, we have seen that an adherence to professional standards should disallow such total obeisance to any one party—especially the client. The fiduciary model of the professional–client relationship assumes that both the professional public relations practitioner and her client will work together to affect the most beneficial solution to the client's problems. However, the balanced relationship between the two primary parties exists only insofar as it does not ignore relevant third parties. The professional is under a special obligation not to harm others in the pursuit of his client's interests.

Although the ideal of advocacy, as it is construed in the legal profession, relies on total client loyalty, neither public relations nor advertising can claim the same status as that profession. Third parties must be considered. The clients of public relations have no constitutionally guaranteed right to representation by a PR agency, nor do the clients of advertising agents. Professionals in both of these fields not only can, but also should turn down client requests that would unduly harm third-party claimants. Professional codes in both advertising and public relations call for a balancing of interests in favor of non-injury to third parties. Articles of those codes that address not lying to the media or to consumers (theoretically on behalf of clients) are examples of the recognition of third-party concerns. However, simply recognizing third-party concerns doesn't imply a caring attitude in the sense of an ethic of care. As we discussed earlier in this chapter, even advocates can, and should, reject client aims that unnecessarily harm third parties.

Educator and theorist James Grunig proposes four models for the practice of public relations: press agentry/publicity, public information, two-way asymmetric, and two-way symmetric. In the *press agentry/publicity* model, the practitioner's role might be that of a press agent, functioning as a one-sided propaganda specialist. The *public information* model presents the practitioner as journalist, carefully disseminating balanced information to the public. Practitioners in a *two-way asymmetric* model are seen as "scientific persuaders," using social science techniques to gather information on attitude and behavior characteristics of their publics and then adjusting their messages accordingly in order to influence those publics. And, finally, the *two-way symmetric* model uses practitioners as mediators between organizations and their publics. One of the key differences among these models is the emphasis placed on either persuasion or mutual understanding as an end.[27]

Grunig proposes the two-way symmetric model as an ideal for public relations. Although he recognizes persuasion as a legitimate function of the public relations role, he posits that mutual understanding ultimately leads to a more beneficial relationship between the public relations practitioner's client and that client's constituencies. More profound associations are built on understanding gained, most often, through communication, negotiation, and compromise. It can be inferred from this model and its goal that care must, at least, be a part of the process leading to compromise (although compromise itself is viewed by some feminist scholars as a by-product of competition and, therefore, a negative outcome). Regardless, some care (perhaps in the form of respect) for the position and views of the "other" is required in this model.

The two-way asymmetric (persuasive) model may also operate under an assumption of respect for both the integrity and the intelligence of the parties being persuaded (as Aristotle's *Rhetoric* suggests). However, the techniques of persuasion can, and often are, used unethically. And any technique that has persuasion as its intended outcome is far more easily open to abuse than a technique having mutual understanding as it goal. The reality of public relations, however, is that persuasion is a recognized and respected communication technique. If we are to accept the traditional ideal of persuasion as a process necessary to the successful application of democracy as a form of government, then we must accept that ethical persuasion is a legitimate approach to coming to grips with different points of view.

This does not invalidate the possibility of incorporating an ethic of care into the persuasive process itself. All that is needed, as Linda Steiner points out, is respect for the dignity and integrity of the receivers of your message. As we have noted throughout this book, coercion and manipulation through communication are decidedly unethical and are actions for which there can be no excuses. Remember that respect, as Kant pointed out, is the least we owe to other human beings; and respect is very definitely a form of caring.

Does this mean that persuasion done in order to sell something other than a political point of view is less than ethical or cannot take advantage of an ethic of care? Ideally, this "respectful" approach to persuasive communication should apply equally to public relations and advertising. A goal of mutual understanding is probably not as appropriate for most advertising as it is for some public relations. Even advertising whose primary purpose is to inform doesn't usually seek or need mutual understanding. It requires only a fairly complete understanding of the needs of the receivers of the information, and that can be gained through audience analysis. Grunig's press agentry/publicity and two-way asymmetric models (although not intended for advertising) are certainly the most appropriate. However, even these models, if practiced conscientiously, can be respectful of audience dignity and integrity. Audiences are often viewed by advertising practitioners as "gullible"; why else would so many ads seek to obfuscate reality? How the advertising professional views the audience dictates the level of respect reflected in the advertisement. The intelligence of a targeted audience is not denigrated by serious advertisers with ethical intent. On the other hand, the harder an ad tries to misrepresent reality for the purpose of deception, the less respect it shows for the audience. Of course, part of the analysis has to be the audience's Qualified Expectation of Reality (explained in more detail in Chapter 6). If they expect the information—or the form of its presentation—to be real and it isn't, they have been intentionally duped.

In the final analysis, media communicators cannot afford to ignore such characteristics as empathy and caring. The often-quoted Chinese philosopher Confucius didn't even have a word for *reason* or *rational* separate from his concept of *emotion*. Or, as Steiner contends, "virtues" such as empathy and caring can and should function alongside concepts such as integrity, fairness, and respect for others. Journalists and advertising and public relations practitioners alike may need to adjust their traditional conceptions of such time-honored practices as near-total objectivity in both informing and persuading in order that some indication that "we are all in this together" be admitted to themselves and to those they affect so profoundly.

Free Speech Theories

The United States has the strongest free speech protection in the world. The First Amendment of the U.S. Constitution states that "Congress shall make no law respecting an establishment of religion, or prohibiting the free exercise thereof, *abridging the freedom of speech, or of the press* [emphasis added], or the right of the people peaceably to assemble, and to petition the Government for redress of grievances." This amendment, along with the rest of the Bill of Rights, was passed in 1791, and we have been debating its efficacy ever since. Although it is most likely true that the free speech component of the First Amendment was originally directed at political expression and designed to prevent government censorship of criticism, it has been much more widely interpreted over the intervening years.

Today, free speech protection has been extended not only to advertising and public relations, but also to night club performances, "pornographic" publications, music lyrics, artwork and other forms of symbolic expression, bumper stickers, and T-shirt slogans. In the words of the legal scholar Stephen Carter, the First Amendment has grown into "an apologetic leviathan, able to shield from community scrutiny everything from violent pornography to tabloid rumor-mongering to hurling racial epithets to burning the American flag."[28] However, it has not been granted to child pornography, sedition (suggesting the overthrow of the government), some instances of privacy violation, speech that incites to riot, and numerous other small and large exceptions. For example, cigarette advertising was banned from broadcasting nearly 30 years ago and is now forbidden on billboards. However, this is not the place to go into the long legal history of Supreme Court cases affirming and, in some instances, restricting free speech. Suffice it to say that the Court has consistently acted out the *theories* of free speech that we will investigate here, and, in some cases, been at the forefront of interpreting those theories.

Freedom of expression in the West has had a long and tumultuous history. The Enlightenment ushered in a new age based on reason and, naturally, on the ability to express the results of rational thought. However, much of that voice was muted during the lifetimes of the philosophers who fought so hard for free expression.

John Milton and the Marketplace of Ideas

The great English poet John Milton (1608–1674), may be singly responsible for one of the most time-honored ideals of Western journalism. In 1644, he published a scathing denouncement of censorship that he titled *Areopagitica* (after an ancient Greek term for a speech given before their highest judicial court). In this brief but immortal address to the English Parliament, Milton defended his right to publish two pamphlets on divorce without government censorship. These earlier publications had angered not only Parliament, but, more importantly, the Anglican Church (which, as you'll recall, apparently granted divorces only to royalty). In fact, Milton's pamphlets on divorce eventually led to a law forbidding any type of publication without church licensing. The real effect of *Areopagitica*, however, was in its defense of free speech and its contribution to the thinking that ultimately led to the near-total protection of expression that exists in the United States today.

In a now-famous construction, Milton envisioned a world in which truth would always win out over falsity. In what has come to be known as "the self-righting principle," Milton held that,

> though all the winds of doctrine were let loose to play upon the earth, so Truth be in the field, we do injuriously, by licensing and prohibiting, to misdoubt its strength. Let her and Falsehood grapple: whoever knew Truth put to the worse, in a free and open encounter?

Thus was born the *marketplace of ideas* concept under which all ideas could, and were expected to, compete with each other in open debate. If truth were as strong as Milton believed it was, it would not need to have its opponents silenced by the government or anyone else. It would win on its own merits. John Stuart Mill, whom we have already visited, gave further impetus to this theory in his treatise *On Liberty*, in which he argues, like Milton, that the truth can best be arrived at through "robust" and open debate. In justifying the marketplace ideal, Mill proposed that (1) if any statement contains truth and we silence it, we lose any chance of having viewed that kernel of truth and possibly exchanging it for error; (2) the result of a clash between two contesting opinions will most likely bring out the truth inherent in both; and (3) even if the opposing opinion is wholly false, by not debating with it, the truth eventually becomes uncontested and unquestioned dogma.[29]

The Marketplace of Ideas in Modern Times

Today, the marketplace of ideas theory is still strongly adhered to by most people working in the media. However, the strength of the argument rests on several assumptions that are being questioned by both consumers and critics of the media. The first is that rationality is probably not as widespread a virtue as the Enlightenment philosophers supposed. (Of course, Plato suspected this all along.) Second, no matter how much we would like to believe that truth will always defeat falsity, the fact of the matter is that we simply can't always tell the difference between the two—especially since the "truth" often seems so subjective. Thus, the marketplace of ideas theory has evolved into one in which the value of any expressed idea lies more in its public acceptance than in its veracity. According to the First Amendment scholar Frederick Schauer, good arguments do not always defeat bad ones.

> While it would be excessively skeptical to think that Gresham's Law operates in the marketplace of ideas, and that bad arguments invariably drive out good ones, it may be excessively sanguine to suppose that we live in the deliberative environment supposed by the rationalists of the Enlightenment, an environment in which sound arguments prevail just because of their inherent soundness. Rather, we appear to exist in a world in which various superficially appealing but deeply flawed arguments all too often carry the day in public debate.[30]

In fact, some critics have pointed out that under the marketplace theory, as it has developed over the years, a single value now justifies and defines the scope of protection for speech: the *successful exchange of information*. This concept assumes that speech is a commodity and that its success in the marketplace depends solely on its ability to compete for acceptance by the public—not on whether it is true or not. In other words, *efficiency* wins out over veracity. Media critic Neil Postman cites efficiency as one of the harbingers of the technical age and discusses its distancing effect on human beings in his book, *Technopoly*. According to Postman, the technological engines of progress work most efficiently when people are conceived of as consumers.[31] He posits that the "I have no responsibility for the consequences of my decisions" argument is a direct result of feeling the pressure of being efficient over that of being moral.[32] The implications of this hypothesis are clear for most media practitioners, especially those whose job it is to produce messages that will compete successfully with other messages—and that's just about everybody in the media. For too many in public relations and advertising, for instance, efficiency is the true measure of success, and success is the only thing that counts. That particular measure is not relegated solely to public relations and advertising, however. Any local TV news show (or network news show, for that matter) knows that it has to compete successfully with every other news show on the air. And, in order to compete, it generally has to become more efficient. And, as mentioned in Chapter 1, the pressure to compete is fast becoming the driving force behind the way news is gathered and presented.

What does this have to do with free speech and the marketplace of ideas theory? If efficiency and the success brought about by being efficient result in one message winning out over another, instead of the truthful message automatically winning out over the false one, then efficiency and success will probably be the hallmarks of protected speech. Under this model, *all* speech would be protected, because only through competition will the speech be either accepted or rejected. The result is that the *market* becomes the sole arbiter of free speech, and, as every marketing student knows, if it sells, it's successful.[33] No tactic is disallowed, no technique is off limits.

The Liberty Theory

An alternative defense of free speech is offered by the *liberty theory*. Developed by C. Edwin Baker as a more logical substitute for the marketplace of ideas approach, the liberty theory holds that First Amendment freedom is essential for furthering four values:

- individual self-fulfillment;
- advancement of knowledge and discovery of truth;
- participation in decision making by all members of the society (which is particularly significant for political decisions but embraces the right to participate in the building of the whole culture);
- achievement of a more adaptable and hence stable community.

In other words, the liberty theory places a positive emphasis on protected speech and on the sanctity of individual autonomy. In a sense, this approach is Kantian in nature, with its focus on the autonomy of both speaker and listener. On another level, it is Aristotelian in that it sees speech worthy of protection as that which furthers self-fulfillment and provides for a stable culture and community.

The liberty theory differs in several areas, but it would be a mistake to think that this approach is more limiting on speech than the marketplace approach. For example, although the marketplace theory would allow speech that harms (except for rare exceptions), it fails to come to grips with a definition of harm that would eliminate debate over certain types of communication, such as pornography. The liberty theory construes harm specifically as coercion, thus clearly stating the reasons for allowing most speech and setting explicit guidelines for limiting speech. Under this theory, speech-caused harms are generally allowed, because speech does not, in most cases, physically harm people. Rather, they are *potentially* harmed only to the extent that they adopt any perceptions or attitudes because of the speech. In other words, the harm-causing speech does not itself interfere with the listener's legitimate decision-making authority (the autonomy of the *listener*). You don't have to listen to it, and if you do, you don't have to change your mind about anything. The listener has no right, then, to control that speech since that would be disrespectful of the *speaker's* autonomy. So, outlawing speech in order to protect people from harms that result simply because listeners might adopt certain perceptions or attitudes disrespects the responsibility and freedom of the listener as well as the speaker.

Under the liberty theory, only if speech is manifestly coercive should it be restricted. In general, speech depends for its power on the voluntary acceptance of the listeners, so speech behavior is normally considered non-coercive. *Coercive speech* would be that which "restricts another person to options that are worse than that other person had moral or legitimate right to expect, or [which] employs means that [the speaker] had no right to use for changing the threatened person's options." Thus, coercion refers to the impropriety of the form of pressure, not to the severity or effectiveness of the pressure itself. Again, like Kant, Baker suggests that motive leads to technique. Improper motive leads to improper technique. It should make no difference if anyone is harmed by the attempt at coercion—coercive speech would be wrong by nature.

> Speech used to influence another person may be coercive if the speaker manifestly disrespects and attempts to undermine the other person's will and the integrity of the other person's mental processes. Both the concept of coercion and the rationale for protecting speech draw from the same ethical requirement that the integrity and autonomy of the individual be respected.[34]

In sum, the liberty theory depicts protected speech as that which (1) represents the freely chosen expression of the speaker, (2) depends for its power on the free acceptance of the listener, and (3) is not used in the context of a violent or coercive activity. Speech is protected because, without disrespecting the autonomy of other persons, it promotes both the speaker's self-fulfillment and the speaker's ability to participate in change.[35]

Free Speech and the Individual versus Society

One of the triumphs of the free-speech principle is that it gives protection to the individual as well as the group. A key interpretation of the free-speech doctrine, as embodied in the First Amendment, is that *no* voice can be silenced—not even the faintest. This emphasis on individual rights has come down to us almost untouched since the time of John Locke. You'll recall that Locke championed the rights of individuals over the power of the government, and, by so doing, presented the founders of the United States with a fully developed concept of government as the agent of the people. *Libertarian theory*, with its extreme focus on the individual, asserts that individual rights may not be violated, and that there is no natural concomitant responsibility associated with any right.

The liberal viewpoint (especially as expressed through libertarianism) holds that the most important political values are freedom and equality—particularly as they relate to individual virtues. The role of government, under this construct, is to ensure freedom and equality, and to promote toleration and freedom of conscience for all its citizens; otherwise, it is to stay out of the affairs of individuals. Society is, thus, governed by an enlightened state working through the tenets of reason, whose actions are not clouded by the ambiguities of culture or the needs of the whole. As Locke proposed, its sole purpose is to ensure individual rights. Under this theory, journalists have the right to publish what they want, and are not answerable to anyone except themselves for what they publish (as long as it's not libelous). Censorship by the government is strictly forbidden by the First Amendment, a journalist's right to information has been validated by such laws as the Freedom of Information Act, and the only responsibility recognized by most journalists is "the public's right to know."

Directly contrary to this approach, the *communitarian* perspective asserts that other values are more important, especially those that regard community as the proper focus of the human being. Communitarians believe that the state's primary role is to ensure the welfare of the community, because it is the basis of all human interaction. They believe that we cannot be simply individuals pursuing our self-interests without regard for the society of which we are an integral part. Under this theory, journalists are responsible to the community of which they are a part. As discussed in Chapter 3, the new trend toward public journalism is a reflection of this increasing concern for the place of the press in fostering community well-being. Under communitarianism, the traditions of culture and society are vital to the realization of the "good life," and we cannot separate ourselves from that whole of which we are a part. In fact, our very roles within that society tie us to the community in ways we could not be joined as mere individuals. We are what we are, in part, because of our roles in society.

In agreement with Confucius, communitarians suggest that our various roles define us. As the Confucian scholar Henry Rosemont, Jr., analogized, the Western individualist is like a peach: Whereas the outside is what most people see and value, what is inside is the real essence of what it means to be a human being. Inside each of us is a center that is wholly ours. We share only that which is exterior to that center. Contrary to that way of thinking, the Confucian sees herself as an onion: Each layer defines her being. One layer may be her role as parent, one as wife, one as colleague, one as employee, one as community member, one as citizen. Thus, the communitarian is defined by her relationship with others, the libertarian by his individuality.

Finally, communitarians disagree that rule by reason alone is sufficient to ensure community health. That can be accomplished only through discourse based on the social goals of the community, as exemplified through its cultural traditions and roles.[36] Again, like Confucians, communitarians hold that communal tradition and one's place within that tradition are vital to the operation of a successful society. In addition, to trust only in reason is to divorce oneself from the reality that human beings are simultaneously thinking and feeling creatures. In fact, Confucius didn't even recognize a separate state of reasoning absent emotion. As pointed out by the religious philosopher Huston Smith,

> The Chinese idiogram for mind designates heart as well, which shows that the Chinese took it for granted that reason functions in a context of attitudes and emotions. Unless our hearts prompt us to cooperate, reason will devise clever stratagems to further self interest.[37]

As might be expected, the debate over free speech rights has not escaped the long-running conflict between these two schools of thought. As suggested by the educator and philosopher John Merrill, most of the major moral philosophers (both past and present) fall into one of these two camps. For example, John Milton, John Locke, John Stuart Mill, and Henry David Thoreau all tend toward libertarianism. Others, such as Plato, Rousseau, and Confucius, favor more communitarian constructs.[38]

One of the most adamant defenders of individual rights over group rights was John Stuart Mill. In his treatise On Liberty, Mill firmly asserted that no individual voice should be silenced, especially by the din of the majority.

> If all mankind minus one were of one opinion and only one person were of the contrary opinion, mankind would be no more justified in silencing that one person than he, if he had the power, would be justified in silencing mankind.[39]

Like Alexis de Tocqueville before him, Mill was concerned with the "tyranny of the majority," and the dangers of operating from a greater-good perspective without consideration of minority opinion. That minority had already been recognized by a number of philosophers, from Plato to Henry David Thoreau, who pointed out in his conclusion to Walden, in 1854, that:

If a man does not keep pace with his companions, perhaps it is because he hears a different drummer. Let him step to the music which he hears, however measured or far away.[40]

This historical emphasis on the individual has, in part, grown from an Enlightenment period distrust of government—especially totalitarian regimes—and a firmly held belief in a social contract construct that gives the individual power over the group. Dissenters, such as Rousseau, have been more often cited for their focus on the dehumanizing effects of mass society than for their belief in a strict allegiance to the well-being of society instead of the individual. In more recent years, philosophers such as Alisdair MacIntyre and Michael Sandel have written forcefully about the dangers of too much emphasis on the individual. MacIntyre, for instance, decries the "cult of individuality" as presenting human beings as free-will addicts with no relationship to society as a whole. This, he says, is a mistake. We are all born into a society and learn to live within its shelter, developing as part of the whole. In this way, we are not (as the libertarians suppose) disconnected entities living wholly for ourselves.[41] Likewise, Michael Sandel argues that human beings simply cannot be considered as separate from their social communities.

We cannot regard ourselves as independent . . . without great cost to those loyalties and convictions whose moral force consists partly in the fact that living by them is inseparable from understanding ourselves as the particular persons we are—as members of this family or community or nation or people, as bearers of this history, as sons and daughters of that revolution, as citizens of this republic.[42]

Sandel says that the "enduring attachments" that arise out of these relationships "partly define the person that I am." This devotion to relationships as the defining force of our existence is common to most communitarian philosophies. And, as we saw in Chapter 2, relationships naturally result in obligations. Obligations, by nature, restrict our actions. Therefore, the various obligations that the media have toward their constituencies constitute another way of looking at conceivable restrictions on free speech—even if those restrictions are self-imposed. If the media are obligated to present news that has some meaning to people's daily lives, and they are obligated to mitigate harm wherever possible, then some restriction on speech is to be expected.

The conflict between the communitarian and libertarian philosophies, like most conflicts, is based on a false either–or dichotomy. It is unnecessary, and probably unwise, to allow all expression free reign. Harm to fellow human beings is one reason for restricting some forms of expression. Child pornography laws attest to our desire to protect our children, anti-sedition laws reflect our desire to protect our country. Slanderous speech is punishable by law, as is speech that incites to riot. We also tend to recognize the inappropriateness of some forms of speech at certain times and places. Some of these restrictions are recognized by the Supreme Court. Courthouses (especially during trials), schools, prisons and jails, and military bases are some examples. Not surprisingly, these exceptions have been made so that order might be maintained in and around these institutions. Additionally, rulings such as those regulating cigarette advertising on television, and now on billboards, have been done for the sake of society as a whole—an entirely communitarian perspective. Social custom dictates other restrictions—but, of course, social customs change. Fifty years ago, it would have been unusual to hear someone swear in public. Today, a walk across any college campus will alert you to how much that piece of etiquette has changed.

On the other hand, John Stuart Mill was probably right when he insisted that no individual voice should be silenced by a "tyrannous" majority. And, as Milton pointed out, that one voice might just contain the real truth, while the rest of us are wrong. The trick is to balance a commitment to free expression with a fair amount of respect for others. This respect can be based on a Kantian notion of natural merit or on a more complex rendering of obligations based on the nature of human relationships. The former is often considered a minimum expectation, and the latter is sometimes referred to as the lynchpin of social order. Whichever way you view it, it is clear that speech rights are not absolute, but are regulated to a very great extent by our social and cultural values—and, if these methods fail, sometimes the law.

Liberty-limiting Principles

Most media practitioners assume that First Amendment protections are inviolable. As we know, such is not the case. Most of the restrictions on speech that exist today have to do with preventing speech-caused harms. Child pornography, cigarette advertising, and libel are all forms of speech restricted because of potential harm to someone. We accept these restrictions, in part, because of an inherent belief in some of the following liberty-limiting principles.

The Harm Principle

In 1859, John Stuart Mill wrote *On Liberty*. In it, he laid out the ethical foundation of democratic individualism. At the same time, Mill considered the circumstances under which individual liberty might be justifiably restricted. Under what has come to be known as the *harm principle*, Mill stated that a person's liberty may justifiably be restricted only in order to prevent harm that the person's actions would cause to others.

> Acts of whatever kind, which, without justifiable cause, do harm to others, may be, and in the more important cases absolutely require to be, controlled by the unfavorable sentiments, and, when needful, by the active interfer-

ence of mankind. The liberty of the individual must be thus far limited; he must not make himself a nuisance to other people.[43]

Following on this principle, the government may limit the freedom of any individual or group if their actions are likely to harm any other part of society. Government prohibitions against murder, theft, rape, and speeding are all examples of this principle. The harm principle is probably the only liberty-limiting principle that is non-controversial and widely accepted.

Under this principle, journalists would have to consider the degree of harm their work causes and then weigh the costs against the benefits of publishing. The same would be true of both advertising and public relations. Ads that had adverse affects on any segment of society could be called into question, as could any public relations communication that might cause undue harm. Of course, defining undue harm is at the heart of the entire debate over harm-causing communication. Part of the problem lies in the inability to draw a correlation between speech and any harm that may have been caused by the speech. For example, a correlation between media violence and social violence has yet to be proven conclusively; however, most of us suspect that there is some link between the two. The most difficult aspect of correlation is that it is easy to ignore or miss altogether variables that might be either the true cause of the harm or, at least, a major contributor. In the case of media violence, for instance, a change in societal mores and the easy availability of guns and other weapons are variables that are very likely affecting the level of violence. As the ethicist Sissela Bok points out, however, just because there may be multiple variables affecting violence in America, that does not absolve the media from their responsibility to do something about it.[44]

The Offense Principle

The offense principle states that an act that offends another person may be prohibited. This principle may account for such laws as those against public nudity, or restricting the sale of pornography to those over 18. This principle is often used to justify complaints about tasteless advertising or offensive photographs in newspapers or on television. The movie industry, a number of years ago, adopted a rating system in order that children will not be surprised by explicit scenes of sexuality or violence. Recently, the Brooklyn Museum of Art lifted its under-17 prohibition, which it had enforced for years to protect the sensitivity of children to some kinds of art. Ironically, a painting many found sacrilegious drew much media and legal attention almost immediately following this lifting of the under-17 ban.

Although the offense principle does have its advocates, it is easy to argue the difficulty of determining exactly what is offensive. Whereas we may agree with Supreme Court Justice Potter Stewart that "I cannot define obscenity, but I know it when I see it," defining harm-causing communication is still at the heart of determining its ethicality. The pure fact is that what offends one person may not offend another. That is primarily why the offense principle is controversial.

The Principle of Legal Paternalism

The *principle of legal paternalism* asserts that we have the obligation to protect others from harm. All governments are paternal to some degree. Laws requiring helmets for motorcyclists or prohibiting suicide are based on legal paternalism. Unlike Ross's obligation of non-injury (discussed in Chapter 2), paternalism requires us to prevent foreseeable harm, not just to refrain from injuring someone. Under this principle, a newspaper would think twice before running a story about a teen suicide that might cause further attempts within the community.

To an extent, all journalists are paternalistic. Every time an editor or publisher decides to "give us what we need," she is acting paternalistically. Each time a news director decides the order of a newscast, he is acting paternalistically in deciding which is the most important story. The legal scholar Stephen Carter points out that news judgment can involve either telling the public what they need to know or telling them what they want to know, but that the two cannot be pursued simultaneously. In fact, Carter points out that "making judgments about what is useful and useless, what it is good to report and what should be ignored, is a central part of the free speech mission."[45] In this sense, paternalism is a positive element of the news business.

However, paternalism also infers that there are those who cannot or will not act on their own behalves. In fact, the American press is premised on the belief that it is the job of the news media to look out for the best interests of the public. This is a somewhat Platonic concept (recall Plato's view of the common people discussed in Chapter 4), and one that clearly considers the public to be either unwilling or unable to look out after itself. In a country in which individualism is so highly prized, you can imagine how popular paternalism is as a concept for protecting the citizenry from harm. And, strangely enough, the press often gets faulted for not being paternalistic enough and for pandering to audience wants rather than needs.

The Principle of Legal Moralism

The *principle of legal moralism* holds that something may be prohibited because it is simply immoral. Of all the liberty-limiting principles, this is the only one based almost entirely on a religious definition of morality. The shortcomings of this principle are immediately apparent: Not all religions agree on what is moral and what is not. Even if they could, the question of whether any religious group should be the arbiter of public morals is a large one.

Most people agree that not only religious groups but also the government should stay out of legislating morality. Such regulations as those prohibiting certain sexual acts between consenting adults are examples of this principle. We have seen repeatedly how difficult it is to define these situations to everyone's satisfaction. Imagine a newspaper not being able to run a story about prostitution because the practice itself might be viewed as immoral, or an advertiser of perfume not being able to suggest that her product induces sexual arousal. The principle of legal moralism is probably the least defensible of the liberty-limiting principles.

How to Choose Applicable Theories

Although the foregoing list of theories and philosophers is far from exhaustive, we can now begin to see where our predisposition to decide in certain ways may have come from. The problem is that, without some coherent method of picking among the various philosophies, we often end up contradicting ourselves or arriving at no satisfactory solution to our dilemmas. Or worse, we manage to rationalize, and thus justify, nearly any action we see fit to take. It is this last that is the most troublesome aspect of having so many differing approaches to moral decision making at our fingertips. Some words of caution need to be voiced here.

The *theory of cognitive dissonance* (yet another theory) tells us that human beings tend to pay attention only to that with which they already agree, and that they simply block out unwanted information (especially if it runs counter to their predisposition to act in a certain way). It is no wonder then, that most of us tend to latch onto the theories that will bolster our already held beliefs. The same is true of moral decision making. Most of us have some idea of what we're going to do before we ever make a formal decision; and, unfortunately, before we've looked at the possible alternatives. The various publics who are targets of the media have probably suspected this for quite some time. It is little wonder that surveys consistently show media professions at the low end of the credibility scale when most people probably believe that media decisions are either standard operating procedure (at best) or knee-jerk (at worst).

Part of the solution is to realize that not every theory is applicable to every situation. For example, a rule in force at a local television news outlet disallowing the use of photos of people who have been arrested but not yet indicted could be an example of either Kantian logic or rule utilitarianism. Either way, we need not apply act utilitarianism to the question of whether to run a photo or not. The decision has already been made. At some point, we had to have asked ourselves what rationale would allow us to run these types of photos. We could have used the Categorical Imperative to arrive at a rule such as "Never run photos of those arrested but not yet indicted." Our reasoning might have told us that we would not want our own pictures run in such a fashion, especially if we were falsely accused. And, if we further reasoned that no rational person would want the same, then we could make a rule to guide us in similar situations in the future. Rule utilitarian logic might have told us that no greater good is furthered by publishing pictures of this type and that the potential harm to the subject might outweigh any benefit to the community at this point.

It is important to remember that we could also arrive at the opposite conclusion by employing at least one of these theories. Rule utilitarianism might tell us that the community's best interest *would* be served by running photos of this sort, since exactly who is suspected of crimes is important information and has some bearing on how people feel about their community and its level of safety. A Kantian approach, however, might still result in the same decision not to run photos since this theory is based, not on consequences, but on a duty to adhere to an already reasoned-out guideline.

As pointed out, the danger here is that we already may be predisposed to run photos of people who have been arrested but not indicted simply because, as a television news operation, we have to rely on images to "sell" our product. In order to make a rule that doesn't reflect this somewhat egoistic reason, we rationalize that the greater good is being served. *Rationalize*, in this sense, means "to devise self-satisfying but incorrect reasons for a particular behavior." It is, therefore, crucial that we understand our *reasons* for preferring one action over another and to admit them to ourselves. Unless we understand our real reasons, we will be content to rationalize our actions by using other means—even if those means are ethical theories. In this case, by recognizing our need to provide images for our stories, we can factor this element into our decision-making process and weigh our egoistic benefits with the benefits to the community versus the potential harm to the subject of the story. Recognizing that egoism is a variable may help us to make a decision based more on the needs of others than on our own perceived needs. Remember, our actions must be justified, never merely rationalized. When we use ethical theory simply as a way to rationalize our decisions, we are doing ourselves and everyone concerned an injustice.

In the next chapter, we will take a detailed look at a method for making ethical decisions based on the theories discussed here.

Chapter 5

A Checklist for Ethical Decision Making

Man is the Reasoning Animal. Such is the claim. I think it is open to dispute.

(Mark Twain)

Throughout the preceding chapters, we looked at a great many theories proposed by some of the finest minds in philosophy. We have also seen how the opposing ideals of professional autonomy and societal obligation can, and frequently do, clash during the process of moral decision making. What we haven't seen is a synthesis of these ideas and philosophies into a working model for decision making. That's what this chapter is all about.

Without a method whereby moral decision making becomes routine—so engrained in our thought processes that we cannot separate it from our other decision-making tools—we will continue to flounder in the waters of inconsistency. Mass media practitioners must learn to approach decisions with ethical ramifications in the same sensible way they do other choices. They must avoid the temptation to answer with pat aphorisms such as "buyer beware," or "the public's right to know." They must resist the urge to hide behind the protection of the First Amendment, for that law protects only legally, not ethically—and it typically protects only the perpetrator, not the victim.

In short, the mass media must consider their actions, and they must show their constituencies that they have done so with the best interests of everyone at heart. Ultimately, the media show that they care by their actions, not their justifications for those actions; however, in the rarified air of the mass communication industries, legitimate justification is often as hard to come by as pirates' gold—and equally valuable. The polls show that the public doesn't respect the media—any part of them. It has been the contention of this book that that lack of respect is often deserved but certainly avoidable.

Any moral decision-making process worth its salt must allow for three things: reflection, justification, and consistency. In order to rationalize our reasons to ourselves, we must reflect on all of the facets of the dilemma we are facing. We must do so without presumption that any particular course of action is automatically appropriate. An honest assessment will provide the only means to an equitable solution. We may be called upon to justify our decisions to others.

We must be prepared to do so with the expectation that we will never satisfy everyone, but with the determination to try. Finally, we must be consistent, for moral consistency is one of the hallmarks of integrity, and integrity may be the most valuable coin of the moral realm.

The following checklist approach to moral decision making has been developed over years of experimenting with both students and professionals. It grew out of the work of others, most notably the former *Washington Post* ombudsman Joann Byrd. It is somewhat involved, but with value to each of its steps—none of which is sufficient without the others. The ultimate goal of this checklist is to allow for the formulation of principles and guidelines by which to make future decisions. At the very least, its consistent use should so educate the user that future moral decisions might become more second nature.

The approach used in this checklist tends to stress the commonalties of the mass media rather than their differences. In fact, this worksheet approach is based on the notion of developing common ground for discussion. For example, although a lie in advertising may bring legal penalties, its moral standing is not far different from a lie in public relations. A free-speech issue having to do with protesters pulling books from a school library has a lot in common with a demand to stifle tabloid journalism. The point is that in discussing a case of whether to fire a perfectly qualified news anchor simply because she is over 40, the theories outlined earlier and the use of this checklist will invariably lead to a resounding "no."

As has been already been stated, blind obedience to any one philosophy is not sufficient for an educated analysis of a moral issue. Therefore, the checklist seeks to pull together the best that these philosophies have to offer. At the same time, the weaknesses discussed throughout this book should be recognized and avoided. Blind adherence to any rule, no matter how well-intentioned, can lead to callousness. By the same token, service always to the greater good can result in tyrannizing a deserving minority. We cannot let our emotions rule our decisions any more than we can let our reason (often cold and calculating) do so. And we must remember that service to our professions and service to society are not always one and the same thing. There are times when each of these may fairly overrule the other. Although it is probably true that we can justify almost any decision using an approach such as the one suggested here, it must be born in mind that we will be judged not solely by our own principles but, to a greater degree, by the principles of those we most affect. As media representatives, it is in our best interest to admit to those principles in order that we may function as a benefit to society and not a burden.

The Checklist

Each of the following points is followed by commentary on its meaning and importance to the overall outcome of the moral decision-making process.

1 What is the ethical issue/problem? (Define in one or two sentences.)

It is important to recognize that every problem has more than one component, and that not every component involves an ethical decision. Therefore, the *ethical* issue involved in the case must be stated succinctly, and it must be made clear that other elements of the problem have not been confused with the ethical component. For example, in a case involving a decision to advertise a product in a certain way, the client's right to advertise must be separated from any ethical question involved in the planned advertisement, and the issue must be stated in such a way that the ethical component is clear. The question, or issue, may not be whether the client should advertise, but whether the client should advertise in a particular manner that might have ethical ramifications.

2 What immediate facts have the most bearing on the ethical decision you must render in this case? Include in this list any potential economic, social, or political pressures.

Only the facts that bear on the *ethical* decision need be listed. For instance, although it may certainly be a fact that a given newspaper employs 500 people, it may have no bearing on its decision to run a story that potentially violates someone's privacy.

The realities of the two most important factors of any decision made within the mass media industry must also be recognized. Very often, economic or political factors are present that, although typically amoral in nature, will probably have a direct effect on the ethical decision-making process. In the world of media industries, "doing the right thing" may very well lead to severe economic consequences, and those consequences must be seriously weighed. This weighing most often leads to compromise. The same is true for political forces affecting a decision. Although most people may not admit to political pressure, its almost constant presence should be noted; and decision makers must be prepared to deal with it and to recognize how it will affect their decisions.

3 Who are the claimants in this issue and in what way are you obligated to each of them? (List all affected by your decision.) Define your claimants based on the following obligations:

- a promise/contract you made (implied or express) (fidelity);
- a wrong you committed that you now have to make up (reparation);
- gratitude for something one of the claimants did for you (gratitude);
- the merit of the claimants when compared with each other (justice);
- your ability to help someone out who needs and deserves help (beneficence);
- your ability to avoid harming anyone unnecessarily (non-injury).

This is the first point at which ethical theory is applied. The notion of moral claimants is tied to both consequential and non-consequential theory. From a utilitarian perspective, for example, majority interests must be considered, thus the majority claimants must be recognized as a group. As Mill would have us consider the rights of the minority as well—since he would limit any liberty that severely affects the rights of others under his "harm principle"—that minority must also be recognized. Duty-based theories (non-consequential) such as Ross's also require us to be aware of all claimants potentially affected by our decisions. His six *prima facie* duties allow not only for a listing of claimants, but also how to decide on who they are by applying his six categories of obligation: fidelity/reparation, gratitude, justice, beneficence, self-improvement, and non-injury. For example, if, as a reporter, you are obligated by the duty of fidelity to honor your implied contract with the public to give them the news they want to read, that reading public must be listed as a claimant on your decision. Likewise, if you are obligated by the duty of non-injury to refrain from violating a person's privacy, that person (perhaps the subject of your story) must be listed as a claimant. At this point, conflicts will begin to show up among various claimants and the obligations to them.

At this stage the decision maker (moral agent) should try to step into the shoes of the various claimants and try to determine, honestly, what their perspective is. One of the hardest tasks in ethical decision making is this. Many philosophers say that to be able to see a problem from another's perspective is a great gift. Philosophers such as John Rawls suggest we step behind a "veil of ignorance" from where we become free of the encumbrances of our existence (social status, education, ethnic/cultural heritage, etc.). It is only from there as "original" people that we can make moral decisions free from the affecting variables of our lives. Although this may seem a bit extreme, the key here is to try to see the problem from as many perspectives as possible.

4   List at least three alternative courses of action. For each alternative, ask the following questions:

- What are the best- and worse-case scenarios if you choose this alternative?
- Will anyone be harmed if this alternative is chosen, and how will they be harmed?
- Would honoring any ideal/value (personal, professional, religious, or other) invalidate the chosen alternative or call it into question?
- Are there any rules or principles (legal, professional, organizational, or other) that *automatically* invalidate this alternative?

It is extremely important to list at least three alternatives. As Aristotle noted, there are always at least two, and these two often represent the extremes. Nothing is ever either black or white, and we must be forced to think in terms of compromise, even if that compromise doesn't exactly conform with our personal notion of what is the right thing to do. A true "Golden Mean" is not simply a watered-down decision. It bears the marks of that internal struggle already begun above, and is the result of hard thinking. We must also be prepared to state where we would go if such a compromise fails. It is not sufficient to state that we would go to a source and ask permission before revealing that person's name to a court of law. We must be prepared to drop back to another option if the compromise option fails. It is also important to realize which options may be most favored by which parties. Although it is probably apparent by this time, putting it down in writing serves to clarify the decision maker's position and shows exactly where it conflicts with the preferences of others involved in or affected by the decision.

Best- and worst-case scenarios: This is a great exercise for discovering whether or not we can live with our decisions. By visualizing the absolute best and worst outcomes for each alternative, the potential effects that decision may have on others may then be assessed. It is important to deal with the probable (not necessarily possible) extremes here since anything may be possible. For example, although it is possible that any person having their privacy invaded might be so distraught as to commit suicide, it isn't very probable.

Harm: Likewise, it is vital to recognize what options will harm which claimants. It is a rare case in which no harm will be done by the carrying out of any option. By listing the options and the concomitant harms, we are made to weigh the amount of potential harm involved with each alternative and to understand that avoiding harm is practically impossible. This might lead, as utilitarians suggest, to choosing the option that will produce the least amount of harm. It might also lead to a closer examination of our values according to, for instance, the ethic of care.

Ideals versus options: The term *ideals*, as defined by Vincent Ryan Ruggiero, refers to "a notion of excellence, a goal that is thought to bring about greater harmony to ourselves and to others."[1] For example, our culture respects ideals such as tolerance, compassion, loyalty, forgiveness, peace, justice, fairness, and respect for persons. In addition to these human ideals are institutional or organizational ideals, such as profit, efficiency, productivity, quality, and stability. So, at this point, we are required to list those ideals that apply to the various claimants.

Ideals often come in conflict with each other, much the same way that the obligations already listed will conflict. We must recognize these conflicts and be prepared to list ideals in the order in which they should be honored. This calls for a serious bout of internal struggling and may be the first time we are forced to consider the ultimate direction our decision will take. For example, if we choose to place the journalistic ideal of providing information our audience wants over the societal ideal of honoring privacy, we are well on the way to deciding to run a story that may, in fact, violate someone's privacy.

Beginning here and continuing through the process, we must winnow our options. The first step is to compare the options with the ideals of all concerned parties. For example, if we have chosen to honor the journalistic obligation of providing the kind of news our readers demand, then an option to withhold a story that would be of vital interest to readers would be invalidated. Again, we are not asked to make a decision yet, only to see how our options stack up against the various criteria.

Rules: The winnowing process continues here by applying what Fritzsche refers to as *conjunctive rules*, specifying a minimal cutoff point for a decision.[2] Principles, defined above, are simply the step that precedes rules and can be viewed as roughly analogous to the rules derived from them. An example of an ethical conjunctive rule derived from a principle might be "any action that would involve lying will not be considered." An example of an actual rule might be Article I of the SPJ code, which states that "The public's right to know of events of public importance and interest is the overriding mission of the mass media." Application of such a rule would clearly invalidate an option of not running a story on an event of public importance.

5   Consider the following ethical *guidelines* and ask yourself whether they either support or reject any of your alternatives.

Guidelines based on consequences: weighing benefits and harms

- Is the "good" brought about by your action outweighed by the potential harm that might be done to *anyone*? (Mill's *Harm Principle*)
- Is any of the harm brought about by anyone other than the moral agent? (Causal Harm)
- Will anyone be harmed who could be said to be defenseless? (Paternalism)
- To what degree is your choice of alternatives based on your own or your organization's best interests? (Ethical Egoism)
- Which of the alternatives will generate the greatest benefit (or the least amount of harm) for the greatest number of people? (Utilitarianism)
- In using utilitarianism, ask yourself if by privileging the majority any injustice has been done to individuals in the minority.
- Does this alternative recognize the interrelationships of the parties involved? Does it help anyone by recognizing legitimate needs? (Ethic of Care)

Guidelines based on the action itself: honoring integrity

- Are you willing to make your decision a rule or policy that you and others in your situation can follow in similar situations in the future? (Kant)

- Does the alternative show a basic respect for the integrity and dignity of those affected by your actions? (Ethic of Care)
- Have you used or will you be using any person as a means to an end without consideration for his/her basic integrity? (Kant)
- Is the intent of this action free from vested interest or ulterior motive? (Kant's "good will")
- Does this action promote the development of character within myself, my organization/profession, and my community? (Virtue Ethics)

This is the final winnowing stage, the point at which the ethical theories come into play. This final stage prior to an actual decision completes the complex reasoning process we have been forced into. We will discover here, as previously, that there is much conflict among these theories. There will be no easy solutions. Whereas one person may use utilitarian theory to support running a story in the interest of the "greater good," another person may cite Kant's proscription against using a person as a means to an end as reason for not running the same story. What is most important is to use only those theories that apply directly to a given decision. The best way to accomplish this is to simply answer the questions honestly while considering all sides of the issue. If a particular theory may not seem to apply from one perspective, it very well may from another.

It is important to note that just because a particular theory seems to justify a certain action doesn't mean that the action is the right one to take. Remember the weaknesses of the various theories discussed in Chapter 4. For example, utilitarianism allows for otherwise egregious actions to be taken in the interest of the majority. Justifying a questionable act just because it benefits a designated majority simply will not wash in the minds of most people. We cannot ignore these problems and must counterbalance them with other theories—in this example, perhaps, the theory of distributive justice or the "harm principle."

In other words, we must not fall into the trap of choosing theoretical justification only because it bolsters an already held position. We must choose it because we have arrived at an option through the "agony of decision making," and the theoretical support we have chosen truly reflects our belief in the rightness of our decision.

6 Determine a course of action based on your analysis.

People often begin the entire decision-making process by coming into a case with a decision already in mind. However, as we proceed through this worksheet, we are forced to look at each case from too many angles to have a fixed position. Remember, the decision itself is not as important as the process. The goal is to provide the tools needed to assess ethical dilemmas and to reason through them. There are no right answers, only well-reasoned answers—which leads us to the final point.

7   Defend your decision in the form of a letter addressed to your most adamant
    detractor.
        As Stephen Carter has pointed out, a person of integrity will be willing
    and able to justify her actions to others. If we have truly thought through
    the process and made a decision based on sound reasoning, then we should
    be able to defend that decision. The most appropriate person to defend it to
    is that claimant who has lost the most or been harmed the most. The very
    least the people out there can ask for is that we, as a media representatives,
    have actually considered our decisions.

An Example

The following case was done by a college student. Although the case is a fairly
typical journalistic problem, it should be stressed again that the worksheet has
broad application and is not limited to a single type of ethical issue. The facts of
the case will become clear through the explication.

1   *Issue:* An activist group composed of concerned parents and several leading
    citizens have found a local paper's series coverage of high school sex and the
    transmittal of sexually transmitted diseases (STDs) offensive. They argue
    that such coverage affects the moral character of high school and other
    students and does not belong in so public a forum as the local the paper.
    They are also concerned that the identities of the students used as "case
    studies" in the series might be discovered, and also that the reputation of
    the entire school district might be harmed.
2   Relevant facts include:

   • Several leading citizens (including two school board members) have
     signed a letter to the editor asking that the series be terminated.
   • Their concern is over the "delicate" nature of the topic in so public a
     forum.
   • Some state that the names of the "sources" should be made known so
     that they can seek medical treatment and not be allowed to "spread the
     disease."
   • The paper is the only one in town.
   • The series is also slated to cover the danger of AIDS and other STDs.
   • The paper has taken care to conceal the names of actual students it has
     interviewed.
   • Readership has dropped with the advent of "soft" news on local TV,
     especially the tabloid-type syndicated programs airing just before prime
     time.
   • As editor and primary decision maker in this case, I am aware that
     my own high-school-aged children face the same problems my paper is
     portraying.

- Special considerations include the need for confidentiality of sources, the general moral tenor of the community (it is fairly conservative), and whether the newspaper is using the series simply to boost circulation.

3 Claimants:
   - *Parents:* Parents seek some measure of control over their children's behavior, especially in the area of sex education. Many would prefer the subject be confined to their households for discussion. Parents of students featured in series are especially vulnerable, even if the students' names are withheld. (Duty of non-injury.)
   - *Students:* They are not naive, but some of them, like their parents, might prefer the topic be discussed in a less open forum, although they might see this as a useful service to their peer group. Students used as sources for the story need to protect their identities and are relying on the paper to maintain their confidentiality. Also, they would probably want their "lessons" to be of some use to others. (Duties of non-injury and fidelity to sources not to reveal names.)
   - *Reporters:* Need to protect their right to gather and print information they feel is important to the public interest, often despite pubic opinion to the contrary. (Duty of self-improvement; duty of fidelity to the profession and the community.)
   - *The paper itself:* Must maintain its viability by producing stories that not only inform the community, but compete well in the marketplace. (Duty of fidelity to the paper and to the community.)
   - *School officials:* Might feel they are being put in a bad "light" since students under their supervision are the ones being featured in this series. (Duty of non-injury; duty of justice.)
   - *Community members:* (Those who do not fit into above categories). They have a right to be kept aware of topics of concern/importance to the community. Despite the letter to the editor, many community members may, in fact, support the story being run. (Duty of fidelity, possibly gratitude.)

4 *The options*, as I see them, are:

   a Continue with the series as is.
   b Discontinue the series.
   c Continue with the series, but offer to reduce offensive language or incidents pictured in the stories to an acceptable level.
   d Continue with the series, and work with student and parent groups toward some resolutions to the problems portrayed in the stories. This way, we are a part of the solution, not just a recounting of the problem.

Favored options:

- Activist parents and citizens clearly would favor option *b*, and wouldn't view option *c* as a complete enough measure.
- The paper would favor *a*, but would probably view *c* as censorship. It might consider *d*.
- Students could go either way, but would probably favor *a*.
- Community would probably favor *d*.

Best- and worst-case scenarios

- *Continuing the series as-is:* Best case—no one gets hurt. The series is respected by community as good journalism. Lives are affected in a positive way. Worst case—could alienate more of my target audience. The paper could lose readership. I could lose my job.
- *Discontinue the series:* Best case—our support among those protesting the series grows. Worst case—some in the community would be pleased if we don't continue the series; however, the paper would lose its journalistic integrity and will have violated its mandate to give the people what they need, not just what they want. We might also be violating the students' trust, since they probably want the story told.
- *Continue the series but with editing for language and graphic content:* Best case—no one is concerned with the editing. The story remains effective despite the editing. Worst case—the editing softens the story to the point that it is ineffective. Editing under community pressure is a bad precedent to set.
- *Continue the series and work with the community toward a solution:* Best case—the series brings the problem to the community's attentions. The paper is recognized as a good citizen. Worst case—people are still angry. The paper shifts its focus to "public journalism" and away from objective journalism.

Harm

Any action would likely cause harm (or perceived harm) to some party, but in differing degrees.

Ideals include: freedom of choice (for readers); freedom of speech (for the paper and its journalists); freedom from harm (for students, the schools and parents); respect for minority opinion; freedom from censorship (by both the paper and the community members who might wish to see the stories).

Conflicting ideals:

- Evidently, some parents and influential citizens favor stopping the series, thus upholding the principles of majority rule (to the extent that it is or may become a majority) and the right to protect their community from what they see as unnecessary exposure.

- The paper's obligation to present information of concern and interest to the community and its right to be free from censorship obviously will conflict at times with some community opinions or ideals.
- Students, parents, and schools who might be harmed from this would complain that their rights to protection from this kind of story are being violated by the paper. After all, isn't it up to the community to say what is best for it?
- The community is likely to favor overall freedom of the press, despite disparate elements within the community who might feel otherwise. The key may turn on how loudly the activist group protests.
- My tendency, at this point, is to honor freedom of the press as an ideal, trying to keep in mind that I must limit, to the best of my ability, the harm that could come from my publishing the series in question. I must also make sure that increased readership is not the *sole* reason for my position.
- No ideal, viewed in context, invalidates any option. Viewed singularly, any ideal will rule out certain options.

Rules

The code of the Society of Professional Journalists, Article I, states that it is the responsibility of journalists to provide news of public importance and interest. In fact, the code states that this is the "overriding mission" of the mass media. I think that this series could be said to be in the interest of the public. Some would call the subject into question, and Article V states that the news media should not pander to morbid curiosity about details of vice and crime. However, I don't believe this series panders to the public curiosity in any way. As to naming the sources of the stories, Article III of the code strictly forbids this. I would say that the SPJ code is on the side of the media in this case.

Ethical theories:

Consequential:

- Mill's "Harm Principle" allows restraints on liberty only if there is harm (or violation of another's liberty). The harm, in this case, has not been demonstrated. Indeed, there is a strong argument that this series will be beneficial to the community since it will help make them more aware of the problem of STDs.
- Egoism could be driving the paper to run the stories because it may help stimulate sales; however, given the SPJ code and the importance

of the subject to the community, I think that the paper is not acting in an egoistic manner here.

- An argument could be made on utilitarian grounds that the objecting citizens *represent* a majority of citizens in the community. However, continuing to publish the series is more in line with the First Amendment's intent, which is also utilitarian by nature and speaks to a greater *societal* good.

Non-consequential:

- There is a clear Kantian rule embodied in the First Amendment: "Don't censor." In fact, and despite the obvious court-sanctioned exceptions, the First Amendment is couched in pretty clear "perfect duty" language.
- Ross's prima facie duties apply in a number of ways. The newspaper owes a duty of fidelity to the citizens of the community. A newspaper operates to bring news to the community that it wants and *needs* to remain an informed citizenry. If it were to publish only that news that the community *wanted*, it would not be doing its civic duty. Non-injury, on the other hand, would have us consider the potential harmful effects of the stories on students. However, I would argue that we do greater harm covering up this sort of epidemic. Beneficence is also applicable since by printing the series of stories we are helping society come to grips with this problem.
- Aristotle's Golden Mean is not especially applicable here since the middle ground would have us partially censor the stories, which goes against our First Amendment position of non-censorship. Plus, I believe that the stories would lose some of their impact if censored.

6   Decision:

I would continue to publish the series, making sure that no sensationalism creeps into the stories in any way. They will be factual and truthful. I will personally respond to the upset citizens of the community via an editorial which will contain much of my defense below.

7   Defense:

The position of those seeking to prevent publication is that citizens, and especially parents, should have some say in the degree to which their children are exposed to unsettling (and possibly sensational) information. This seems reasonable. However, as the only newspaper in town, we are obligated to present the community not just with news it wants, but also with news it needs. In an open, democratic society, this means exposing them to a variety of issues, some which potentially conflict with some individuals' standards. In every controversial story, there will be something that someone finds objectionable. Although you may disagree that some of the issues we choose to bring to your attention are worthy, we reserve the right, as citizens ourselves, to work on your behalf in presenting the news. We admit the paternalistic nature of this arrangement; however, we will continue to listen to you and to try to respond to your complaints while reserving the right to make the kind of judgments our training has prepared us to make. In short, we wouldn't print a story we thought was not in the best interest of the community of which we are an integral part. Most importantly, we believe that any limitation on the freedom of expression in this country is counterproductive and can only lead to further restrictions of our most valued liberty.

What Does It All Mean?

Applying ethical thought to the mass media decision-making process requires two vital components: a rudimentary grounding in the relevant ethical theories, and a structured approach to analyzing the issues on a case-by-case basis. It is clearly impossible to bring every relevant theory to bear on every case; however, there are certain thinkers whose theories have contributed immensely to the ethical foundations of modern American mass media. The common ground is the democratic system in which the media professions operate. Therefore, the primary theorists are those who have proposed ethical guidelines based on the sanctity of the individual as an active citizen in a society in which he or she may exert some control. However, other theorists went beyond these considerations to the nature of virtue and good will that ultimately guides our decisions, adds so much to our deliberations, and limits our blind obedience to the greater good. We must also not forget that community plays an increasingly vital role in our lives, and there are those who deem community the most important consideration, not necessarily subservient to individual will. Taken as a whole, these theorists and others are but the building blocks to a more complete understanding of the role of ethics in our decision-making processes.

We are not an either–or society when it comes to ethics. We staunchly defend individual rights, yet complain that any sense of community is vanishing in these hectic, and often confusing times. It is clear that we should value both individual autonomy and community interests. Ethical decisions need not ignore individuality in order to recognize community, or favor community over personal autonomy. We simply must realize that often both can be served simultaneously if we are simply willing to communicate and compromise. We should also recognize that there will be times when one need will override the other. In these instances, we must exercise special caution that those affected by our decisions are not unduly injured. The only way to accomplish this is to hold both individual rights and community needs as valid media concerns. And the only way to do this (to paraphrase Fred Friendly) is to make the agony of decision making so intense that we can escape only by thinking.

Decision making can more easily become a part of our lives if it is the product of a structured method of analysis focusing on the things we all have in common and viewed in the light of the relevant ethical theories. We can be taught to think in a logical fashion by forcing ourselves, at least initially, to conform to this step-by-step analysis. Hopefully, this will lead to an ability to do the same in the day-to-day routine of deadline-based decision making. Previously considered cases can then be used as reference points for future decisions. And those issues that do not follow from previous exposure to similar circumstances can be analyzed on their particular merits based on familiarity with this decision-making model. The lessons learned in every decision-making situation should serve not only to better our ethical skills, but also to better our professions, and, by extension, all of society.

Chapter 6

Meta-issues Across the Media

When in doubt, tell the truth.

(Mark Twain)

We have seen in preceding chapters how the various media professions differ in such areas as loyalty and goals. These differences set them apart from each other ethically as well. That doesn't mean that lying in a news story isn't the same as lying in public relations or advertising. What it does mean is that there are issues unique to each medium that require different ethical approaches. That is what we'll be discussing in this section of the book. In this chapter, we will be exploring the meta-issues of truth telling and harm and how those larger issues play out within the three mass media professions—public relations, advertising, and news journalism.

To Tell the Truth

Of all the possible virtues a media practitioner would like to be known for, truth stands out as preeminent. Hardly anyone doubts that the media go to great lengths to tell the truth. With the exception of the tabloid press, who typically run stories on alien births and Elvis spottings, most media base their reputations on their veracity. In fact, the few laws that limit freedom of speech have mostly to do with protection from harm caused by some form of lying. Laws against libel, slander, defamation, and so on, all deal with false or misleading speech. These laws apply equally to both public relations and advertising. In addition, both public relations and advertising are subject to very strict Federal Trade Commission guidelines governing deception in print and broadcast ads. In short, truth is the default position for all serious media, both legally and ethically. However, as we will see, truth is defined somewhat differently for journalism than it is for public relations and advertising, and on that definitional difference turns a great deal of controversy.

Can the media's allegiance to the truth be bent or even broken in the name of public interest? Do public relations and advertising have to adhere to the same strict standard of truth telling that the news media do? These questions, and others, are probably the most important ones facing the media today. And these are the questions we will take up here.

Truth as a Legal Concept

Remember that the law is the ultimate formalization of societal and cultural values and ideals. The fact that we have enacted laws that deal with truth shows that, as a society, we value communication that is truthful and tend to restrict communication that potentially harms others. Although the law doesn't pretend, nor does it need, to cover every potential communication-caused harm, it does deal with the most egregious. It is also worth mentioning that most of these laws apply equally to individuals and to the media. For example, *slander* is generally applied to the communication of individuals whereas *libel* is reserved for published communication. As an individual, I may slander someone else if I harm them in some way because of something I've said to a third party. Libel would occur if the harm were caused by my publishing the same communication.

The First Amendment is not inviolable. Laws exist that clearly disallow certain types of speech, and all those who deal in public communication are bound by these laws. For the most part, these laws protect others. We are all familiar with the First Amendment rights allowed the press in this country. But, as with most rights, there are concomitant obligations—chief among them is the obligation not to harm others through communication. The most important "don'ts" in the media concern slander or libel (defamation), and invasion of privacy.

Defamation

Although it is variously defined (each case seems to bring a new definition), *defamation* can be said to be any communication that holds a person up to contempt, hatred, ridicule, or scorn. One problem in defending against accusations of defamation is that there are different rules for different people. It is generally easier for private individuals to prove defamation than it is for those in the public eye. Celebrities and politicians, for example, open themselves to a certain amount of publicity, and, therefore, criticism. Whereas a private individual suing for libel need only prove negligence, a public figure must prove malice. In order for defamation to be actionable, five elements must be present.

- There must be communication of a statement that harms a person's reputation in some way—even if it only lowers that person's esteem in another's eyes.
- The communication must have been published or communicated to a third party. The difference here is that between slander and libel. *Slander* is oral defamation, and might arise, for example, in a public speech. *Libel* is written defamation, though it also includes broadcast communication.

- The person defamed must have been identified in the communication, either by name or by direct inference. This is the toughest to prove if the person's name hasn't been used directly.
- The person defamed must be able to prove that the communication caused damage to his or her reputation.
- Negligence must also be shown. In other words, the source of the communication must be proved to have been negligent during research or writing. Negligence can be the fault of poor information gathering. Public figures must prove malice—that is, the communication was made with knowing falsehood or reckless disregard for the truth.

There are defenses against defamation. The most obvious is that the *communication is the truth*, regardless of whether the information harmed someone's reputation or not.

The second defense is *privilege*. Privilege applies to statements made during public, official, or judicial proceedings. For example, if something normally libelous is reported accurately on the basis of a public meeting, the reporter cannot be held responsible. Privilege is a tricky concept, however, and care must be taken that privileged information be released only to those who have right to it. Public meetings are public information. Only concerned individuals have a right to privileged information released at private meetings.

The third most common defense is *fair comment*. This concept applies primarily to the right to criticize, as in theater or book critiques, and must be restricted to the public interest aspects of that which is under discussion. However, it also can be construed to apply to such communications as comparative advertising.

We should remember that laws are extensions of our moral beliefs, codified so that we, as a society, must follow them. In this way, laws are similar to what Kant would call perfect duties. We must refrain from such acts as murder, stealing, and—most importantly for our purposes here—lying. It is often pointed out that being legal doesn't necessarily mean being ethical; however, if we understand that many of our common laws were designed to help us live together successfully as a society, we should also see that those laws reflect the commonalties in our moral standards. All that is legal may not be ethical, but legality is a good starting point for many ethical situations.

Defamation and privacy issues (covered in Chapter 10) are at the heart of legal protection from untruthful and harmful speech, and these types of speech are certainly morally troublesome as well. What follows, then, is a discussion of the additional ethical considerations necessary for all media in order that they fulfill both their professional and their social obligations.

Truth and the Act of Communication

You would think that in any act of communication, truth would need to be an essential ingredient. After all, what kind of society would we have if lying rather than telling the truth were the default position? When you ask a stranger on the street if he has the time, you don't expect him to lie to you. When you ask the price of a pair of socks, you expect the store clerk to give you a truthful response. In fact, in nearly all of our everyday dealings with fellow human beings, we assume the truth of their statements unless we have good reasons to believe otherwise. As human beings, we naturally seek a state of cooperation, and cooperation can be gained in the long run only by telling the truth. However (and here's the rub), what constitutes "telling the truth" varies definitionally as well as functionally. Suppose you ask if a particular item is expensive. The store clerk answers that it's not. You ask the price. It's a real killer—at least according to *your* paycheck. Was the clerk lying? It depends. Maybe the clerk is used to selling high-priced items and this is one of the least expensive of the items she sells. But you're not used to buying high-priced items, so your definition of "expensive" may be different from the store clerk's. Can we say the same thing about the definition of "truth"?

There is certainly no lack of definitions of truth (and lying, for that matter); however, we must always recognize the limits of those definitions and realize our own limitations in pinning them down. One of the most useful definitions of truth comes from the philosopher Sissela Bok, who suggests that lying is a form of coercion. That is, to lie to someone is to lead them to act in a manner in which they would not have acted had you told them the truth. For example, a politician lies to his constituency concerning his stand on a particular issue. His constituency votes for him based, in part, on that stand. They have been encouraged to act in a way they might not have had they known the truth. Recall C. Edwin Baker's description of coercive speech from Chapter 4. He holds that coercive speech is that which undermines another person's autonomy in decision making.

Telling the "truth" also implies that the teller believes what he is saying as well. This is especially important if the professional communicator is repeating what someone else has said and has no reason to doubt the veracity of that information. In recent years, both public relations and advertising professionals have been called to account for falsehoods they furthered on behalf of their clients. In fact, many agencies now require a contract that includes a "no fault" clause absolving them from blame if they unknowingly pass on false information on behalf of a client. All media professionals, including journalists, must believe in the basic truth of their statements and the accuracy of their information; realizing, at the same time, that there is always the chance they may be proven wrong. The British philosopher Mary Midgley explains how important it is to be committed to what we believe to be true, because commitment doesn't carry any claim of infallibility.

> Commitment of this kind is necessary for effective discourse, because if everybody holds back from endorsing everything they say, no speech is reliable and we lose the advantage of speaking at all. (Someone who kept adding,

"Of course this may not be true", to every sentence would simply be a public nuisance.) Words like "certain" and "know" and indeed "truth" are part of this language of commitment. Perhaps the strongest from of commitment is to say something like, "I am as sure of this as I am of anything".[1]

Without getting into deep philosophical debates over the nature of language, perception versus reality, and truths of reason versus truths of fact, let's take a look at the possible different ways the media might define truth and put it into practice.

Journalistic Truth

Mark Twain once said that his job as a journalist was to "corral" the truth. When a journalist talks about the truth today, she is generally speaking of the elements that contribute to journalistic truth (ways in which it can be corralled). Among these elements are accuracy, context, and balance.

- *Accuracy* has to do with getting the facts straight. Despite deadline pressures, nearly every journalist will tell you that accuracy is of utmost importance to the "truth" of a story. Although the term "fact" itself may often be disputed (especially by philosophers), a journalist will strive to verify the "facts" of a story through sources, background, records, experts, and other methods before deciding on their veracity. Some will argue, of course, that truth (including facts) is relative. For instance, once people believed that the world was flat. For all intents and purposes, it was a fact for quite a long time. Of course, it was later disproved and now we all accept the "fact" that the earth is round (or nearly round). But a journalist upon learning from the coroner that a victim was killed at approximately 2:00 a.m. will almost certainly take that information as fact and pass it on as such. And although other facts are more difficult to ascertain, part of a journalist's job is to do just that, using his power of perception and his training to decipher, as much as possible, fact from fiction.

   A second factor contributing to accuracy is the care with which direct quotes are treated in journalism. No self-respecting journalist would alter a quote. In fact, whereas some journalists feel that cleaning up grammar is acceptable, others hold that a quote is accurate only if repeated exactly the way it was uttered. Of course, even an accurate quote can be deceptive if taken out of context.

- *Context* is vital to the understanding of a story. We all know how damaging taking quotes out of context can be, for instance. When General William Westmoreland (the former U.S. supreme commander in Vietnam) sued CBS News for libel, he based his case almost exclusively on his quotes having been taken out of context by *60 Minutes*. Another way to look at context, however, is to say that to place any element of a story out of context is to leave out information vital to the understanding of that story—and to do that would be tantamount to lying by omission. Journalists strive, or should strive, for understanding. After all, mere facts alone don't constitute understanding. This sticking point is also central to the debate over the supposed objective nature of journalism—a subject we will deal with more fully later.

- *Balance* is integral to the truth of a story because it bears on the concept of fairness, and fairness is viewed by many as essential to ethical action of all sorts. To a journalist, balance simply means presenting as many sides of a story as it takes to achieve a complete picture. So, in a very real sense, balance is related directly both to accuracy and to context. Part and parcel of being objective is to seem not to take sides. It may be for this reason as much as any sense of fairness that most journalists strive for balance. To present an unbalanced account would be to leave yourself open to accusations of partisanship. Either way, it is certain that balance contributes to the truth of a story by strengthening its context.

Truth in Advertising and Public Relations

Many people would say that the area of truth telling is where journalism and advertising and public relations definitely part company; however, from a professional perspective, truth is just as important to advertising and public relations as it is to journalism. The truth of an advertising claim is quickly verified once the product is tested by the consumer. In the same way, the truth of a public relations claim is likewise verified by proof in the form of action. (For example, a political candidate's claims are quickly confirmed once he takes office.) Both advertising and public relations generally rely on a legal definition of truth to determine whether or not they have erred. But, although a legal definition of truth is useful, it does not begin to cover the gray areas produced by vagueness, ambiguity, and puffery.

Puffery is defined by Ivan Preston as "advertising or other sales representations which praise the item to be sold with subjective opinions, superlatives, or exaggerations, vaguely and generally, stating no specific facts."[2] A soft drink commercial showing young people frolicking on the beach doesn't really tell us anything about the soft drink itself. It merely creates an ambience in which the soft drink plays an apparently critical role. Some, including Preston, consider puffery to be unethical by nature; however, anyone who has ever had to come up with an idea for a product that is exactly like every other product of its kind knows that image can be everything.

Carl P. Wrighter in his book *I Can Sell You Anything* defines words that have a vague meaning and seem to say something other than what they really mean as *weasel words*. Such advertising claims as "part of a balanced breakfast," "helps prevent gum disease," and "leaves your dishes virtually spotless," have little meaning when weasel words such as *part of*, *helps*, and *virtually* are fully defined. Both *part of* and *helps* actually indicate that something else plays a part in the success of the product, and *virtually* literally means *almost*.[3] Although use of these words is not, on the face of it, unethical, we should be aware that there is a certain equivocation involved in using them at all, and that ambiguity in both advertising and public relations is usually intentional. Is that tantamount to lying? Possibly not. Unless the claim is absolutely false or the information inaccurate, the truth is not being altered—the message is merely being selectively presented. Selectivity of information and the way in which it is presented is what sets advertising and public relations the farthest apart from journalism. One of the ways to discover the basic differences among the various media is to compare the criteria for truthful communication used in journalism with those in advertising and public relations.

Applying the Accuracy Criterion in Public Relations and Advertising

If we were to compare the journalistic definition of truth with that of advertising and public relations we would discover that on the criterion of *accuracy* they would approximately match. Accuracy is just as important to advertising and public relations as it is to journalism. The accuracy of information disseminated by advertising is central to the success of its endeavor. Inaccurate information could be considered a false product claim, which is illegal. At the very least, it could lead to consumer dissatisfaction. For public relations, inaccurate information could result in, for instance, lack of credibility, the ultimate goal of media relations. For both advertising and public relations, intentional inaccuracy would be considered unethical (and possibly illegal), just as it would in journalism. When it comes to quotes, however, there is a major difference.

Whereas quotes used in journalism must be absolutely accurate, quotes in public relations can be, and often are, literally made up. What does a speech-writer do? She makes up quotes. How, then, do those quotes become an accurate reflection of the person for whom the speech is written? That person gives the speech. At that point, the quotes become his, not his speechwriter's. What about the corporate or political speech that is handed out prior to the actual speech being given, as with the State of the Union address given by the President each year? The same thing applies. The quotes, once passed on to the intended audience, are then validated as having been spoken by the person for whom they were written. The same thing applies to quotes appearing in press releases. These are often made up in order to enhance the credibility of the release or simply to get the name of some executive into the release. Once the person to whom the quote is attributed approves the quote, it is legitimate. The key in both instances is the approval of the quoted person. This form of writing, often referred to as *ghostwriting*, presents a number of ethical pitfalls. Richard Johannesen proposes a series of guidelines that would remove some of the potential for ethical error from this process.[4]

- *What is the communicator's intent and what is the audience's degree of awareness?* In other words, does the communicator pretend to be the author of the words he speaks or over which his signature appears? And how aware is the audience that ghostwriting is commonplace under certain circumstances? If we assume, as most do, that presidential speeches are ghostwritten, then the only unethical act would be for the President to claim to author his own speeches.

- *Does the communicator use ghostwriters to make himself or herself appear to possess personal qualities that he or she really does not have?* In other words, does the writer impart such qualities as eloquence, wit, coherence, and incisive ideas to a communicator who might not possess these qualities otherwise? The degree to which the writing distorts a communicator's character has a great deal to do with ethicality.

- *What are the surrounding circumstances of the communicator's job that make ghostwriting a necessity?* The pressures of a job often dictate that a ghostwriter be used. Busy executives, like busy politicians, may not have the time to write all the messages they must deliver on a daily basis. However, we don't expect the average office manager or university professor to hire a ghostwriter. Part of the answer to this question lies in the pressures of the job itself, and the other part has to do with the need and frequency of communication.

- *To what extent do the communicators actively participate in the writing of their own messages?* Obviously, the more input a communicator has in his or her own writing, the more ethical will be the resultant image. We really don't expect the President to write his own speeches, but we do expect that the sentiments expressed in them will be his own.

- *Does the communicator accept responsibility for the message he or she presents?* When former president Ronald Reagan's press secretary, Larry Speakes, disclosed in his book that many of the quotes attributed to the president were, in fact, either made up or "borrowed" from someone else, he caused quite an ethical uproar. Part of the problem with the Larry Speakes revelation was that the President denied the accusations. In other words, he claimed he never approved Speakes' work. Most communicators simply assume that whatever they say or whatever they sign their names to is theirs, whether written by someone else or not. This is obviously the most ethical position to take.

Applying the Context Criterion in Public Relations and Advertising

Context is a more ambiguous concept for advertising and public relations. Whereas a news story needs to appear within the broader context of its setting in order to enhance understanding, the contextual setting of information for both advertising and public relations can be much narrower. For example, a television ad need only be placed within the context of its own reality, and that reality is often created just for that product (in literature, this is called *verisimilitude*). The make-believe world of the ideal nuclear family is the context from which we are most often sold laundry detergent, bath soap, kid's juice drinks, floor waxes, and dozens of other similar products. Does this created context enhance understanding of the typical uses of the product? Of course it does. Is the context true? Possibly not; however, if it actually shows the most typical use of the product, even in a make-believe setting, it does not alter the veracity of the product claim.

For public relations, context may be even more important. The context within which a claim is made or an argument offered decidedly influences the reactions of the receiving audience. Claims not placed within context generally cry out for support. Intelligent listeners typically reject such vacuous statements. For example, a political candidate claiming that violent crime is a problem so great in scope that only severe measures will work to prevent its uncontrolled spread would do well to place that claim within the context of national crime statistics or risk loss of credibility. By the same token, context is sometimes narrowed in order to give an argument more strength. For instance, an impassioned plea for gun control by a state legislator following a school shooting may be placed within the local context for greater effect. It may even be placed within the larger national context, given the "epidemic" of school shootings in this country, and still succeed. However, if placed within the totality of violent crime, which is on the decrease, or if compared with the relative safety of nearly all of our schools (hundreds of thousands in number), the argument may lose some of its edge. So, selective context for public relations, as for advertising, is purposeful and generally done to enhance the marketability of a product, service, or idea.

Applying the Balance Criterion in Public Relations and Advertising

On the criterion of *balance*, advertising and public relations diverge widely from journalism. The objective nature of journalism demands balance. The highly subjective nature of advertising and public relations results in no such requirement. In fact, the act of persuasion requires that a side be taken. And although a persuasive claim may very well present both sides of an argument, it will certainly support only one. We must also remember that persuasion is not unethical by nature. As mentioned earlier in this chapter, persuasion within a democratic environment is entirely necessary for that endeavor to succeed. As long as the message isn't intentionally deceptive, important facts are not misrepresented or left out, and blatant lies are not told, advertising and public relations communication can be said to be truthful.

Finally, it should be noted that it would be a mistake for us to hold all media to the same standards as news writing. We must remember that journalistic writing, in its present form, is an invention of the past 80 years or so and uses standards of objectivity not suited to persuasive writing. In fact, the ideal of objectivity is being argued by many as an unsatisfactory one even for journalism. Regardless, we must be cautious not to assume unethicality simply because of a difference in style or intent.

Can We Tell Truth From Fiction?

As far as advertising and public relations are concerned, the question of whether we can tell truth from fiction is crucial. We expect journalistic descriptions and reports to be "real"—that is, factual and accurate representations of reality. Thus, we are shocked to learn that a news story has been fabricated, as in the infamous Janet Cooke–*Washington Post* scandal of over 20 years ago. We are outraged when we learn, for instance, that NBC News would rig a truck to blow up to prove a crash-test point. We *expect* the news to be real. But what about docu-dramas, "reality" cop shows, entertainment "news"? These somewhat gray areas, as well as a great deal of advertising and public relations, require a closer inspection of what constitutes truth. Such a discussion also requires that we take sides in the age-old debate over whether people are intelligent enough to make such distinctions or are, as Plato suggested, simply an uneducated mob.

The Qualified Expectation of Reality Test

Ethics scholars Tom Wheeler and Tim Gleason have developed a test for ethicality in photo manipulation that is based on the idea of an audience's expectation of reality. They claim that one way to test this ethicality is to ask the viewer/reader if the photograph is plausible. "Or, is the fictional content immediately obvious?"[5] This recognition factor allows for a fairly liberal interpretation of what is misleading. It relies on two tests: (1) whether or not the image is implausible and, thus, readily obvious, and (2) if not, if it is appropriately labeled.

This *qualified expectation of reality* test (QER), then, is the determinant of ethicality—at least for manipulated photographs. Following on this guideline, we might expect that a photo on the cover *of Mad Magazine* would more likely be manipulated than one on the cover of *Time* magazine. That is why, for instance, the now-famous O. J. Simpson photo that appeared greatly altered on the cover of *Time* several years ago drew so much negative attention. The cover was labeled a "photo–illustration" on the masthead and showed a heavily touched-up police mug shot of Simpson with a decidedly darkened countenance. Racial overtones aside, most people felt that the cover of a "news" magazine was not the place to fool around with reality. The determinant is whether an average reader or viewer would expect the image to be real or not. If he does expect reality, then any manipulation must be admitted in order not to, either intentionally or unintentionally, fool him.

The QER test also can be useful for determining the "truth" of advertising and public relations claims—as regards image and context—as well as information programming that blurs the lines between fact and fiction. How plausible is the image of a skier screaming down the side of a skyscraper, or of huge draft horses playing football, or of frogs talking with lizards about beer? Do we really believe that the product they are selling is reflected in the image they are using, or are we merely amused? Do we really prefer Pepsi over Coke because of all those clever commercials? Clearly, the examples cited here fall into the implausible category; however, there are many that are not so easily recognized as fiction. Magazine ads that depict young women as unnaturally tall and thin may appear to be real when, in fact, they are subtly manipulated to enhance already gaunt features. What about the celebrity spokesperson who endorses a product he doesn't use? Do we believe him or not? What about the seemingly real testimonial from a person who turns out to be an actor? Do we believe that the "vintage" film footage of Dean Whitter urging his employees to care about their customers is what it purports to be? Or do the advertisers think we'll instantly recognize it as an artistic prop meant simply to catch our attention? Is that Jeep really on top of that mountain peak? Is that hamburger really that big? What are our expectations?

So, although selective presentation, as mentioned earlier, may not be inherently unethical, much depends on the receiver's qualified expectation of reality. The clichéd advertising response of *caveat emptor* (buyer beware) covers only so much transgression. If we follow the model suggested by Wheeler and Gleason, our obligation is to remove all doubt concerning the reality of the context of our message. And although the law has already insisted on some indicators (labeling dramatizations, for instance), our goal should be to eliminate any potential for misunderstanding. If our goal is to intentionally blur the lines between fact and fiction, we are acting unethically.

Consumers: Victims or Informed Choosers?

You'll remember from our earlier discussion of Plato and Walter Lippmann that not everyone has viewed the "people" as intelligent enough to look out for themselves. This is an important point to come to grips with since much of the justification for the type of communication that both advertising and public relations engage in is predicated on the notion that listeners are intelligent enough to discern true from false. According to this concept, the views of the likes of Milton and Locke are correct in that truth will prevail in an open marketplace, in part, because autonomous and rational individuals will be able to discern the difference between truth and falsity. This belief in the rational abilities of the people who receive media messages is directly responsible for such precepts as *caveat emptor*. "Buyer beware" assumes that an intelligent consumer will be able to discern nuances in messages—nuances that the designer of the message may have intentionally obscured. And this turns up the other side of the coin: Why do those advertising and public relations practitioners who say they believe in the intelligence of the average consumer try so hard to cloud their messages? Could it be that, like Plato and Rousseau, they really believe that the masses are easily deceived by the "shadows on the cave wall"?

Think of the huge numbers of infomercials airing on television these days. A great many of them are "performed" before a live audience as if the "guest" were appearing on a talk show. Does the average consumer know that these audiences are paid to be there? Can viewers tell that the "programs" are really commercials posing as talk shows? Why do you suppose the FCC requires these lengthy commercials to carry the disclaimer that they are paid advertising? Why do phrases such as "dramatization" have to appear on commercials in which actors pose as "real" people? Because some believe that average consumers just might be duped by such tactics as fake talk shows and dramatic recreations. This also accounts for the labeling of news images not actually taken during the unfolding of the story being discussed but at some time earlier as "library footage," or "file footage."

As the line between entertainment and information becomes increasingly blurred, catch phrases such as *caveat emptor* may no longer provide sufficient warning. Additionally, such techniques as the QER test have to be based on a pragmatic assessment of the abilities of the consumer to discern what is real from what is not, especially in instances in which they are expecting "reality." Whether you agree with Plato or with Milton, placing the onus of recognition of reality solely on the receiver of your message is failing to live up to your own moral obligations. Intent is still the ultimate measure of truth telling. If, as a media practitioner, you *intend* to deceive, then you are acting unethically; however, if someone is misled by a message you never expected would be misleading, then your actions may be excused. Likewise, we don't tend to criticize advertising that is clearly fictional. (We don't really believe that frogs and lizards talk—do we?) But if we are led to believe that someone stands for something she does not, or that a product performs in a way it ultimately does not, or that something fake is something real, then we have been deceived—and deception is unethical.

The Ultimate Truth

It must be remembered that advertising and public relations are not, by nature, unethical. Neither is the act of persuasion. The ultimate determinant of the ethicality of a persuasive technique is the degree to which the practitioner intends to deceive in order to manipulate an audience. Manipulation is the same as coercion—the result of telling an outright lie. In both cases the communicator is intentionally altering reality in order to force another person into believing or acting in a way she would not have but for the deception or the lie.

To fail to respect the autonomy of another person goes against most of the principles on which American democracy is founded. It violates the Kantian imperative to treat all human beings with respect; it ignores Mill's caution against bullying the minority; it runs counter to the Liberty Theory of free speech; and it violates the natural rights of individuals that Locke was so set on protecting. Even the Greek philosophers, who recognized that rhetoric implied persuasion, held that to lie or to mislead by false logic was inherently wrong. Both Plato and Aristotle had little use for sophists, the group of professional philosophers who specialized in dialectic, argumentation, and rhetoric and who were often known for their elaborate and specious arguments. In fact, the word *sophistry* has come to mean "a plausible but misleading or fallacious argument." In the final analysis, it is best to remember that persuasion is ethical, manipulation is not.

The same is ultimately true for journalism. While journalists continually hold up the truth as an icon, they also stoop to consistently newer lows each time they use deception to gather news without first considering alternative methods. At first blush, it may seem that using deceptive techniques in advertising and public relations is so obviously self-serving as to be undeniably unethical. At the same time, deception used in the name of the public's "right to know" appears to carry a sense of higher purpose. However, if we realize that the news "business" actually is a business, then it is less clear whether deception is being used on behalf of the public or merely to stimulate consumption of the news product.

The growth spurt in television news magazine shows is proof enough that investigative reporting draws viewership. When all the major networks are competing head-to-head on weeknights with amazingly similar products, the push to go for the spectacular is great indeed. And with this rise in competition comes a parallel rise in the temptation to use deceptive techniques to gather the story. Nothing condemns quite like a hidden camera or an ambush interview. As in any war, in this battle to achieve the highest ratings, truth is usually the first casualty.

How can we avoid this trap? For all of the media, truth has to become the paramount concern. Deception must not be used in advertising and public relations at all. And in investigative reporting, deceptive news-gathering techniques must be limited to instances in which a vitally important story cannot be gathered in any other way. In the final analysis, the media cannot afford to lie—in any way, for any reason. If we cannot be assured that the default position is always the truth, then the media will continue to slide in esteem, along with their ability to affect lives in positive ways.

We have seen so far in this chapter that the road to truth is filled with obstacles. Most of these can be avoided easily; some take more effort. Ultimately, the result is worth the effort, for the media are known by the truth they tell—whether it is about a product, a political candidate, or a school shooting. We rely on the media for practically everything we know about the world that we haven't experienced first hand. It is vitally important that the truth be the rule and not the exception.

Avoiding Harm

We have all heard the phrase, "the truth hurts." This simple adage illuminates one of the most controversial areas of media ethics: the avoidance of harm. The media, in fulfilling their role as disseminators of information, often face the invariable conflict between providing news or respecting rights. As mentioned in Chapter 1, values and ideals come into conflict all the time. A citizen's right to privacy can be, and often is, ignored by the news media. Every tragedy has its victims and tragedy is news. Unfortunately, so are the victims. The recent rash of high school shootings has illustrated the extremes that some reporters will go to get a story. In the aftermath of the shootings at Thurston high school in

Springfield, Oregon, in 1998, reporters obtained the home addresses of the victims and pursued their stories right into the families' homes in some cases. One reporter for a national news outlet even posed as a doctor in order to get nearer the hospitalized shooting victims.

When *USA Today* ran a story making public the fact that the tennis great Arthur Ashe had AIDS, a great deal of harm was done to both Ashe and his family, who wanted the information kept private. *USA Today*, and a number of journalistic defenders, pointed out that Ashe was a public figure and a role model for a great many people, and that this was, thus, a newsworthy story. Others, journalists and non-journalists alike, countered that the story was merely voyeurism, and that there are times when respect for others should outweigh public curiosity.

To what extent does the obligation of the news media to gather and disseminate the news outweigh their personal obligation to respect the rights of others? Can personal standards override professional standards?

As far back as Hippocrates we have been advised to avoid harming other human beings. However, to what extent, if any, is harm an allowable by-product of communication? As individuals, we probably consider harm to others high on our list of proscriptions; however, a great deal hangs on our definition of harm. Do we harm a friend by not telling her the truth about her partner's infidelity? Do we harm ourselves by overeating or drinking too much? Do we harm our children by allowing them to watch television? Do we harm our employers by taking sick leave when we're not really sick? These, and a thousand other questions concerning potential harms, are not as easily answered as we might suppose. And when the harm is potentially great or affects the lives or attitudes of large numbers of people, the answers are even more difficult to obtain.

Communication-caused harm has the potential to affect both individuals and multitudes. The harm caused by the publication of Arthur Ashe's condition was restricted to Ashe, his family, and his friends. Yet all of us are harmed, in a way, when a single person's privacy is violated on our behalf. Remember: The rationale for the news media exposing another's private life is generally the "public's right to know." When Princess Diana died in an automobile accident in France in 1997, the blame quickly fell on the media "vultures" who were constantly following her around. However, little was said about her courtship of that same media when she sought the spotlight for her own personal messages. And little was mentioned about the seemingly voracious appetite of a celebrity-hungry public that keeps both the tabloids and the "legitimate" media in business.

Can the media operate under a proscription of "do no harm"? Probably not. Stephen Carter points out that Milton "argued that truth would win out, he did not contend that nobody would get hurt in the process."[6] Advertisers regularly harm their competition every time a successful ad results in increased sales for the product being advertised. Public relations practitioners certainly harm competing political candidates' chances each time their own candidate moves higher in the polls because of their aggressive campaigning. It may very well be that, as some scholars propose, the persuasive act naturally causes harm to someone every time it is practiced. And yet we accept these "harms" as a necessary by-product of a democratically sanctioned competition. The nature of both democracy and capitalism is competitive, and competition almost always implies a winner and a loser—with some degree of harm visited on the loser. The question then becomes: How much of that harm is avoidable rather than necessary?

"If . . . harm is done in the service of a greater good, . . . then it is an acceptable side effect." Thus say the ethicists Stephen Klaidman and Tom Beauchamp in their book *The Virtuous Journalist*.[7] However, they warn that, unlike medicine, in which the patient is consulted before any harm is committed (such as a leg amputation to save a life), in journalism the subject of a story is rarely, if ever, consulted. In addition, "the risk of harm to a person or institution being reported on is rarely disclosed, not always evident, and virtually never refusable." And the potential beneficiary is not the subject of the story who will suffer the harm; it is generally the public.[8]

Klaidman and Beauchamp rely on a definition of harm borrowed from the ethicist Joel Feinberg. "Harm involves thwarting, defeating or setting back an interest including: property, privacy, confidentiality, friendship, reputation, health and career."[9] The strength of this definition lies in its breadth. According to this approach, a person may be harmed in a number of ways, not just physically or psychologically—the most commonly assumed types of harm. Under this construction, USA Today could be held accountable for its unwarranted disclosure in the Arthur Ashe case because it did not honor his privacy. However, if journalists were to avoid any story in which some form of harm might be visited on the subject, very little news would be forthcoming to the public whom they serve. It is very clear that some type of harm follows from much of what journalists produce as news, and that, in many cases, that harm is either a necessary by-product or literally unavoidable.

Causal Harm

For the journalist, then, harm may very well be a necessary concomitant of gathering and disseminating the news. However, are journalists absolved of any blame for causing harm? Before answering that question, we need to differentiate between causal and moral responsibility. In Chapter 1, we discussed the difference between responsibility and accountability. Recall that not every act can be blamed on the person directly responsible for the act. A bank teller robbed at gunpoint is not accountable for the money he hands over. In the same sense, a manufacturer of toasters is not accountable if someone uses the appliance cord to hang himself. In the first case, the teller is being forced to hand over the money. In the second, the manufacturer could not have reasonably anticipated the misuse of that particular product. In the same way, journalists, and advertising and public relations practitioners cannot be held accountable for every potential harm they may cause through their communications.

Part of the reason for this is the difference between causal and moral responsibility. *Moral responsibility* refers to being held accountable for an action. So, if an advertiser develops an ad campaign for a liquor manufacturer that deliberately targets a minority population known for its misuse of alcohol, she is complicit in any harm that might be caused by that campaign. She cannot simply declare *caveat emptor* (buyer beware). Conversely, if a journalist reports on a story about a public official arrested for drunken driving, he is not causing the harm—the official brought it on herself. This is called *causal harm*. All media practitioners must ask themselves this vital question: Does the action being taken actually cause the harm or does it merely augment an already present harm?

That question was probably asked over and over again during the year-long media frenzy over the Clinton–Lewinsky affair in 1998–1999. Did the President of the United States deserve to have his private life dragged before the public, over and over again? Part of the answer to that question can be answered by asking another: Did he in any way bring this upon himself? The answer to that question is decidedly, yes. The harm had already been done. The president had violated a private and public trust by abusing his position, and the story was already known in some circles. Did that give the press free rein to report anything they wanted? Possibly not.

The usual test in cases such as this is whether the private information being reported affects the public figure's public performance. Every journalist has to ask this simplest of questions in advance of releasing any privately held information. However, if the answer is no, does that automatically mean that the information will remain private? It probably should, but it often does not. And when the media decided to go against this most basic of guidelines, did they end up contributing to the very problem they were reporting on? Yes, especially because the release of that information, in and of itself, probably affected the President's public performance—in this case especially (at least according to opinion polls taken at the time). So, in some cases, such as this one, the harm that results from covering a story can both add to existing harm (causally related to the subject's actions) and create additional harm due to, among other things, extended coverage. In the latter instance, some blame must fall on the press.

On the other hand, the concept of causal harm coincides nicely with that of distributive justice. You'll recall that distributive justice rests on giving to those who deserve and withholding from those who do not. In this light, exposing the ineptitude or moral failings of public officials could be seen as a form of justice. Despite the fact that most media practitioners don't see themselves as judges, the result of exposing corruption through media coverage can be ethically justified through both causal harm and distributive justice concepts.

Professional Responsibility

According to Klaidman and Beauchamp, "To be morally blameworthy, . . . a harm must be caused by carelessness resulting from failure to discharge a socially, legally, or morally imposed duty to take care or to behave reasonably toward others."[10] As noted earlier, professionals incur a number of obligations by virtue of having taken on professional roles. As professionals, media practitioners must conform to the minimal expectations of the profession of which they are a part. Failure to do so could result in accusations of professional negligence, or malpractice. Malpractice is most often associated with the legal and medical professions; however, every professional is expected to operate within certain ethical parameters. For journalists as well as advertising and public relations practitioners, these parameters should include avoiding unnecessary harm.

Professional negligence can be charged in instances in which the professional has not exercised "due care" in carrying out her responsibilities. Negligence or "careless" action can be analyzed in terms of the following essential elements:

1 an established duty to the affected party must exist;
2 someone must breach that duty;
3 the affected party must experience a harm; and
4 this harm must be caused by the breach of duty.[11]

As we have seen, duty (or obligation) is a natural consequent of social relationships. And, as Kant stated, discharge of duty is of paramount importance if we are to maintain moral standing. Breach of duty almost always indicates a lack of integrity, and results, at the very least, in lack of trust between the harmed party and the instigator of the harm. When this occurs in a professional–client relationship, the client is far less likely to respect the professional's autonomy and more likely to question his motives. And, if the professional continues to violate this trust, the client is very likely to call for restrictions on professional autonomy. Censorship is one such threat that is nearly always the result of perceived over-zealousness on the part of the media.

Mitigating Harm in Journalism

"Act so that you treat humanity, whether in your own person or in the person of any other, always as an end and never as a means only." With this prescription, Immanuel Kant set the stage for the championing of individual autonomy and integrity. He specifically meant that we should avoid, as much as possible, harming other human beings. However, even Kant realized that total avoidance of harm is probably impossible. The question then becomes: If we cannot avoid harm altogether, can we at least mitigate its effects?

Writing in the now defunct media criticism magazine *Brill's Content*, newspaper editor Mike Pride of the *Concord Monitor* in Concord, New Hampshire, cited an instance in which he was getting ready to publish a story concerning the suicide of a local teenager. The victim's family appealed to him personally not to publish the story because of the emotional harm and public embarrassment it would cause them. At their request, and completely against journalistic character, he let them read the story prior to publication. They asked for a single change in copy: omitting an opening paragraph detailing the method of death. Pride realized how little the story would be affected by the deletion of this information and how much pain could be avoided by censoring his own story. The story ran, but without the detailed first paragraph.[12] Was harm avoided altogether? No. Was it mitigated or lessened without a loss of journalistic integrity? Yes.

In the inevitable clash between personal and professional ethics, the weight is usually on the professional side. The reason is that a person takes on the role of a professional willingly, with eyes supposedly open to the potential conflicts inherent in the work itself. For example, a person enlisting in the Army who is not aware that part of the commitment of military service is a possible battlefield assignment is basically self-delusional. By the same token, any journalist who does not acknowledge the likelihood that personal standards concerning privacy, for instance, will come into conflict with the professional obligation of newsgathering is likewise fooling herself. It is wise to remember that, for journalists, the duty to serve the public usually overrides any duty to observe the individual rights of the subjects of their stories. This does not mean that all compassion and civility should be thrown out the window, however.

The editor/publisher and media critic Steven Brill worries that journalists are so insulated from the rest of society that their decisions are made from within a "cocooned" environment resulting in a "warped sense of their own conduct that renders them unaware of the consequences . . . of what they do."[13] In a 1999 survey profiled in *Brill's Content*, the Editor, Eric Effron, observed that the media's reluctance even to consider self-regulation in problem areas such as invasion of privacy renders them at great odds with the public they purport to serve—a public that has indicated an "overwhelming support for some simple common courtesies on the part of the media."[14] The power of the press, likewise, results in what Stephen Carter calls "a special First Amendment arrogance."

> The First Amendment, in its current guise as an excuse for everything, makes decisions on what to publish or broadcast virtually risk-free, and thus, almost inevitably, corrupting as well.[15]

Carter also warns against the kind of "emotional pornography" that many in journalism indulge in every time they conduct an ambush interview or confront a grieving family member. He points out that the media understand completely that this is "where the money is," and calls for "genuine moral reflection before making a difficult decision."[16]

Others believe that the only answer to media abuses is written guidelines. In addressing the privacy debate, Steven Brill strongly suggests such guidelines.

> The real point is having *some* guidelines, something that gives the public a benchmark from which to hold media organizations accountable—not

legally, but in a way that compels them to put their decisions to the test of explaining them when asked.[17]

In fact, guidelines do exist at most news organizations and in several professional codes. As noted earlier, however, codes are often vague when it comes to dealing with day-to-day ethical issues and tend to speak only to the generalities of professional conduct. As Brill suggests, the best use of such policies might be to give the public recourse to an ethical benchmark from which to ask informed questions concerning media activities they consider questionable. As he points out, however, the existence of such guidelines has never prevented the media from violating them.

A central question in any process of decision making about whether to withhold publication will continue to be: How much does the public need the information, and how successfully does that need compete with the principle that we should avoid the harm that would result from its publication?[18] For journalists, this simple test must be performed whenever release of information has the potential to cause someone harm. By the same token, it would be impossible for editors to perform this balancing act for every story being considered. However, it is not too much to expect that the most obvious cases should require such a weighing of interests. Too much is rationalized on the basis of "the public's right to know." As we have seen, that rubric, like *caveat emptor*, is a poor excuse at best. Again, Steven Brill writes that

> the privacy of those who are entitled to it is best protected by editors who understand the fine line between individual rights and the public's right to know, between fairness and decency on one hand and the commercial impulse on the other.[19]

Mitigating Harm in Advertising and Public Relations

For those in advertising and public relations, the task of mitigating harm is even more demanding. In Chapter 3, we discussed the concept of public service as it relates to professional obligation. You'll recall that the fiduciary model best epitomizes the proper balance of client/professional control over decision making. When the professional is allowed to exercise his decision-making authority (based on education, training, and experience) within a framework of professional standards, he cannot easily ignore third-party obligations. However, the fiduciary model assumes a good deal of professional autonomy. By contrast, the advocacy model allows minimal autonomy to the professional who works almost exclusively at the behest of the client. Advocates are at a distinct disadvantage because of the necessary subordination of their standards to their client's wishes. Given that advertising and public relations, alike, work from within both fiduciary and advocacy models, how can harm to third parties be avoided or, at least, mitigated?

A Suggested Process

What we need is a framework that allows the function of advocacy to remain a professional role obligated to client interests, professional interests, and personal ethics. Although the role of autonomous professional assumes objectivity, the role of advocate assumes a certain amount (if not a great amount) of subjectivity. The terms, although often mutually exclusive, are not necessarily at odds; and the professional advertising or public relations practitioner may, in fact, be both objective and subjective. The key is the order in which objectivity and subjectivity are applied. Certainly, consulting professionals objectively evaluate potential clients before taking them on. This earliest stage of the consulting process is also the first line of defense against possible ethical conflicts. Objectivity should also be brought to bear in the early stages of campaign development—the period in which a thorough understanding of the issue is obtained. It is during this stage that the professional will examine the ramifications of the proposed actions and its effect on *all* parties, especially the ethical concerns.

During this *objective stage*, the communications professional may apply any of several applicable ethical theories to the proposed act in order to determine if the act itself (means) and the outcome (ends) are morally responsible. Several standards may be applied, including:

- a determination of the legality of the act (whether it violates existing laws or applicable regulations);
- company procedures and policies or organizational codes;
- and any codes or standards existing for the profession (relevant advertising and/or public relations codes).

Although this procedure will merely provide guidelines, assuming that all that is legally or professionally permissible may not be ethically permissible, these will allow the professional to advance to succeeding evaluative stages.

The communications professional may also apply standard cost–benefit analysis to the issue, determining the potential financial consequences of the act to the client and the affected third parties. Beyond these monetary considerations, he may attempt to determine societal effects. If, after such applications, the professional determines that the act itself and the intent of the act are morally acceptable, then he may proceed to the succeeding subjective stages of advocacy.

Even after the professional has decided to move on to the role of advocate, that role does not absolve the advertising or public relations practitioner from moral culpability. As we know, the moral guidelines under which the advocate operates presuppose loyalty to one's client or employer; however, the obligation of non-injury is still in effect based on non-consequential moral duties. The same rules used prior to the decision to become an advocate may be used at this stage to determine individual actions.

According to non-consequential ethical theory, the obligations assumed as part of a role are of prime importance in making moral decisions. If there are rules governing decision making within an organization, for instance, and those rules say that one should not dispense false information, then an advocate who has been ordered to falsify information can and should refuse to do so based on existing rules. No consideration need be given to the consequences of the act itself. It is sufficient that the rule exists prohibiting it. For the advocate, non-consequential considerations might include whether an act is illegal or not. Certainly, refusing to perform an illegal act is within the moral scope of even the most loyal advocate.

The existence of a set of guidelines in the form of a code of conduct or ethics is imperative at this stage as well. For the practitioner lacking a formal code within the organization for which she works, an outside, professional code might be cited as legitimization for refusal to carry out an immoral act. An advocate lacking recourse to a professional code might appeal to consequential ethical theory. Lacking any clear-cut guidelines in the form of rules, she may precipitate a complex analysis of both short- and long-term consequences.

In summary, the advocate generally assumes a primary responsibility to the client and to the client's purpose because of the nature of the role of advocacy. However, as precursor to that role, the professional retains his objectivity throughout the exploratory stage in which the issue is defined and the claimants are identified. It is in this early stage that communications professionals must become aware of the affects of their potential actions on all third parties. Both at this stage and in the latter stages of advocacy itself, advertising and public relations professionals must continue their vigilance by constant referral to written codes within their own companies and the professions they are a part of. Lacking any clear written guidelines, the advocate may undertake to stand behind the moral shield of protecting the greater good. Ultimately, the major determinant may be the personal morals of the advocate and his willingness to stand up for or forgo them under certain conditions. The approach proposed here suggests that the advocate, like his journalistic counterpart, resort to the traditional use of objectivity in order to determine, without bias, who the moral claimants are in any given situation.

But, whereas objectivity is still very much the legitimate step-child of Enlightenment reason, some have proposed that there might be an alternative view of those affected "others" that rests not on objectivity, but on subjectivity.

What Does It All Mean?

No mass medium is free from the obligations of truth telling and non-injury, and no mass medium should be purposely devoid of care and respect for those it affects with its words and pictures. Telling the truth and avoiding harm are often one and the same thing; however, the delicate balance involved in telling the truth while avoiding harm requires, at times, the equilibrium of a high-wire walker.

Can we expect that no one will ever be harmed by a media act? Probably not. But we should expect that the media will do no unnecessary harm and that, as far as possible, they will respect the dignity and integrity of everyone whose lives they touch. It really isn't impossible to believe that those who choose to become media professionals do so because they care. They care about letting us know what is going on in our lives and how to deal with it. They care that we think about and how we understand the world we live in. And they care about whether we're using a bath soap that makes us "feel" clean and fresh (not a bad thing, really).

However, the perceived value of autonomy, as Steven Brill has pointed out, tends to hobble the media through fear of interference in their discharge of a constitutionally guaranteed right of expression—even if that "interference" is self-imposed. As professionals, media practitioners expect to be free to choose their own ends, without having them dictated or altered by others. As we have seen, however, we are not necessarily locked into a moral system devoid of care for others. As the philosopher Michael Sandel has argued,

> By insisting that we are bound only by ends and roles we choose for our-selves, [modern Western liberalism] denies that we can ever be claimed by ends we have not chosen—ends given by nature or God, for example, or by our identities as members of families, peoples, cultures, or traditions.[20]

If we accept, even tacitly, the tenants of communitarianism, we must allow obligation to others a higher priority than either a strict adherence to personal autonomy or blind allegiance to professional duty. Even the consideration of this point of view during the deliberative process is a step in the right direction.

The point is, if the mass media really care about doing their jobs well, shouldn't they automatically worry about telling the truth and avoiding harm? As media legend Fred Friendly once said to a panel of journalists and public relations practitioners, "Stop thinking about what you have the right to do, and start thinking about what is the right thing to do." The two shouldn't be mutually exclusive, and, with some concentrated effort on the part of media practitioners, they won't be.

Chapter 7

Meta-issues in Public Relations and Advertising

All of us contain Music & Truth, but most of us can't get it out.

(Mark Twain)

In this chapter, we will look at the ethical issues that public relations and advertising have in common. First, we will look at how the Supreme Court views the differences between the two and the way they use their free speech rights. Then, we'll take a close look at the act of persuasion. It is this communication act that binds public relations and advertising most closely and is also the most ethically problematic. The most frequent complaint against any form of communication is that it is trying to persuade unethically, usually through some form of deception. Both public relations and advertising frequently suffer from this charge. But first, we need to see how public relations and advertising differ before we discuss the ethical issues they have in common.

What's the Difference between PR and Advertising?

Although many people don't understand the difference between public relations and advertising, those within the business see a pretty clear distinction. Here are a few of the primary differences.[1]

Paid for or Publicity

- Public relations doesn't usually have to pay for placing messages in the media. Although a good deal of money is spent in PR on such things as "corporate advertising" (basically promoting the image of the company, not its products), the bulk of its messages are publicity. Publicity is basically free coverage provided usually by the media and instigated by such message vehicles as press conferences, press releases, and product publicity (trade magazine articles, etc.). Of course, this turns over control of the message to the media in which it will appear. They may edit it as they wish, run it where and when they wish, or not run it at all. This is called "uncontrolled information," and is both the blessing and the bane of public relations.

What this also means is that public relations practitioners must be acutely aware of how news is produced and what its requirements are.

- Advertising almost always pays for placing its messages. The advantage is that the advertiser has complete control over what the message will say and how, where, and when a message will be placed—because they're paying for that privilege. That's the upside. The downside is that advertising costs of lot of money.

A Different Primary Audience

- Although public relations messages are ultimately targeted to a specific public, they must generally go through the media to reach that audience. Thus, the primary audience for most PR messages is generally the media itself. That's why these messages are crafted in the style of the medium for which they are intended. A press release written for a local paper will mimic hard news style (inverted pyramid). A release for an entertainment industry magazine will be more feature-oriented.
- Advertising is aimed directly at the potential adopter of the product, service, or idea. Although the advertising message is crafted to fit the medium, it is actually designed to appeal directly to the audience that uses that medium. For example, major network news programs attract older viewers, so we tend to see commercials for health aids, insurance, travel, and other interests specific to that target audience.

Repetition

- Most public relations messages have a short life span. Press releases are about something that is happening right now. After that, they become old news. And because their effectiveness depends so often on the news media, old news is basically no news. In addition, there is generally no repetition factor as in advertising. A press release will only be run once in the local paper. That's why PR people try to expand coverage by placing information in as many media as possible. This is called using a "media mix." People who don't read newspapers may get the message from television, or from the radio, or on the internet.
- Advertising is based on repetition. Think of how many times you watch the same ad on TV, or in a magazine. The theory is that the more you see it, the more the message is reinforced. Of course, the advertiser pays for all those repetitions.

Transparency

- Public relations messages are not always as transparent as they could or should be. You never know, for instance, whether that news story about a local company was produced entirely free of influence by the company or not. It could have been stimulated by a press release, furthered by an interview with the company president set up by the PR person for that company, and fleshed out through a carefully prepared backgrounder on the company produced in-house by the PR staff.

- For the most part, advertising messages are recognized by consumers for being what they are—sales pitches. That allows the consumer to take these messages with a grain of salt, setting up the necessary defenses talked about in the last chapter. This doesn't always sit well with advertisers, who are already complaining that television viewers can now "zap" their commercials out with digital recording devices. The result is an increased reliance on not-so-transparent methods, which we'll discuss later.

Public Relations, Advertising, and the First Amendment

In order to understand how the First Amendment affects the practices of public relations and advertising we first need to understand the differences between protected and non-protected speech and how they apply.

Commercial Speech

A number of federal agencies have at least some control over advertising. The Federal Trade Commission (FTC) deals mostly with untruthful or deceptive advertising, and the Food and Drug Administration (FDA) watches over the advertising of drugs and medical devices. Although the "truth" of advertising is covered more or less adequately by these two bodies (and others at the state and local levels), the nature of commercial speech itself is a vitally important concept. The burning question, for quite a long time, has been whether the type of "speech" engaged in my public relations and advertising should garner the same protection as other speech protected by the First Amendment.

The gradual evolution of speech as a commodity has been lent legitimacy by several Supreme Court decisions, most notably *Virginia Pharmacy Board* v. *Virginia Consumer Council*, in which Justice Harry Blackmun concurred with the majority when he noted that consumers' decisions needed to be "intelligent and well informed," and that the "free flow of commercial information is indispensable" to that process within a free enterprise economy. In so stating, he likened commercial speech (specifically advertising) to other information competing for attention within the marketplace of ideas, and suggested that some consumers might even prefer commercial information over political information—a point made as well by Walter Lippmann (although more critically). Lippmann had noted in *Public Opinion* that the public appetite for the trivial spelled the death knell for any idealized democratic involvement in the political process. In his view, citizens were more concerned with their individual needs than with the state of the nation. Nonetheless, Blackmun's comment was but one of many along the twisting road toward a doctrine of commercial speech.

Commercial speech was originally an exception to the First Amendment stemming from a Supreme Court decision in 1942 in which the phrase "commercial speech doctrine" was coined. In brief, the doctrine exempted such speech from any First Amendment protection. In the case, the distribution of handbills on the streets of New York City had been banned. The dividing line seems to have been that such information posted or handed out for the purpose of commercial and business advertising didn't deserve the same protection as information "devoted to 'information or a public protest.'"[2]

This exemption of all commercial speech from the First Amendment's protections remained pretty much intact for a number of years, until the 1970s. During that decade, the Supreme Court made several rulings narrowing the definition of commercial speech and granting it greater protection. In an effort to broaden that protection, the Court, in 1980, set out a four-part test for determining whether commercial speech can be restricted:

- First, the commercial speech "at least must concern lawful activity and not be misleading." Otherwise, it can be suppressed.
- Second, if the speech is protected, the interest of the government in regulating and limiting it must be assessed. The state must assert a substantial interest to be achieved by restrictions on commercial speech.
- Third, it must be determined whether the regulation directly advances the governmental interest asserted.
- Fourth, it must also be determined whether an imposed restriction is more extensive than is necessary to serve that interest.[3]

Finally, in 1993, the Court summarized the general principles underlying the protection of commercial speech:

> The commercial market place, like other spheres of our social and cultural life, provides a forum where ideas and information flourish. Some of the ideas and information are vital, some of slight worth. But the general rule is that the speaker and the audience, not the government, assess the value of the information presented. Thus, even a communication that does no more than propose a commercial transaction is entitled to the coverage of the First Amendment.[4]

It is important to note that the Court has also recognized "different degrees of protection" accorded to commercial speech. This applies directly to different categories of commercial speech. For example, the first test means that false, deceptive, or misleading advertisements need not be permitted.[5] This allows the government to require such additions as warnings and disclaimers in order to prevent deception.

Another important product of this series of rulings is that "the court recognized the difference between purely commercial speech such as advertising and noncommercial corporate speech such as that used by public relations practitioners."[6] This means that the standards used to define commercial and non-commercial speech are different, which is especially important when trying to decide whether something is purely advertising or public relations. This allows a corporation, for example, to prepare public relations materials, such as brochures, newsletters, press releases, etc., for distribution to its various target publics without restriction—allowing basic First Amendment protection. At the same time, advertising of that corporation's product or service may be less protected. The determination of exactly what is commercial versus non-commercial, however, is still a bit vague. For example, what is the difference between what is referred to as "corporate advertising" (image advertising that has little or nothing to do directly with product sales) and commercial advertising?

The distinctions have been further blurred in recent years over the findings in the case of *Kasky* v. *Nike, Inc.*, which began in 2000.[7] Nike, whose logo has become a worldwide symbol of athletic shoes and gear, produced a public relations campaign to counter growing criticism that some of its products (notably, shoes) were manufactured in overseas "sweat shops." In answer to these allegations, Nike placed paid-for advertisements in newspapers and sent letters to athletic directors at major universities stating their side of the debate. The company was subsequently sued by a private citizen in California under that state's unfair competition law and false advertising law. Recall that false advertising is exempted from First Amendment protection. In response, Nike claimed that its statements did not constitute commercial speech and were therefore afforded protection.

After both the California superior court and the California Court of Appeals both dismissed the claim, it was taken up by the California Supreme Court. That court developed its own test to determine whether this particular speech act was commercial or not. The three-part test involves the speaker, the intended audience, and the message content. The upshot of this test is that "where there is a commercial speaker, an intended commercial audience, and commercial content in the message, the speech is commercial."[8] The Court held that Nike's speech was commercial because (1) the company is engaged in commerce, thus a commercial speaker; (2) its statements were directed expressly to actual and potential purchasers of its products; and (3) Nike's statements were of a commercial nature because it described its labor policies in factories in which its commercial products were made.[9] The Court, in effect, suggested that Nike's statements, although bordering on non-commercial speech, were not so intertwined with its commercial message as to be inextricable from it. When the U.S. Supreme Court declined to hear the case, the parties settled, leaving the question of what is commercial and what is non-commercial speech unanswered.

The bottom line for public relations seems to be that corporate speech is protected depending on its content. In other words, the right of a corporation to speak out publicly is limited only by what is being said. As Karla Gower, educator and ethics expert says:

> The Supreme Court has determined that corporations have important contributions to make in public debates and the content of such speech should be protected . . . Commercial speech, which does no more than propose a commercial transaction or is solely motivated by the desire for profit, receives less First Amendment protection than corporate speech.[10]

There are, however, those who disagree that commercial speech deserves even moderate protection. The First Amendment scholar C. Edwin Baker, in his Liberty Theory of constitutionally protected speech, points out that although commercial speech (such as advertising) is protected under the marketplace theory, the liberty theory would not offer it like protection. The reason is that the success of commercial speech is determined by economic market forces. It is not a necessary component of self-fulfillment (one of his criteria for protected speech) since its content is likewise determined by success in the market and not by any abiding sense of value felt by the copywriter. Its purpose is to sell a product or idea and not the discovery of truth or even the participation by all members of society in any decision-making role except as that of a consumer, which, contrary to what the Supreme Court has suggested, is not equivalent to the role of citizen. In this, the liberty theory is consistent with its own claim that the marketplace approach is based entirely on an economic model rather than a human value model. A *human value model* would presume that not everything is reducible to the status of a product—some values are intrinsic (have worth of their own) and need not compete for attention or recognition of worth.

The marketing professors Menette Drumwright and Patrick Murphy also point to a confusion among advertising practitioners about how the First Amendment functions in relation to advertising. In a study conducted among working professionals in the field they found that many cite the free speech clause as justification for not self-censoring their product.[11] Drumwright and Murphy call this a kind of naiveté. They suggest that the First Amendment "does not stand for the proposition that all speech is equally worthy and should be uttered or encouraged, or that speakers should not be condemned for the speech that they make." They point out that, under the marketplace theory, falsity is supposed to be exposed as what it is and justifiably condemned. What they discovered through their research is that many in advertising believe, mistakenly, that the free speech clause exonerates them from personal and professional responsibility. They agree with the proposition reiterated throughout this book that all purveyors of information "have a responsibility to make judgments about speech," and that "[t]his becomes even more the case as the Supreme Court lessens the distinction between commercial and noncommercial speech."[12]

Ethics and Persuasion

Nearly 2,500 years ago, Aristotle wrote *The Rhetoric*, outlining techniques for persuasive communication that have been studied and used ever since. For our purposes, however, it is most important to note that Aristotle placed no moral value on the techniques of persuasion themselves. In fact, he pointed out that they could be used for good or ill, depending entirely on the intent of the user. In other words, the character of the person using these persuasive techniques would determine the ethicality of the persuasive act. Aristotle accepted persuasion as a natural product of democracy. It was a tool needed to offer arguments and counterarguments that would be sorted out by the audience, who would then make the final decision. Persuasion depends now, as it always has, on the acceptance of the persuasive idea by the audience and on their ability to make their own choices free of coercive pressure.

One of the primary differences between journalism and advertising and public relations is that we *expect* the last two to be biased in their points of view. Both advertising and public relations use language to persuade, and, as already mentioned, persuasion is not unethical by nature.

Those who believe persuasion is unethical by nature generally also believe in a very strict version of the "marketplace of ideas" theory—that is, if you provide enough unbiased information for people, they will be able to make up their own minds about any issue. Although our political system is based on this theory to some extent, it is also based on the notion of reasoned argument—including persuasion. People who believe fervently enough in a particular point of view aren't going to rely on any marketplace to decide their case. They're going to get out there and argue, persuasively, for their side.

Persuasion and Coercion

The rhetorician and scholar Richard Perloff defines persuasion this way:

> Persuasion is a symbolic process in which communicators try to convince other people to change their attitudes or behavior regarding an issue through the transmission of a message, in an atmosphere of free choice.[13]

From an ethical perspective, the last part of this definition is vital. By "free choice," Perloff means that "a person . . . has the ability to act otherwise—to do other than what the persuader suggests—or to reflect critically on his choices in a situation."[14]

According to the First Amendment scholar C. Edwin Baker, "speech generally depends for its power on the voluntary acceptance of the listeners." Thus, speech would *normally* be considered non-coercive. Baker contrasts this normally benign nature of speech with its counterpart, coercive speech.

In general, a person coercively influences another if (1) she restricts another person to options that are worse than that other person had moral or legitimate right to expect, or (2) she employs means that she had no right to use for changing the threatened person's options.[15]

How then does persuasion differ from coercion? Persuasion deals with reason, and sometimes emotional appeals, whereas coercion typically employs force. Coercion is a technique for forcing people to act as the coercer wants them to act, and presumably contrary to their preferences. It can employ a threat of some dire consequence if the actor does not do what the coercer demands, but it doesn't have to. In the sense we're talking about it here, coercion refers not to how severe or effective the pressure or influence applied is but to the impropriety of the *form of pressure*. For example, deceptive speech may intentionally leave out vital information needed by listeners in order to make an informed decision. Without complete information, the listeners are limited in their choices and literally forced to decide in a predetermined way, presumably the way the speaker would like them to decide. Seen in this light, coercive speech would force another into a position they would not have been in but for the act of the communicator. Further, Baker suggests that speech may be deemed coercive if a "speaker manifestly disrespects and attempts to undermine the other person's will and the integrity of the other person's mental processes."[16] This is certainly in line with Kant's insistence that we respect others through our actions.

Some believe that persuasion, like lying, is coercive, thus harmful by nature. The feminist theorist Sally Miller Gearhart holds that persuasion is, in fact, "an act of violence." Like a number of other feminist scholars, Gearhart views some communication techniques as reflecting a masculine-oriented approach. Persuasion, in particular, represents a "conquest/conversion mentality."[17] This approach, according to Gearhart, uses persuasive techniques to convince the persuaded that they are better off accepting a particular point of view. The persuaded, under this model, may or may not be willing to change their points of view. She holds that those who are willing will be self-persuaded when presented with the necessary information, and that others should be left to their own beliefs. Gearhart proposes that we develop a "collective" mode, focusing on listening and receiving rather than the "competitive" mode common to the masculine perspective.

Clearly, this runs counter to the assumption of the ancient Greek rhetoricians, who held that persuasion was a necessary concomitant of democracy. And it seems a bit harsh for other feminist theorists as well. Sonja Foss and Cindy Griffin accept persuasion as one among many techniques that can be used ethically given the right context. They point out, however, that persuasion based on a model of "domination" is decidedly not the ethical approach. Rather, they suggest that persuasion be grounded in a belief that the most desirable outcome of the persuasive act is one of equality and autonomy among the parties. Their ideal persuasive model is one in which all sides are invited to view the alternatives and decide for themselves. Under this model, the likelihood of change is as great for one party as the other.[18] This same model shows up in other communication theories, such as those of the public relations scholar James Grunig. Grunig proposes that the ideal model for public relations is one that provides for mutual understanding as its goal. This "two-way symmetric" communication model presupposes that all sides of an issue are amenable to change, and that change will come with an increased understanding of all points of view.[19]

We must realize, however, that the "traditional" approach to persuasion (whether it is a masculine orientation or not) is the approach that is in effect today, much as it has been for several thousand years. Advocates of all sorts (legal, commercial, and editorial) still subscribe to the tenants of persuasion set forth by the likes of Aristotle and Cicero. And, because this traditional approach is in effect, we must be prepared to deal with the potential for unethical use of both the intent and the techniques of persuasion.

In summary, then, *the ideal persuasive act is one in which both the ends sought and the means employed by the persuader are ethical, and those being persuaded are allowed the opportunity to reflect critically on the available options and to make an informed and free choice.*

The Ethics of Means and Ends in Persuasion

In assessing the ethicality of persuasive activities, we need to look both at the means of persuasion (the techniques used) and at the ends (the results sought). The public relations scholars Benton Danner and Spiro Kiousis provide us with a "taxonomy of means and ends" that charts the possibilities in four categories.[20]

1 *You can engage in ethically justifiable persuasive acts in an ethical manner* (good ends, good means). This type of act occurs in two manifestations:

- A *morally permissible act*: One in which the moral agent is neither required by ethics to perform the act nor prohibited ethically from performing the act; that is, to perform the action is moral and to not perform it is also moral.

   An example of a morally permissible act in the realm of public relations might involve a public health campaign designed to persuade a public of the benefits of appropriate cardiovascular exercise. Although this is a good act, there is no obligation to perform it—what Kant would call an "imperfect duty."
- A *morally obligatory act*: An act that the agent has a moral obligation to perform. To not perform the act would be unethical.

   For example: Suppose you are the vice president of public relations in a corporation that manufactures children's clothing. You have discovered information that conclusively shows that the children's pajamas manufactured by your company are highly flammable. As the public relations chief for your company, not only would you have a moral obligation to attempt to persuade management to reveal this information (so that the danger can be publicized and appropriate recalls initiated), but if you fail in the attempt to persuade superiors to reveal the defect, you would have a moral obligation to reveal the defect yourself (often referred to as "whistle blowing").

2   *You can engage in persuasion that is ethically unjustified, but do so in an ethically proper manner* (bad ends, good means). Although you could argue that the means justify the ends, you would be on shaky moral ground.

- For example, you could use ethical means of persuasion to attempt to convince others of the benefits of selling or using methamphetamines or crack cocaine.
- You could promote racism by using completely acceptable persuasive tactics—say a speech in which all the rhetorical techniques are ethically sound.

3   *You could engage in unethical tactics of persuasion in a persuasive act that is itself morally justified* (bad means, good ends). Because you are using morally suspect means to achieve a good end, you might be able to argue for the ethicality of the entire act; however, the questionable tactics would taint your achievement.

- For example, you might engage in lies in order to solicit donations for a charity that legitimately helps the homeless. Kant would not see this as a permissible act since the ends, in his view, never justify the means. To tell the truth, regardless of the outcome would be a perfect duty.

     However, Danner and Kiousis suggest another set of cases under this category that may be morally permissible. These are instances in which the ends pursued are extremely significant—for example, the lives of a large number of people are at stake. For instance, would you lie to save the lives of a great many human beings? Kant would have said no, but our basic humanness would probably disagree with him on this one.

4   *Neither the persuasive act itself nor the means employed in persuasion are morally permissible* (bad means, bad ends). Acts in this category will always be morally prohibited.

- For example, you could be employed by a tobacco company and engage in deceptive persuasive acts designed to entice children to start smoking.

To summarize:

- When the means and ends of a persuasive act are each morally sound, the overall act will be ethical. The act may be either *ethically permissible* (that is, ethics permits one to perform the act) or *ethically obligatory* (that is, ethics requires that one perform the act).
- When the persuasive means are unethical but the ends sought are ethically justified, the ethicality of the act as a whole isn't as clear. The justification for using unethical means would have to be a strong one.
- When the means are ethical and the ends are not justified, an argument can be logically made in defense of the act, but bad ends are rarely justifiable.
- When both the means and the ends of persuasion are ethically unjustifiable, then the persuasive act itself is unethical (that is, it would be unethical to perform the act).

Guidelines for Ethical Persuasion

The ethical determinants of most of advertising and public relations messages are, thus, those of responsible rhetorical techniques. A number of scholars in the field of rhetoric and persuasion have provided excellent guidelines for determining the morality of both the act of persuasion and the content of persuasive messages. Following is one such checklist for the measurement of the persuasive act itself.[21]

- Is the communication act or technique right in general and/or right in this specific situation?
- To what extent is the argument valid?
- Are the best interests of the audience considered?
- Does society hold the communication act or technique to be right in general and/or in this situation?
- Does the communication act or technique appeal to values the society holds to be morally good or bad?
- Are the "real motives" behind the act or technique admirable or at least legitimate?
- What would be the social consequences of the act or technique if it were to become widely practiced by others?

Obviously, these questions reference a number of ethical theories including utilitarianism and Kant's Categorical Imperative. Consequently, they serve to provide the persuader with a checklist for motives when developing, as every public relations and advertising professional must, a proper marketing mix for the dissemination of a persuasive message. This checklist, or another like it, can be applied both to the act itself and to the communication technique. One of the admonitions contained in the PRSA Code of Professional Standards, for instance, forbids the corruption of media channels. This checklist also speaks to that problem.

The message itself also has the potential for corruption. Obviously, moral intent and ethical technique do not necessarily guarantee subsequently ethical communication. For this purpose, these eight guidelines for evaluating the degree of ethicality in argumentation and persuasion might be useful.[22]

- A message should be *accurate*. It should stay both within the facts and within relevant context, and neither exaggerate nor make false claims.
- It should be *complete*. Although advocacy implies bias, it is necessary that all arguments be at least recognized. This also refers to the proper attribution of sources.
- Material should always be *relevant*. Superfluous information only serves to cloud the message.
- *Openness* implies that alternatives be recognized even if the intent of the message is to promote only one of them.
- The message should be made *understandable* through the minimization of ambiguity, avoidance of oversimplification, and distortion of accuracy.
- Sound *reasoning* should be in evidence, containing only appropriate appeals to values, emotions, needs, and motives.
- *Social utility* should be promoted.
- Communicators should demonstrate *benevolence* through sincerity, tact, and respect for dignity.

Propaganda versus Persuasion

What is Propaganda?

The term *propaganda* has a long and checkered history. Beginning with the Catholic Church, several hundred years ago, the term originally meant to spread the faith. More contemporary definitions indicate how far that original concept has fallen. Ted Smith, editor of *Propaganda: A Pluralistic Perspective*, calls propaganda:

> Any conscious and open attempt to influence the beliefs of an individual or group, guided by a predetermined end and characterized by the systematic use of irrational and often unethical techniques of persuasion.[23]

The atheism proponent and secular humanist Austin Cline defines propaganda as:

> any organized effort to persuade large numbers of people about the truth of an idea, the value of a product, or the appropriateness of an attitude. Propaganda isn't a form of communication which simply seeks to inform;

instead, it is both directional (because it often seeks to get people to act in some fashion) and emotional (because it seeks to condition certain emotional reactions to specific situations).[24]

Cline also points out the basic difference between arguments (in the sense in which rhetoricians use the term) and propaganda. According to Cline, the key difference is that:

> while an argument is designed to establish the **truth** of a proposition, propaganda is designed to spread the **adoption** of an idea, regardless of its truth and always in a one-sided manner. [emphasis in original][25]

Although there doesn't seem to be much connection between what public relations says it does and propaganda, the very nature of persuasion can easily lend itself to less than ethical practices. And most of public relations is still about persuasion.

So, does the act of persuasion through the mass media naturally equate with propaganda? Part of the answer has to do with our own ability, and willingness, to investigate the complexities of issues rather than just accept the simple explanation frequently offered by propaganda. A couple of important psychological theories come into play here, both of which have ethical ramifications.

Theory of Cognitive Dissonance

Dissonance theory, formulated in the 1950s, says that people tend to seek only messages that are "consonant" with their attitudes; they do not seek out "dissonant" messages. In other words, people don't go looking for messages they don't agree with already (who needs more conflict in their lives, right?). This theory also says that about the only way you are going to get anybody to listen to something they don't agree with is to juxtapose their attitude with a "dissonant" attitude—an attitude that is logically inconsistent with the first. What this means (theoretically) is that if you confront people with a concept that radically shakes up their belief structure, you might get them to pay attention. For example, this is the technique employed by some anti-abortion activists when they force us to look at graphic images of aborted fetuses. Although the experience may be truly uncomfortable, it does remind even the most ardent pro-abortion of those among us of the costs of the procedure. The attempt is to shock unbelievers into questioning their loyalties.

Later research revealed that people use a fairly sophisticated psychological defense mechanism to filter out unwanted information. This mechanism consists of four "rings of defense":

- *Selective exposure:* People tend to seek out only that information which agrees with their existing attitudes or beliefs. This accounts for our not subscribing to the *New Republic* if we are staunchly liberal Democrats.

- *Selective attention:* People tune out communication that goes against their attitudes or beliefs, or they pay attention only to parts that reinforce their positions, forgetting the dissonant parts. This is why two people with differing points of view can come to different conclusions about the same message. Each of them is tuning out the parts with which they disagree.
- *Selective perception:* People seek to interpret information so that it agrees with their attitudes and beliefs. This accounts for a lot of misinterpretation of messages. Some people don't block out dissonant information; they simply reinterpret it so that it matches their preconceptions. For example, whereas one person may view rising interest rates as an obstacle to her personal economic situation, another may view the same rise as an asset. The first person may be trying to buy a new home; the second may be a financial investor. Both are interpreting the same issue based on their differing viewpoints.
- *Selective retention:* People tend to let psychological factors influence their recall of information. In other words, we forget the unpleasant or block out the unwanted. This also means that people tend to be more receptive to messages presented in pleasant environments—a lesson anyone who has ever put on a news conference understands.

The Elaboration Likelihood Model

Some people seem easy to persuade and tend to believe almost anything, whereas others seem resistant to persuasion, have their own opinions, and often argue with those trying to persuade them. The fact is that audiences, or publics, exist in multiple forms and use multiple methods of reasoning out decisions, two of which have caught the attention of researchers over the past 30 years or so.

In 1980, Richard E. Petty and John T. Cacioppo developed what they called the *Elaboration Likelihood Model of Persuasion* in which they sought to explain these differences. They suggested that persuasive messages were transmitted and received through two different routes: the *central route* and the *peripheral route*. The central route is used by those people who think about messages extensively before becoming persuaded. In other words, they "elaborate" on a message and will be persuaded only if the message is cognitively convincing. The peripheral route is used by those who are unable or unwilling to spend time thinking about a message. Instead, recipients using peripheral processing rely on a variety of cues to make quick decisions, most of which don't bear directly on the subject matter of the message. For example, when President George W. Bush made his famous "Mission Accomplished" speech on board a naval aircraft carrier wearing a military pilot's flight suit, he was using several cues (the uniform and setting, among others) to reinforce his persuasive message.

Petty and Cacioppo stress that the central route and the peripheral route are poles on a cognitive processing continuum that shows the degree of mental effort a person exerts when evaluating a message. They are not mutually exclusive approaches. The more listeners work to evaluate a message, the less they will be influenced by cues not relevant to the message itself. The greater the effect of cues not relevant to the message, the less impact the message carries.

For central processing receivers, the cognitive strength of the argument being presented is extremely important. For these receivers, thoughtful consideration of strong arguments will produce the most positive shifts in attitude. In addition, the change will tend to be persistent over time, resist counterpersuasion, and predict future behavior. However, thoughtful consideration of weak arguments can lead to negative boomerang effects (the weak arguments are shown to be exactly what they are and the idea loses the respect and attention of the receiver).

According to Petty and Cacioppo, however, most messages are processed through the peripheral route, bringing attitude changes without actually thinking about the issue. Peripheral route change can be either positive or negative, but it won't have the impact of message elaboration and the change can be short-lived.

What does all this mean? For those in the business of persuasion, it means the job isn't as easy as it seems. And it means that the temptation to come up with newer, more inventive types of persuasive communication is compelling. That can also mean taking ethical shortcuts in order to achieve the kind of persuasion necessary to sell an idea. See the case study and discussion in the next chapter concerning the Edelman/Wal-Mart scandal for an example of how ever-newer persuasive strategies carry with them some dangerous moral pitfalls.

Propaganda Again

The media ethicist Jay Black suggests several insights based on a lengthy investigation into the concept of propaganda, which can be applied to the producers of propaganda, the contents of propaganda, and the consumers of propaganda. These relate closely to the theories just discussed, and show how important the role of the receiver is in the process of persuasion. On one hand, the person who is easily persuaded by propaganda:

> is probably seeking psychological closure whether rational or not; appears to be driven by irrational inner forces; has an extreme reliance on authority figures; reflects a narrow time perspective; and displays little sense of discrimination among fact/inference/value judgment.[26]

In other words, he is seeking information that he already agrees with, and is probably using the peripheral route to gather it. On the other hand, the person who is not easily persuaded by propaganda:

> faces a constant struggle to remain open-minded by evaluating information on its own merits; is governed by self-actualizing forces rather than irratio-

nal inner forces; discriminates between and among messages and sources and has tentative reliance on authority figures; recognizes and deals with contradictions, incomplete pictures of reality, and the interrelation of past, present, and future; and moves comfortably and rationally among levels of abstraction (fact, inference, and value judgment).[27]

These traits are what Petty and Cacioppo have suggested as a defense against "peripheral cues," distracting and often unrelated information designed to persuade, often unethically. For example, picking a spokesperson solely on the basis of appearance is ethically questionable, but it may work on those using the peripheral route. For those central processors, it would be easily recognized as a cheap trick.

Black also suggests that propaganda contains characteristics generally associated with dogmatism or closed-mindedness. Conversely, ethical (and, as Black calls it, "creative") communication will expect, even encourage, its audience to investigate the validity and credibility of both the message and the source. Further, propaganda is characterized by at least the following six specific characteristics which make it more easily recognizable:

1   a heavy or undue reliance on authority figures and spokespersons, rather than empirical validation, to establish its truths, conclusions, or impressions;
2   the utilization of unverified and perhaps unverifiable abstract nouns, adjectives, adverbs, and physical representations rather than empirical validation to establish its truths, conclusions, or impressions;
3   a finalistic or fixed view of people, institutions, and situations divided into broad, all-inclusive categories of in-groups (friends) and out-groups (enemies), beliefs and disbeliefs, and situations to be accepted or rejected in toto;
4   a reduction of situations into simplistic and readily identifiable cause and effect relations, ignoring multiple causality of events;
5   a time perspective characterized by an overemphasis or underemphasis on the past, present, or future as disconnected periods rather than a demonstrated consciousness of time flow;
6   a greater emphasis on conflict than on cooperation among people, institutions, and situations.[28]

And finally, Black concludes with this sage advice:

A fully functioning democratic society needs pluralism in its persuasion and information, and not the narrow-minded, self-serving propaganda some communicators inject—wittingly or unwittingly—into their communications and which, it seems, far too many media audience members unconsciously and uncritically consume. Open-mindedness and mass communications efforts need not be mutually exclusive.[29]

What Does It All Mean?

Public relations and advertising are not the same thing; however, they do share similar ethical concerns because of the nature of the communication act they share. The act of persuasion, common to both practices, is fraught with ethical complications. Whenever we seek to persuade, the potential to manipulate is a very real temptation. And, as we have learned, manipulation is coercive in that it puts the target of the persuasion in a position that limits his freedom of choice. This can be accomplished through outright lying or, more often, through withholding information vital to a complete understanding of an issue.

Although bias is usually assumed in persuasive acts, that does not mean that information will necessarily be restricted or choices limited. The ethical persuader is transparent at every level: who they are, who they represent, what they are "selling," and why. Incompleteness in any of these areas has the potential to turn persuasion into propaganda. Respect for those who are the targets of persuasion is paramount if either public relations or advertising is to be considered ethical. As we will see in the next two chapters, there are a number of obstacles to ethical action, and more than a few temptations to do that which is other than completely ethical. It is often in the grey areas that unethical action is rationalized. We will need to work all the harder if we are to shine the light of morality into those corners.

Chapter 8

Ethics and Public Relations

> Honesty is often the best policy, but sometimes the appearance of it is worth six of it.
>
> (Mark Twain)

What is Public Relations?

That's not an easy question to answer. If you were to think that public relations is about putting a client's best foot forward, you'd be right. If you proposed that public relations is about dealing with the media (keeping your client's name either in the media or out of it), you'd be right as well. If you believed that public relations is helping clients and organizations get along with their constituencies, you'd be right again. In fact, public relations can involve all of these and more. Public relations involves everything from planning complex communications campaigns to writing a letter to the editor. It involves any activity that enhances the reputation of your client, mediates disputes between various publics and your client, helps to achieve mutual understanding among all parties involved in an issue, advocates on behalf of a client or cause, provides guidance and direction, and results in positive and mutual well-being.

In fact, modern public relations is an eclectic package encompassing a great many job descriptions, titles, and functions. The federal government even forbids the use of the term "public relations" to refer to roles whose functions in the business world would be identical. The practice is rife with terms synonymous with, yet subtly different from, "public relations." "Press agentry," for instance, is usually taken to mean the role of providing media exposure, whereas "promotion" combines media exposure with persuasion. "Public affairs" most often refers to those who deal with community or government relations; and the federal government's chosen replacement term is "public information."

Whatever definition you choose to describe public relations, it is always about communication and, as we have seen, there are a great many ethical considerations involved in the communicative act. Many would say that public relations is a breeding ground for unethical behavior; however, that would be a gross generalization at best and literally misleading at worst.

What's Good about Public Relations?

Nearly 20 years ago, Apple computers ran a campaign for the, then new, Macintosh computer. Its slogan was, "For every voice, a means to be heard." For many in public relations, this is the goal of the practice. Despite the fact that most people when they hear the phrase "public relations" think of corporate cover-ups and government spin, a great many others know that public relations, like persuasion in general, is only a tool. It's the purpose you put it to that dictates its morality. For example, the goal of socially responsible public relations is to better society by, among other things, allowing disparate voices the opportunity to join in the conversation. Certainly, this is true in a literal sense, because most of what we call "social service" organizations (the Red Cross, Greenpeace, Doctors Without Borders, etc.) have public relations functions that project their voices globally, and pitch their messages of a world motivated by compassion. From 1996 to 2006, the number of charitable non-profit organizations (NPOs) in the United States alone grew 69 percent, to nearly 100,000. And they all use public relations in some form to get out their messages. For instance, a 2004 study showed that the 100 largest NPOs in the U.S. were effectively using the internet to "present traditional public relations materials and connect with publics."[1]

A good international example is non-governmental organizations (NGOs). These are typically, but not exclusively, organizations created privately, frequently volunteer-based, that often deal with humanitarian issues in developing countries. The World Bank categorizes them into "operational" (those that work in delivering services, such as medical aid or food, or develop service programs on-site) and "advocacy" (those that promote a cause through typical public relations tactics). Most NGOs, especially those engaged in advocacy, couldn't survive without public relations. They must maintain an ongoing and positive relationship with their various publics in order to be successful. Depending on the focus of the NGO, typical public relations goals might be fundraising, political awareness and influence, recognition of social causes, etc. Among the numerous examples of NGOs are Amnesty International and the International Committee of the Red Cross.

In addition, it would be fair to say that the ideal of public relations, whether for profit-making or non-profit organizations, is to build relationships among constituents that will help the organization fulfill its goals—goals hopefully designed to benefit not just the organization, but also the various publics it serves. After all, organizations exist to provide either a product or service, which implies that is something the public needs or wants. Good public relations should make delivery of those products and services run more smoothly by keeping the overall image of the organization in good shape. Ideally, successful, ethical public relations will help both the organization and its publics achieve their mutual goals. In order to accomplish this, the ethical imperative of public relations has to be congruency between reality and image. In other words, what public relations says about a client or organization must match what is really going on.

One way to look at the paradigm of image versus reality is to view the three elements that make up successful and ethical public relations as regards image construction and maintenance. First is the reality itself—what the client or organization actually is, its product or services, its environmental practices, relationship with employees, the community, etc. Second is what it says about those things through its public relations. Third is what receivers of the message believe the client or organization to be. So, there are several possibilities:

- If the reality of the client or organization matches (is congruent with) the message it produces by its communication about itself, and the receivers of the message believe it, that would represent *ethical* and *successful* public relations.
- If the reality of the client or organization matches (is congruent with) the message it produces by its communication about itself, and the receivers of the message *do not* believe it, that would represent *ethical* public relations—but not necessarily *successful* public relations.
- If the reality of the client or organization is intentionally *not represented accurately* by its communication about itself, then the public relations is *unethical*, whether the receivers of the message believe it or not. This is the worst case as far as public relations ethics goes. And the worst part of the case is that, if the receivers *believe* the inaccurate information to be accurate, there are those clients, and their public relations representatives, who will still think they did a "good job."

So, What's the Problem?

Two primary concerns come up when people complain about public relations: It has too much influence on the news media, and it's just plain deceptive by nature (the final possibility in the paradigm of reality versus image above). On the first count, public relations does influence news—sometimes in positive ways, and sometimes in purely self-serving ways. Estimates have varied over the years of how much of what we see and hear on the news is prompted by public relations; whatever the number, it's probably a big one. We shouldn't assume that the "influence" is all bad, however. Business editors, for example, have to fill their pages some way, as do financial publications, and the myriad "trade publications" that serve everyone from golf aficionados to computer geeks (think *Golf Digest* or *Macworld* here). Companies such as PR Newswire and Business Wire make a living delivering public relations driven information to thousands of news outlets around the world every day. Their clients foot the bill—the media get the service for free. On the one hand, public relations information such as this can be one of many sources journalists use for background into stories they are researching. On the other hand, the pure information overload can be distracting, and tempting. Although most journalists and editors assiduously edit information originating from public relations practitioners, the need to fill time and space is a very real one.

Recent research by the journalism and advertising professors Jim Upshaw and David Koranda suggest that non-editorial content is beginning to seep into television newscasts. They found that 90 percent of the 294 newscasts analyzed had at least one instance per newscast of what they called "stealth advertising." Overall, they found 750 instances of "commercial influences," about 2.5 per newscast averaging 1 minute 42 seconds long.[2] What they were looking for was advertising; however, what they found was much closer to what is being discussed here. Their examples were composed, to a great extent, of what this book classifies as public relations. This is not an uncommon phenomenon among academics and others unfamiliar with the distinctions between PR and advertising. In fact, it might be said that much of what is transpiring in advertising today, especially on the internet, is actually public relations. That's the claim from the marketing consultants Al Ries and Laura Ries, whose book *The Fall of Advertising and the Rise of PR* is based on the premise that public relations has the ability to generate discussion about a product, as publicity (which is generally free).[3] This is referred to these days as "buzz." They make a number of points that are salient to our discussion here.

- Advertising draws attention to a product. It tells you what it is. PR insinuates messages about the product into the conversation going on in the real world beyond advertising. For example, you may see an new product advertised heavily on TV, and then start to see seemingly unprompted blog postings from users talking about the product. Chances are, the postings aren't entirely unprompted. They're part of a PR product publicity campaign.
- Advertising shouts its message. PR whispers. It's about information, albeit usually intentionally filtered, that aids the consumer in making a purchase decision. This is part of what is known as the *diffusion process.*

The theory of diffusion suggests that the adoption process goes through several stages ranging from the initial attention-getting stage through to the final reinforcement stage (following adoption). Advertising usually takes care of the first stage and the last. Everything else can, and often does, involve public relations. An important part of the process involves talking about the product or idea with other people who are asking the same questions or have already tried it themselves.

- Public relations tends to be "other directed." That is, its messages are passed on—through the media by means of positive publicity, and, increasingly, through word of mouth via consumers. Because public relations messages are often passed through intermediaries to end-users of the information (consumers), the credibility is usually higher. If you hear about a new product through the news media, you will attach more credibility to the product itself. The same goes for if you get it from friends and neighbors, even if they are "friends" only in a broad, MySpace sense.

When a small-town newscast includes information about a local company hiring 200 people, it is news. When the bulk of the story comes from the local company, including interviews with the CEO, other officers, and new employees, public relations is going to be involved at some point. The fact the new company gets positive press makes the story successful public relations. Because the story is newsworthy, it's news. The danger comes when journalists and editors rely too heavily on public relations-generated information.

As we will see later in this chapter, transparency is the key. Public relations *masquerading* as news is unethical. If viewers and readers *know* it is public relations, it's ethical. Openness and disclosure are vital. Although public relations may certainly influence news, PR people often view it as their jobs to try to do so. Journalists, on the other hand, need to be cautious in relying too heavily on pre-packaged "news." For example, a recent survey of journalists suggested that blogs are having an impact on the way they gather information and on the tone and direction of their subsequent reporting.[4] This is good news for public relations practitioners looking for new ways to get their clients' messages out, but sounds a cautionary note for journalists looking for stories.

Another area in which public relations attempts to influence news is in the coverage of negative news about a client. An old adage used to be that the primary job of PR was to keep the client's name out of the paper. Today, that usually means only if it becomes associated with bad news. There is no denying that the job of *media relations* (a specific function within public relations) involves both getting good news out and dealing with bad news when it happens. Obviously, the most ethical approach to dealing with bad news (if it's true) is to admit it, say what your client is going to do to rectify the situation, and move on. However, as we will see later in this chapter, some who work in public relations don't always see ethical problems when they occur, or are hired simply to deal with them in the most efficacious way for the client, and only the client.

These "spin doctors" put the best face possible on a negative situation using techniques that can generally be classified as a type of equivocation. *Equivocation* is essentially the use of ambiguous language to either conceal the truth of something or to avoid admitting to a wrongdoing. Examples of this approach are: responding to journalist's inquiry by referring to an accusation as "ridiculous" or "absurd" without actually stating why, or impugning the source of the accusation, or refusing to respond at all by seeming to be offended by the very idea of being accused (e.g., "I'm not going to dignify that with a response"). All of these techniques are really dodges of the truth, and irritants for journalists. Technically, equivocation is not lying, but it is deceptive. Which is not to say that public relations people don't ever lie outright—and that brings up our second major complaint.

In 2000, the industry trade publication *PRWeek* presented the findings of a survey of 1,700 public relations executives asking about the ethics of the PR industry. The headline on the story read, "One out of Four Pros Admits to Lying on Job." The survey showed that 25 percent of the executives admitted they lied on the job, and 39 percent said they had exaggerated the truth.[5] These were tough findings for an industry forever in need of polishing its own image. Of course, the respondents on the survey were probably referring to everything from small, "white" lies to deception through withholding information. And, although all lies are unethical by nature, some, as the philosopher Sissela Bok noted, are far worse than others. What follows here is one of the most talked-about instances of public relations deception in the past 20 years. It represents what ethical public relations is decidedly *not* about.

On August 2, 1990, Iraqi troops invaded Kuwait. By January 1991, a coalition of international forces, including the United States, engaged the Iraqi military, and by February the First Gulf War was over. In hindsight, it seems simpler than it actually was. Although the United Nations officially sanctioned military action against Iraqi, the success of selling the idea to the American public wasn't a foregone conclusion. Even though polls conducted following the war showed a high level of support (around 80 percent), at the time of the Iraqi invasion and subsequent buildup and engagement by American and coalition forces, support hovered at around 50 percent or less.[6] What wasn't so clear is how the American public arrived at such a high level of support in such a short period of time. There are more than a few, including many in the public relations industry, who believe it was PR that tipped the scales.

In a public hearing of Congress's Human Rights Caucus on October 10, 1990, a 15-year-old Kuwaiti girl named Nayirah presented some startling testimony. She said she had seen Iraqi soldiers remove babies from hospital incubators, leaving them to die on the floor. Her stunning testimony was repeated worldwide and cited frequently in the ensuing national debate in the U.S. over whether to commit American troops to the Middle East conflict. President George H. W. Bush mentioned it frequently as he drummed up support for military action. As journalist Ted Rowse put it two years later, "It was a major factor in building public backing for war."[7] Shortly after the war ended, however, NBC news interviewed Kuwaiti hospital officials who flatly denied any such thing had ever happened. Almost a year later, a story by *Harper's* magazine publisher John R. MacArthur appearing on the *New York Times* op-ed page revealed that Nayirah was the daughter of the Kuwaiti ambassador to the U.S. and had not even been in Kuwait at the time she claimed the atrocities occurred.[8] It seems that all of this had been part of a complex public relations campaign mounted by Hill & Knowlton (HK)—at the time, the world's largest PR firm. HK had been talking with the government of Kuwait since just after the Iraqi invasion began and had taken over the operation of a "front" group called Citizens for a Free Kuwait, financed almost entirely by the government of Kuwait (which also paid HK $11.5 million to get its message out). Thanks in large part to HK's public relations campaign on behalf of the Kuwaiti government, the United States entered the war, on a 52–47 vote. Although HK denied any wrongdoing, observers both inside and outside the field of public relations have denounced the use of deception, and it has become a case study in what not to do if you want to be considered ethical.

What follows next is an examination of some of the ways experts in public relations ethics have considered the problems covered here, and more.

Ethical Approaches Specific to Public Relations

During the past 40 years or so, those in the field of public relations, both practitioners and academics, have been fairly self-reflexive in addressing their own ethical issues. Next to news journalism, public relations is probably the most aggressive in pursuing a working "ethic" of proper behavior. This is probably on account of its drive toward professionalism, as detailed in Chapter 3. Serious philosophical research into public relations ethics has been going on since at least the 1980s, and has increased over time.

Much of this research incorporates elements of the classical theories of moral philosophy discussed in Chapter 4. In addition, there are a number of theoretical approaches that have been suggested over the years that are specific to the nuances of the practice of public relations. Following are some of those.

Five Baselines for Justifying Persuasion

The ethicist Sherry Baker outlines five different models that she says are most often used to justify persuasive communication. They range from the questionable to the ethically useful. Among the ethically useful models are the following:[9]

Enlightened Self-interest

- Under this model, the interests of both the client and the professional are best served by ethical behavior.
- Businesses do well (financially) by doing good (ethically). Ethical behavior makes good business sense. Doing good gives a corporation a competitive edge. Businesses should therefore engage in good deeds and ethical behavior.
- Willingness to forgo immediate benefits results in future benefits.
- Ethical behavior will prevent government regulation.

Social Responsibility

- This model recognizes the interdependency of persons in society—of persons as communal beings.
- Corporations have a responsibility to the societies in which they operate and from which they profit; they have obligations of good citizenship in

contributing positively to the social, political, environmental, and economic health of society.

- The focus of this model is on responsibilities rather than on rights.

Kingdom of Ends

This model is based on the philosophy of Immanuel Kant, and even borrows it name directly from one of Kant's major concepts—respect for persons.

- Individuals act as if they were members of a *kingdom of ends*—an ideal community in which everyone is always moral, one in which all people are treated as ends in themselves rather than as means to someone else's ends.
- Individuals treat others as they would wish to be treated and as others would wish to be treated.
- Individuals take responsibility for the moral conduct of the organizations with which they work.
- Individuals pursue the moral ideal with dignity and integrity, despite the behavior of those around them.
- Persuasive appeals are made to the decency in people and with respect for their rights as rational self-determining beings.
- Individuals and corporations take responsibility to promote and create the kind of world and society in which they themselves would like to live.
- Professional communications should dignify rather than debase society. Communicators function under the guiding maxims of a moral community engaged in the harmonious and cooperative pursuit of the good.

Responsible Advocacy

This theory of public relations proposes that the best way to practice public relations ethics is through the ideal of *professional responsibility*. This idea is in line with our discussion of professionalism in Chapter 2. According to Kathy Fitzpatrick and Candace Gauthier, "Modern day public relations efforts include both self-interested persuasive tactics as well as genuinely benevolent initiatives."[10] Their contention is that these imperatives can work together if we consider the public relations practitioner as a professional. The key points of this theory are:

- Public relations practitioners' greatest need for ethical guidance is in the reconciling of their conflicting roles of professional advocate and organizational social conscience.
- Public relations professionals best serve society by serving the special interests of clients or employers.
- First loyalty is always to the client, but public relations professionals also have a responsibility to voice the opinions of organizational stakeholders.[11]

According to the authors, three principles that could provide the foundation for a theory of professional responsibility in public relations are:

The comparison of harms and benefits: Harms should be avoided, or at least minimized, and benefits promoted at the least possible cost in terms of harms.

Respect for persons: Persons should be treated with respect and dignity.

Distributive justice: The benefits and burdens of any action or policy should be distributed as fairly as possible.

Fitzpatrick and Gauthier note the importance of recognizing these as *prima facie* (accepted as correct until proved otherwise), and not absolute, principles. They are principles that hold generally unless they conflict with one another. When only one of the principles is implicated in a moral choice, that principle should be taken as the controlling guideline for ethical conduct. However, moral dilemmas often involve conflicts between the principles. In these cases, the decision maker must employ his or her own values, moral intuition, and character to determine which principle is most important and most controlling in the particular context.

Two-way Communication and the "Corporate Conscience"

James Grunig proposes a model of two-way, symmetrical communication as the best way to achieve ethical decisions. Following a functional systems perspective, he bases his theory on the following assumptions:[12]

- Collaboration, working jointly with others, is a key value in ethical decisions.
- The process of dialogue with different people allows for both listening and arguing.
- Not everyone will get what they want, but dialogue will lead to the most ethical outcome.

This approach requires public relations practitioners to balance their role as advocate for their client with their role as *social conscience*. It also assumes that organizations will be voluntarily socially responsible instead of egoistic. From a systems perspective, mutual cooperation requires adaptation to the environment, which may be the most harmonious method of maintaining balance. However, it does recognize the possibility that controlling an environment may also be necessary for needed change to occur and a new and beneficial balance to be realized. For example, it may be necessary for a company to pursue its interests, knowing that the final outcome would be beneficial for most of the other systems in its relevant environment, even if some of those systems disagree with the change initially. Think of the Social Security Act of 1935. President Franklin Roosevelt pushed it through during a very dark time in the United States and against some very strong opposition. Most agreed later that it turned out to be a good idea.

Grunig's theoretical approach, and many who use this approach as a basis for their own, assumes that public relations will become the "conscience" of an organization. The rational is that, because of PR's responsibility for maintaining communication linkages with corporate constituents, it is in a unique position to understand the myriad points of view presented by these publics. Generally speaking, other elements within an organization have a less holistic view of these publics. So, it makes sense to locate the "corporate conscience" within the public relations function.

Some important recent research by the ethics scholar Shannon Bowen seems to show that there are potential problems with assigning the role of "corporate conscience" to public relations practitioners.[13] In her study, a number of public relations practitioners were questioned using a combination of personal interviews and focus groups. The findings showed two fairly distinct and "entrenched" categories of practitioners when it came to the role of public relations, especially that of ethical counselor: those who were "antiethical" and those who were "proethical."[14] Bowen describes the results this way:

> Antiethical conscience role practitioners are often in favor of a professional perspective relying on codes of ethics or legalism [it's not about ethics; it's about what's legal]. They do not see ethics as germane to public relations counsel. Many public relations practitioners cite the fact that they do not have any training in ethics, feel ill-equipped to counsel others on such issues, or simply believe it is a matter better left to legal counsel. Others report that their reluctance stems from lack of access to the dominant coalition [primary organizational decision makers] or from an overwhelming number of other job responsibilities.[15]

Members of this group tended not to recall many ethical dilemmas. Bowen suggests that this could result from either an actual lack of ethical problems or an inability to recognize one when they encountered it. (Similar findings crop up in advertising as well, as explained in Chapter 9.) Those who viewed public relations as an advocacy function or a purely professional endeavor showed little desire to take on an ethics role. A contributing factor seemed to be their general lack of input into strategic decision making.[16] On the other hand:

> Proethical conscience practitioners often find themselves in this role through the demand for such counsel and the experience they hold with external publics. Many public relations professionals report that CEOs are initially reluctant to include them except when absolutely necessary, such as in matters of crisis. However, once their worth as ethical conscience is illustrated, they become an indispensable part of the dominant coalition.

The proethical practitioners tended to combine strong moral values with practical business sense, a position they believed would result in a more profitable company in the long run. Their approach seemed to be one of trust-building, believing that "ethical counsel and careful attention to ethical actions improved the reputation of the organization as credible, reliable, and ethical, and built 'public trust.'"[17]

Even though Bowen's findings turned up two distinct categories of practitioners with seemingly intractable points of view, nonetheless she maintains that the "corporate conscience" model of public relations is viable, perhaps even preferred. She notes that the data:

> strengthen the argument that public relations can contribute to an organization's strategic management, and by incorporating ethical decision-making and counsel that role can not only enhance organizational effectiveness but also contribute to the stature of public relations counsel as an ethical and valued voice in the dominant coalition.[18]

However, she points out that:

> For public relations to take strategic management responsibility at the organizational policy level, knowledge of ethical deliberation and active ethical counsel is absolutely required.[19]

The TARES Test

In their continuing effort to supply guidance to professional persuaders with useful ethical guidelines, Sherry Baker and David Martinson have outlined an elaborate test for judging the ethicality of persuasive communication.[20]

They suggest that the appropriate foundation of ethical persuasion is a clearer understanding of the difference between means and ends. They argue that "the end must be formulated in a way that places an emphasis on respect for those to whom particular persuasive communication efforts are directed."[21] They propose a five-part test of *prima facie* duties that they say "defines the moral boundaries of persuasive communications and serves as a set of action-guiding principles directed toward a moral consequence in persuasion."[22] They are:

Truthfulness of the Message

"The Principle of Truthfulness requires the persuader's intention not to deceive, the intention to provide others with the truthful information they legitimately need to make good decisions about their lives."[23] Among the considerations are:

- The communication should be factually accurate. It should not be deceptive in any way. It should present a complete picture and avoid communicating only part of a message, especially if omissions are intended to deceive.
- No false impressions should be communicated by the use of selective information.
- No information should be withheld that is needed by the audience in order for them to make an informed decision, especially if the omission of this information results in harm.

Authenticity of the Persuader

This has to do with the integrity, personal virtue, motivation, commitment to principle, and moral independence of the persuader. Among the considerations are:

- The action, or communication, should conform to the highest principles and personal convictions, and should arise from noble intentions. As Kant said, it should be done out of a sense of good will, not out of vested interest. The intent of the act should promote the well-being of everyone potentially affected. This means that loyalties need to be appropriately balanced.
- Persuasive communication, especially advocacy, should reflect the personal beliefs of the persuader. If you would be ashamed to be revealed as a participant in a persuasive campaign, then you shouldn't be doing it.

Respect for Those Being Persuaded

This principle requires that no one's autonomy be violated. Your audience must be free to make their own decisions, based on truthful and complete information. Among the considerations are:

- Persuasive messages should appeal to the higher natures of people, not pander, exploit, or appeal to their baser inclinations.
- Messages should exhibit a sense of caring for those being communicated to.

Equity of the Persuasive Appeal

This principles requires a "parity between the persuader and persuadee in terms of information, understanding, insight, capacity, and experience, or that accommodations be made to adjust equitably for the disparities and to level the playing field."[24] Among the considerations are:

- The persuasive act should be fairly carried out and should be just and equitable for all concerned. If there is a lack of understanding among any of your audiences, you should clarify and educate in order to reduce confusion.

- Vulnerable audiences should never be targeted with messages that are designed to exploit that vulnerability.
- All arguments should allow for reflection and counterargument.
- It should be clear to everyone that persuasion is being attempted. Persuasive activities should never masquerade as information-only campaigns.

Social Responsibility

This principle recognizes the professional obligation to act in the public interest and to balance loyalties among claimants. Among the considerations are:

- Any persuasive action should be responsible to society and to the public interest by working to improve life within the social realm.
- Potential harms that may result from the communication should be recognized and eliminated or reduced.
- Understanding should be promoted among all publics involved in the issue.

A Kantian Approach

Shannon Bowen suggests an approach to public relations ethics, specifically within organizations, that is based solidly on Kantian philosophy, especially his notion of autonomy and respect for persons.[25] Her model proceeds through several phases.

- *Phase 1* is issue identification, in which the PR practitioner must determine the importance of the issue. Typically, only complex issues move through the succeeding phases. Smaller issues are usually handled immediately, but can benefit from the complete process.
- *Phase 2* involves issues managers meeting in teams to discuss the issue, collect more information and research, or bring in experts to help analyze the issue. This is the point at which alternatives are discussed. It is also the first point at which ethical dimensions are considered. Because this theory is rules-based (deontological), it asks the decision makers to "do what is right" based on their duty to universal norms—usually concepts of fairness and rights.
- *Phase 3* engages the Kantian "law of autonomy," which refers to the moral conscience of the decision makers and reminds them not to submit to undue pressure from other organizational functions. It also allows decision makers to act according to their moral duties "without fear of harmful repercussions."[26] Each decision maker should be allowed to express himself freely, and that expression should be respected by the others involved in the decision. This argues strongly for an autonomous public relations function within organizations. This phase also requires us to ask if we are acting on

the basis of reason alone and not because of political influence, monetary influence, or pure self-interest.

- *Phase 4* applies the Categorical Imperative and asks questions such as "Could we obligate everyone else who is ever in a similar situation to do the same thing we are considering?" or "Would I accept this decision if I were on the receiving end?"[27]

- *Phase 5* asks the organization to consider its duty, its intention, and dignity and respect for the organization, publics, and society. This would imply a willingness to be open to the input of all stakeholders, and it would validate the Kantian notion of acting out of a good will. It asks the question, "Does this decision make us worthy of earning trust, respect, and support from our publics?"[28] "Publics and stakeholders are more likely to be satisfied with a decision when the intent of the organization toward them is based on a good will rather than when other interests taint it."[29]

- *Phase 6* calls for symmetrical communication about the results of the decision-making process. This approach works well in conjunction with phase 5 in that it allows for ongoing communication and contributions to the process by all parties.

Dialogue as the Ethical Component

The public relations ethics scholar Ron Pearson has developed a theory of public relations ethics based on the ideal communication situation as dialogue.[30] Pearson suggests that "establishing and maintaining dialogical communication between a business organization and its publics is a precondition for ethical business practices."[31] Both Pearson and Carl Botan[32] were among the early advocates for moving toward a dialogic, relational manager model of public relations. Botan summarizes their view as follows:

> A dialogic view of public relations . . . [is] humanistic, communication-centered, relationship-focused, and ethical. This perspective focuses on communicative relationships rather than on technical skills. Traditional approaches to public relations relegate publics to a secondary role, making them an instrument for meeting organizational policy or marketing needs; whereas, dialogue elevates publics to the status of communication equal with the organization.[33]

Pearson argues that organizations have a moral duty to engage in dialogue. He proposes two rules (using the Kantian "imperative" format) of ethical public relations:

- It is a moral imperative to establish and maintain communication relationships with all publics affected by organizational action.
- It is a moral imperative to improve the quality of these communication

relationships, that is, to make them increasingly dialogical (two-way symmetrical).[34]

The first of these rules essentially specifies that it is necessary for an organization to take consequences on publics into account when it makes strategic decisions. The second states that organizations have the moral obligation to communicate with those publics even though the organization cannot always accommodate the public.

James Grunig and Larissa Grunig included Pearson's obligation of dialogue in their discussion of ethics, using symmetry as a way of satisfying that obligation. Recall the earlier discussion of Grunig's model of two-way symmetric communication. They have translated Pearson's two moral imperatives into an ethical theory of public relations that incorporates both a consequential and a duty-based perspective:[35]

- *Consequential*: Ethical public relations professionals ask what consequences potential organizational decisions have on publics.
- *Duty-based*: Ethical public relations professionals then have the moral obligation to disclose these consequences to publics that are affected and to engage in dialogue with the publics about the potential decisions.

A Virtue Ethics Approach

Karey Harrison and Chris Galloway, Australian theorists, suggest a virtue-based approach to dealing with the complexities of public relations ethics.[36] They contend that simply having a practicable ethical model, such as an ethics code, to apply to decision making won't insure good ethical decisions. Rather, they propose that the virtue, or character, of the moral agent is more important. They believe that the environment in which public relations operates is often "murky" and this murkiness leads to moral confusion all around. Following on Aristotle's theory of virtue, they suggest that virtuous action results in a good feeling for the moral agent and, thus, becomes desirable over time. Moreover, the person of virtue values the intrinsic worth of right action (i.e., virtue is its own reward); whereas the person who lacks virtue might feel discomfort in being forced into right action, or even see no harm in avoiding it.[37] Achieving excellence in a practice, such as public relations, means doing something good for its own sake, and requires and develops the virtues of justice, honesty, and courage. They cite MacIntyre's requirements of these virtues:[38]

Justice demands that we:

- recognize the skills, knowledge, and expertise of other practitioners; and
- learn from those who know more and have greater experience than we do.

Courage requires that we:

- take self-endangering risks;
- push ourselves to the limits of our capacities; and
- be prepared to challenge existing practice in the interest of extending the practice, despite institutional pressures against such critique.

Honesty asks us to:

- be able to accept criticism; and
- learn from our errors and mistakes.

In order for individual virtues to be realized, the organization in which the individual works must develop an environment conducive to the development of good character—much in the way Aristotle suggested that the best form of government was one that would do the same. In order to actualize these virtues, the focus of right actions should be the public interest.

> If excellence and virtue are related to community, as Aristotle suggests, then public relations' chief internal good is its contribution to maintaining and enhancing the community's health. This may be the health of the community in the sense of everyone who lives in a particular place, or the firm as a community through facilitating mutual adjustment and adaptation between organisations [sic] and their publics.[39]

If this sounds a bit too idealistic, then, at the very least, "public relations practitioners may participate in and contribute to the internal good of organisations they choose to work for, as long at the organisation's focus is on doing something that is good for its own sake."[40]

Special Issues in Public Relations Ethics

As with all those who work in the mass media, those who practice public relations will encounter ethical dilemmas unique to their chosen profession. Although there are certainly similarities among the media requiring that some issues, such as truth telling, be dealt with in a similar fashion, there are also differences in objectives and the approaches used to achieve those objectives that will incur unique ethical responses. Some of the most common of those are listed here.

Conflict of Interest

Conflict of interest cuts across the media professions, but is especially important in public relations. Basically, a conflict of interest occurs when a professional has interests, usually either professional or personal, that come into conflict with another obligation. This is usually considered as affecting the professional's impartiality. For example, a public relations firm attempts to take on two competing clients—perhaps two cell-phone companies. The question each of those companies is going to ask is whether the PR firm can possibly devote its full energy to pursuing their individual client's interests and maintain the confidentiality level required between the competing companies. If you were the CEO of company X and you found out that your public relations agency was courting a competitor, company Y, wouldn't you be concerned?

Types of Conflict of Interest

What's most troublesome about conflict of interest is that even the appearance of it can cause concern, and a conflict could possibly exist even if no improper or unethical acts result from it. There are a number of manifestations of conflict of interest, mostly having to do with a conflict of roles or a problem sorting obligations among claimants.

- A situation in which public and private interests conflict. For example, a PR professional working in a firm is required to take on a client account for a company he knows to be a notorious polluter. Perhaps the PR person is environmentally aware. His personal beliefs come into conflict with his obligation to serve the client.
- A situation in which outside employment may be in conflict with the primary occupation. In the example above, perhaps the PR professional also volunteers for a local environmental group. What then? Whose interests is he supposed to serve?
- A situation in which personal interests, such as family, come into play. For example, a public relations practitioner working for a corporation is asked to job out the monthly newsletter to a freelancer. It happens that her spouse is one of the best newsletter editors in town and makes a good living producing a number of corporate newsletters. Should he be denied the opportunity to bid on the job just because he's married to the person making the decision?
- A situation in which a professional receives compensation beyond salary for work either performed or to be performed. All media professionals need to be aware of the potential pitfalls of taking extracurricular "gifts" from clients. For example, a PR practitioner receives a free golf vacation from a client who owns a resort in Palm Springs. He is already being paid by his firm to handle the client's business, and this trip isn't necessary to the completion of his job in a professional manner. Should he accept it?

Ways to Mitigate Conflicts of Interests

The best way to handle conflicts of interest is to avoid them entirely—even the appearance of a conflict. Short of avoiding conflicts of interest, there are several other common ways to deal with conflicts of interest:

- *Disclosure:* Professionals are often required either by rules related to their professional organization, or by legal statute, to disclose an actual or potential conflict of interest. In some instances, the failure to provide full disclosure is a crime (in medicine and the law, for example). In financial public relations, for instance, violations of conflicts of interest over stock transactions are governed by the Securities and Exchange Commission and carry legal penalties.
- *Recusal:* Those with a conflict of interest are expected to recuse themselves (abstain) from decisions where such a conflict exists. Sometimes this is written into the code itself as a guideline or, at the very least, covered as a caution with examples explaining typical potential violations (see below).
- *Codes of ethics:* Generally, codes of ethics forbid conflicts of interest. Codes help to minimize problems with conflicts of interest because they can spell out the extent to which such conflicts should be avoided, and what the parties should do where such conflicts are permitted by a code of ethics (disclosure, recusal, etc.). Thus, professionals cannot claim that they were unaware that their improper behavior was unethical. As important is the threat of disciplinary action to minimize unacceptable conflicts or improper acts when a conflict is unavoidable.

Many codes have self-policing mechanisms; however, this too may be cited as a potential conflict of interest because it often results only in eliminating the appearance of the conflict rather than the actual offense. Such internal mechanisms often serve to hide the conflict of interest from public view.

PRSA's Take on Conflict of Interest

The Public Relations Society of America's "Member Statement of Professional Values" covers the subject this way:

Core Principle

Avoiding real, potential or perceived conflicts of interest builds the trust of clients, employers, and the publics.

Intent

- To earn trust and mutual respect with clients or employers.
- To build trust with the public by avoiding or ending situations that put one's personal or professional interests in conflict with society's interests.

Guidelines

A member shall:
- Act in the best interests of the client or employer, even subordinating the member's personal interests.

- Avoid actions and circumstances that may appear to compromise good business judgment or create a conflict between personal and professional interests.
- Disclose promptly any existing or potential conflict of interest to affected clients or organizations.
- Encourage clients and customers to determine if a conflict exists after notifying all affected parties.

Examples of Improper Conduct Under This Provision

- The member fails to disclose that he or she has a strong financial interest in a client's chief competitor.
- The member represents a "competitor company" or a "conflicting interest" without informing a prospective client.

In summary, conflict of interest, whether real or imagined, is a problem. Because public relations, to a great degree, is the business of image making and maintaining, it seems logical that appearances would be extremely important. It might be wise to follow the advice of Paul's letter to the Thessalonian Christians: "Abstain from all appearance of evil."

Withholding Information

Selective communication is morally suspect when it is intended to mislead or when it is used to conceal information that others need to make their own life decisions. Yet, not everything that is known, believed, or communicated within an organization needs to be made public.[41]

When is withholding information unethical? For example, journalists who do not present clear context may, unintentionally, be omitting information vital to understanding. Certainly, if this omission is unintentional, then the outcome can be said to be potentially harmful but the action not necessarily unethical. Remember, as many philosophers have pointed out, intent is vital to determining the ethicality of an act. Thus, when information is withheld, we need to determine the reason before we can condemn the act as unethical.

Advertisers and public relations professionals have long been accused of presenting information that is incomplete; and, as we have already discussed, that is not necessarily unethical because, by nature, both of these practices are supposed to be biased in favor of the client. No one expects an advertisement, for example, to include every detail of a product or its potential uses (although multiplying the uses of a product is usually a good thing. Think of Arm & Hammer baking soda. Who knew you could put it in your refrigerator to dispel odors?). However, the recent laws regarding the advertising of pharmaceuticals reflects the growing concern with advertisers leaving out information vital to understanding the whole range of a product's potential effects. No prescription pharmaceutical may be advertised as having a specific positive effect unless it is accompanied by information concerning its negative side effects. The result has been commercials that are sometimes ludicrous in their happy-voiced disclaimers that, although the product may relieve your allergy symptoms, it may also cause nausea and vomiting.

And think of the countless times a political candidate's omissions of wrongdoing have been "found out" by the press despite an army of news secretaries painting an opposite image. Or the corporate PR people who routinely cover for mistakes and misdeeds. What were the PR people at Enron thinking while their company was going to pieces before their eyes? Did the public relations agencies for such companies as Enron and Firestone simply buy into their clients' lines of a solid investment or a safe product? When we think of company executives lying about their products or the value of their stock, where do we place their spokespeople in the hierarchy of deception? Surely, there has to be some culpability on the part of their media representatives. However, as stated throughout this book, it is not always easy to know every detail about a client or that client's product or company, and those gaps in knowledge may, ultimately, have disastrous consequences. At the very least, a PR firm's reputation may suffer during and following such disclosures.

There are times, however, when withholding information may be thought of as *not* unethical. As discussed in Chapter 3, consulting professionals generally maintain client confidentiality in order to defend them from competitors. Not everything needs to be made public. A company's research and development projects are clearly in this category, as are their plans to go public with their stock offerings (a position dictated by the Securities and Exchange Commission), potential expansion projects, or a myriad other "secrets" that ensure the privacy so needed in industries in which competition is high. Where, however, do we draw the line? When does discretion need to become disclosure?

The ethicist Michael Bayles delineates instances when breaching confidentiality (disclosing rather than withholding information) is usually thought to be ethical. He lists three kinds of reasons that can be given for a professional violating confidentiality: the best interests of (1) the client, (2) the professional, or (3) other persons.[42] Bayles considers disclosure in the best interest of the client to be rare and unadvisable since this could lead to a paternalistic stance rather than the ideal fiduciary position between client and professional.

Confidence can be breached, however, in the best interest of the professional in two kinds of situations: "when it is necessary for professionals (1) to collect a just fee or (2) to defend themselves against a charge of wrongdoing."[43] For our purposes, the second is the more important. Bayles suggests that clients will typically not wish to have information disclosed that might show they have done something wrong. The onus of correcting the wrongdoing is, then, placed squarely on the professional in order to prevent harm to innocent third parties, which, concomitantly, injures the professional's reputation and credibility. For this reason, many in both advertising and public relations require disclaimers in their contracts that absolve them of blame should a client lie about a wrongdoing causing that lie to be passed along by the professional representative.

In the third instance, Bayles suggests identifying and weighing the values and interests of the client against those of affected third parties to arrive at a rule that can, then, be used in similar circumstances in the future. Further, all professionals may disclose confidential information to prevent illegal conduct.[44]

The somewhat tricky relationship between client and professional makes the decision to violate confidentiality a serious one. This step should be taken only when it is clear that:

1 the client has violated the law;
2 the client has done something that would harm the reputation and credibility of the professional; or
3 the client has done or plans to do something that will harm innocent third parties.

As we discussed in Chapter 6, avoiding harm is one of the primary obligations of the media professional. This is especially true of advertising and public relations because of their tendency toward client loyalty.

The PRSA's Take on Disclosing Information

Core Principle

Open communication fosters informed decision making in a democratic society.

Intent

To build trust with the public by revealing all information needed for responsible decision making.

Guidelines

A member shall:
- Be honest and accurate in all communications.
- Act promptly to correct erroneous communications for which the member is responsible.
- Investigate the truthfulness and accuracy of information released on behalf of those represented.
- Reveal the sponsors for causes and interests represented.
- Disclose financial interest (such as stock ownership) in a client's organization.
- Avoid deceptive practices.

Examples of Improper Conduct Under this Provision:

- Front groups: A member implements "grass roots" campaigns or letter-writing campaigns to legislators on behalf of undisclosed interest groups.
- Lying by omission: A practitioner for a corporation knowingly fails to release financial information, giving a misleading impression of the corporation's performance.
- A member discovers inaccurate information disseminated via a Web site or media kit and does not correct the information.
- A member deceives the public by employing people to pose as volunteers to speak at public hearings and participate in "grass roots" campaigns. [This will be discussed in more detail below under "new media."]

Corporate Social Responsibility (CSR)

Corporate social responsibility (CSR) is the latest concept in a long line of philosophies aimed at ensuring that companies and corporations accept the notion of being responsible to society beyond merely providing goods or services that benefit the public on a functional level. As pointed out in Chapter 2, social responsibility, at its most basic level, is about ensuring that what a company produces is useful to those for whom it is produced. Beyond that, however, there has always been an underlying belief that organizations should also act in a responsible manner in other areas, such as environmental stewardship, safety issues, and philanthropy. In the last decade or so, a movement has been afoot defining more broadly the level of responsibility expected of corporations in areas beyond those already noted, as well as an increased emphasis on ethics.

According to one of the many groups now consulting with organizations on how to adopt a CSR approach,

> Corporate social responsibility (CSR) is about how businesses align their values and behaviour [sic] with the expectations and needs of stakeholders— not just customers and investors, but also employees, suppliers, communities, regulators, special interest groups and society as a whole. CSR describes a company's commitment to be accountable to its stakeholders.
>
> CSR demands that businesses manage the economic, social and environmental impacts of their operations to maximise the benefits and minimise the downsides.[45]

Put more broadly, CSR

> generally refers to transparent business practices that are based on ethical values, compliance with legal requirements, and respect for people, communities, and the environment. Thus, beyond making profits, com-

panies are responsible for the totality of their impact on people and the planet.[46]

Or, as the executive vice president for Ogilvy Public Relations Worldwide puts it, "CSR is about one thing: that regardless of whether or not people are consumers of a given company's goods or services, they should benefit, ideally, from the very existence of the company. They certainly should not suffer from it."[47]

In a working paper from the John F. Kennedy School of Government at Harvard University, Jane Nelson, Senior Fellow and Director, argues that public trust in business has been undermined by corporate scandals and the perceived rise in power in the private (corporate) sector.[48] As anyone in public relations will tell you, actions speak louder than words. This has been true for a very long time. The poet Ralph Waldo Emerson once remarked, "What you are stands over you the while, and thunders so that I cannot hear what you say to the contrary."[49] The "bottom line" of CSR is about action, not so much about words. The big question plaguing CSR is whether it really is a movement dedicated to social change and welfare, or merely more of the same "PR."

Critics of CSR have suggested that it is virtually impossible to engender social good while enhancing the bottom line. A Stanford University report states bluntly that companies trumpeting CSR are sometimes the same companies engaging in activities that could be said to be less than honorable.[50] For example, Wal-Mart's success in the marketplace belies the fact that the company has continuously been sued over poor labor practices.[51] On the opposite side of the coin, Costco's employee benefits package is apparently seen as a bit too beneficial by its own shareholders, who are pressuring the chain to cut it in order to be more competitive with Wal-Mart. In other words, some have argued that the demands of the stock market provide a *disincentive* for doing too much social good. "When shareholders interests dominate the corporate machine, outcomes may become even less aligned to the public good."[52]

CSR and "Greenwashing"

Other criticisms cover the various methods sometimes used by corporations to affect a CSR attitude without actually engaging in CSR. The most recent example of this is called "greenwashing." Essentially, greenwashing is the act of literally pretending to be an environmentally friendly organization or of producing products or services beneficial to the environment. Sharon Bader, an Australian academic and expert on science and technology, says that "Greenwashing, Greenscamming and Greenspeak are all different terms for public relations efforts to portray an organisation [sic], activity or product as environmentally friendly."[53] The term relates primarily to environmental issues (which, if dealt with properly, are by definition a form of CSR), and is thus relevant both to public relations and to advertising. Speaking specifically of greenwashing, Sheldon Rampton, research director for the Center for Media and Democracy (a media watchdog organization) writes of a "degraded information environment" in which some corporations intentionally put up green fronts while continuing to practice the opposite. Rampton calls greenwashing "ultimately an attempt to obscure awareness of environmental pollution by polluting language and thought itself in an attempt to stop people from thinking clearly about the issues they face."[54]

> The attempt to provide a "green" and caring image for a corporation is a public relations strategy aimed at promising reform and heading off demands for more substantial and fundamental changes and government intervention. Public relations experts advise how to counter the negative perceptions of business, caused in most cases by their poor environmental performance. Rather than substantially change business practices so as to earn a better reputation many firms are turning to PR professionals to create one for them. This is cheaper and easier than making the substantial changes required to become more environmentally friendly.[55]

Although there are a great many companies that are practicing legitimate environmental stewardship both as part of CSR and more directly through their products and services, the fear among critics is that (1) the incentive is more bottom line than altruistic and (2) some are paying only lip service to it with small but splashy public relations and advertising campaigns. In public relations theory, this technique is sometimes called *hedging and wedging*. The theory, originally developed by Keith Stamm and James Grunig, plays off the notion that public relations programs are often used to change attitudes, usually from negative to positive. As we already know from cognitive dissonance theory, people tend to ignore information they don't already agree with, so someone who holds a negative opinion of a company (say, for its poor labor practices) is not likely to attend to any positive spin concerning the issue, especially if it issues from the organization itself. However, if this same person holds no opinion of the company's environmental practices, its public relations effort might try refocusing attention on a potentially positive aspect of the company's practice, which, in turn, might distract from the negative aspect caused by its other practices.

According to the theory of hedging and wedging, human beings are completely capable of holding conflicting opinions, so when a person holds a "wedged" (firmly held) view and is confronted with a contrary view, he or she may then "hedge" his or her views. This is a cognitive strategy, usually completely subconscious, that prevents dissonance. Knowing this, a retail chain that has developed a poor reputation for labor practices might be able to divert attention somewhat by developing a "green" strategy not related to its labor practices. People who are concerned about its labor practices might, simultaneously, applaud the company's efforts on the environmental front. If the company's positive practices gain enough attention, the negative opinion might eventually be pushed out or, at the very least, mitigated.

Although not all companies are using this approach when they become environmentally aware, there are some that do—so many, in fact, that a number of watchdog groups have sprung up to identify them. In addition to the ones already mentioned here, notable is Enviromedia's *Greenwashing Index*. Enviromedia Social Marketing is a Texas-based corporation that consults with clients on how to make their environmental efforts truly green. Its sponsored web site asks consumers of media to report on greenwashing attempts and to post them online, thus making even more consumers aware of the real versus the fake.[56]

Where Does Public Relations Fit In?

The corporate consultant Zena James says that "[T]he danger . . . is in paying lip service to CSR or 'using' it in a way that is not transparent. Badly thought through CSR practice will inevitably destroy trust, erode goodwill and damage reputation."[57] According to James, the role of public relations is to keep everyone informed throughout the process. Her key points, as relate to our discussion, are:

- Help the organization demonstrate its fundamental approach to CSR (which should include transparency and accountability).
- Ensure that efforts are not misinterpreted as tokenism or a part of marketing.
- Make sensible use of existing internal and external communications tools to substantiate the organization's commitment, to create dialogue, to respond to concerns, and to demonstrate direction.

Further, there are several important questions to be answered concerning the role of public relations in CSR. First, how much does a public relations/marketing plan relate to the reality of what the company actually practices? Second, if public relations plays a part in CSR, what, if any, are the ethical pitfalls of doing so? In order for public relations to be accountable either for the praise garnered from successful CSR or for its failure, it must be seen as somehow responsible. If we follow the model proposed by James Grunig—public relations as the corporate conscience—then it is either directly responsible for suggesting CSR as the high road to corporate good deeds or accountable for not doing so. However, if we view public relations as but one of many corporate mechanisms for managing communication, then we must investigate the intent behind the messages and the methods used to impart them, including messages about CSR. As stressed throughout this chapter, the obligations of public relations professionals are not only functional but also moral, and on that front we have a lot of guidance.

The Ethical Bottom Line for CSR

Ethically responsible public relations professionals will reject the notion of making claims that are either completely false or even somewhat misleading. To avoid real issues while focusing on distractions is decidedly not ethical. It is a form of deception. Public relations is in a unique position within most organizations in that it has a broader view of issues than most other entities. It needs to be informed in order to inform others. In discharging its obligation to the consumers of its messages, it must not engage in deception of any kind, even if it benefits its own client or organization. Thus, corporate social responsibility messages must accurately reflect the reality of the activities they are supposed to represent. If they do not, they are misleading. And, if these attempts are merely window dressing designed to distract from more complex and potentially problematic conversations, then they are also misleading. It may be true that a company is observing some form of environmental concern. It may also be true the same company is price gouging or treating its employees poorly. One does not offset the other. Good deeds should be recognized. Bad deeds should be redressed. It is the moral obligation of public relations professionals to recognize reality and to reflect it accurately in everything they do.

Public Relations Ethics and the "New" Media

The introduction of new methods of disseminating information and persuading audiences are changing the landscape of media ethics. Most, but not all, of these "new" media are computer-generated or computer-assisted. The allure of a democratized media has resulted in an internet presence that is both gratifying and alarming. According to a long-time web-content guru, Gerry McGovern,

> Traditionally, public relations was about honing a silvery message that communicated exactly what the organization wanted us to hear. Now, we can hear all sorts of voices on the subject. It's true democracy at work.[58]

Virtually anyone with access to a computer (or a device that can be linked to the internet) can voice his or her opinion instantaneously, and to millions of people. As you might imagine, this ease of transmission has great potential for abuse. As Aristotle pointed out in response to the argument that his rhetorical guidelines for persuasion could be used for evil ends, the ultimate use of any tool is up to the person who uses it. So it is with the new media. The most important thing to remember is that all of the approaches to ethical communication apply to the new forms as well. A hidden agenda on a blog site is still a hidden agenda. The rules for ethical persuasion still count, no matter the format in which the persuasion appears.

Public Relations and the Internet

Recent changes in technology have allowed organizations to reach out to their constituencies in ways never before imaginable. The computer has not only spawned word processing and desktop publishing, but also allowed us to reconfigure our communications and our modes of delivery. Additionally, technology has expanded the scope of both internal and external communications beyond that of traditional media. The role of everything from the news release to the corporate magazine has been broadened by the ability to make what was once a static delivery system now interactive. There are a number of relatively new methods for getting a public relations message out over the internet, including intranets, web sites, weblogs (blogs), web seminars (webinars), online newsletters, and podcasts. All have great potential for clarifying information and for persuading audiences. They also are burdened with predictable pitfalls—most, simply new versions of old evils. We are going to concentrate here on blogging, but it is indicative of the types of ethical problems associated with much of the new media.

Blogging—The Need for Transparency

Blogging is a relatively new phenomenon which has managed to catch on very quickly. In what is known as *conventional blogging*, anyone can write anything they want any time. It has become a haven for the verbose, highly opinionated, and often uninformed. Obviously, this is not what blogging in public relations should represent. The key difference is that PR people don't represent themselves. They represent their clients and/or organizations. In addition, public relations messages have to be economical and to the point, and, above all, accurate.

Blogging can be a less formal way of keeping people informed than many other media options. It's a low-cost publishing tool that has the advantage of being able to get company news out quickly. Unlike email, blogging is literally "broadcast" simultaneously to anyone who wants to read it. It is also egalitarian in a way that much of public relations communication is not. Blogs allow for instant responses, multiple conversation threads, and a sort of accessible history of issues that can be referenced, added to, and corrected at any time. However, there are disadvantages.

- Most people don't have very much to say that's interesting or the ability to write down their ideas in a compelling and clear manner.
- [It's often true] that the people who have most time to write have least to say, and the people who have most to say don't have enough time to write it. Thus, the real expertise within the organization lays hidden, as you get drowned in trivia.
- Organizations are not democracies. The Web makes many organizations look like disorganizations, with multiple tones and opinions. Contrary to what some might think, the average customer prefers it if the organization they are about to purchase from is at least somewhat coherent.[59]

Blogging is a perfect example, then, of both the benefits and the potential problems often inherent in public relations communication. In addition to the functional disadvantages of blogging, there are several ethical problems that can arise in relation to this new form of communication.

For example, one of the major disadvantages of blogs not mentioned above is the tendency to want to respond immediately to queries and comments posted by other people. This often leads to not very well thought-out responses, which, for public relations professionals, is not a good approach to communicating with publics. Moral decision making requires a certain degree of reflection—time in which to consider the ethical ramifications of your actions. Immediate responses, by nature, are not reflective. But perhaps the most troublesome aspect of blogging, and with many of the new technologies now used in public relations, is the lure of anonymity.

What is Anonymity?

To be anonymous is to present yourself or your opinion publicly without disclosing your true identity. Historically, there have been many good reasons for people to remain anonymous. In societies in which free expression is limited, anti-government positions have often been stated publicly by anonymous writers in order to protect themselves from harm. Benjamin Franklin used anonymity under various pseudonyms to poke fun at both people and institutions, with the serious aim of improving society. Anonymity, in this sense, has been a mainstay of democracy in the United States since its founding. The Federalist Papers, which argued for ratification of the U.S. Constitution at a time in which it was being hotly debated, were written by James Madison, John Jay, and Alexander Hamilton, but under the joint assumed name of *Publius*. This anonymity allowed them to express more openly their views without fear of censorship or retribution. In an important 1995 Supreme Court decision, the Court held that:

> Protections for anonymous speech are vital to democratic discourse. Allowing dissenters to shield their identities frees them to express critical, minority views . . . Anonymity is a shield from the tyranny of the majority . . . It thus exemplifies the purpose behind the Bill of Rights, and of the First Amendment in particular: to protect unpopular individuals from retaliation . . . at the hand of an intolerant society.[60]

In other words, following on the writings of John Stuart Mill, a democratic society can often be as intolerant of minority opinion as an authoritarian one, but in a democracy it is incumbent upon the people to allow for such opinion. In the marketplace theory of free speech, all information is welcomed—even if it is presented anonymously. However (and this is a big "however"), anonymity also allows for abuses without accountability. It is easy to say something that others find objectionable when you cannot be held accountable for your words. More importantly, it complicates the issue of credibility.

For example, suppose you read some information online suggesting that a local politician has been having a sexual relationship with a married man. The information has been posted anonymously on a blog site you frequent. How do you know the information is legitimate? How can you evaluate the reliability of the information without knowing the credibility of the source? Or the motivation of the source? Remember that Kant said the only moral act was one done from a good will—that intention was everything. Recall the Elaboration Likelihood Model discussed earlier. Those tending to decipher persuasive attempts cognitively will always ask about source credibility, seeking to know the source of the information in order to determine the expertise and, even more importantly, the motivation of the sender of the message. Those using the peripheral route will often accept ideas they already agree with or simply be convinced by cues, such as *seeming* expertise on a subject, without necessarily considering motivation. We are often convinced by a seemingly well-constructed argument, especially if we don't stop to consider the motivation behind it.

What is Transparency?

Being transparent in public relations (or any form of public communication) means that both your identity and your motivation are apparent to those whom you are trying to persuade. The media ethics scholar Patrick Plaisance suggests that "Transparent interaction is what allows us as rational, autonomous beings to assess each other's behavior. Our motivations, aspirations, and intents are fully set forth for examination."[61]

> [C]ommunication is based on the notion of honest exchange. This norm of forthrightness, or being "aboveboard," is what is known as being transparent. And society would not be possible if we did not place a premium on the spirit of openness, or transparent behavior.[62]

Using a Kantian approach, Plaisance points out that communication that is intentionally opaque as regards the sender's identity and motive manifestly disrespects the humanity and autonomy of the receiver. In other words, the receiver is being used as a means to an end. Transparency in media communication, or in all communication for that matter, is the mainstay of human interaction. It is the mortar that binds us to each other in mutual respect.

> [T]ransparent behavior can be defined as conduct that presumes an openness in communication and serves a reasonable expectation of forthright exchange when parties have a legitimate stake in the possible outcomes or effects of the communicative act. It is an attitude of proactive moral engagement that manifests an express concern for the persons-as-ends principle

when a degree of deception or omission can reasonably be said to risk thwarting the receiver's due dignity or the ability to exercise reason.[63]

In a practical sense, transparency in public relations means being up front with your identity as a PR professional and with the identity of those whom you represent. However, in order to avoid the automatic defense mechanism that most of us employ against a persuader's vested interest, some in both public relations and advertising are moving into an old use of new media—the anonymous identity, or, worse yet, the fabricated identity.

THE WHOLE FOODS CASE

For six years, John Mackey, the CEO and co-founder of Whole Foods, a nationwide organic grocery chain, appeared as a regular blog poster on *Yahoo Finance* stock forums.[64] During that time, he posted dozens of negative attacks on his company's biggest competitor, Wild Oats. He questioned their corporate structure, verbally berated their management, and generally denigrated the value of their stock, often suggesting it was overpriced. At the same time, he praised his own company, its management, and even predicted its success in the stock market. On the face of it, this would appear, at worst, an unseemly display of corporate precociousness. The catch was, he was posting anonymously. He used the pseudonym Rahodeb (an anagram of his wife's name, Deborah) and hid behind the mask of anonymity to bash his competition.

His vehemence eventually began to attract attention. When questioned by other bloggers, he steadfastly asserted his innocence as just another anonymous poster. Once it became clear who he really was, the Federal Trade Commission published some of his online comments in an anti-trust suit filed against Whole Foods in its bid to take over Wild Oats. Mackey maintains that he was simply acting as a private citizen, and has a right to do so. While his anonymous postings were being written, he simultaneously maintained regular postings under his real name on the Whole Foods blog site. Although he denied it, many believe that this was all part of a larger, and intentional, corporate strategy to lower the value of Wild Oats so that a buyout would be easier and cheaper.

The question for us is whether this type of deception is ethically acceptable; to answer that, we need simply to question motivation. The discussion of conflict of interest earlier is also applicable here. When someone argues a point of view from a vested interest (they can benefit from the decision they promote) we naturally suspect them. When they do so from a position of anonymity, and with a sense of expertise, we are left not knowing whether to question their motivations or not.

Would we have been more suspicious of John Mackey's arguments condemning his competitor had he been open about his identity? Probably. We would have realized he had a very vested interest in trashing his competitor and would have taken his comments with a huge grain of salt. In other words, our defenses would have gone up immediately. Recall that ethical persuasion requires that the person being persuaded have all the facts she needs to reflect critically on a situation and make an informed decision. That includes the identity of the persuader and his motivation. Without that complete information, we are being effectively deceived.

GOVERNMENT PR POSES AS NEWS

In 2004, a number of news organizations reported that federal investigators were looking into television segments in which the Bush administration had paid people to pose as journalists.[65] Their segments included praise for the new Medicare law, especially its prescription drug benefits, which had been highly controversial. Several of the segments included pictures of President Bush receiving a standing ovation from a crowd as he signed the new Medicare bill into law.

These taped "news" segments were actually produced by the Department of Health and Human Services and intended for use by local television stations, who often have difficulty filling news holes with local-only stories. This type of product is typically called a video news release (VNR) and should have been labeled as such by the company who produced them, along with the name of the company and its client. In fact, the sources of these "news" segments were not identified, and two of the videos ended with reporter-like sign offs—"In Washington, I'm Karen Ryan reporting." As it turned out, the "reporter" was a hired actor paid to read a script prepared by the government.

In addition to the unlabeled VNRs, a script accompanied the tapes that could be used by local news anchors to introduce what the administration later described as a "story package." One such script suggested that anchors use this language:

> In December, President Bush signed into law the first-ever prescription drug benefit for people with Medicare. Since then, there have been a lot of questions about how the law will help older Americans and people with disabilities. Reporter Karen Ryan helps sort through the details.

Lawyers from the General Accounting Office reported to Congress that the television news segments were a legal, and effective, way of educating the public on this new Medicare law—despite their admission that the source of this information campaign was intentionally omitted and the "reporters" had been paid actors. And, even though federal law prohibits the use of federal money for "publicity or propaganda purposes" not authorized by Congress, the Department of Health and Human Services suggested there was nothing wrong with their approach to disseminating this information. Their spokesperson went on record as saying, "The use of video news releases is a common, routine practice in government and the private sector. Anyone who has questions about this practice needs to do some research on modern public information tools."

In fact, VNRs have been used for years to promote both products and ideas. Pharmaceutical companies, especially, have used them to promote their products by placing them within a narrative framework, or human interest environment. These short segments (usually "feature-length," 90 seconds to three minutes) are easily sandwiched into local news programs to fill empty news holes. As more local stations cut newsgathering budgets in the late 1980s, the use of VNRs became more prominent. The real problem was that the sponsors, and the producers, of the segments were not always mentioned, giving the false impression that these were either locally produced, legitimate news segments, or nationally produced segments "shared" with the local station.

Although it may be perfectly legal to produce and to run VNRs without citing the source, it violates the ethical requirement of transparency, thus it violates the trust relationship between the public and its information sources. This violation occurs at several levels. First, any public relations firm that produces VNRs for a client is morally obligated to make it clear that it is a video "news release" and indicate who the client is. Without this information, we are left either to question the credibility of the piece (especially if we are central-route processors), or simply to accept it as legitimate news based mostly on its news-like presentation (peripheral-route processors). In either event, we are cheated out of information vital to our understanding of the issue and to our subsequent decision-making ability.

It is important to note, however, that the onus of disclosure doesn't rest solely with the public relations firm originating the VNR. It is shared by the news organization that runs it. It is incumbent on local news stations to reveal the sources of their stories. News directors must distinguish between news and public relations, both for themselves and for their audiences. Their integrity is as much at stake as that of the PR people who produced the information in the first place. It is certain that much of the information generated by public relations professionals is newsworthy; however, astute journalists need to distinguish the difference between pure publicity and news value, and ensure that their final product is composed entirely of the latter.

THE EDELMAN–WAL-MART SCANDAL

Another, perhaps better-known example, is the so-called " 'Wal-Mart' " scandal involving Edelman Public Relations, one of the nation's largest PR firms. A pair of seemingly independent travelers drove their recreational vehicle around the country, stopping overnight at Wal-Mart stores everywhere they went. (Wal-Mart allows RV parking for free in their lots overnight.) The pair subsequently interviewed Wal-Mart employees at these stores and posted glowing blog accounts of these happy individuals and the wonders of working for Wal-Mart. This blog and another, also seemingly independent and ostensibly set up by Wal-Mart "families," eventually came under suspicion. A *New York Times* story revealed that both blogs were supported by Wal-Mart and developed by Edelman Public Relations as part of a "'stealth'" marketing plan. In fact, one of the blogs was written almost entirely by Edelman employees posing as Wal-Mart employees. For many in public relations, this was a big step over the line. In responding to questions about the fake blog (flog) scandal, Emmanuel Tchividjian, the executive director of Ethics Consulting Practice of the public relations firm Ruder Finn, described the problem this way:

> [T]here is something new at work when it comes to the Internet, in terms of morality and ethics. The big element here is that of anonymity. When we complain that someone lied to us, we say, "He lied to my face. He looked at me and lied." That factor of human interaction is gone when it comes to the Internet. You can use an assumed name and nobody can trace you. This goes to the whole issue of transparency. If you follow the PRSA code, for example, you wouldn't do that.[66]

As with the other examples cited here, the question is not so much whether what is being said is true. The question is whether the people who are giving us information have a vested interest in the outcome, and, if so, why they are hiding their identities. Public relations, in order maintain its own integrity, must be entirely transparent and above board. Hiding behind the free speech right to anonymity may be all well and good for whistle blowers and others fearing for their livelihood, reputations, or even their lives, but there is no acceptable reason for anyone engaged in public relations on behalf of a client to act anonymously.

What Does It All Mean?

Public relations is an eclectic practice with a great many job descriptions involving myriad functional obligations. As we have learned, along with these functional obligations, there will always be accompanying moral obligations—either directly or indirectly related. As the message vehicles available to public relations professionals evolve and increase in number, there will always be a temptation to avoid moral obligations in favor of the purely functional. As noted, these ethical lapses are often discovered by the very audiences involved in the communication. In the case of Whole Foods' CEO, it was initially the other bloggers who suspected the ruse.

Public relations, more than any other media industry, is entering with gusto into the realm of new media, especially the opportunities provided by the internet and the concept of social marketing. However, public relations professionals must continue to follow the dictates of their already established standards, either codes provided by professional organizations such as PRSA, to the idea of social responsibility, or to their own personal ethics. A basic rule of thumb is that, if it was unethical before, it will be unethical now. Despite the advent of new ways to communicate with people, respect is still respect. The only way to ensure ethical practice is to practice ethics in everything you do.

Chapter 9

Ethics and Advertising

Many a small thing has been made large by the right kind of advertising.
(Mark Twain)

In a special issue of the *Journal of Business Ethics* in 2003, Richard Beltramini of Wayne State University introduced the group of articles by asking whether advertising ethics was an oxymoron. Citing the numerous complaints regularly leveled against advertising, Beltramini argues that it draws so much attention precisely because it is "the most visible business tool today, exposing the public to thousands of messages each day."[1] He rightly suggests that the emergence of new technology and delivery methods have posed new ethical problems that will naturally require a reassessment of the methods used to evaluate ethicality in the past. He issues a call for action for practitioners to "adhere to potentially even higher standards of ethical conduct than other business functions."

What follows in this chapter is a recounting of some of the charges leveled against advertising, and an exploration of the research into possible answers. As with public relations, we cannot assume that advertising is unethical by nature. But, in order to prove that, we must point out not only its faults, but also its value to the economic well-being of and its potential contribution to society.

What Is Advertising?

John Phelan, a professor of communications and media studies and media reform activist, defines advertising as a three-part process including the advertisement itself, the advertising agency that produces and places it, and the entity who pays for and sanctions the process and the outcome (the advertiser).[2] First, there is the *advertiser*. This is the client of the agency:

> Usually a corporate seller of commodities, the advertiser can also be a political party, a government, a public utility, a religion, a social movement, a charity. Any entity which chooses some medium of the public forum to reach large numbers of the public with a message and is willing and able to pay to do so.

Then there is the advertising *agency*—the entity that solicits, creates, and places advertisements and, frequently, measures their effects. Finally, an *advertisement* is any public form of announcement, usually a commodity, aimed to promote the acceptance or purchase of or a preference for the commodity. The commodity can be a product, service, idea, entity, or person.

Phalen points out that most advertisements are pretty straightforward—simply announcements about the availability of basic commodities, along with their attributes and prices. In addition to these are a "culturally significant" smaller number of ads promoting everything from political parties, candidates, and issues to those creating favorable images for various industries, organizations, or ideas—usually to dispel (or distract from) some unpopular belief about them. Finally, there are that small number of ads, often highly visible, that call attention to whatever it is they are selling by using emotional appeal and other cues that attract the less cognitively inclined among us (the "peripheral" processors of the ELM model discussed earlier).

What's Good about Advertising?

There is no denying that advertising does good things. Among them, advertising supports a free press. In the United States, most media (both entertainment and news) are supported by advertising dollars. Given their aversion to government control (prevented by the First Amendment), the various media must seek support elsewhere. Although subscriber fees (magazine and newspaper subscriptions, cable television fees, and burgeoning internet pay-to-access sites) defray a portion of costs, these media, and others, simply wouldn't be viable without other means of support. And that support almost always comes in the form of advertising. Very little of the media in the U.S. today exists free of advertising revenue, including the new media, which are struggling to come up with a workable business model—so far, still based on advertising income.

Advertising is also necessary to the functioning of a free-market economy. It informs the public about the availability of new products and explains the benefits and improvements of existing products, services, and ideas. It helps sustain the healthy competition necessary to such an economy and contributes to general economic growth by so doing. It can result in lowering prices and a general participation by the public in the process of normal consumption. As mentioned previously, the Supreme Court has even equated consumers with citizens, saying, in essense, that in some instances the decisions we make as consumers can be more important to our daily lives than those we make as citizens. To that end, advertising can also inform citizens about the ideas of political candidates, their policy decisions, and often something of their character, and it can bring candidates to our attention who might not otherwise be known.

Finally, advertising, in and of itself, is often viewed as an art form. It employees millions of people who plan, design, write, and create the messages and images we see every day in thousands of advertisements. As with any art form, the best of advertising is witty and entertaining, uplifting and inspirational.

So, What's the Problem?

Because media are so dependent on advertising revenue for survival, an increase in advertisements and commercials is inevitable, even unavoidable. The result is that we are bombarded with advertising messages, causing what has often been called "information clutter." Well over 50 percent of all newspaper pages are filled with advertising, roughly the same number for magazines, and a lesser quantity, but more intrusive in many ways, for radio and television. The average television entertainment half-hour is really only about 20 minutes of programming. The remainder is filled with advertising. Most recently, radio has begun to digitally compress news interviews and talk shows in order to cram in even more advertising. Internet pages are quickly becoming filled with annoying pop-ups, distractingly busy images, and even sounds—including outright sales pitches using both video and audio. Access to news stories frequently pass through "welcome pages" with full-screen, animated advertising acting as road blocks between us and the information we are trying to access.

A side effect of the media's dependency on advertising dollars is that, in order to survive, media must reach the type of audiences sought by their advertisers, and produce the type of programming and information content that will attract the largest numbers of that audience. This raises a multitude of issues including the cultural and social implications of both advertising and the programming it supports.

Before we tackle those issues, let's first take a look at some of the approaches to ethics in advertising suggested by modern research. What follows are several ways of looking at modern marketing/advertising communications from a "big picture" perspective. Following that, we will discuss some of the specific issues that constitute much of the potential ethical problems associated with advertising.

Ethical Approaches Specific to Advertising

Advertising is a much-studied industry. Much of that research is related to the effectiveness of advertising and is industry-generated; however, a fair amount of research is given over to ethics. Recent research has also begun to focus on such topics as advertising on the internet and the effects of direct-to-consumer (DTC) advertising, especially pharmaceuticals. Some of these will be addressed later in this chapter. First, however, we will look at some of the more general approaches to studying ethics in advertising.

Moral Myopia

Minette Drumwright and Patrick Murphy have coined the phrase "moral myopia" to describe the position of many in advertising towards ethics.

[M]oral myopia as a distortion of moral vision, ranging from shortsightedness to near blindness, which affects an individual's perception of an ethical dilemma. Moral myopia hinders moral issues from coming clearly into focus, particularly those that are not proximate, and it can be so severe that it may render a person effectively morally blind. If moral issues are not seen at all or are somehow distorted, it is highly unlikely that sound ethical decision making will occur.[3]

In personal interviews with advertising professionals in eight large metropolitan areas across the country, Drumwright and Murphy found two kinds of practitioners: those who are ethically sensitive and those who are not. For the latter group, ethical issues simply do not "appear to be on the radar screens." In most cases, these practitioners either thought that ethical issues didn't apply or, if they noticed them at all, did not discuss them. This is owing to either a failure to see an ethical problem at all or a tendency to rationalize a problem, further distorting its ethical dimensions.

Drumwright and Murphy categorize a number of reasons (or excuses) for avoiding ethical issues. The following stand out.

- *An unwavering faith in consumers*—A belief that consumers are too smart to fool through unethical practices, thus advertising messages need not be evaluated for ethicality. The paradox is that advertising is created to persuade, and admitting that it is powerless in the face of smart consumers seems contradictory.
- *Passing the buck*—Putting the onus of ethicality on parties other than the advertising practitioner (parents, peers, the media, clients, etc.). In other words, society is to blame if something unethical is slipping into advertising. This raises anew the question of whether advertising creates or reflects societal mores. More importantly, it absolves advertising of any responsibility in the creation of these messages. As we have seen previously in this book, responsibility and accountability are shared throughout the communication process.
- *Legality equals morality*—A belief that laws governing advertising are sufficient as ethical guidelines. This also leads to the notion that advertising legally sanctioned products (cigarettes, for instance) leaves the moral decision up to the consumer (buck passing). The law, however, only covers the most blatant offences within society. The nuances are much harder to deal with. Ethics is full of nuances, and typically requires a determined conversation to ferret them all out. In other words, ethics covers what the law does not,

and requires hard work. Assuming that what is legal is also the sum of what is ethical is a lazy response to a complex problem.

- *Moral muteness*—The tendency to not rock the boat. Even if advertising practitioners feel there is an ethical problem, there is often a reluctance to bring it up in order to avoid confrontation—which could lead to losing the client. This phenomenon is defined as a situation in which advertising practitioners "do not recognizably communicate their moral concerns in settings where such communicating would be fitting."[4] This "muteness" is manifested in several ways: not blowing the whistle or questioning unethical decisions; not speaking up for ethical ideals when that action is clearly called for; and not holding others accountable for their actions.[5] The authors subsequently identified several excuses that are most frequently used to rationalize moral muteness. Among them are the following:

  - *Compartmentalization*—Separating personal ethics from occupational behavior. This results in at least two sets of standards. As discussed in Chapter 3, the tension between professional and personal ethics is always present; however, if ethics is avoided altogether in one's professional life, the conflict between personal beliefs and what one must do on the job can be very great indeed—and cause a great deal of dissonance. In addition, this compartmentalization is often the result of assigning different virtues to what one does as a professional from what one would ascribe to a "good" person. For example, if an advertising practitioner's primary (functional) virtue on the job is creativity, then other (moral) virtues, such as compassion, may be ignored simply because, when one is at work, the proper measurement of success is usually considered to be functional. According to Drumwright and Murphy, compartmentalization leads to the avoidance of responsibility for the negative effects of advertising.
  - *The client is always right*—The agency model of the client–professional relationship discussed in Chapter 3 privileges functional over moral responsibilities. There is an inclination in advertising to put the clients at the very top of the list of claimants purely because they pay the bills. This leads to a lack of critical judgment, especially as regards ethics. The authors call this a "please-o-holic" tendency, which places the agency in a subordinate position to the client, and, to an extent, absolves it of any moral responsibility (passing the buck, again). As we have seen, the proper relationship between professional and client is a fiduciary one in which decisions as well as responsibility are shared.

Finally, Drumwright and Murphy discovered a second group of advertising practitioners "who typically recognized moral issues and talked about them inside the agency with their co-workers and outside the agency with their clients and potential clients."[6] Although this was a smaller group, comparatively, they were "notable exceptions" that they labeled "seeing, talking" practitioners. The authors noted that the most significant difference between these and the previous group seemed to be the moral climate in which they operated. They worked within agencies that "appeared to have some authentic norms regarding ethical behavior that were widely held and clearly articulated by members of the community."[7] In line with the major premise of this book, the "seeing, talking" advertising practitioners tended to adhere to a more formal moral decision-making framework involving recognition of the issue, communication about it, and the decision itself.

- *Recognition*—This group of practitioners seem to recognize moral issues when they encounter them, and count on their clients to view issues similarly. Thus, these practitioners "did not conceive of their roles as merely doing their clients' bidding. Instead, their roles encompassed making judgments and asserting opinions, as would be expected of a trusted partner."[8] In other words, they follow the fiduciary model outlined in Chapter 3. However, for most of those interviewed who fall into this "seeing, talking" group, the issues they were most likely to recognize were discrete, narrowly focused on the immediate and not on long-term or unintended social consequences. They suggest, in agreement with other, earlier research into advertising, that societal issues are perhaps thought of as too vague and the results difficult to calculate—one of the primary drawbacks to considering a broader definition of social responsibility among organizations in general.
- *Communication*—The "seeing, talking" practitioners also believed in open and direct communication, including that concerning ethical issues, which included plainly stating their own ethical values to potential clients to make sure that those of the client would match up favorably with theirs. They also cited the importance of agency-wide values initiated by those in charge and officially stated as part of the agency culture. These were frequently codified and prominently displayed, not merely as window dressing, but as an affirmation of a recognizable moral climate.
- *Decision*—Another hallmark of this group was the willingness and moral courage to say no, to each other and to their clients. This is in direct contrast to the sentiments of the other group of practitioners for whom the desires of the client were law—ethical or not.

According to Drumwright and Murphy, the "seeing, thinking" practitioners "appear to have mastered the various aspects of Rest's model of four psychological components determining moral behavior: '1) moral sensitivity (interpreting the situation), 2) moral judgment (judging which action is morally right/wrong), 3) moral motivation (prioritizing moral values relative to other values), and 4) moral character (having courage, persisting, overcoming distractions, implementing skills).'"[9] The result is what they call "moral imagination"—"being able to see and think outside the box, envisioning moral alternatives that others do not."

On the whole, the research conducted by Drumwright and Murphy, and their accompanying analysis seems to confirm what others have suggested and point to new methods of understanding advertising practitioners and the way they deal with ethical issues. Ultimately, the importance of a moral community/culture can't be overstated, for only within a nurturing environment can moral action be unabashedly practiced. The authors end with a list of propositions, among which are the following suggestions about what sort of working environment is most conducive to a higher level of moral sensitivity.

- Leaders who create a context in which moral imagination can flourish in the offices in which they work.
- Agencies with a highly communicative corporate culture.
- Agencies with frequent internal communication about core values.
- Agencies with frequent communication between upper management and lower-level employees about tough ethical issues.
- Agencies with formal ethics policies that have been widely disseminated within the organization and discussed among co-workers.

A Philosophical Approach

Christopher Hackley and Phillip Kitchen, British academics in business and marketing, claim that modern marketing communications have evolved into a "Leviathan," much in the way Hobbes described government. That is, today's marketing environment is a vast and omnipresent element of modern society. As such, it deserves more than an examination of mere professional responsibility and simple "moral decency in human exchange relationships."[10] They view the ubiquitous nature of modern marketing as having an overall societal effect of "circumventing the moral development of citizens."[11]

They begin by assuming, as do many others, that advertising "does not, in general seek to promote the advancement of human moral sensibility."[12] They point out that one of the major dangers of marketing is that it is able, and quite willing, to combine emotional and rational appeals, suggesting that, in most cases, the emotional reaction to marketing precedes the rational. Recall the discussion of the Elaboration Likelihood Model in Chapter 6 that supports the notion that consumers of persuasive communication tend to process information either cognitively or peripherally, or by using a combination of the two methods. For Hackley and Kitchen, the real question is whether modern consumers process the overload of information presented by marketing by falling into "confusion, existential despair, and loss of moral identity," or "adapt constructively . . . and become intelligent, cynical, streetwise, circumspect Postmodern Consumers who are just as savvy as advertisers who are trying to persuade them."[13] Drumwight and Murphy's argument presented above seems to support the notion that many in advertising tend to believe this latter construction of consumers.

Hackley and Kitchen argue that even if the consumer has developed certain avoidance strategies, the sheer weight of marketing communications ultimately confuses consumers, thus "disarming critical and evaluative faculties, and impairing the presumed moral and economic quality of buying decisions."[14] Another variable in modern consumer culture is the blurring of the lines between marketing communications and entertainment. The influence of the symbolic in film has led, they believe, to an entertainment-based advertising medium in which products are more likely to be sold based on symbolic context rather than literal descriptions of their salient features. In other words, a bar of soap becomes a refreshing spring day rather than a head-to-head competitor with other bar soap with differences defined in actual qualities instead of images.

For an answer to this problem, the authors suggest we look at the classical philosophical perspectives relevant to the modern consumer and the marketing "Leviathan." They begin with Plato, who, as you recall, didn't have a lot of faith in the people to run their own society. He believed that the masses had neither the education nor the experience to make complex decisions and were ruled mostly by emotion. Plato believed that the information people obtain from their senses, and which they tend to use in making life choices, was merely the result of the projection of reality, not reality itself (remember the parable of the cave?). For Plato, education was the answer—free of the "corrupting influences of popular drama, poetry, and personal property."[15] According to Hackley and Kitchen, we can infer that Plato would view modern marketing communications as "as a wasteful and corrupting force for evil incompatible with stability and social justice."[16]

Plato's most famous student, Aristotle, had a notably different take on the place of "things" in the lives of human beings. Unlike Plato, Aristotle conceived of life as including a sufficient supply of "goods," without which people would be forced into a life of asceticism, sustained only by intellect. On the contrary:

> [An ethical man] is an individual who seeks personal happiness in this world as if life is a skill to be mastered, and a sense of deep responsibility toward others is as inherent a part of such a man as is a sense of responsibility towards himself.[17]

Because Aristotle places responsibility for moral development on the individual and not on the state (except as a supporting environment), he would probably view modern marketing communications as simply another dilemma to be investigated and solved by the morally mature person in the same way as life's other challenges.

John Stuart Mill, in the nineteenth century, suggested that freedom of speech was a paramount consideration in modern society. Private behavior, according to Mill, cannot and should not be restrained by either government or society itself. Rather, individuals should remain free to explore the natural limits of their potential through the normal experiences of life and a natural give and take of the various influences that make up a personal and self-fulfilling life. This approach is, of course, reflected in Mill's "Harm Principle" discussed in Chapter 4.

> Postmodern consumers would simply have to regard the Communications Leviathan as an opportunity for personal development. In a process of cultural laissez faire, some would fail to cope and be 'cretinized' by the mass communicators: others would evolve into morally mature, critically aware individuals who might not have done so without the intrusive and challenging presence of the Marketing Communications Leviathan.[18]

On the other hand, given that modern marketing communications is ubiquitous in its nature and has definite social ramifications, Mill might have viewed it as "an instrument of oppression rather than one of liberty,"[19] thus requiring some sort of social or government intervention. The "tyranny of the majority" that Mill warned about, on this view, could be (or maybe should be) applied to the Leviathan of modern marketing communications.

The authors conclude by noting that the cumulative effect of modern marketing communications may impair both the critical and moral reasoning of individuals flooded with an endless barrage of messages on a daily basis. And, although a normative ethical approach to this problem can be derived from the works of classical philosophy, its multi-dimensional aspects probably require a closer look at political science as well for further insight into the political-economic model that fosters the modern marketing "Leviathan" in the first place. Ultimately, they suggest that the persistent ethical issues

> concern the intellectual bases for the construction of normative ethical approaches concerning the formation of the legal framework for marketing communications, the conduct of professionals within the industry in designing marketing communications strategies, and the role of the Leviathan in framing the behaviour [sic] and values of the Postmodern consumer.[20]

Approaches to Professional Ethics

Johannes Brinkmann, a Norwegian sociologist and business ethicist, suggests that marketing ethics would be best viewed as a professional endeavor, allowing it to be subject to the various approaches common to professional ethics. Assuming the criteria of professionalism (as described in Chapter 3 of this book) are met, more or less, by marketing, he outlines four approaches to *professional* ethics that are typically used in business and marketing (and, by extension, advertising).[21]

The *moral conflict approach* recognizes that for most professionals ethics is a pretty abstract concept, until they are forced to face an ethical dilemma.

[B]usiness ethics can be an abstract issue for most ordinary business people unless it is experienced in the format of urgent and threatening conflicts and dilemmas.[22]

The problem with this approach is that, unless there is a conflict, very little attention will be paid to ethics in general.

The *professional code approach* suggests that moral dilemmas are best handled by the implementation of rules, typically set down as codes.

Such codes draw maps of expected conflicts, expected or suggested solutions and, perhaps, predictable sanctions. Codes try to exploit the positive functions of legal regulation by institutionalizing rules and laws which are valid for organization members who accept the rules by signature when joining or when passing exams.[23]

Strengths of the code approach include the above-mentioned plus such additions as peer pressure from those in the profession, limitation of power, and a broadening of social responsibilities. On the downside, codes are sometimes imprecise, heavy on symbolism, and difficult to enforce.

The *professional role morality approach* views ethics from the perspective of rights and obligations inherent in the role itself, as opposed to personal ethics. Given that professionals are typically considered to be relatively autonomous in their actions, they are also more responsible for their actions. Conversely, because professional roles generally limit choices to those requiring *professional* expertise only, moral responsibility can be reduced somewhat. Thus, professionals may, when faced with criticism, simply blame the role. For example, the degree of obligation owed a client can outweigh the degree of obligation owed a third party. Or, as Brinkman points out, the professional could simply say, "I withheld information, or even lied as a *professional*, not as a *person*."[24] The major drawback to this approach is that the role becomes the sole arbiter of ethical action rather than the moral agent acting as a "subject with free choices."[25]

The *moral climate approach* posits that ethics is best understood as being part of an overall climate or culture that a professional is socialized into. A moral climate both shapes and is shaped by its participants.

Derived from a work climate definition, moral climate has been defined as "stable, psychologically meaningful, shared perceptions employees hold concerning ethical procedures and policies existing in their organizations."[26]

The strength of this approach is that it is holistic—it includes the entirety of the cultural and social context in which decisions are made, allowing for a broader consideration of issues, causes, conflicts, and affected parties. The weaknesses of this approach are that it is dependent on the degree to which the individuals internalize the goals of the moral climate (make it a part of their personal and professional ethical system), and the possibility that any given moral climate may be biased in its values in favor of the organization.

Brinkman suggests that these various approaches are not mutually exclusive, and, in fact, are complementary and can be combined—with moral climate being the best approach as a base for incorporating the others.

> Moral climates can prevent and handle moral conflict and can be learned by newcomers together with rules and roles. Climates are more or less dependent on ethical codes. Role players produce and reproduce moral climates. Many moral conflicts can be understood as role conflicts, codes describe role rights and duties, etc.[27]

Special Issues in Advertising Ethics

As with the other media discussed in this book, advertising has a number of flashpoint issues that seem to recur as areas of concern and subsequent investigation. The ethics scholar John Alan Cohan takes the position, often stated in this book, that,

> in itself, advertising is neither morally good nor bad. The ethics of advertising has to do with an evaluation of the content and techniques deployed in given bits of advertising, or prestige value of material things.[28]

Many of the ethical issues discussed here have to do with content and techniques. Others are broader and deal with larger societal issues, such as consumption being equated with happiness. For example, in a report on ethics in advertising produced by the Vatican (yes, the Vatican), the overarching concern appears to be that advertising often generates its own values or, at the very least, is extremely "selective about the values and attitudes to be fostered and encouraged, promoting some while ignoring others."[29] And advertising can sometimes promote values that are not necessarily compatible with a healthy society (healthy on many levels). For example, advertising tends to focus on material gain. In fact, much of advertising promotes a blatantly consumer-oriented culture. For those with enough income to pursue such goals, this might not be a problem (functionally, at least). However, for those millions of society's members who have trouble enough making ends meet, the feeling of being left out or of needing to compete in the acquisitions race can be problematic. As Cohan puts it, "Advertising often fosters the philosophy that human happiness depends on the possession or prestige value of material things."[30]

However, the historian Michael Schudson suggests that "People's needs have never been natural but always cultural, always social, always defined relative to the standards of their societies."[31] Recall that Aristotle would not have us live without the material things that make life comfortable and aesthetically pleasing. On the other hand, he would also not have us value the acquisition of material goods above the acquisition of a good character, which ultimately is what leads to a good life. Regardless, we must also accept that advertising is required by its very nature to paint such a picture—consumption leads to pleasure, which leads to happiness. Whether this is literally true or not, we must remember that advertising is an otherwise valuable element and a mainstay of a free-market economy. It is also capable of doing so without disrespecting those to whom it appeals—consumers.

Following, then, is a short list of some the most common ethical concerns associated with advertising. Note that these are not mutually exclusive and often overlap.

- *Advertising often attempts to bypass rational thinking and, in so doing, sometimes creates a sort of fiction by avoiding the literal truth.* Much of advertising is aimed at peripheral processors, especially for those products that are difficult to distinguish among, thus requiring the creation of images in order to sell them (perfume, soap, colas, etc.). Because of this requirement, advertising uses all the techniques of entertainment at its disposal to both attract the consumer to products and distract the consumer from consideration of the rational and definable differences among products—which creates grey areas that truth-in-advertising laws don't cover, and which are vague enough to be ethically troubling.

  Some of these grey areas include "puffery," the use of vague words or phrases such as "the best" or "most desirable." Carl P. Wrighter called these "weasel words" and warned that they can seem to say something that they don't literally mean.[32] For example, "helps your body grow" doesn't really answer the question of how it helps, or what exactly it's helping—good eating habits, exercise, steroids?

  Another, much larger, problem is the creation of images or a kind of *symbolic ambience* in order to sell products, services, or ideas when comparing actual product attributes doesn't seem to suffice. *Symbolic ambience* can be defined as the use of emotional images and cultural symbols to create a context for a product, essentially void of actual product attributes.[33] For example, scenes of crowded, upscale bars full of young, good looking people are a time-honored technique for selling certain types of beer. Or snowy landscapes equal "pure" products. Or a fun day at the beach means that you're obviously enjoying the right brand of cola. These, and hundreds of other similar ambience-creating methods, all avoid the more difficult chore of a straightforward comparison of products.

- *Advertising tends to classify audiences by type, sometimes leading to stereotyping.* Because audiences are typically classified by a generic typing (typically using demographics), there is a tendency to ignore the subtleties of human character in favor of the most obvious characteristics of a group. The result is that often advertising paints too simplistic a picture of some people, which can be misleading and, sometimes, even offensive. For example, in recent years television has created a genre of men on numerous sitcoms who could only be classified as "the bumbling husband" type. Advertising, in turn, has mimicked this stereotype by picturing both boys and men as incapable of understanding the mysteries of laundry, or cooking a family meal without purchasing it in a bucket, or keeping themselves clean more than a few minutes at a time. Examples range from Homer Simpson to the title character on *Everybody Loves Raymond*. It may seem silly, but doesn't this lower in some way the expectations women have of men in a home setting?

The converse of this is that advertising often ignores certain audiences because they don't fit the demographic. Because advertising, and marketing in general, rely on demographic information (age, education, income, habits of buying and consuming, etc.) to determine their audience, there is a temptation to ignore certain segments simply because they don't fit into the required demographic—the very young, the very old, the poor, for example. If you belong to one of these groups, you may begin to feel that you are not important. The sad fact is that some groups wouldn't appear at all if it weren't for stereotypes. For example, how many Native Americans have you seen in television commercials who weren't stereotyped in some way? Now, ask yourself why they don't appear.

- *The increasing sophistication of advertising can lead to a lack of transparency.* Consumers have traditionally been able to avoid advertising, but in the "old days" it was much harder. You literally had to skip the advertising in magazines (which was pretty difficult to do), get up and go to the kitchen for a snack during commercials on TV, switch stations on the radio whenever an ad came on, or just generally ignore what was being shouted at you from every sign on a block of retail stores. Of course, advertising countered with increasingly intrusive techniques to gain your attention, including placards on grocery carts and bathroom stalls, unending rows of kiosks at shopping malls, louder and flashier television commercials, and increasingly larger advertising supplements in newspapers and direct mail.

With the advent of digital media, advertising seized on yet another chance to get your attention; however, the new technology has also created new ways of avoiding advertising—zapping commercials with digital recorders, setting pop-up and spam blockers on computers, etc. The important thing to note here is that, up to this point, consumers have mostly been able to recognize advertising for what it is, and avoid it as they saw fit. We know from both elaboration likelihood and cognitive dissonance theories that, if we recognize that a communication is persuasive, we can set up psychological defenses against it. But, what if we don't know it's a sales pitch? In response to technological advances that have allowed consumers to avoid certain types of persuasive messages, advertisers have responded with increasingly sophisticated means of calling attention to their products, including methods that avoid the appearance of advertising altogether. This raises the important ethical concern of whether advertising masquerading as "friendly conversation" (or anything other than what it truly is) is deceptive or not. Advertising within social media (sometimes called "viral" marketing) is one of those techniques that will be discussed below.

- *Advertising can be offensive and tasteless.* Because of the need to get the attention of audiences, advertisers often resort to techniques designed to "cut through the clutter."[34] This generally means ads designed to get your attention, and nothing gets attention like shocking visuals or copy. In addition, sometimes advertising that we may find offensive has been deliberately designed to "push the creative envelope"—often a euphemism for "you're not hip if you think this ad is offensive." Other times, advertising professionals are charged with selling products that, by their nature, require approaches that may offend some people. For example, how does one sell perfume or cologne when the main purpose of the product is to attract someone sexually? In order to deal with these issues, many involved in advertising take an approach described earlier as moral subjectivism—everything is a matter of personal opinion or taste, thus it really isn't legitimate to say an advertisement is tasteless or immoral.

Let's turn now to dealing with some of these concerns in more detail beginning with those grey areas where truth often becomes the victim of creative presentation.

Creating the Image: Between the Truth and the Lie

Advertising isn't just about information dissemination; it's also about persuasion, and, as we know, the act of persuasion is fraught with ethical dilemmas. For example, advertising can be outright deceptive, as in all those weight-loss ads claiming remarkable results literally overnight, or the myriad products advertised to enhance sexuality (your spam filter probably handles most, but not all, of these). In the cases where the veracity of the claim is clearly in doubt, intelligent consumers tend to discount the advertisement and the product immediately. For most of us, our "qualified expectation of reality" negates the more blatant attempts to fool us. However, there will always be those, either desperate or merely gullible, who will be fooled. Advertising practitioners cannot simply rely on the old adage *caveat emptor* (buyer beware) when deliberately attempting to mislead consumers. In these cases, the various laws and agencies controlling advertising can be called on to intercede between consumer and advertiser. But these very obvious ethical, and legal, violations are not the most troubling aspects of potentially deceptive advertising.

The real difficulty comes in the grey areas of advertising—somewhere between the absolute truth and the absolute lie. Much of advertising is designed to *motivate* people rather than to *inform* them—either to buy something, adopt an attitude conducive to consuming, stick with a product or idea, or to literally adopt a way of thinking that can lead to the acceptance of an entirely new idea or product. On the face of it, this is not unethical; however, a potential problem occurs when advertising switches from enumerating actual differences among competing brands to creating a *symbolic ambience* through the use of such things as cultural symbols (American flags), music (your favorite rock song), emotional narratives (happy puppies frolicking with happy nuclear families), and sexual images (always young, barely clothed, and in provocative poses) in order to distinguish their product from other, similar products.

This might be called *advertising through implication*. The *New Oxford American Dictionary* defines *imply* as to "strongly suggest the truth or existence of something not expressly stated." For example, in 1990 the Leo Burnett agency produced a short television commercial for the investment firm Dean Witter. It was composed of seemingly original 1920s newsreel-style footage of a man obliquely identified as Dean Witter giving a fatherly pep talk to a small group of businessmen sitting and standing around a table in a richly appointed office, sipping coffee. The footage was a faded black-and-white, scratchy, jerky, piece—complete with jump cuts and tinny sound. A quiet, East-coast-accented voice emanates from a gentle, bespectacled man we suppose is Dean Witter, advising his comrades that "We measure success one investor at a time." The commercial subtly implies that this footage was shot in a time before advertising learned to manipulate the truth—a time when even businessmen were kind and gentle. Of course, the footage was shot in 1990, using actors, and intentionally designed to look authentic. It's also unlikely that Dean Witter had an East cost accent, given that he was raised and lived in California, but that's the sound we expect, because that's what nearly everyone in movies from the period had. It came to be called "Mid-Atlantic English"—slightly reminiscent of a British accent—and was widely used by both film actors and broadcasters of the period preceding World War II. The point is, no one says the accent is authentic. No one says the footage is authentic. No one says the man speaking is actually Dean Witter. But it is *implied*. Notably, nothing is expressly said as to why anyone should invest with Dean Witter. What the ad does is create an "emotional bond" between the brand and the potential consumer of the product.

According to the advertising researcher Rosalinde Rago, the classical approach to marketing has traditionally been to compare products by "performance advantage." However, with the rise of new technology and proliferation of ever-newer channels of communication, "product differentiation based on functional differences has become increasingly difficult."[35]

> [A]s brand clutter increases and functional benefits become less distinct and less likely to be acknowledged, marketers have had to rely more on those intangible characteristics of a product and its advertising that serve to establish a unique relationship—or emotional bond—between the brand and the target consumer.[36]

Because of the ease with which consumers can avoid commercials in this new environment, "Advertising today cannot argue. It must entice. It must seduce. It must present an attitude about the brand that insinuates itself into consumers' lifestyle aspirations and self-perceptions."

> More and more advertising is being developed, which, in addition to illuminating the functional benefit, is designed to engage the viewer in the commercial tale. It demands that the viewer participate and, himself, supply some of the meaning.[37]

This approach is especially important for *parity products*, those whose attributes are shared broadly with competing products, thus making differentiation more difficult—if not impossible. These include such items as soap, shampoo, cola drinks, beer (especially mass-produced American beer), athletic shoes, perfume and cologne, laundry detergent, and investment firms—to name just a few. The result has been that advertising agencies frequently resort to creating an image that then has to compete with other images for other products. By relying on image rather than actual product attributes, the focus is shifted from the product to an illusion of a better life associated with the purchase of the product. Consumers are left to judge, if they can, the actual differences among products, and are sometimes the poorer for not understanding exactly what they are buying other than an image.

Take cola drinks as an example. Most people have a preference and, subsequently, can identify their favorite in a taste test. On the other hand, sugar content seems to have played a significant factor in the early days of taste testing, in which Pepsi typically came in ahead of Coke. In reality, most cola drinks look alike, taste somewhat the same, contain similar ingredients (including caffeine), and are difficult to differentiate through advertising according to their actual physical properties. The result is that we have an ongoing battle between cola cultures, with the prize an increasingly younger, hipper audience. Because the content is not the issue, image becomes the selling point. Recently, an Australian research team found that adding caffeine to a soft drink does not enhance flavor. The obvious question then becomes, "Why is it being added?" According to the head of the research team, Russel Keats, it is "unethical" because it is simply being used to addict young people to sugary drinks.[38]

> Children don't have the cognitive ability to understand why they may be getting moody or irritable because their caffeine high has waned over time and they're wanting more.
>
> If it's there purely not as a flavouring [sic] but as an addictive agent or to promote caffeine dependence, then that would be unethical.[39]

The point is, advertising a product based on a created image while avoiding the realities of the product's contents couldn't be said to be entirely ethical—

especially if the contents are unhealthy. Obvious products in this category include, for instance, cigarettes, which historically were sold based on image alone while consumers were led to believe that image trumped reality. But think about the health factors involved in fast food, alcohol, soft drinks, candy, and myriad other products sold almost entirely through the creation of cultural images. How many of us think of the content of a fast-food sandwich while we're watching a fast-food commercial late in the evening after having skipped dinner? But is it entirely up to us to weigh the pros and cons of running out to the nearest drive-in for a burger and fries?

Some in advertising have also noted the movement toward fuzzier product identities. Brad VanAuken, a professional consultant on brand strategy, suggests that advertising has become too reliant on emotion as a sales technique. He cites the Continental Airlines slogan "More airline for the money" as an example of branding through an easily recognizable performance characteristic—a reason to choose them over other airlines. Then their slogan was inexplicably changed to "Work hard. Fly right," which, according to VanAuken, not only doesn't mean anything, it's also "silly."[40]

He also points out that, even if we are sold products through emotional appeal, we still want "reasons" other than emotional stimulus before we go into debt over a $50,000 BMW or a $10,000 Rolex. We may not need a more expensive car or expensive jewelry in order to live completely productive and satisfying lives. However, if we were to at least consider quality and performance, then our decisions would be based on legitimate differences that perhaps meet our actual needs. After all, a BMW is a great performance car, and a Rolex "takes a year to build."[41] We can justify purchases as being based on other than emotional satisfaction, but we must have access to that other information presented and available to us in order to do so.

Puffery

Even if an advertisement does present attributes or performance claims, it doesn't necessarily follow that the claims are legitimate. It may be only mildly frustrating to consumers to notice that the claim a dandruff shampoo "fights dandruff" doesn't say it eliminates it altogether, or that "Four out of five dentists surveyed recommend sugarless gum for their patients who chew gum," is so over-qualified as to be meaningless as a statistic. However, advertising that sets up a false impression of a product or a product's benefits to the consumer by seeming to promise actual performance characteristics is acting unethically.

For example, a few years ago, the advertising agency for KFC produced an ad series that was eventually taken out of play on the order of the Federal Trade Commission (FTC). Kentucky Fried Chicken had already opted for calling itself KFC in order to remove the "Fried" part from its image. But they took a giant step backward when an ad claimed that "Two Original Recipe chicken breasts have less fat than a Burger King Whopper. Or go skinless for 3 grams of fat per piece." According to Bob Garfield, who writes a regular feature for *Advertising Age* on TV commercials, this was an example of "desperate and sleazy tactics" prompted by the upsurge in consumer willingness to "put their money where their arteries are."[42] As if to slip under the legal wire, fine print briefly flashed the message that KFC is "not a low fat, low sodium, low cholesterol food." The reality is that there is a five-gram difference between the two fast-food mainstays, and that neither product is especially good for you. The point is that KFC wasn't actually saying their deep-fried chicken is good for you—they were saying that it had less fat than another fatty, fast-food product. They were *implying*, however, that it was good for you, and that's the problem.

In response, the FTC charged the company with making false claims concerning nutritional value, weight-loss benefits, and health benefits that are not substantiated. Eventually, KFC withdrew the claims. However, this case exemplifies the problem of making direct comparison claims for products that are significantly the same (nutritionally at least) and helps explain why so many such products are marketed using images rather than facts. It also points to the problems inherent in exaggerating claims, whether through image cues or simply "fuzzyfying" the facts.

The KFC case is pretty easy to understand as ethically problematic. But what about those claims that are not patently false yet seem to say something about a product that isn't exactly provable? Techniques ranging from annoying to downright unethical allow for product claims to be made in ways that are either too vague to be understood or too misleading to be considered the literal truth. This is often referred to as "puffery," which the FTC has defined as a "term frequently used to denote the exaggerations reasonably to be expected of a seller as to the degree of quality of his product, the truth or falsity of which cannot be precisely determined."[43] This would include such claims as:

- We make the world's best mattress (Serta)
- America's favorite neighborhood (Applebees restaurants)
- Nobody does breakfast like IHOP does breakfast
- Fly the friendly skies of United

What these, and thousands of other claims like them, have in common is that they express subjective rather than objective views, and are based on the notion that a "reasonable person" would tend not to take these claims literally (the *qualified expectation of reality* test). As with most such definitions, however, what constitutes a "reasonable person" is open to interpretation. The advertising critic and scholar Ivan Preston wants to know if the FTC chooses to "protect only reasonable, sensible, intelligent consumers who conduct themselves wisely in the marketplace? Or does is also protect those who act less wisely?"[44] He argues that the defining factor separating a reasonable person from anyone else should be that "in the given context . . . [the latter] are poorly informed or utterly uninformed. They have not obtained all of the information that can affect the decisions they will make."[45]

Preston is bothered by advertisers' seeming assumption that such claims are not false—that "who's to say you won't experience a sense of utter freedom while driving that new car?" is a legitimate matter of opinion and it *could* happen. However, Preston asserts that these features are "attached to products in an entirely arbitrary manner, there because the message says they are, and *only* because the message says they are."[46] He calls such claims as "Reebok believes in the athlete in all of us" *social-psychological representations*. Claims such as these imply that a product "possesses a feature that in truth exists only in consumers' social environments or within their own personalities or mental states of mind."[47] The problem with claims such as this is that expressions of self-image

> [are] not truly part of the product, but [are] associated with the product only in the representation. The message implied to the consumer, however, can be that the feature will accompany the product with such certainty that it may be treated as if it were an actual part of the product.[48]

Unfortunately, the law doesn't cover these vague areas of illusory attributes and implied promises. The law says a claim must be false to be harmful. Preston insists that "The question is not whether [puffery] is false . . . but whether it is deceptive."[49]

The Ethical Bottom Line for Creating Symbolic Ambience

Does selling a product by creating an image using emotion or other cultural or social cues in order to avoid outright product comparisons necessarily constitute unethical behavior? That would be too harsh a judgment; however, advertising professionals must realize that they have an obligation to present products in such a way as not to build a false impression of what a consumer may expect from a product or to create a "need" based solely on an image. That advertising may create a desire is not necessarily damning. What is questionable is the exploitation of emotions or the circumvention of rational thought processes—which is manipulative. When that happens, a consumer's freedom of choice is limited and her autonomy is violated.

Remember, respect for those with whom you communicate dictates that they understand fully the content of your message. They may not be fooled by talking frogs or football-playing Clydesdales. But they may actually believe that buying a diamond ring designed exclusively for a woman's right hand which says, "me" instead of "we" (which is what the one on the left hand apparently says) somehow makes a woman independent and in charge. After all, the same company that came up with this idea also came up with the concept of the diamond engagement ring some 80 years ago (yes, only 80 years ago) and marketed it through one of the largest advertising agencies of the time. Today, more than 80 percent of American brides receive a diamond engagement ring at an average cost of $3,200.[50] Can advertising create a need? Yes. Can it do so by simply creating an image? Yes. Is there anything potentially unethical about this? Yes.

Fudging facts and playing with words and images to create a picture that is not quite true is an obvious ethical violation. However, sidestepping reality by projecting an illusion of a product is also problematic, and a dubious practice at the very least. When we do this, we run the risk of misleading our audiences, especially if what we create doesn't address the real needs of the people paying money to participate in our fantasy. Contrary to what some believe, advertising is not in the business of selling dreams. It is in the business of selling things. To the extent that advertising agencies can avoid images that say little or nothing about the actual product, service, or person being "sold," they should do so. At the very least, such images need to be based on real assumptions about the actual affects of the product, not merely on a created illusion.

A Reflection or a Creator of Reality: Stereotyping

Happy, good-looking, thin, mostly white, heterosexual, young people inhabit the world created by advertising. Although many have argued that advertising merely reflects the society and culture inside of which it is produced, the question of exactly what parts of society, which of its cultures, and what values of that society and those cultures are chosen to be portrayed is a big one. Others argue that advertising is extremely selective about what it shows us as reality. Common complaints are that certain values and cultures are virtually ignored. The Vatican report suggested that

> the absence from advertising of certain racial and ethnic groups in some multi-racial or multi-ethnic societies can help to create problems of image and identity, especially among those neglected.[51]

Over the years, we have seen an increase in the inclusion of some ethnic minorities in advertising; however, recent research into television commercials suggests that, as far as the largest minority segments go (blacks and Hispanics), there is still serious underrepresentation. Some have pointed out that, despite an increase in representation of some minorities, others are ignored.

> It is clear that minority groups represent important segments to all types of companies that provide goods and services to Americans. However, advertisers' recognition of the importance of the groups is inconsistent. Many advertisers do not specifically target any minority group. Most advertisers that specifically target minority populations identify Hispanics as their primary minority group target, with Asians identified as their second most important target and with blacks, the largest group, as their third priority. Other groups, such as Native Americans, are rarely targeted.[52]

Because of the lack of representation in advertising (and other media, for that matter), we are often left with an incomplete or erroneous image of some members of our own society.

> Consequently, to the extent that members of the host society are denied an opportunity to learn about minorities through the media (either in programming or through advertisements) due to insufficient frequency of appearance, or are provided with mainly stereotypical representations, the effect may be to perpetuate stereotypical attitudes toward minority groups, as well as to interfere with the acculturation process of those minorities.[53]

If we don't see ourselves in the media we consume, or we do see ourselves, but in a way that doesn't really represent who we are, can we then say that those media are truly a reflection of society? Can we legitimately blame advertising, for example, for its abbreviated view of our world? What are the constraints that have led to the incomplete and often inaccurate image that we see when we look into the mirror that is modern advertising?

What is Stereotyping?

The way we most commonly use the term is an outgrowth of a concept first proposed by the journalist, media scholar, and critic Walter Lippmann in 1922.

He believed that people simply are not equipped to deal with the subtlety and variety presented by the "real environment" in which they live. Instead, they must construct simpler models of that environment so that they can better manage it. Stereotypes are those models. However, they are not individually constructed. Stereotypes are the Platonic shadow-show put on by our own culture—a figment of reality at best. As Lippmann put it,

> For the most part we do not first see, and then define, we define first and then see. In the great blooming, buzzing confusion of the outer world we pick out what our culture has already defined for us, and we tend to perceive that which we have picked out in the form stereotyped to us by our culture.[54]

Lippmann's work was primarily in reaction to a world driven in part by a burgeoning new media whose "screech, blare and color" were simultaneously clamoring for the public's attention. He suggested that it was with the help of stereotypes that a media-based society transmitted its cultural canon and explained the complexities of modern life. The narratives that people need to put their world into perspective were created, in part, by these stereotypes.

For Lippman, stereotypes were the domain of unconscious thought and preceded reason insofar as they are created without our direct experience or involvement.

We are told about the world before we see it. We imagine most things before we experience them. And these preconceptions, unless education has made us acutely aware, govern deeply the whole process of perception. They mark out certain objects as familiar or strange, emphasizing the difference, so that the slightly familiar is seen as very familiar, and the somewhat strange is sharply alien.[55]

This is a view of stereotypes as being inherently dangerous in that they sidestep rational thought in favor of a shadowy illusion of life, leading the masses clinging to a culture they barely understand while rejecting out of hand that which is foreign to them. Lippmann's vision of how people use the "pictures in their heads" to construct reality, especially a reality they have not experienced first hand, has remained pretty much intact as a concept. He believed that stereotypes were an inevitable by-product of modern existence. In a sense, he was right. They are inevitable—especially in advertising.

Advertising and Stereotyping

The average American will spend one and one-half years of his or her life watching television commercials. The ads sell a great deal more than products. They sell values, images, and concepts of success and worth, love and sexuality, popularity and normalcy. They tell us who we are and who we should be. Sometimes they sell addictions.[56]

How does one go about explaining an important concept, a product's salient attribute, or the complexity of a cultural ritual in 30 seconds? The limitations of space and time are a very real constraint on advertising. Is it possible for a wedding photographer, for instance, to develop a one-page print ad for her services without using stereotypical images of the traditional, Western-culture wedding? Probably not. Would we consider those images harmful? Probably not. But they are limiting, present only a single cultural picture, and reinforce certain cultural expectations at a number of levels. Nonetheless, stereotypes allow advertising to shortcut lengthy explanations by setting a context everyone already understands and moving directly to the sales pitch.

On the face of it, stereotyping is a neutral tool; however, because advertising both reflects and creates an image of society, it has the power to reinforce the positive or the negative, the helpful or the harmful. Obviously, then, stereotypes can be problematic. They can:

- reduce a wide range of differences in people to simplistic categorizations;
- transform assumptions about particular groups of people into "realities";
- be used to justify the position of those in power;
- perpetuate social prejudice and inequality.[57]

The most troublesome aspect of advertising is its potential effects on how we view ourselves and others. How many believe that the Irish are heavy drinkers, that Mexicans are lazy, that blondes are dumb, that white men can't jump? Far too many, actually; but those are the most egregious stereotypes, and more easily recognized for what they are. What about the more subtle stereotypes? How do we come to a place in our society where young women believe that what constitutes "normal" weight is barely enough to sustain life? Or that being a male in today's society means being macho, muscular, athletic, and in charge? Or, conversely, that being a male means not being capable of doing anything remotely domestic? Two theories can help us understand why this can and does happen.

Cultivation theory suggests that repeated exposures to media portrayals of a stereotype may result in public acceptance of the stereotype as reality. Over time, the ubiquitous nature of television may tend to provide a consistent, if inaccurate, picture of reality. For example, television sitcoms and commercials both frequently present women as nurturing—to their husbands, children, neighbors—while men are seen as bumbling, sloppy, self-absorbed. Sure, it's funny, sometimes endearing, and cues on what we may already believe. And, if we see this enough, it may eventually become a permanent part of our way of thinking about women, men, and marriage and its concomitant roles. That is the problem. If we accept these stereotypes as reality, how narrow is our understanding of actual women and men and actual marriages, and who ultimately suffers because of that?

Expectancy theory states that repeated media portrayals can build or reinforce expectations that are held for a group. For example, if we are exposed to the same stereotypes repeatedly, we come to expect that people who belong to the group being portrayed consistently in a stereotypical manner will, in fact, act that way in real life. If we belong to that group, we may even begin to believe that we should act that way. The more limited the exposure we have to anything other than the stereotype, the more we will tend to imprint the stereotype on the real individual. If you are a young woman and you consistently see women portrayed as air-headed "shopaholics," you may, over time, begin to adopt that cliché as a way of life. According to the advertising scholar and researcher Kim Sheehan, the actual effects of these theories are mitigated by the degree to which three variables are present.[58]

- *The range of stereotypes presented over time*—Although it may be true that portraying young women as addicted to shopping constitutes a stereotype, whether we tend to believe the stereotype is accurate may depend on how many other "types" we are exposed too. For example, if the shopping addict is only one of a number of stereotypes of young women we see consistently over time (e.g., as aspiring student, young professional, romantic partner, family member), then we will have a more complete picture of what constitutes a "young woman."

- *The frequency of portrayals of individual stereotypes*—This links closely with the range of stereotypes because a single image not repeated consistently over time is not likely to become a stereotype. In order for that to happen, it must be repeated to the exclusion of other possible images, ultimately presenting a one-dimensional portrait of a type.
- *The valence of the stereotype*—Are the portrayals negative or positive? Although a positive stereotype is still a stereotype, it is less likely that the results of viewing the stereotype will be harmful. A negative stereotype consistently presented over time (frequency) without balancing, contrary, or compensating images can cause a negative image to be imbedded in the life-view of those watching it. As Sheehan puts it:

> Seeing one single, consistent portrayal of a group of people can affect how we perceive all members of the stereotyped group, either while we are creating advertising messages or when we encounter members of the group in the real world.[59]

Although stereotypes abound in advertising, we'll address only one here as an example of how they work and their potential affects. The lessons learned from this example are applicable to all stereotypes and the solutions are the same.

Portrayals of Women and Girls

> Desperate to conform to an ideal and impossible standard, many women go to great lengths to manipulate and change their faces and bodies. A woman is conditioned to view her face as a mask and her body as an object, as things separate from and more important than her real self, constantly in need of alteration, improvement, and disguise. She is made to feel dissatisfied with and ashamed of herself, whether she tries to achieve "the look" or not. Objectified constantly by others, she learns to objectify herself.[60]

Advertising plays a very large role in what the media activist Jean Kilbourne describes as the selling of women to the cosmetics, clothing, and lifestyle industries. The combined messages these industries send out via advertising define a version of "beauty" that is "unattainable for all but a very small number of women."[61] The perfect woman is chic, free of blemishes (in theory, mostly thanks to makeup, but in practice thanks to digital photo manipulation), sexually desirable, vulnerable, and, above all, painfully thin. In fact, we rarely see "real" women in advertising at all, resulting in a kind of invisibility of normalcy that can leave the majority of women staring into a cultural mirror and seeing nothing at all that resembles them looking back. The result is that over time women begin to internalize these stereotypes and subsequently reject their own reality as something in need of constant adjustment.[62]

This process often begins startlingly early. The average North American girl will watch 5,000 hours of television, including 80,000 ads, before she starts kindergarten.[63] In 2002, an Australian study showed that teenage girls who watched television commercials in which underweight models appeared lost self-confidence and became more dissatisfied with their own bodies, and that girls who spent the most time and effort on their appearance suffered the greatest loss in confidence.[64] The National Institute on Media and the Family cites studies showing that the way girls are portrayed in the media, and advertising in particular, have an overall negative effect.[65] For example, at age 13, 53 percent of American girls are "unhappy with their bodies." This grows to 78 percent by the time girls reach 17.[66]

In addition to body image, girls are confronted with images that portray them as sexually erotic at increasingly young ages. Stereotypical images show young girls not only as sexual but also as powerless and as victims. Young women who consume these images over time are strongly influenced by "stereotypical images of uniformly beautiful, obsessively thin and scantily dressed objects of male desire."[67]

> The pressures on girls are exacerbated by the media's increasing tendency to portray very young girls in sexual ways . . . [T]he fashion industry has begun to use younger and younger models, and now commonly presents 12- and 13-year-old girls as if they were women. Camera angles (where the model is often looking up, presumably at a taller man), averted eyes, wounded facial expressions, and vulnerable poses mimic the visual images common in pornographic media.[68]

Other research has found that the images presented to girls are so narrow as to present a mostly stereotypical picture of who they should be. For example, a study analyzing Saturday morning toy commercials showed that, with regard to work roles, no boys had unpaid labor roles, and girls were mainly shown in traditional female jobs or roles of unpaid labor.[69] Another suggested that "media also presented an overwhelming message that girls and women were more concerned with romance and dating . . . while men focus on their occupations."[70]

Women and girls are bombarded with images of thin, sexual, and often powerless and passive, versions of who they should be. Both cultivation theory and expectancy theory are at work here, and the overall effect is painfully evident. A photograph of a teenage girl appeared on a blog site recently. She was wearing a T-shirt that read, "If found, return to the nearest mall." She was smiling.

The Ethical Bottom Line for Stereotyping

Advertising practitioners aren't likely to give up using stereotypes, nor should they. As already mentioned, the physical and temporal constraints on advertising literally require that a shorthand method of presenting information in context be used. Nonetheless, given the potential for problems associated with stereotypes—inaccurate or negative portrayals of entire social and cultural groups being the most prominent—advertisers should err on the side of caution. As with any media form, we need to consider any potential harm that is being done, intentionally or otherwise, by our messages. For advertising in general, and stereotyping in particular, harm is a highly potential by-product of the message. Advertising professionals cannot ignore that potential. This doesn't mean that stereotypes should be eliminated altogether. Lippmann was right—a part of our world view is, of necessity, based on these stereotypes. We simply can't know everything about everything. However, we must resist the urge to classify too narrowly that which we don't know. By doing so, we automatically reject the nuances of life. Advertising should help us understand those nuances, relying on stereotypes only when absolutely necessary.

As Sheehan suggests, one of the best ways to do this is to present a range of images more fully representative of reality. Given that in order for most advertising to be effective it must be repeated over time, there would seem to be enough leeway to expand on any portrayal of any group so that a rounded, not a flat, image is created. Another, often cited, suggestion is for advertising agencies to hire people who are members of audiences that are consistently being stereotyped. At the very least, these people may bring an enhanced sensibility to potentially stereotypical messages.

As to the neglect shown to some groups within society who appear only as stereotyped sidebars to some advertising (the old, the very young, the poor)—until advertisers get out among the people who inhabit the real world not reflected in their demographic analyses, those groups will continue to be underrepresented or misrepresented. Ultimately, the best way to get rid of stereotypes is to meet the real people you are portraying. This can be accomplished by simply consulting with groups who represent your target audience and asking them their opinions. Respect for others as ends and not just as means to an end, as Kant reminds us, is the real bottom line.

Advertising and the Need for Transparency

Problems arise when advertising shifts from being obvious, thus avoidable, to being hidden or disguised as something else, so as not to be so easily avoided. As mentioned earlier, new technology has made avoiding advertising, especially on television, much easier, forcing advertisers to come up with ever newer approaches to getting your attention. Many of those approaches utilize techniques more often associated with public relations; however, they still fall under the rubric of "marketing." There are a wealth of terms currently in use to describe these related techniques: Buzz Marketing, Word-of-Mouth-Marketing (WOMM), Viral Marketing, Stealth Marketing, and Social Media Marketing.[71] They all refer to roughly the same technique—spreading the word about a product or idea by using the consumer to help promote it for you. An article published by the

Wharton School of Business at the University of Pennsylvania notes that this technique

> assumes that a person-to-person marketing message is much more powerful because it is so personal—and that it could potentially reach more people than a broadcast message, if only it is buzzed about in great quantity by people who have very long contact lists and no qualms about promoting products to anyone who will listen.[72]

Although these techniques can be practiced ethically, there are numerous pitfalls associated with them, all having to do with transparency. As the Wharton article points out, these tactics raise "the specter of a paranoid future where corporate marketers have invaded every last niche of society, degrading all social interaction to a marketing transaction, where no one can be certain of anyone else's true opinions or intentions."[73]

Definitions

Viral marketing or *advertising* refers to using existing blogs and social networks (MySpace and Facebook, for instance) to increase the level of brand awareness of a product. *Viral* is an unfortunate word choice in that it is most often associated (at least in the past) with the spread of sickness or disease. The idea is the same, though. Marketers put out information in various forms on blog sites and other seemingly amateur venues in order to spread the word throughout the internet much faster (and cheaper) than traditional advertising can—thus the term *word-of-mouth* marketing. We will treat "word-of-mouth marketing" here as the overarching term under which the others described below fall. The driving concept is that people will pass on or "share" information, especially if it is exciting or creative. The rise of YouTube to the status of a multi-million-dollar business in just a few years is a testament to this approach. The ethical down side is that information disseminated this way can take on a false credibility because it seems to come directly not from an advertiser but rather from people just like you and me. As the marketing professor Jerry Wind notes, "For years, people recognized the power of word-of-mouth in convincing, influencing, affecting consumer behavior. It has more credibility than traditional advertising."[74]

Buzz marketing is essentially the same concept, except that the advertising aspect is more hidden beneath layers of person-to-person communication. The technique attempts to make advertising seem more like a conversation between friends in which information is exchanged spontaneously. This may even include actual marketing representatives posing as members of the target audience, often in chat rooms or specific blog sites devoted to the topic under discussion. This more insidious form of buzz marketing is called *stealth* or *guerilla marketing*. According to the Canadian law firm McMillan, Binch, Mendelson, stealth marketing is "marketing that promotes a product without disclosing any direct connection between the advertiser and the message."[75]

Stealth marketing involves a marketer engaging with customers without disclosing that they are in fact paid by the business for which they are marketing a product or service. For example, a business might hire an actor or charismatic person to use a certain product visibly and convincingly in locations where target consumers of such product are located. While using the product in the location, the actor will also discuss the product with people he or she meets in that location and possibly hand out samples. The actor will often be able to sell consumers on their product without those consumers even realizing it.[76]

This approach is based squarely on the understanding that people will drop their defenses to persuasion if they don't think they are actually being pitched to. In other words, people are more likely to accept at face value recommendations about a product, service, or idea if (1) it comes from someone they know, even tangentially, and (2) they thus believe that the person has no vested interest or ulterior motive in presenting them with the information.

As traditional outlets (such as TV and magazines) decrease, become saturated, or are ignored, advertisers must seek ever-newer venues in which to sell their products. Social media outlets are an obvious choice, especially for the various forms of word-of-mouth marketing. *Social media* can be defined as an integration of technology with social interaction. Some have called it the "new democracy." Internet forums, message boards, blog sites, etc., are all forms of social media. Obvious examples are such sites as MySpace and Facebook, popular among college students and, increasingly, others. These are places in which people share everything from their personal lives to heated political commentary to creative work. It is also a place in which, increasingly, advertisers seek to become your friend, and that is what we will focus on here.

To Disclose or Not to Disclose: Is There Really Any Question?

That probably depends on whom you ask. In 2005 the non-profit watchdog group Commercial Alert filed a complaint with the Federal Trade Commission citing what they saw as a deeply disturbing marketing trend. The complaint stated that

> companies are perpetrating large-scale deception upon consumers by deploying buzz marketers who fail to disclose that they have been enlisted to promote products. This failure to disclose is fundamentally fraudulent and misleading.[77]

Commercial Alert cited several instances of what they called "stealth marketing." The most familiar (probably because of a *New York Times* article) was the 2002 campaign initiated by Sony Ericcson Mobile for its T68i mobile phone and digital camera. The initiative, called "Fake Tourist," involved placing 60 actors posing as tourists at attractions in New York and Seattle to demonstrate the camera phone. Some of the actors asked passersby to take their photo, which demonstrated the camera phone's capabilities.[78] Others frequented trendy lounges and bars, engaged strangers in conversation, and found reasons to use their new mobile phones to elicit interest. In neither case did the actors identify themselves as representatives for Sony Ericsson.[79]

Most notably, the complaint also targeted the number-one maker of household products in the United States—Procter & Gamble (P&G). In 2001, P&G started "Tremor," a word-of-mouth marketing program that actively recruited teenagers to pitch P&G products to their friends.[80] By 2006, some 225,000 teens were enrolled in the program. The teens were provided with such incentives as coupons, discounts, free downloads, and product samples. The idea was that they would then play up the use of P&G products to their social networking friends. The "connectors," the name used to define their function, were free to disclose that they were working for P&G, but were not required to do so. In 2005, P&G broadened its focus to include "moms." Again, this group wasn't required to disclose their affiliation with the company or let on that their praise of its products was somewhat "induced."

Commercial Alert's complaint criticized P&G's policy of not requiring transparency in their marketing efforts. According to *BusinessWeek*:

> Without such disclosure, Commercial Alert Executive Director Gary Ruskin sees the danger of the basic "commercialization of human relations," where friends treat one another as advertising pawns, undercutting social trust.[81]

P&G countered that by not requiring its "connectors" to disclose that they are working for the company, they are put completely in charge of what they choose to tell their friends. However, others point out that such disclosure would jeopardize the sales pitch by undermining the credibility of the "connectors."[82]

In December, 2006, the FTC, in a staff opinion, denied the request to investigate P&G's marketing techniques. They did, however, agree that "companies can deceive people by deploying 'sponsored consumers' who hide that they are paid to promote products."[83] The Commission stated that

> in some word of mouth marketing contexts, it would appear that consumers may reasonably give more weight to statements that sponsored consumers make about their opinions or experiences with a product based on their assumed independence from the marketer . . . In such circumstances, it would appear that the failure to disclose the relationship between the marketer and the consumer would be deceptive unless the relationship were clear from the context.[84]

But, what if that relationship is not completely opaque, only a little blurry? In an article for CNET News.com, the journalist Stefanie Olson deals at length with the growing problem of the blurred line between "friends and flaks" on MySpace.[85] The major concern is that although ads on most web sites are "typically set off from editorial and clearly labeled . . . [on] social networks, ads and marketing pitches can come in any form, without a label. Even stickier on My Space, it can be difficult to tell a genuine member from a marketer."[86] According to a report from the research firm eMarketer, social networking sites such as MySpace are full of marketing campaigns set up as "profile pages" for hundreds of advertising "partners," none of whom identify themselves as such to visitors. Instead, they offer free music downloads, celebrity gossip, comic books, games, coupons for products, and myriad other opportunities to become subtly exposed to products. Olson cites Renee Hobbs, director of the media education lab at Temple University, as pointing out that

> [m]ost American teens perceive the presence of bands, celebrities and comics on MySpace not as marketing, but as an opportunity for friendship. Teens' response to these marketing messages is linked developmentally, because they are at an age where they are using relationships to develop a sense of identity.[87]

But, what if the relationship isn't even a relationship? What if those passing on the sales pitch aren't even aware they are part of the marketing plan? In 2000, Fallon McElligott, the ad agency for Lee Dungarees, came up with an idea to make their clent's product more appealing to 17- to 22-year-olds.[88] Playing on the amateur multi-media-author appeal, they created a series of three, grainy, apparently home-made video clips. The small films were sent out over the internet to some 200,000 web surfers in the target age group. The videos were designed to appeal to the quirky, naïve nature of budding MTV music video producers who would, of course, pass them on to their friends all over the web. The films directed the receivers back to the sites of the "creators" of the clips, who had fully formed internet lives and lots of quirky interests (one was a 24-year-old race car driver). The problem is, they weren't real. Instead, they turned out to be the fictional creations of a marketing plan. The plan, however, worked. Some 100,000 surfers visited the three sites the first week and, when the ruse was intentionally disclosed a few months later, unwitting participants were already hooked. It was revealed that the characters were actually part of an online video game in which the only way a player could reach the advanced level was to go out to a store and retrieve the product identification numbers ("secret code") off Lee jeans and other items. Sales of Lee products rose by 20 percent in 2000.

The one thing all of these cases have in common is that the marketing tactics they use are purposefully designed to create a sense of security for the consumer. However briefly, they believe they are sharing an experience with someone free of motivation other than friendliness.

[T]he gambit essentially is the same: to slip into the conversational pathways of those who heavily influence their peers. That way, instead of coming from a faceless and distrusted corporate conglomerate, the marketing message seems to emanate from the most powerful endorser possible: your coolest friend.[89]

The Ethical Bottom Line for Word-of-Mouth Marketing

The fact is, word-of-mouth and buzz marketing work and, because they work, advertisers will continue to use them. As the business professors Andrew Kaikati and Jack Kaikati note:

> Despite the criticisms from various quarters, stealth marketing is here to stay. It has a powerful role to play when it is tastefully implemented. As traditional television advertisements continue to lose their effectiveness, brand managers are being pressured to think outside the box by going undercover to reach consumers. To capture the attention of jaded, fickle consumers, they will continue to devise new approaches that are harder to detect. Brand managers are gambling that the benefits of stealth marketing will outweigh the castigations by critics.[90]

These authors, like the myopic advertisers defined earlier, seem to believe that the marketplace is full of intelligent and independent-minded citizens who "can choose the messages they want to engage with while ignoring the vast majority of ad clutter."[91] They believe that the ethicality of the new marketing tactics will ultimately be decided by these "savvy consumers" who will "determine when stealth marketing has crossed some ill-defined line."[92] Their only fear seems to be that, as these tactics become more popular, they will lose their stealth value, forcing advertisers to "seek even more creative tactics to stand out in the competitive marketplace."

The "ill-defined line" being crossed here is not so fuzzy as to go unnoticed by others in the field, however. The Word of Mouth Marketing Association (WOM-MA), a leading organization representing marketers who practice this brand of advertising, has developed a code of ethics aimed specifically at such practices as stealth marketing. It clearly calls for what it terms "honesty of identity," which includes:

- Clear disclosure of identity is vital to establishing trust and credibility. We do not blur identification in a manner that might confuse or mislead consumers as to the true identity of the individual with whom they are communicating, or instruct or imply that others should do so.
- Campaign organizers should monitor and enforce disclosure of identity. Manner of disclosure can be flexible, based on the context of

the communication. Explicit disclosure is not required for an obviously fictional character, but would be required for an artificial identity or corporate representative that could be mistaken for an average consumer.

- We comply with FTC regulations regarding identity in endorsements that state: "Advertisements presenting endorsements by what are represented, directly or by implication, to be 'actual consumers' should utilize actual consumers, in both the audio and video or clearly and conspicuously disclose that the persons in such advertisements are not actual consumers of the advertised product."
- Campaign organizers will disclose their involvement in a campaign when asked by consumers or the media. We will provide contact information upon request.[93]

In addition, the organization has developed a "tool kit" composed of a set of 20 questions that can be used to judge the ethicality of a word-of-mouth marketing campaign. It includes such advice as always insisting on disclosure, making sure the opinions expressed by advocates are honest ones, and instructing advocates in ethical practices and behaviors.[94]

The WOMMA code and the increased scrutiny of word-of-mouth practices have encouraged some agencies, such as BzzAgent, one of the largest and most visible buzz marketing agencies in the U.S., to adopt policies that require its agents to disclose their identities. But, as with much else in media ethics, the functional results often dictate the moral response. It seems the practical aspects of disclosure suggest that word-of-mouth campaigns are generally more successful with identity disclosure than without. Apparently, credibility vanishes once people find out they've been duped, and the backlash from consumers can be detrimental to the overall campaign, and the product being sold.

Regardless of the practical motivations behind disclosure, advertisers have a moral obligation not to hide their identities. As previously noted, the ethics scholar Patrick Plaisance argues that transparency

is an attitude of proactive moral engagement that manifests an express concern for the persons-as-ends principle when a degree of deception or omission can reasonably be said to risk thwarting the receiver's due dignity or the ability to exercise reason.[95]

In other words, we violate the dignity and autonomy of our audiences when we seek to deceive them, and many forms of word-of-mouth marketing do exactly that. If we are to act as morally responsible communicators, we must treat the "other" as if he or she actually were our friend.

Offensive Advertising

The code of Advertising Ethics and Principles of the American Advertising Federation states that, in the matter of taste and decency, "Advertising shall be free
of statements, illustrations or implications which are offensive to good taste or
public decency."[96] That's a tall order. And a little vague. What exactly are "good
taste" and "public decency" and who gets to define them?

A Matter of Taste?

Is offensive advertising truly in the eye of the beholder? Some would have us
believe so. Certainly, many in advertising adhere to the tenets of ethical subjectivism, believing that there is no such thing as offensive—it is all just a matter of
taste. And, as the Romans said, *de gustibus non disputandum* (there can be no dispute over matters of taste). There is also no disputing that advertising sometimes
produces material that some find offensive. The first question we need to ask is
why it is offensive to some and not to others.

James Barnes and Michael Johnson, both professors of marketing, suggest
that ads may appear as offensive to some because of either the nature of the
product itself (condoms, sanitary napkins, etc.) or their creative execution (using
sex to sell, for instance).[97] The fact of the product itself being offensive is not
generally under the control of the advertising agency—except that it can always
decline to take the account. In addition, social mores, including taste, change
over time, affecting the first factor. For example, advertising condoms was once
considered pretty much off limits. Today, ads for condoms appear regularly in
a number of mainstream magazines, though not as much on TV. Exposure to
the product can be thus controlled to some extent by placement. On the second
factor, creative execution, the agency can be said to have much more, if not total,
control. The Australian marketing professor David Waller found that even if a
product itself might be considered "controversial," it doesn't necessarily follow
that advertising it would be viewed as offensive.[98] If it was considered offensive,
it is more likely that something else about the ad was offensive other than the
product itself. For example, Waller found that people tended to be offended by
such associative aspects as sexist images, violence, stereotyping, indecent language, anti-social behavior, and nudity—aspects over which advertisers usually
have control.[99]

The adverting professor Timothy Christy, however, argues for a more holistic
approach. He suggests that variables such as the descriptions of the product, the
execution being used, the medium in which it is displayed, and the audiences
that are least/most likely to be offended should be considered as a whole. For
example:

> the use of nudity by itself may be offensive to some, but if nudity is used
> to promote a product associated with sex to certain audiences in a medium

that includes sexual content, the likelihood of offense is lessened. This example alludes to the importance of understanding consumers and tailoring messages to target audiences accordingly.[100]

He suggests that advertisers can control the level of potential offense in an ad by better understanding how consumers are offended in the first place—in other words, understand your audience. This, he argues, is a by-product of the fact that advertisers are often quite different from those to whom they advertise—a point also relevant to stereotyping.[101]

In Great Britain, the advertising industry has set up an independent body to police the rules laid down in their various advertising codes—a self-regulatory system. A 2002 report on serious offence in non-broadcast advertising (magazine, billboard, etc.) found that "the majority of the population are quite positive towards advertising, but some feel that sometimes ads just go too far."[102] The findings suggest that the reaction to offensive material can be broken down into "emotional" offense and "rational" offense, roughly corresponding with the way people process advertising (e.g., the elaboration likelihood model). For example, an ad depicting a blatantly violent image might elicit an emotional reaction whereas one using subtle yet harmful stereotyping might prompt a more rational objection. Additionally, people seem more likely to be offended "by proxy" (on behalf of someone else) than to be personally offended; for instance, passing a public billboard containing a sexual image while walking with a child. Not surprisingly, the research showed that offense differed with the age of the viewer.

> Younger people tended to be less sensitive in relation to "traditionally" offensive areas, such as sexual images, violence and bad language; but they tended to be more sensitive than older people when thinking about how groups and individuals were portrayed, and were more concerned about the negative portrayal of vulnerable groups.[103]

All groups seemed to agree that the most sensitive images were those that sexualized children or degraded, demeaned, or humiliated vulnerable groups (ethnic minorities, seniors, women, the poor, etc.). However, over three quarters of the people surveyed also felt that it is wrong to use sex to sell unconnected products. Similarly, the majority agreed that violence should never be portrayed in advertising.

Probably the most important finding, and one supported by a number of researchers, is that context affects the level of offense experienced. In other words, the location and type of media were crucial in deciding whether someone was offended or not. If an ad using overt sexual images were placed in a magazine targeted to adult readers, children would be less likely to see it, as would members of religious groups—thus the ad would be less offensive. Choice also plays an important part, because people can choose whether to buy or read certain publications (or prohibit their children from doing so) and thus avoid being offended. Conversely, offensive advertising placed in public places (billboards, posters, store signage) is most likely to be viewed negatively.

Finally, what's being advertised plays a role as well. People are less likely to be offended by advertising produced by charities (non-profits) for "good" causes even if it uses "shocking or distressing" images. For example, an ad for AIDS awareness stressing condom usage probably would not offend, whereas an ad *for* condoms by the manufacturer might. So where does that leave us? According to the advertising professor Kim Sheehan:

> Images that are shocking, disrespectful, or out-and-out disgusting must be evaluated within the context of where they will appear. The sensibilities of the target audience who will see the message must also be considered. This recognizes that a message that is completely appropriate to one target audience may be inappropriate for another.[104]

However, is advertising's only responsibility as regards offensive material to place it where those most likely to be offended won't see it? Or is it a much larger issue of what the Yale Law professor Stephen Carter calls "the coarsening of society" in general, and the part advertising plays in that process?[105]

Whom Are We Offending, and Why?

A 2007 ad by the Italian fashion house Dolce & Gabbana, appearing in *Esquire* magazine and elsewhere around the world, was pulled by the company after being banned in Italy and Spain following protests. In the ad, a woman,

> fully clothed in a tight dress and spiked heels, lies on her back, hips raised as a bare-chested man holds her down and four other men look on. The menace in the situation is underscored by the fact the woman is blankly unsmiling and some of the men appear to have slight sneers on their faces.[106]

Consumer groups and women's organizations immediately took offense. Kim Gandy, president of the National Organization for Women, called it "a provocative ad," but one that is "provoking things that really are not what we want to have provoked. We don't need any more violence."[107] Wally Snyder, president and CEO of the American Advertising Federation, says that the ad ran afoul of what he calls "taste and decency," and certainly does not "advance the image of the advertising industry."[108]

Another area of advertising that walks a very thin line is "shock advertising." *Shock advertising* can be defined as an appeal that "deliberately, rather than inadvertently, startles and offends its audience."[109] The business professor Darren Dahl says that this tactic purposely elicits offence through the process of "norm violation," by literally flouting law or custom (obscenity or indecent sexual references) or moral or social codes (profanity or vulgarity), or simply by outraging the moral senses (violence, disgusting images).[110] For example, the clothing giant Calvin Klein began outraging consumers in the early 1980s with blatantly sexual images of adolescent models such as Brooke Shields (blue jeans) and a childlike Kate Moss (Obsession perfume). In 1995, a campaign featuring "pubescent models in provocative poses caused major controversy and debate when they crossed the line between fashion and pornography."[111]

> The advertising campaign—which used images of models who were reportedly as young as 15—was meant to mimic "picture set" pornography of the '60s. In the magazine ads, young models posed suggestively in a sleazy suburban "Rec Room," complete with cheap paneled walls, a paint splattered ladder, and purple shag carpeting. The TV spots left little doubt that the images intended to imitate pornography.[112]

Eventually, the Justice Department launched an investigation to determine whether the ads violated child pornography laws. The ads were subsequently withdrawn, but not before Klein's reputation for "cool" had skyrocketed. In 1999, another Calvin Klein campaign targeted even younger children, photographed in black and white, frolicking in their underwear. Again, experts pointed out that the images were pornographic because children were sexualized by the particular style of the ads. The ads were pulled within 24 hours.

By contrast, consider an ad campaign that ran in 2000 sponsored by the Breast Cancer Fund. The posters, which ran in public venues such as bus stations, mimicked typical magazine ads in *Cosmopolitan* and catalog images such as those in *Victoria's Secret*. The models, clothed in trendy underwear, were seen revealing mastectomy scars where their breasts would normally be. The copy read, "It's no secret society is obsessed with breasts, but what are we doing about breast cancer?" One billboard company that had originally donated space refused to use the posters at all. Several other posters were removed following complaints. As we have seen, potentially offensive advertising used in a "good" cause is less likely to be viewed negatively; however, that doesn't mean that it won't offend people at all.

So, what's the difference? We can look back at Chapter 7 for part of the answer. In judging the use of certain means to reach a desired goal, we have to ask ourselves whether the goal itself is moral and whether the means used to achieve it are moral. The variables that concern us here are whether the goal, or ends, of advertising a particular product are morally worthy and thereby mitigate the use of morally questionable means. If the end is not viewed as morally worthy, then the use of morally suspect means is questionable. Let's assume, for argument's sake, that the goal of simply selling a product or gaining brand recognition in and of itself is basically amoral—that is, it is neither moral nor immoral. It is an economic goal. Further, let us argue that raising awareness of breast cancer and its effects is a good thing—a moral act.

The question posed at the head of this section, "whom are we offending, and why?" now comes into play for both scenarios. Advertisers can rather easily predict whether a campaign will be offensive, and who is most likely to be offended. The part of the question that goes to the morality of the act is the "why" part. By applying the criteria of means and ends, we could say that using shock advertising to draw attention to a moral cause is *probably* ethical—remembering that unethical techniques are still suspect, even in a good cause. However, if we accept that selling a product or simply drawing attention to a brand is an amoral end, then the morality of using potentially offensive tactics to accomplish that end deserves a much harder scrutiny. As David Waller reminds us:

> For those involved with controversial products or controversial campaigns, it appears that they should be aware of the potential to offend the public . . . [They] should also be aware of what issues are the ones that offend their customers, and be socially responsible enough to refrain from openly being offensive.[113]

Further Use of the Means–Ends Paradigm in Advertising

We can use the means–ends paradigm detailed in Chapter 7 and applied above as a good starting point from which to investigate ethicality in advertising overall. We can look at the means used (how are we doing it?), and the ends sought (why are we doing it?) in order to judge the ethicality of an action. A good end does not necessarily justify questionable means, but it does help (the breast cancer example). Conversely, an ethically unjustifiable end (selling cigarettes) cannot be vindicated by ethical means. We must use a modicum of caution, however, in judging the validity of both means and ends. If we take too critical a stance regarding the purpose of advertising, almost nothing can be justified. For example, if we assume that the practice of advertising naturally subverts personal autonomy, or produces, de facto, a society of mindless consumers, then no amount of moral justification will suffice. On the other hand, if we conceive of advertising as a necessary component of a free-market economy and as an important contributor to the "marketplace of ideas," then we must regard it as also capable of acting ethically—indeed require it to do so. As the Vatican report suggests, "[a]dvertising can violate the dignity of the human person both through its content—what is advertised, the manner in which it is advertised—and through the impact it seeks to make upon its audience."[114]

In using the means–ends paradigm, however, we must also consider the important role of intent. Aristotle defended his how-to book on persuasion (*Rhetoric*) by arguing that the act of persuasion is neither good nor evil. Only the person using it can determine its morality by his intent. A person of good character would not perform an evil act. Likewise, Kant argued that an act can be judged moral *only* by the intent of the actor. Thus, a moral act is one that is intended by the actor to do good, not evil. How do we factor intent into the equation? The following example will help illustrate.

An end might be viewed as morally unjustifiable by most people—such as selling cigarettes. However, the means used to accomplish the selling could be entirely above board. For instance, some cigarette ads even mention the health risks or include information on how to quit. So, if the goal (or end) of advertising is to sell a particular product or idea, then we can first ask whether that end is, in itself, morally justifiable. If we assume that the *act of selling* is itself neither moral nor immoral (amoral), then we must ask if the *product* being sold is questionable. For example, if cigarettes are thought by many to be a bad (even evil) product, can any tactic used to sell them mitigate that fact? *An immoral end cannot be justified by moral means.* On the other hand, alcohol abuse is epidemic within certain groups in our society. Is it the alcohol that is bad, or is it the act of selling it to those who are most vulnerable to its abuse the immoral part of the equation? In this case, the tactic used to sell the alcohol (means) is beside the point. If we cannot judge the ethicality of an act by either its ends or its means, we must question its intent, which goes to the act itself. When the very act of selling something is questionable (it *could* cause harm) but not necessarily morally unjustifiable (the use of alcohol, unlike tobacco, is not necessarily harmful), then it cannot be amoral. That is, morality can then be attached to the act. In this case, the act of selling alcohol by intentionally targeting at-risk groups is unethical.

We can use this same paradigm to explore each of the problems in this chapter by asking if:

- the act itself is morally *unjustified*: the selling of harmful products such as cigarettes;
- the act itself is morally *justified*: making people aware of the breast cancer epidemic;
- the means are questionable: use of potentially offensive images, or the creation of misleading images instead of the use of simple facts, or the use of stereotypes that might prove harmful over time to certain groups within society;
- the intent is honorable or not: concealing the identity of product "advocates" in order to deceive consumers into believing they are talking to "regular people."

What Does It All Mean?

Of all the media discussed in this book, advertising is probably the most criticized, and, sometimes, the most maligned. We should remember, however, that advertising is not inherently unethical any more than public relations or journalism. It contributes to the culture in which we live, both by reflecting it and by contributing to it. As the Vatican report on advertising puts it, "[A]dvertising can, and often does, play a constructive role in economic growth, in the exchange of information and ideas, and in the fostering of solidarity among individuals and groups."[115] Advertising can be creative, often humorous, and even uplifting at times. Many consider it an art form.

We must also remember that what advertising seeks to accomplish, in most cases, is the sale of a product or the adoption of an idea (often leading to the sale of a product). Advertising affects the consumer directly, in myriad ways—some good, some bad. Because of this, a "fundamental principle" is enjoined: "[T]hose who commission, prepare or disseminate advertising . . . are morally responsible for what they seek to move people to do."[116]

The ethics of advertising don't boil down to simply recognizing shady tactics. It is a matter of wanting to do the right thing. As we have seen, that is most often effected by working from within a moral climate in which ethical issues are recognized and dealt with.

> The indispensable guarantors of ethically correct behavior by the advertising industry are the well formed and responsible consciences of advertising professionals themselves: consciences sensitive to their duty not merely to serve the interests of those who commission and finance their work but also to respect and uphold the rights and interests of their audiences and to serve the common good.[117]

Chapter 10

Ethics in News Journalism

That awful power, the public opinion of a nation, is created in America by a horde of ignorant, self-complacent simpletons who failed at ditching and shoe-making and fetched up in journalism on their way to the poorhouse.

(Mark Twain)

In 1947, the Hutchins Commission of Freedom of the Press presented its report on a "Free and Responsible Press." In it the commission called for a press that today might be deemed "socially responsible." The five obligations of modern media, according to the Hutchins Commission, were:

- To provide a truthful, comprehensive, and intelligent account of the day's events in a context that gives them meaning.
- To serve as a forum for the exchange of comment and criticism.
- To develop a representative picture of the constituent groups in society.
- To be responsible for the presentation and clarification of the goals and values of society.
- To provide full access to the day's intelligence.

In other words, not only should media do their job and attend to the ramifications of carrying out that job, but they should also involve themselves in the well-being of society as a whole. As stated by the journalists Bob Kovach and Tom Rosenstiel, "The primary purpose of journalism is to provide citizens with the information they need to be free and self-governing."[1]

Journalism today is a diverse package of offerings including print (newspapers and magazines), broadcast (radio and television) and, increasingly, the internet. The face of news journalism is changing, literally every day. According the Project for Excellence in Journalism, "The Web is becoming a more integral part of people's lives. Eight in 10 Americans 17 and older now say the Internet is a critical source of information."[2] According to the same survey, more Americans identified the internet as a more important source of information than television, radio, and newspapers. And the number going online regularly for news is growing. In late 2007, more than seven in 10 Americans said they went online for news.[3]

Probably the most important change instigated by the internet is "citizen" or "participatory" journalism. The growing phenomenon involves "ordinary" citizens playing an active role in gathering and reporting news. Mark Glasser, a freelance journalist, says:

> The idea behind citizen journalism is that people without professional journalism training can use the tools of modern technology and the global distribution of the Internet to create, augment or fact-check media on their own or in collaboration with others.[4]

How this movement will affect mainstream journalism (practiced by "professional" journalists) has yet to be seen. What is clear is that any form of journalism will encounter ethical issues. Many of these problems are bound to plague the "new" journalism as well, but many new issues are bound to surface as journalism changes. What follows in this chapter is mostly the thinking concerning traditional journalistic practices that have developed over the past 100 years or so. However, as has been noted throughout this book, what has been considered unethical in the past will probably still be unethical today. Media practitioners must use the lessons of the past to inform their actions now and in the future, especially if they want to avoid the mistakes of the past.

Meta-issues in News Journalism

Before we begin a detailed look at the research and the ethical issues specific to journalism, we will look at two larger meta-issues that inform the practice in the United States and, to a large extent, the Western world. These will include the concept of objectivity, upon which the modern practice of journalism is grounded, and media bias, a topic directly related to objectivity and a cause for much concern among journalists, their audiences, and their critics.

Objectivity

As we learned in Chapter 4, subjective claims are based on individual feelings, personal opinion, or taste. In other words, the subjective view of reality is relative to the observer. However, not everything we can observe is relative. Some of it is just plain fact. Water still boils at 100 degrees Celsius, regardless of who observes it. In order to observe objectively, then, we must accept the notion of a "reality" that can be both identified and described accurately. At the same time, we must remember that, as human beings, we still tend to view the objective world through a subjective lens. The trick to being objective is to recognize this inclination and understand that there will be different accounts of reality that must then be judged as either adequate or inadequate based on facts and reason, not on personal perspective.

Philosophically, objectivity has acquired several different meanings over time.

The basic meaning distinguishes objectivity from subjectivity, which means to remove all "human judgment . . . , usually with the aid of some appropriately rigorous methodology."[5] The second sense of the word conveys disinterestedness or neutrality, which is generally used to denote the difference between objectivity and advocacy of a particular idea (e.g., political). An important use of the term was suggested by the pragmatist philosophers Charles Peirce and, later, John Dewey. They argued that objectivity could be attained only as part of a collective decision formed by a "community of the competent."[6] In other words, it was useless to exclude the active participation of the observer from the subject of observation. It was only through an interaction between the two that we could arrive at a common understanding of the world. "[K]nowledge came from an active community of inquiry in which individuals tested themselves against and contributed to an evolving collective understanding."[7]

Objectivity, as used in news journalism, incorporates all of these approaches; however, which gets higher billing often depends upon whom you ask. It is generally accepted that journalistic objectivity refers to being without prejudice or bias, presenting information fully and in context, and with an eye to being fair and balanced. Julia Fox, a professor of broadcast news, characterizes objective reporting as

> being neutral, unbiased, and balanced and void of personal ideology and values, opinions, and impressions. Journalistic objectivity is a professional norm seen by journalists as both an individual responsibility of the reporter and a collective responsibility of the profession.[8]

She notes, however, that this is a relatively new phenomenon, pointing out that there was a fiercely partisan press in the United States for much its history. The historian Michael Schudson agrees that the press remained "deeply partisan" until the end of the nineteenth century, and suggests that the modern notion of an objective press dates more accurately to the 1920s.[9]

It was during and after this period that Walter Lippmann argued for a new form of journalism in which objectivity would replace what he saw as an ingrained, often unconscious, bias in the press. This was also a time, following World War I, when propaganda began to be more fully understood, and increasingly used by a developing new occupation called "public relations." Journalism, according to Lippmann, was being practiced by "untrained accidental witnesses" whose personal opinions superseded reality in favor of preconceived stereotypes—thus creating and perpetuating the "pictures in our heads."[10] Michael Schudson says Lippmann believed this problem was exacerbated by the public's limited access to first-hand experience of the world.

> When these pictures come from distant places, brought to us by a press without much self-discipline or sophistication or intellectual weight, our

actions—our votes, our choices—are at the mercy of the flawed picture of the world that various media provide.[11]

Lippmann believed that the crisis in journalism was reflective of the crisis of democracy as a whole. The modern world was just too complex for personal understanding, thus only knowable second-hand—and second-hand information was a muddle of pre-conceived stereotypes. How could democracy function if citizens couldn't understand its intricacies and the media were unable or unwilling to explain them?

His solution to the problem was twofold. First, he argued that journalists should acquire a "scientific spirit." By this he meant that they should arrive at a common method of gathering, analyzing, and reporting the events of the day, relying exclusively on verifiable fact, not opinion or speculation. He knew this would not be an easy task; however, he noted it was precisely "because news is complex and slippery [that] good reporting requires the exercise of the highest scientific virtues."[12] According to the Project for Excellence in Journalism, the original intent of Lippmann's proposal was to develop a "consistent method of testing information—a transparent approach to evidence—precisely so that personal and cultural biases would not undermine the accuracy of their work."[13] They note that "In the original concept . . . the method is objective, not the journalist. The key was in the *discipline* of the craft, not the aim."[14]

This discipline of verification is what separates journalism from other modes of communication, such as propaganda, fiction or entertainment.[15]

The second part of Lippmann's solution was based largely on Plato's observation that most people couldn't figure out reality on their own. They had to rely on the intelligent elite for guidance. In the *Republic* Plato suggested a government composed of "philosopher kings" who would wisely guide the masses in the best way to live and prosper. In the same vein, Lippmann imagined a "specialized class" of elites who would form information agencies, or, as he termed them, "political observatories," that would then inform both government and, through the press, the people. In other words, reality would be interpreted by those most able to understand it. The press would play a vital role in this function because of its shift from opinion to factual reporting. According to Schudson, it was around this time that

the objectivity norm became a fully formulated occupational ideal, part of a professional project or mission. Far more than a set of craft rules to fend off libel suits or a set of constraints to help editors keep tabs on their underlings, objectivity was finally a moral code. It was asserted in the textbooks used in journalism schools, it was asserted in codes of ethics of professional associations.[16]

Problems with Objectivity

The most persistent complaints about objectivity are that it doesn't truly exist, or that it does exist, but it's the wrong approach for journalism. We needn't go into the epistemological argument over whether reality is objective or entirely subjective; however, that long-debated topic does inform the discussion over whether it is even possible to be objective as a journalist. The idea of an attainable objectivity in journalism rests on the "commonly held view that there is some fixed reality which can be observed and recorded without bias."[17] However, as the Australian educators Rick Iedema, Susan Feez, and Peter White note:

> The way events are observed, interpreted and reported will always be conditioned by the social background and ideological perspective of journalists, editors and management. Even the most ostensibly "factual" report will be the product of numerous value judgments. These will have determined, for example, that this event, rather than some other, deserved to be covered, how prominently it was to be featured, the way in which the event was to be described, which part of the event received primary focus, which experts, eye witnesses or participants were called upon for comment, which viewpoints were regarded as authoritative, and so on.[18]

Most of those who work in journalism agree that true objectivity is more an ideal than an obtainable reality. However, because of the belief of those outside journalism that the objectivity standard so often touted by the field is part of an unwritten contract that journalists have with their audiences, a recurring complaint against the press is that it *lacks* objectivity. Journalists Evan Thomas and Suzanne Smalley, writing for *Newsweek*, say that "the criticism is fair, in the sense that it is almost impossible to be completely objective."

> Subjectivity always creeps into the choices made by reporters and editors on what to include or what to emphasize in a story. News people are all too human, and sometimes they are not even aware of their biases. But on the whole, the mainstream press does try, with imperfect results, to be fair.[19]

As we saw in Chapter 6, truth in journalism relies on a combination of factors: accuracy, context, and fairness/balance. Objectivity has often been viewed similarly, especially as regards fairness and balance, in the belief that by being fair and balanced, neutrality (thus, objectivity) is achieved. Remember, however, Walter Lippmann argued that objectivity is not a result; it is a method. The journalist need not be neutral, but her method of gathering, analyzing, and reporting should be. Objectivity of method can produce news that may at once be both informationally accurate and complete, and present a point of view. Neutrality, then, is not the issue, and, in fact, can be abused.

[T]he impartial voice employed by many news organizations, that familiar, supposedly neutral style of newswriting, is not a fundamental principle of journalism. Rather, it is an often helpful device news organizations use to highlight that they are trying to produce something obtained by objective methods . . . [T]his neutral voice, without a discipline of verification, creates a veneer covering something hollow. Journalists who select sources to express what is really their own point of view, and then use the neutral voice to make it seem objective, are engaged in a form of deception.[20]

Adopting a neutral stance, in other words, is only a fiction of objectivity. The ethics scholar Stephen Ward defends the concept of objectivity, but says that the concept he defends

is not the traditional idea of objective reporting as a neutral description of "just the facts." Instead, [it is] a theory of objectivity that stresses the testing of journalistic interpretations in various contexts.[21]

Ward's "pragmatic objectivity" fits well with John Dewey's assertion that what is ultimately objective is determined by a combined communicative effort involving both journalists and their audiences. In this interpretive mix, both parties reason about and with values that are, in a sense, subjective, but, in a larger sense, are "part of good inquiry, a coherent life, and a democratic society."[22]

As Lippmann pointed out, there is a difference between the method of objectivity and an objective result. We must remember that journalists are human beings, and, as such, they use language to construct reality. As with all such constructions, subjectivity informs the result. It is entirely possible to use the method of objectivity and still present a subjective viewpoint. Many newspapers around the world do this regularly. Facts are still facts. They can and should inform opinion, but opinion follows facts. It should not precede them. According to the public journalism advocate Philip Meyer, good journalism should be concerned with "objectivity of method, not objectivity of result."[23] This is scientific method applied to the practice of journalism.

Scientific method was developed to protect human investigators from the unconscious tricks of self-deception that afflict us all. Its procedures of peer review, replicability, and falsifiable hypotheses protect journalists as well.[24]

Meyer argues that a journalism that does not involve community in its deliberations is not acting responsibly in its function as a disseminator of information.

Objectivity, as defined by the knee-jerk, absolutist school of media ethics, means standing so far from the community that you see all events and all viewpoints as equally distant and important—or unimportant. It is implemented by giving equal weight to all viewpoints and assertions—or, if not all, an interesting variety within a socially acceptable spectrum. The result is a laying out of facts in a sterile, noncommittal manner, and then standing back to "let the reader decide" which view is true.

This, in effect, is objectivity of result, defining objectivity not by the way we go about our business of gathering and interpreting the news, but by what we put in the paper. It can be measured out: so many lines for this group, so many for that. In an effort to be fair, we sprinkle our resources to produce as even an effect as we can.[25]

What Meyer proposes is a press that involves community discourse in its search for the "truth," recognizing that a more subjective relationship with community and the realities that affect it may result in a "kind of truth that is different and in some ways better than the truth arrived at by more objective methods." This does not negate the need for such things as investigative journalism, or the use of objectivity as a method. What it does is allow the news media the leeway to recognize the difference between good and bad ideas (perhaps even promoting the good ones) and to note that difference without appearing to be biased in favor of the good ones. He argues that modern journalism has evolved into a "race apart, distant, detached, and uninfluenced by anything but a dogged desire to discover and impart the truth regardless of its consequences."[26] These journalists prefer to tell the *objective* truth and "let the chips fall where they may; give light and the people will find their own way."[27] What Meyer ultimately argues is that objectivity of method can, and often should, result in subjectivity of result. As Rick Iedema, Susan Feez, and Peter White suggest, "The difference between describing events 'objectively' and dealing with them 'subjectively' is a difference in the degree of our commitment to the truth value of what we are saying."[28]

The case both for and against objectivity rests not only on the debate over whether or not reality can be accurately described, but also on the ability of journalists to represent any given reality as free as possible from bias, but not necessarily from subjectivity. As the communications scholar Howard Myrick says,

[T]o the extent that [journalists] move in a positive direction on the continuum from speculation, innuendo, yielding to extraneous pressures, and the sloppiness of depending on press releases and staged press conferences which too frequently are designed to manipulate public opinion rather than inform, to that extent they will be regarded as responsible journalists. When they reach the point on the continuum that is defined by accuracy, integrity, and honesty, to that extent the prerequisites of objectivity will be achieved. It is a goal well worth pursuing, for the good of the profession of journalism and, more importantly, the good of the nation.[29]

Structural Biases in News Journalism

Andrew Cline, a professor and former journalist, observes that the press is often thought of as a "unified voice with a distinct bias," usually either politically right- or left-leaning, depending on the critic.[30] In order to avoid political bias (or any sort of bias, for that matter), journalists invoke the ethics of objectivity and fairness. Objectivity, in turn, is sought through attempting to be fair to those concerned with the news, and through a "professional process of information gathering that seeks fairness, completeness, and accuracy."[31] He describes the job of journalism as applying a "narrative structure to ambiguous events in order to create a coherent and causal sense of events."[32] However, he notes that journalists often go about their jobs without reflecting on the possibility that some biases are built into the practice—that there are certain premises and assumptions that go unnoticed in the work of news journalism.

In categorizing the potential forms of those biases, Cline notes that bias does not suggest that a message is necessarily false or unfair, but that consumers of information, nonetheless, need to be aware that those biases exist. He suggests that the real biases of journalism are *structural*. That is, they are inherent within the structure of modern, particularly American, journalism. He also notes that the kind of bias he is referring to is accurately described as "framing," which presents a particular viewpoint—a viewpoint that is not always immediately apparent, but, nonetheless, colors the way we view the world. What follows is a distillation of Cline's categories.

Commercial Bias

Increasingly, the business of news is making money. As news outlets are bought by large conglomerates and become only one of many interests in a vast business empire, there can be a disconnect between the ideals of news journalism and the imperatives of the marketplace. Large corporations typically demand a return on investment that some in the news business believe is unreasonable. With the proliferation of news outlets (the internet being the most noticeable) comes an new incentive to deliver what will be the most profitable "product" in an increasingly cluttered media market. As we saw in Chapter 9, the media have long been supported by advertising. This symbiotic relationship between news journalism and advertising requires, to some extent, that programming appeal to the target market of the advertisers. Because the network must be profitable for its owner, the news segment must draw viewers. Decreased viewership of news programming means fewer eyes on the advertising that supports that programming.

The State of the News Media 2008 report saw viewership fall for network nightly newscasts across the board.[33] In addition, the demographics for much of both network and cable news are changing. In 2007, the audience for network news was visibly aging, with a median age of 61. According to the report, "younger viewers are important to the network news programs because marketers generally pay higher ad rates for them, specifically those in the 25-to-54 demographic."[34] Because of the need to remain commercially viable, news must continue to satisfy existing audiences and attract new ones. Although recent tactics have included adding heavier doses of "soft news" (feature stories, human interest, entertainment-oriented content), probably the most time-honored tactic is to provide stories featuring conflict, because, as Cline points out, conflict draws readers and viewers. The effect of this tactic will become clearer as we elaborate on bias below.

Temporal Bias

The news media are biased toward the immediate. Although we have always suspected that news happened all the time, even when we were asleep, we were trained by the media to expect it at certain times of the day. At one time, "immediate" meant you had to wait for the evening paper to find out what was happening in the world. The advent of radio altered that somewhat as broadcasts could be "beamed" literally at any hour of the day or night; however, in the first few decades of radio, most stations simply signed off at midnight. Television was initially the same story. Television network news has traditionally been presented in the early evening, matching the schedule held first by newspapers and then by radio. It wasn't until the advent of 24-hour programming in general that the concept of an around-the-clock news channel even became viable—the advent of which literally changed the face of journalism. The rise of cable news has signaled a rise in expectations among audiences seeking news. No longer will they be content to wait until the evening to get their daily dose of news. They expect it when they turn on their televisions, and, increasingly, when they turn on their computers. The notion of what's new has been altered irrevocably by technology. However, the fact of news is that there isn't always a story to be covered or, even if there is, there aren't always the resources available to do so. It's one thing to have a 24-hour news operation. It's quite another to fill all that time with news. As the State of the News Media report reveals:

> For all the time it has to fill, roughly 18 hours of original programming each day, cable news has become in many ways a niche medium that offers viewers narrow formula rather than a broad-based agenda of the events of the day. That formula in 2007 was a combination of controversial opinion, a dose of tabloid-tinged crime and celebrity, edgy personalities, and, during the daytime, a focus on the immediate.[35]

Nonetheless, the expectation that there will always be something of interest drives news outlets to present "news" even when there's nothing to present.

Expediency Bias

Closely related to temporal bias is expediency bias. Because of the intense deadline pressure faced by most journalists, there is extreme pressure to be first with a story—to "scoop" the competition. The 24-hour news cycle exacerbates the situation as news operations increasingly compete for market share and viewer attention. As a result, there is a bias toward "information that can be obtained quickly, easily, and inexpensively."[36] The result is the hurried call to a veteran "expert" or official for a pithy quote or opinion in a hurry. Well-known sources become regulars on talk shows, or are often quoted in news stories—as much because they can be accessed quickly as for the validity of their opinions.

Visual Bias

Television has always been biased in favor of moving images. After all, television contains all the elements that Marshall McLuhan once called a "hot medium"— sight, sound, and, most importantly, motion. This puts news stories that aren't accompanied by interesting visuals at a distinct disadvantage. Compare, for instance, what you see on a televised newscast with what you might observe by watching CSPAN (Cable Satellite Public Affairs Network), which offers non-stop coverage of government proceedings and public affairs programming. Although what is happening in a senate hearing might ultimately affect your life more than a story on a car chase covered by helicopter news teams, it's less likely that viewers will nod off during the latter.

What this means realistically is that much news of import may be pushed aside in favor of potentially lighter fare with more interesting visuals. Another result is that we are often treated to ludicrous images of the exterior of court houses in which proceedings are occurring from which the media have been banned, or to still photographs of celebrity weddings, or to the myriad images of politicians shaking hands with visiting dignitaries in front of banks of microphones.

It is not only television that has fallen prey to the "no image, no story" syndrome. Newspapers, in order to compete, long ago adopted full-color photography, and have continued to increase the number of visuals they present in order to attract and hold the attention of readers. And, with the advent of broadband internet capabilities, even newspapers and radio news programs have now been able to offer, for the first time, digital video and slide shows to their audiences. In one sense, this has surely added to the level and quality of information we have access to. But, in another sense, it still biases news in favor of the visual, whether that visual actually adds anything to the story or not.

Bad News Bias

As Cline so aptly puts it, "Good news is boring (and probably does not photograph well, either)." The old adage, "If it doesn't bleed, it doesn't lead," still holds sway over too much of news. Watch any local newscast and see what it leads with. If there is a story about a stabbing in a community, it is much more likely to lead the newscast (and dictate the tone of the teasers leading up to the newscast) than a story on a new business that may employ hundreds of community citizens in a tight job market. This preference for bad news tends to make the world we live in seem much more dangerous than it is.

A 2001 study by the Berkeley Media Studies Group found that, historically, depictions of crime in the news are not reflective of the rate of crime generally, the proportion of crime that is violent, the proportion of news content devoted to crime, the proportion of crime committed by people of color, or the proportion of crime committed by youth. The study proposed that:

> The problem is not the inaccuracy of individual stories, but that the cumulative choices of what is included—or not included—in the news presents the public with a false picture of higher frequency and severity of crime than is actually the case.[37]

There are several reasons for this.

Newspapers and television tend to emphasize violent crime, especially the more unusual forms—mass or serial murders, crimes against children, torture, etc. Violent crime, according to the findings, is covered more than any other topic on network newscasts. In fact, television crime reporting was found to be the inverse of crime frequency. "That is, murder is reported most often on the news though it happens the least."[38] Finally, the study also showed that often the rate of crime coverage increased while real crime rates dropped.

The reasons suggested by the study for this bias toward the reporting of violent crime are that the stories are easy to do and perfect for the deadline-driven newsroom. "They are often about life and death—'good stories,' full of drama and emotion—that keep audiences attentive."[39] In summary, the study suggested that

> The steady diet of violent crime, coupled with the absence of nonviolent crime and general context, means that the rare crime looks like the normal crime; homicide is the prototypical crime in the news. Further, increased coverage of crime in general and homicides in particular while crime and homicides are declining gives the viewing public a skewed view of crime trends.[40]

Narrative Bias

The Greeks, including Aristotle in his *Poetics*, proposed that stories (or narratives) be composed of a number of elements. First, they must have a plot with a beginning, middle, and end. All "good" stories follow the progression of introduction, rising action, climax, and falling action—leading to a finale in which loose ends are typically tied up neatly in order for the audience to achieve dramatic closure. This narrative form has been passed down to the modern storytellers of today, the news media. The problem is that real life isn't exactly carried out in the same manner as a Greek play, or a modern novel or movie. According to Cline,

"Much of what happens in our world . . . is ambiguous." Leading the media to "apply a narrative structure to ambiguous events suggesting that these events are easily understood and have clear cause-and-effect relationships."[41]

In addition, because good storytelling requires drama, journalists often seek it out for their stories, whether it is actually present or not. And, since drama is often the result of conflict, journalists often match competing interests against each other, usually in the form of experts or officials with differing points of view, in order to create a sort of false conflict. This is often done under the guise of "fairness," covered next.

Narrative bias also leads to the creation of master narratives. "They tend to be set story lines with set characters who act in set ways."[42] Jay Rosen defines "master narrative" as the story that "generates all the other stories."[43] For example, the Enron scandal wasn't so much about important economic news as it was a tragic story of "corporate criminality," replete with villains and victims and climaxed by a tragic ending. Likewise, political campaign coverage becomes a "horserace," with the focus on winning more than on the issues. "Winning, then, is the story that produces all (or almost all) the other stories,"[44] and only candidates who are capable of winning become news. Rosen says that the master narratives of the news media are never talked about, or even recognized for what they are. The point is that once a master narrative has been set, it is very difficult to either recognize or alter.

For example, following the onslaught of hurricane Katrina in 2005, the city of New Orleans was devastated. Television was filled with images of flooded streets and thousands of homeless, desperate people. There were also images of people scavenging through deserted stores looking for food and other necessities. A now infamous photograph taken by the Associated Press showed a young African American wading through the flooded streets with a bulging plastic garbage bag in his hands. The caption read, "A young man walks through chest-deep flood water after looting a grocery store in New Orleans on Tuesday, Aug. 20, 2005." A similar photo taken by Agence France Press showed two White people doing exactly the same thing captioned, "Two residents wade through chest-deep water after finding bread and soda from a local grocery store after Hurricane Katrina came through the area in New Orleans, Louisiana." At first glance, this could be viewed as blatant racism; however, on closer inspection we see a master narrative at work.

This particular narrative had been formed over many years in the U.S. by similar scenes following riots, usually involving African Americans, in places such as Wilmington, Detroit, Watts, Chicago, and Baltimore. In the news coverage of many of these riots, people were frequently shown looting stores—and most of these people were Black. Thus, a narrative was constructed, many years in the making, composed of a breakdown of civil authority, African Americans, and looting. When hurricane Katrina came along, we were presented with the same images complete with all the elements of the master narrative in place; however, the cause of the civil breakdown and the reasons for the "looting" were very much different. Despite this, the media tended to offer up the stereotyped narrative that had been constructed over all those years. To their credit, many news operations quickly rethought the use of the term and began to recognize that most of the activities that had been labeled as "looting" were instead survival tactics resulting from a natural catastrophe. After all, if you can't buy food at the local grocery store because it is largely destroyed and deserted, and you are starving, what choice do you have? Nonetheless, there is some evidence that public charitable response to the disaster was based in part on the perception of rampant crime in New Orleans and the "racial cues embedded in news coverage."[45]

Fairness Bias

One of the hallmarks of journalistic objectivity is fairness. So much so that the search for balance sometimes results in a sort of faux conflict. The result is that, if someone presents a viewpoint in a news story, editors and journalists are compelled to dig up an opposing viewpoint in the name of balance, regardless of whether the opposing point of view is needed or even logical. This compulsion for fairness has resulted in a conflict-driven media filled with pundits from opposing sides literally shouting each other down in the name of balance. And, although screaming matches between political pundits can be chalked up to "theater," as the comedian Jon Stewart so aptly put it as a guest on CNN's now-cancelled *Crossfire*, the effects of the fairness bias infect even the most innocuous news stories. For example, if a candidate running for office says something newsworthy, then the media generally attempt to get a reaction from a the opposition candidate. According to Cline, "This creates the illusion that the game of politics is always contentious and never cooperative."[46] So that, even if the point being made by the first candidate is valid and widely accepted as true, the media are compelled to present an opposing viewpoint. This sort of balance game can create an illusion of legitimacy for a viewpoint that isn't warranted.

An excellent example of this is the Terri Schiavo case. Schiavo was a young woman who had been kept alive artificially for over a decade following a car accident. The case became public when her husband tried to have her removed from life support so that she could die. Her parents steadfastly refused to cooperate and brought the case to court. Based on the media coverage, one would have believed that there was a nationwide debate over Schiavo's fate. The journalist Eric Boehlert says the press was "allowed to stick to its preferred narrative that the Schiavo story had sparked a divisive 'debate' about the right-to-die issue," based largely on its need for conflict and its bias for fairness.[47] In reality, national polls were showing overwhelming support for the husband's cause.[48] When Schiavo was eventually taken off life support and subsequently died, Boehlert wrote on Salon.com, "It was fitting that reporters were in danger of outnumbering pro-life supporters outside Terri Schiavo's hospice . . . Has there ever been a set of protesters so small, so out of proportion, so outnumbered by the press, for a story that had supposedly set off a 'furious debate' nationwide?"[49] Ultimately, Boehlert puts the blame on the media for their invention of a conflict that didn't exist, at least on a national level. He says that "The excessive media coverage of the Schiavo story wasn't the most disturbing part. It was how, too often, journalists appeared to be afraid of the facts."[50]

Glory Bias

Geraldo Rivera has developed a reputation as an investigative reporter and talk-show host, and, most notably, by being controversial. As an "embedded" reporter with the 101st Airborne during the early stages of the Iraq war, Rivera was denounced by the U.S. military for disclosing troop movements on live television. He had literally drawn their positions in the sand during a report on Fox News. Initially, there was some confusion over whether he was expelled from Iraq officially and would be shifting his base of operations to Kuwait. When MSNBC mistakenly reported that he had been immediately forced to leave Iraq, Geraldo responded on Fox News from Iraq by saying:

> It sounds to me like some rats at my former network, NBC, are spreading some lies about me. You know, they can't compete fair and square on the battlefield, so they're trying to stab me in the back.[51]

At that point Geraldo Rivera became the story.

We all recognize certain reporters and news anchors because we frequently see them on television. In fact, the State of the News Media 2008 report referred to an increase in what it called "a host-oriented culture," particularly in prime time, which translates into:

> notably different agendas and character even among programs on the same network. Not only does Lou Dobbs have a news agenda of his own on CNN, but so does Anderson Cooper versus Wolf Blitzer on CNN, and Shepard Smith versus Brit Hume on Fox News.[52]

However, simply being well-known and opinionated doesn't necessarily represent glory bias, although it comes pretty close.

By the very nature of their jobs, journalists are close to important and newsworthy events and people. The temptation to insert themselves into the stories they report on is therefore great, especially for television reporters. This most often happens because of their proximity to important and often unfolding events or to the politically powerful, the decision makers, the elite sources they rely on so heavily. According to Cline, "This bias helps journalists establish and maintain a cultural identity as knowledgeable insiders."[53] We see it every time a local TV station produces a promo for its news programming, complete with stirring music and anchors posing as if they were celebrities imbued with a special knowledge gained only through their ability to be close to the important events of the day and to the movers and shakers who control those events. When the people reporting those events and covering the powerful elite become as, if not more, important than the stories themselves, then we see the effects of glory bias.

Ethical Approaches Specific to News Journalism

Because of the vital role the press has played historically as a purveyor of opinion, a harsh critic of government and politics, and a provider of citizen-centered information, it has been continually monitored over the years to make sure it is fulfilling its function. Not everyone has been kind. Even the staunchest defender of a free press, Thomas Jefferson, had his moments. Near the end of his presidency, Jefferson showed his growing disaffection from the press when he wrote:

> Nothing can now be believed which is seen in a newspaper. Truth itself becomes suspicious by being put into that polluted vehicle. The real extent of this state of misinformation is known only to those who are in situations to confront facts within their knowledge with the lies of the day.[54]

It shouldn't be surprising, then, that of all the disciplines we've discussed so far, news journalism is probably the most researched, especially in the area of ethics. According to Clifford Christians, who compiled a bibliography of books in media ethics, more than half the books written on the subject have emerged in the last decade.[55] In addition to the scores of books, hundreds of scholarly articles on the subject have been published covering nearly every imaginable aspect of the practice.

We will begin with some of the propositions put forth on how best to address the overall subject of journalistic ethics. Many of these will reference much already presented in this book, but in more detail and specifically related to journalism, both traditional and modern. As the ethicist Stephen Ward puts it, "The ethics of journalism is the never-ending task of inventing and reinterpreting its moral framework, because the project of journalism is ever changing."[56]

Shared Values: An Antidote to Relativism

The ethics scholar Deni Elliot says that many outside journalism might deduce that reporters tend toward ethical relativism because they typically hesitate to impose their moral viewpoints on other journalists. She suggests, instead, that "journalists do hold moral standards by which they judge professional behavior," and that, "without such standards, journalism would not be recognizable as a discreet [sic] industry."[57] Journalists, like other professionals, are motivated to use the "shared values" of their profession in doing their jobs, and it is by the standards that result from those values that journalists are judged.

Elliot lists several "essential shared values" that she says provide the basis for journalistic standards. First, news accounts should be accurate, balanced, and complete—for these are the elements that others often point to as lacking when they speak of ethical problems. The second value is the avoidance of harm in the publishing of news stories. The third, and what Elliot calls "deciding value," is that journalists should provide readers with information they need. This value is particularly important because it can serve as a counterbalance to harm. In other words, some harm can be justified if the story is important enough. Take the Clinton–Lewinsky scandal for example. Exposing the President's dalliance with an intern would certainly harm the President, his family, and the intern; however, that harm could be offset by the fact that the story is important simply because it involves the President of the United States and speaks directly to his character.

Elliot also proposes a test to determine whether or not a shared value is essential to a particular profession. For instance, if we remove the above three values from the profession of journalism, what remains? We would have a press that *could* produce inaccurate, unbalanced, and incomplete stories—developed without thought as to whether the stories are important or not and whether any harm would come from them. In fact, we would have a press much like the one that existed prior to the twentieth century in the U.S. However, she reiterates that values alone are not sufficient for ethicality. It is the motivation to act on the shared values of the profession that ultimately results in ethical journalism.

Finally, Elliot points out that what may be taken as relativism by some is really pluralism. That is, journalists are willing to give each other some leeway in decision making—but "within the limits of essential shared values."[58] She points out that journalism is decidedly not relativistic, and, in fact, a "complete ethic for journalism is likely to contain a smattering of various ethical theories."[59] As we shall see below, others have thought the same thing.

A Contracturalist Approach

Stephen Ward proposes a "contracturalist" approach to ethics in journalism. Drawing on the notion of social contract, he suggests that ethics understood this way is a set of "legitimate but fallible principles" that guide the actions of journalists in their role as purveyors of information vital to public understanding and discourse.[60] Because these principles are determined by journalism's social obligation to society—via the social contract—critiques of journalistic ethics should then be based on the implicit and explicit promises made by journalists to their audiences as part of that contract. If journalists break these promises, they jeopardize the special protections they receive—for instance, under the First Amendment. Among these "promises" are that journalists act as "independent communicators for the public at large," and are not the mouthpieces of special interests or of the government.

The professional journalist is obligated to speak to the public in a manner that is different from partisan public communicators such as the social advocate, the government official, the lobbyist, the public relations person promoting a product, or the lawyer representing a client. Professional journalism is the organized, socially recognized activity of communicating to the public for the public, from the impartial perspective of the public good.[61]

As part of his contracturalist approach, Ward proposes three foundational principles:

- The claim of credibility: "All journalists (and news organizations) have the ethical duty to provide the public with credible news and analysis, within the limitations of newsgathering."[62] This goes to the expectation that information presented will be truthful to the extent it is as "accurate and verifiable as can be expected, given the constraints of deadline, conflicting views, and incomplete information."[63]
- The claim of justifiable consequence: As with other professions, one of the primary obligations is to mitigate any potential harm that might be caused by the actions of the professional. This is usually dealt with in a utilitarian manner, balancing the potential harm to individuals against the potential benefit to society as a whole.
- The claim of humanity: "Journalists owe their primary allegiance to humanity, not to parts of humanity."[64] Because Ward is building a global journalism ethic, this claim is an important one in that it requires journalists to act as if the whole of humanity were their audience, thus affected by their actions. In his words, "Loyalty to humanity trumps other loyalties, where they conflict."[65]

The three claims capture what are arguably the most general and important features of journalism's social contract: reliability, impact, and allegiance. Ward suggests these three principles because they accurately reflect the expectations of society as regards the news media, via the social contract.

It is likely that many publics would agree that the news media should report what is accurate and verified, that news media should consider their impact, and that journalists should maintain allegiance to a public interest that is greater than their own personal interests. The three principles state the basics of a plausible social contract for global journalism.[66]

The Consequentialist Approach

As with the other media we have discussed throughout this book, journalism has likewise been involved in the debate over how to construct a working ethic. Part of that debate has centered around the use of consequences to determine ethical action versus a system of recognized duties and obligations which determine action. In other words, it is a debate between consequentialism (primarily utilitarianism) and theories of obligation (Kant and others). Many have suggested that utilitarianism is a flawed concept because it considers only the greater good in its calculations, leaving no room for individual choice or integrity.

Deni Elliot, however, contends that utilitarianism is widely misunderstood, and does, in fact, allow for a broader consideration of issues and constituents beyond mere calculation of the "greater good." She differentiates between the "greater good" and the "aggregate good." Aggregate good can be defined as "the overall good for the community as a whole, or for all of the people who can be identified as being affected by a particular action."[67] According to this view, the good of the whole community, including those potentially harmed by an action, must be considered. Thus, any harm caused to an individual can be justified only if it serves the good of the entire community—even the person being harmed. And the only way to insure this approach is for the moral agent—in this case, the journalist—to "make the determination with dispassionate objectivity."[68] In other words, impartiality must be the hallmark of ethical decision making if the community is to be served.

Elliot assures us that Mill was concerned with minority opinion and argued that only public discussion could discover truths. Thus, the aggregate good must be sought over any simple arithmetical good. Cold calculation of numbers alone cannot suffice when deciding on moral action. The moral agent must have developed sense of benevolence toward the entire community, free of personal interest, yet aware that the community includes *everyone*, not just the majority.

> It would follow that the good journalist and good news organization acting well have the good of the community as a practical priority. Certainly the First Amendment allows news organizations to publish whatever they want—and Mill would enthusiastically support this liberty. But . . . Mill answered the question of what one is supposed to do with all of that freedom. The answer is promote the good of all.[69]

In order for utilitarian decision making to succeed, Elliot proposes a "Utilitarian Decision Tree" based on the principles of justice provided by Mill and outlined in Chapter 6 of this book. These principles are justified, Elliot says, "because of their utility in advancing the aggregate good."[70] Any exception to these principles can only be allowed because the exception contributes to the aggregate good. A decision tree founded on Mill's theory of utilitarianism would look like this:[71]

1 What is the intended action?
2 Will it cause harm?
    If not, no analysis needed.
    If yes, review principles of justice.

3   Is someone being denied legal rights?
     If so, action is unjust.
4   Is someone being denied moral rights?
     If so, action is unjust.
5   Is the person being harmed getting what s/he deserves? Or is the person being helped getting what s/he deserves?
     If so, action is just.
6   Has the person being harmed had a promise broken to him/her?
     If so, action is unjust.
7   Has everyone in the situation been treated impartially?
     If so, the action is just.

In the rare occasions that exceptions to following these rules are justified, it is essential to show how the exception will lead to the aggregate good and how following the rule will not lead to the greatest good for the whole group.

Only if the action has been determined to be just do we advance to the utilitarian calculus:

8   How will harming this individual promote the overall good of the community? Consider whether the community will be better or worse if everyone knows that individuals can be harmed in this way for this reason.
9   How will the community be harmed if the proposed action is not taken? Consider whether the community will be better or worse if everyone knows that individuals will *not* be harmed in this way for this reason.

A Critique of the Utilitarian Approach

Clifford Christians says that "Utilitarian ethics is enormously influential in North American society," and is especially prevalent in the media professions.[72] Its attraction is due, in part, to its claim that all moral judgments are based on utility—the degree to which actions are either harmful or beneficial. It is particularly appealing to journalists because of its requirement of neutrality on the part of the moral agent—an almost scientific objectivity that allows the agent to make judgments on behalf of society rather than individuals. At the same time, under John Stuart Mill's construction, it allows for individual freedoms to be determined by majority decision, with all individuals able to participate in that decision. Utilitarianism, because it appears to focus on the majority well-being, has become a mainstay argument for journalists seeking to serve the "public's right to know."

However, Christians argues that utilitarianism may no longer be useful in ethical decision making in journalism. He cites, for instance, the vagaries of new media such as blogging, and the difficulty of accurately assessing their long-term effects. If effects can't be determined, then utilitarianism becomes an ineffective decision-making tool. Additionally, he points out that not all issues are soluble through consequential deliberation.

> In some media situations, consequences are a reliable guide. But in many of the most crucial issues we face at present, utility is not adequate—for understanding distributive justice, diversity in popular culture, violence in television and cinema, truth telling, digital manipulation, conflict of interest, and so forth. We face the anomaly that the ethical system most entrenched in the media industry is not ideally suited for resolving its most persistent headaches.[73]

He notes that in utilitarianism only the future seems to count, whereas, in many moral dilemmas, it is the present or the past that needs to be addressed. For example, W. D. Ross's duty of gratitude is based on past actions, as is the duty of fidelity (keeping promises).

What Christians proposes as an alternative to utilitarianism is a *dialogic duty ethics*. Dialogic ethics, simply speaking, involves decision making that incorporates the community—in other words, it is a social ethics of duty based on dialogue among its members.[74] He says that "Moral agents need a context within which to assess what is valuable, and values are nurtured in particular settings,"[75] specifically, within the community. Other theories support this notion, Christians says, including the ethic of care, which supposes the framework of moral action as being our subjective interrelationships with others. Our obligations, or duties, thus arise out of our relationships with others—even with the entire community of which we are a part.

As part of this construction, Christians argues that the idea of objectivity, involving neutrality and detachment (both utilitarian ideals), is sorely outdated.

> Objectivity as a one-dimensional framework of rational and moral validation accounts for some of the goods we seek in community, such as minimal harm, but those issues outside the objectivity calculus are excluded from the decision-making process. The way power and ideology influence social and political institutions, including the press, is largely ignored.[76]

Dialogical ethics, instead, calls for "authentic disclosure" wherein the complexities of society and culture can be fully accounted for only through the involvement of community and its varied voices. As Christians puts it, "Moral duty is nurtured by the demands of social linkage and not produced by abstract theory."[77] He decries the "reasoned calculation" involved in utilitarian thinking and calls for a broadening of journalistic concerns that involve the subjective community as a whole.

A Duty-based Approach

As discussed earlier in this book, and as Christians argues above, ethical decisions based on a sense of duty or obligation have been viewed historically as an alternative to consequential approaches such as utilitarianism. Probably one of the most useful of those approaches is the *prima facie* system proposed by W. D. Ross (and used to define moral claimants in Chapter 2). Christopher Meyers argues that Ross's approach, in fact, links both consequential and non-consequential theories and provides a reasonable basis for decision making in journalism.[78]

Recall that Ross believed certain moral duties could be intuitively known as being literally self-evident—such as, "Persons should keep their promises." Although many have since argued that intuition is far too vague a concept on which to base moral principles, Meyers proposes that, from an applied ethics perspective, it doesn't matter where the principles come from—what matters is *why* they are valid.[79] He also says that Ross successfully bridged the gap between consequential and duty-based ethics. Although Ross is clearly in the duty camp when it comes to motive and obligation as the driving force behind moral decision making, Meyers points out that some of Ross's duties, especially non-injury and beneficence, are forward-looking, based on probable outcomes of actions—in other words, an obligation to produce benefit or to avoid harm. So, Ross's duties contain both duty-based admonitions "rooted in motives and reasoning," and obligations based on predicted, if potentially unforeseeable, outcomes.[80]

A key element of Meyers' analysis of Ross is the notion that decisions based on conflicting duties and resulting in honoring one above another also provoke further duties. For example, if a journalist decides not to run a story, based on non-injury to the subject of the story, she must still ask if that decision affects any of the other duties—for example, fidelity to the readers to provide them with information that may be vital to their understanding of an important topic. What if the story is about an AIDS victim, and the reporter decides not to run it in order to prevent harm to the subject of the piece? Don't readers gain something from learning more about the disease and its consequences within their community? Is the reporter then further obligated, by, say, the duty of reparation, to provide something else that serves the purpose of keeping the community informed on such important issues as AIDS awareness—perhaps a series on the disease, or a deeper investigation of the causes of it locally? As Meyers points out, it was Ross's position that all moral dilemmas were a conflict among duties, and that any decision among conflicting duties was bound to further obligate us. But it is exactly this process that makes Ross's duties attractive. The fact of conflict among duties makes the application of them "wholly contextual, with each situation bringing different moral facts," potentially requiring a privileging of one over another.[81] At the same time, it requires us to consider, at the deepest level, our obligations to each other and the consequences of our actions.

Meyers concludes that Ross's duties combine the key elements of both consequential and duty-based approaches. From duty-based approaches, it draws on the primacy of motive in acting on obligations that, in and of themselves, have apparent moral value. And motives, as we have seen, are key to ascribing accountability. At the same time, Ross clearly recognizes the importance of potential effects of certain duties, namely non-injury and beneficence. Finally, Ross recognized the importance of relationships and how they affect the context of decision making, thus the determination of which duty is paramount in a given situation. As Meyers puts it, "The theory thus emerges as a viable tool for engaging, even resolving, real world problems, including those in media ethics."[82]

Virtue Ethics

Virtue, or character, ethics concentrates not on the action itself, or the consequences. Rather, it focuses on the moral agent and the characteristics that make that person capable of making a right decision. As a concept, it is particularly appealing to certain constructions of professional ethics. As the philosopher Alisdair MacIntyre notes, any area of human endeavor, such as professions, in which standards of excellence guide the production of societal goods is an "appropriate locus for the exercise of the virtues, and the virtues are those qualities that allow practitioners to excel in their roles."[83] MacIntyre also suggests that three basic virtues are common to most endeavors. As previously noted in Chapter 6, they are:

- *justice*, which demands that we recognize the skills, knowledge, and expertise of other practitioners, and that we learn from those who know more and have greater experience than we do;
- *courage*, which requires that we take self-endangering risks, push ourselves to the limits of our capacities, and be prepared to challenge existing practice in the interest of extending the practice, despite institutional pressures against such critique;
- *honesty*, which asks us to be able to accept criticism and to learn from our errors and mistakes.[84]

Virtue ethics also seems to align nicely with what moral philosophers call "role morality." As Kevin Gibson explains it, "The notion of role morality suggests individuals may adopt a different morality depending on the roles they undertake."[85] For instance, a journalist may be put in the position of violating someone's privacy because of a story. As an individual, the journalist may feel that, under normal circumstances, such a violation would go against his individual moral beliefs. However, journalists are regularly required to visit some harm on the people they cover, and the "morality of the role" they have chosen allows this in, say, the pursuit of the greater good.

For others, the key benefit of virtue ethics is that it supports democracy. Recall that the concept was originally developed within a democratic system—that of ancient Athens over 2,500 years ago. As the media ethicist Elliot D. Cohen says:

Within a democracy, the virtues of journalists include character traits that are conducive to the stated end of journalistic practice . . . [T]hese character traits can be defined as habits or dispositions to act in manners that advance the end of a democratic press. These habits involve dedication to principles of conduct that follow from the journalistic end of serving democracy. Insofar as this end is a moral end, these virtues and their corresponding principles are also moral.[86]

Cohen suggests that such virtues as being responsible, loyal, fair, impartial, honest, and courageous in reporting news are all part of "what it means to be a competent journalist."[87]

Another proponent of using virtue ethics as a foundation for journalistic ethics is Aaron Quinn, educator and ethicist. He proposes that ethical decisions are best made when internally derived (as from the elements of good character) rather than externally derived (as from rules or guidelines).[88] Following Aristotle, Quinn suggests that the virtues, values, and principles that will guide journalists ethically are best provided by education and life experience.

Quinn proposes two primary virtues for journalists: justice and integrity. The first is what he calls an *agent-neutral* virtue—one "that calls for equal application to all persons, with no special consideration for an individual or discreet [sic] group."[89] Justice was recognized by Aristotle as an overarching virtue that affected the running of a good society, treating citizens not equally, but according to their merit (distributive justice). A journalist possessing the virtue of justice would be able to judge efficiently the merits of others in a given situation and decide whether they deserved to be treated in a certain way or not. For example, a drunken driver who caused an accident might deserve less privacy consideration than his victim who was an innocent pedestrian.

Integrity, on the other hand, is *agent-relative*—"the moral value of the virtue in a given case relates directly to its relevance to a specific person or discreet [sic] group of persons."[90] Integrity is integral to moral action. This is especially true under virtue ethics because of its focus on character. Integrity means being consistent in one's actions by upholding one's principles. A consistent character is the hallmark of a virtuous person. Thus, good character drives good action.

Finally, Quinn proposes what is known as a *regulative ideal*, "a standard by which one ought to judge one's actions both in a general sense—what it is to be a good journalist—or in a particular circumstance, how ought a journalist to act in this situation, right now." A regulative ideal requires internalization of a standard of conduct, a conception of excellence, by which to guide one's motivations and judge one's own actions. For example, a good journalist may have developed, over the years, an internal ideal of what defines excellence in journalism. This ideal will then serve to regulate her actions by checking her motives against the ideal in each situation—thus guiding her actions. Quinn suggests that the process of developing a regulative ideal allows journalists to bolster certain key virtues, such as justice and integrity, while continually testing and adjusting their actions. The novice may require constant comparison of the ideal against the impulse. The seasoned journalist, on the other hand, may have reached a point of character development in which the right action has become second nature. This is completely in line with Aristotle's notion of character being the culmination of education and life experiences—a place from which the golden mean is always the obvious choice.

Special Issues in Journalism Ethics

As we have already seen in this chapter, the practice of news journalism comes with its own set of ethical issues. Some of those have already been discussed earlier in the chapter. Here, we will discuss only two additional areas, deception and privacy; however, they are two areas often cited as being troublesome for journalism. They also subsume many of the offences people outside journalism focus on, including topics such as sensationalism (a result, perhaps even a goal, of some forms of investigative reporting and privacy invasion). In addition, we will, as in the other chapters, deal specifically with new media and the potential for ethical problems there.

Journalistic Deception

Exactly what constitutes journalistic deception? Most ethicists agree that both outright lying and misleading through the withholding of information constitute deception, especially as it relates to journalism. Lying means to literally say something that is provably not true. Withholding information relevant to a complete understanding of something can mislead at a level that sometimes can be even more of a moral problem than outright lying.[91] For example, a woman asks her husband, "Are you cheating on me?" He responds, "No. I am not cheating on you." What he withholds is that he *was* cheating on her, but he broke it off. His direct answer is therefore not a lie; however, his withholding of information is potentially as deceptive as any outright lie. Deception, then, is more than just lying. It also includes any action that would lead someone to believe something that is not true. It is this definition that we will assume here.

The ethicists Deni Elliott and Charles Culver have identified several conditions for deception.

- Acting with the *intention* to deceive, even if the deception is ultimately unsuccessful—because the attempt to do something unethical is still morally suspect, regardless of the outcome.
- Actively lying verbally or by other non-verbal means. Examples of non-verbal deceptions might be altering appearance, as in a reporter masquerading as a physician in order to gain access to a shooting victim. Or nodding your head to indicate "yes" when the truth is "no."

- Withholding information so as to alter perception. For example, a journalist might leave out certain facts about the subject of a news story that so as to make him seem more heroic at an accident scene. The subsequent picture of him will thus be one manufactured in part by not having presented a complete story of events.[92]

Because withholding information is often a grey area in deception, Elliott and Culver give it special consideration. They outline three key areas in which journalistic deception is most likely to occur.

1 *Investigative deception* refers to deceptions carried out during the news-gathering process. For example, a reporter poses as someone she is not in order to gain access to information.
2 *Interrogative deception* may take place during interviews, even when the people being interviewed know they are talking to a journalist. For example, pretending to be sympathetic to a subject when you may, in fact, be hostile. Or intimating that your broadcast interview is being taped when, in fact, it is live.

  An infamous example of this type of deception took place in 1995 during an interview between Connie Chung, then CBS host of *Eye to Eye*, and the mother of Newt Gingrich, Republican Speaker of the House. During the interview, Mrs. Gingrich indicated that she couldn't say what her son thought of then first lady, Hillary Rodham Clinton. When Chung suggested to her that the information would be "just between you and me," the House Speaker's mother indicated that her son thought Clinton was a "bitch." Reaction not only to the slur but also to the way in which it was extracted was immediate and condemnatory. "What we have here is a short-term rating gain for CBS and a long-term black mark for media credibility," said Everette Dennis, then executive director of the Freedom Forum Media Studies Center at Columbia University.[93] He classified Mrs. Gingrich as an "innocent" when it came to dealing with the media, and suggested that Chung, and CBS, had exploited that fact by intimating that the Gingrich comments would be off the record.

  It is exactly this sort of problem that cause Elliot and Culver to argue that journalists "have a duty to relate information about the procedural features of [an] interview to the source," including the following:[94]

- A duty to tell the source that an interview for publication is taking place (including a duty to relay more detailed information to less sophisticated sources).
- A duty to tell the source how the information is being recorded.
- A duty to tell the source if, through some misunderstanding and resultant action on the part of the source, the source becomes more likely to be harmed than he or she knows.

3　*Informative deception* takes place when a reporter either intentionally includes false information in a story or withholds information, thereby allowing the reader to initiate or sustain a false belief. This is probably the rarest form of journalistic deception because so much of what constitutes good journalism has to do with completeness. Deception of this type generally denotes bias. An example might be withholding information about an alleged act of sexual harassment by a congressional representative on the eve of an election in order *not* to prejudice the outcome.

That's the excuse used by the Portland *Oregonian* in 1992 when the then Oregon Senator Bob Packwood was accused of sexual harassment in a *Washington Post* article. It was only after the publication of that article that it became obvious that the senator's own home paper had avoided the story. The *Oregonian's* editor admitted to the *Post* that his paper "should have been a little more aggressive . . . We were worried about ruining a man's career."[95] It also came to light that the senator had even kissed one of the *Oregonian's* own reporters during an interview—a fact that was kept quiet by everyone who knew about it. A bumper sticker at the time read, "If it matters to Oregonians, it's in the *Washington Post*."

The effects of the paper's misstep with the Packwood story has lasted for years. During a more recent brush with similar issues, the now political editor of the *Oregonian* noted that editors at the time "flat-out knew the senator harassed women, one in their own office no less, and, with eyes open, they passed on a story that could have affected his re-election."[96]

Finally, as Elliott and Culver argue, the bottom line in defining deception is that withholding information is every bit as much of a problem as outright lying in journalism. The authors reiterate that the act of deception is always, on the face of it, immoral. And the burden of proof is always on the journalist to show justification.

The Case For and Against Deception

Now that we have a definitional handle on what constitutes journalistic deception, the ultimate question arises: Is it ever proper for a journalist to lie in order to get a story? This is the primary question every journalist must ask when deciding whether to engage in investigative reporting, especially undercover reporting, which is the area we will focus on here. The question is not a new one. At the turn of the century, the reporter Nellie Blye (a pseudonym) posed as an insane woman so she could expose New York City's notorious Women's Lunatic Asylum. Carrying on in that tradition in the 1960s, Gloria Steinem became a Playboy Bunny in order to give readers an inside look at what the women employees of the Playboy Clubs had to go through earn a living. In the 1970s, the reporter Carol Lynn Mithers posed as a man to get a job on a sports magazine and then published the results of her investigation in a *Village Voice* article called

"My Life as a Man." The *Chicago Sun-Times* sent female journalists into clinics in downtown Chicago that performed costly abortions on women who were not pregnant. Even the venerable Walter Cronkite once voted under false names twice in the same election to expose election fraud. And, in 1977, in probably the most famous undercover scam in decades, the *Chicago Sun-Times* set up a fake bar called the *Mirage*, run completely by undercover journalists, in order to record dozens of city officials engaged in bribe taking.

In the now-famous Food Lion case, ABC's *Prime Time* went undercover to expose what it suggested was the giant grocery store chain's practice of selling tainted meat and fish and ignoring expiration dates on other food products. When Food Lion sued ABC in a North Carolina court, it based its legal position on the fact that ABC undercover reporters had lied on their employment applications in order to gain access to Food Lion stores for the purposes of surreptitious filming. The jury awarded Food Lion $5.5 million in damages (later reduced to just over $300,000, and ultimately dismissed). Both journalists and non-journalists came down on opposite sides of the issue. Writing in *USA Today* magazine, Joe Saltzman painted a picture of investigative reporting as a time-honored tradition, fighting both big government and big business on behalf of the American people.[97] Whereas most journalistic accounts of the case were in this vein, David Wagner, writing for *Insight on the News* (a *Washington Times* publication), saw it differently. Citing possible collusion between ABC and the United Food and Commercial Workers International Union (UFCWIU), Wagner contended that the report was simply a concerted effort to "get Food Lion" because it had repeatedly resisted pressure to unionize.[98] Eventually, an appeals court threw out the original verdict and exonerated ABC. Despite this new ruling, the Food Lion case exemplifies the problems caused by undercover reporting using deceptive practices. The question of using deception to gather information is a sticky one that has troubled journalists for a very long time.

The Society of Professional Journalists (SPJ) code of ethics advises journalists to:

> Avoid undercover or other surreptitious methods of gathering information except when traditional open methods will not yield information vital to the public. Use of such methods should be explained as part of the story.

The argument in favor of using questionable means to gather news deemed of value to the public welfare is based solidly on utilitarian grounds. According to the utilitarian view, deception must be used at times to further the public interest. Supporting this position, Sissela Bok, in her seminal work, *Secrets: On the Ethics of Concealment and Revelation*, holds that journalistic deception, like lying in general, is not an either–or proposition. Rather, it is best viewed as operating along a continuum from unnecessary to necessary.[99] Thus, journalistic deception that clearly benefits the public welfare could be seen as permissible, whereas deception that results in a story that merely titillates or satisfies the public's curiosity over some matter is clearly suspect. However, since the guiding ideal in journalism is to tell the truth, any deviation from that ideal must be able to stand up to the closest scrutiny. In other words, the burden of proof for using deceptive techniques in newsgathering is squarely on the journalist.

According to the educator and ethicist Louis Day, investigative techniques such as undercover reporting and the use of hidden cameras should be employed only after a full and deliberate discussion in which the decision makers:

1 are convinced that the information sought is of compelling public importance;
2 have considered all alternatives to the use of deception;
3 are convinced that the benefit to be derived from the deceptive practice outweighs the possible harm to the various parties involved; and
4 are willing to disclose to their audience the nature of the deception and their reasons for using such tactics.[100]

This test, although not solving all the problems associated with undercover reporting, certainly requires a hard look at the justification for using such techniques. Conversely, Bob Steele, resident ethics scholar at the Poynter Institute, identifies five criteria that *do not* justify deception.

- winning a prize;
- beating the competition;
- getting the story with less expense of time and resources;
- doing it because "others already did it";
- the subjects of the story are themselves unethical.[101]

The last two are of particular importance because of recent events in which NBC was sued over the suicide of a subject covered in a televised sting operation in 2006. In November of that year, an assistant district attorney in Rockwell, Texas, made arrangements to meet privately with someone he was led to believe was a young boy he had reportedly been sending sexually explicit messages to over the internet. The "boy" was, in fact, a volunteer posing as a chat-room participant for NBC's *Dateline* news magazine program. *Dateline* was in the act of producing another segment of a series of televised sting operations based on the exploits of a group called Perverted Justice that had been conducting similar stings via the internet and that had already gained quite a bit of notoriety. Perverted Justice was a paid consultant for the NBC program. The idea was to lure subjects to a house where they would be confronted by TV cameras and the show's host.

Although the subject in this instance never showed up for the rendezvous, the local police attempted to arrest him at his home after being encouraged by NBC (according to the lawsuit). As the police and camera crews entered his home, he shot himself in the head.[102] The lawsuit was settled in 2008. *Dateline* hasn't produced another episode of "To Catch a Predator."

This much-talked-about ethical lapse fits Steele's last two unacceptable criteria for undercover reporting. The show was an offshoot of what had already become a highly controversial internet operation—one that had subsequently been mimicked by local TV news crews around the country, and one that FBI spokesman Jeff Lanza called an example of "vigilante justice."[103] Perverted Justice's position, and that of most of the news outlets using their model to run their own stings, is that the people exposed through these methods were themselves immoral, and so deserved to be outed. However, Charles Davis, director of the Freedom of Information Coalition at the Missouri School of Journalism, noted that when this kind of story is gathered through undercover means, "You're moving from an observer of fact and recorder of history into someone who's creating history."[104]

Deception of any form is a shaky practice, especially for journalists, whose primary obligation is to tell the truth. Although there may be some debate over the usefulness of deception in newsgathering, it is ultimately up to journalists to make the call, keeping firmly in mind the potential for abuse this tactic brings with it—and the potential for tragedy if it is used unwisely.

Photo Manipulation: A Special Case of Deception

The public may well be losing faith in photojournalism. Part of the problem is that so much we see today in the way of photographs is obviously manipulated digitally: magazine covers, advertisements, posters, billboards, etc. And we are increasingly treated to the digital manipulation, and creation, of moving images on television and movies. The last bastion of "photographic truth" may well be news photography; however, even that is coming under assault as photographs are increasingly altered, often in the most minor ways, in order to present just the right story.

For example, in April 2003, the *Los Angeles Times* photographer Brian Walski was fired over a photograph he submitted from the field in Iraq. It turns out that the photograph he submitted to the *Times* of a British soldier directing civilians under fire from a mortar attack was actually a composite of two photographs. An employee of another paper, with whom the photograph was shared, noticed that there was duplication of some of the people in the crouching crowd being directed by the soldier. Further investigation revealed that two images had been combined to produce the dramatic photo. Walski admitted that he had manipulated the photos on his laptop computer in the field in order to "improve the composition."[105] The *Times* Director of Photography, Colin Crawford, reacted this way:

> What Brian did is totally unacceptable and he violated our trust with our readers. We do not for a moment underestimate what he has witnessed and experienced. We don't feel good about doing this, but the integrity of our organization is essential. If our readers can't count on honesty from us, I don't know what we have left.[106]

Why all the furor? Because, despite our cynicism, we still want to believe that what we see in a newspaper or otherwise presented by a news outlet is an accurate reflection of reality. That means that where it appears directly affects our expectations. In judging the ethicality of photographs, context becomes an all-important factor. Twenty years ago, the ethics scholar Edwin Martin pointed out that the "vehicle of presentation" indicated to viewers the level of reliability of the photograph in representing the reality. He argued that "advertisements, fashion magazines, art galleries, and newspapers provide contexts of varying inferential license"—that is, what a photograph infers as being true will vary according to its context.[107] None of us expect the cover of a humor magazine to represent reality, much less print advertisements in magazines. However, photos appearing in newspapers, in fact "infer" reality, and, in that sense, have a greater "assertional" force—they effectively assert that what they represent is unaltered reality.[108]

Tom Wheeler, a former magazine editor and photo manipulation expert, points out that there is a fine line between reality and what can be presented in any photograph purporting to reflect reality.[109] However, it is the job of the journalist to interpret the world in ways that correspond as closely as possible to reality. He refers to this type of photography as *editorial* photography. In his book *Phototruth or Photofiction*, Wheeler argues that news photographs are "assumed to have captured objects or events that have happened in real time and space."[110] As noted in Chapter 6 of this book, Wheeler has developed what he calls the "qualified expectation of reality" test (QER) based on whether the viewer of a photograph expects it to depict reality or not, particularly given its context. Thus, a cover for a fashion magazine would have a lower QER than a front-page photo in a newspaper. In delineating the instances in which QER will play a determining role, Wheeler proposes several tests for photographers, especially editorial photographers, to use when determining the ethicality of their photographs.

The first is the *viewfinder test*. Wheeler argues that viewers don't typically expect that an editorial photograph actually *is* reality; "only that it *corresponds* in some sense to reality, that the objects it portrays are no more or less than those that were seen through the viewfinder."[111] This test allows for traditional processing and editing techniques and allows, to some degree, interpretive influences of the photographer herself. It does not allow for certain alterations to the photograph after exposure—such as addition, removal, rearrangement, or substantial alterations of material objects within the frame. This would disallow such practices as the removal of a fence post in a famous photo of the Kent State shootings in 1970. The photo, taken by a student photographer, subsequently won a Pulitzer Prize. It was later altered by *Life* magazine to remove the post that seems to grow out of the head of the primary focus of the photo.[112]

The *photojournalist's process test* assumes that certain decisions made by the photographer "in the field" are understood by viewers, thus their QER is adjusted by this realization. For instance, despite the fact that photographers typically frame subjects, select a lens, adjust aperture, etc., viewers expect that this is part of the process of photography and accept it. Even the use of special lenses, such as fish-eye, are understood as acceptable special effects, in the same way they know that, just because a photographer chooses black and white film, reality is not black and white. The same is true of some post-exposure techniques such as cropping or dodging and burning (used to lighten or darken exposure). None of these "traditional" methods tend to violate what viewers expect in an editorial photograph.

The *technical credibility* test basically notes that most people will recognize manipulated photographs that are amateurish in their execution. An infamous attempt to place the former presidential hopeful John Kerry alongside the one-time anti-war activist Jane Fonda and pass it off as an Associated Press photo failed simply because it looked exactly like what it was—a digital cut-and-paste job. However, with the increasing sophistication of digital editing software, telling a fake photo from a legitimate photo is becoming much harder to do. A recent *Time* magazine cover depicting a tearful Ronald Reagan garnered a lot of attention, despite the fact that the masthead carried a credit for the artist who painted in the tear on the late president's face. There were many who believed the emotional moment had been captured in reality some time during the Reagan presidency; therefore, the use of it to illustrate the turmoil in today's Republican party was nothing short of disrespectful.

Finally, Wheeler proposes the *obvious implausibility* test—or, more tongue-in-cheek, the "pregnant Bruce Willis" test. The latter term is based on a cover perpetrated by the now defunct *Spy* magazine—a publication focusing on political and celebrity satire. The cover featured a photograph of actor Bruce Willis, naked and obviously pregnant. It was a pointed parody of an earlier *Vanity Fair* cover in which his wife at the time, Demi Moore, was featured pregnant and naked. Wheeler's point is that if the fiction of a photograph is immediately obvious, then QER is completely suspended.

All of these tests allow for audience expectation of reality to come into play. The bottom line is: If the audience expects the photograph to represent reality, then it shouldn't have been altered in any way not already assumed as legitimate by that audience. On the other hand, if the manipulation is obvious, then there can be no expectation of reality. However, if the photograph has been altered, and the audience expects it to reflect an unaltered reality, then something must be done to apprise them of the alteration. Wheeler suggests written disclosure appropriate to the degree of image alteration. For example, if the substance of the photograph hasn't been significantly altered (say, the removal of an awkward phone line obstructing someone's face) then a simple disclaimer stating that alteration, is probably sufficient. However, when the image has been altered significantly, as in the now infamous O. J. Simpson *Time* cover, then a fine-print disclaimer on the inside masthead probably won't serve.

Wheeler offers some final suggestions for the profession as a whole.[113]

1   Embrace a broad definition of "editorial photography" as being photographic images published for news, editorial or documentary purposes.
2   Treat the reader's Qualified Expectation of Reality as a sacred trust; we can suspend it altogether with immediately obvious photofiction, but otherwise we cannot violate it.
3   In measuring the QER, consider the tests discussed above.
4   Publish no editorial photography that falls into all of the following categories:

   •   It is photofiction.
   •   It fails one or more of the QER tests.
   •   There is no appropriate disclosure.

5   In determining appropriate disclosure, consider whether the fiction is a detail, requiring only a brief mention in fine print, or is the essence of the image, requiring an identification sufficiently prominent to mislead no one; the extent to which the publication's commercial potential depends on the photo-fiction.
6   Remember that the ultimate test is one of honesty and perception: Do we mislead our consumers? Do they think we mislead them? When in doubt, let us err in favor of the public trust.

Privacy and the News Media

Information is power. At no time in history has this been more true than today. Our personal autonomy is greatly affected by how much others know about us, and we seem to be increasingly willing to let them know. In today's "performance" culture, in which existing at all seems to mean existing publicly, the concept of privacy is radically different from the one delineated by past generations. Social networking sites such as MySpace and Facebook are filled with private moments made public. Rowdy party pictures compete with deeply private love notes for public attention. The television screams reality at us from shows designed to embarrass even the most hardened souls. The private lives of public officials and celebrities are the stuff of common gossip on internet blogs and entertainment "news" programs. Can journalism help but be affected by the trend toward disclosure? Up until very recently, presidents' private lives were a matter of private concern. Franklin Roosevelt's life-long relationship with another woman as well as John F. Kennedy's alleged frequent dalliances were virtually ignored by the media of their day. Compare this with the Clinton–Lewinsky story of the 1990s, when the frenzy with which the media reported even the most sensitive details of a White House sex scandal literally dominated the news for months. Some imagine this was a historically recent trend, but journalism wasn't always as chaste as it appeared during much of the twentieth century.

Privacy has a muddied history in journalistic ethics. The nature of the early press in the United States pretty much guaranteed that subjects of news stories, particularly political figures, would have little or no privacy. During Thomas Jefferson's presidency, opposition newspapers regularly reported on rumors of his alleged sexual relationship with his slave Sally Hemings. Andrew Jackson shared a similar fate when his mistimed marriage to Rachel Robards became the stuff of press gossip on the eve of his election. It wasn't until the twentieth century that the privacy laws we are familiar with today were enacted, protecting citizens from the prying eyes of the media.

Privacy as a Legal Concept

Privacy has no single legal definition; however, the simplest definition does come from a jurist. In 1888, Judge Thomas Cooley defined privacy as "the right to be left alone."[114] Subsequent definitions refined the concept somewhat. In 1890 Samuel Warren and Louis Brandeis argued for the creation of a legal remedy that would allow citizens the right to sue over invasions of privacy, worrying (prophetically) that "what is whispered in the closet shall be proclaimed from the housetops."[115] The modern definitions of privacy also assume a sense of place, distinguishing between the private and the public sphere. For instance, this "right" is generally restricted to places in which a person might reasonably expect privacy, such as home, or a hotel room. Most people, including journalists, assume that anything that happens in a public space is, by definition, public, especially if the disclosure is voluntarily made (think of loud cell-phone conversations here). The same applies for information already a matter of public record, such as arrest records.[116]

Although there are early examples of privacy as a legal concept, especially in the form of trespass laws, the privacy constructions we are most familiar with are historically very current.

- *Intrusion* is most cited by people as "invasion of privacy." It basically refers to the sanctity of an individual's private space being "invaded" by an uninvited intruder, and covers such acts as wiretapping, looking through windows, and physical trespass. As regards journalists, it is most often about physical trespass and the use of such intrusive techniques as telephoto lenses to capture private moments. In 1999, the Supreme Court ruled that journalists have no right to enter a person's home without being invited by the person dwelling there. This ruling put an immediate damper on the production of the myriad "cop" shows in which alleged criminals were caught and arrested in dramatic fashion on camera, often in their own homes.
- *Publication of embarrassing private* facts limits the rights of journalists to print or otherwise reveal facts, even true facts, about individuals that will cause them embarrassment. This could include information about their personal finances, sexual relations, medical treatment, personal correspondence, etc.

However, this prohibition has been often tested in court with the result that public figures have much less protection than private individuals—a distinction that has dominated legal findings concerning privacy.

- *Publication that might place someone in a false light* deals with possible distortions or outright falsehoods that could leave a false impression of someone. This is similar to defamation in that it would have to be proved intentional or done out of careless neglect to be legally actionable. Nonetheless, certain instances do occur in which individuals are harmed in this way. For example, a photo of a person taken to illustrate one story might appear alongside an unrelated story in a newspaper leaving the impression that the unrelated story and the photo are connected. This is especially troublesome if the story is a negative one.

- *Appropriation* has to do more with advertising than journalism and involves the use of person's name, picture, or likeness without that person's permission, usually for commercial exploitation. So, if you see an image of a celebrity tied to a product, it's almost certain that the advertising agency has permission to use it as an endorsement. Otherwise, they could be sued.

In order for invasion of privacy to be legally actionable, two criteria must be met. First, the newsgathering or publishing process must have violated certain legal principles that protect the individual (one of the above torts). Second, it must be clear that the action isn't protected under First Amendment privilege. As with libel cases, there may be a sort of "constitutional excuse" granting immunity for some articles or broadcasts.[117] This is especially true in cases involving public figures, or, in some cases, information gathered in a public place. It may also be argued that the information published is of legitimate public concern. As the ethicist Louis Hodges notes, "It is just for a journalist to violate the privacy of an individual only if information about that individual is of overriding public importance and the public need cannot be met by other means."[118]

Privacy as an Ethical Concept

In order to discuss the ethical aspects of privacy, we must first understand the human need for it. Sissela Bok defines privacy as "The condition of being protected from unwanted access by others—either physical access, personal information, or attention."[119] But why do we value privacy at all? Louis Hodges asks us to visualize privacy as "circles of intimacy," at the center of which we exist alone with our "fantasies, unarticulated hopes, memories."[120] In the second circle, we occupy a space with someone we know personally and with whom we are willing to share certain intimacies—generally in a one-to-one relationship, as with a spouse. The third circle includes a larger group of friends, but friends with whom you are still willing to share information about yourself that you would not necessarily want to become public—a sort of trust relationship. The circles continue outward until they encompass all of humanity, with the level of intimacy lessening as we move farther from the center. The idea is that we need to maintain some control over these circles of intimacy by determining who enters and who does not. Hodges suggests that our need to control these circles of intimacy stems from psychological needs, such as the need to develop and maintain a sense of self while simultaneously constructing boundaries between ourselves and others in order to protect our notion of who we are as individuals. This allows for what Kant would call "individual autonomy"—control over our own destinies.

The philosopher Candice Gauthier proposes several classical models for addressing the ethics of privacy, including a *Kantian model* based on respect for persons. From this perspective, "Invading a person's privacy treats that person as a mere means by interfering with the choice to keep certain information private."[121] This typically initiates a dilemma between reconciling the rights of individual subjects of news stories with the rights of the consumers of news, who must also be recognized as rational agents and who require "relevant information in order to make reasoned choices."[122] The deciding factor on honoring the Kantian ideal would have to be a weighing of interests, thus suggesting that a recognition that respect for persons is perhaps not an absolute rule. Rather, it is one that must be tempered by the balancing of needs. Gauthier argues that

> invading the privacy of some and interfering with their choices regarding the release of information may be necessary in order to permit others access to information needed to make equally important choices in their lives.[123]

She does note, however, that respecting the privacy rights of individuals should be the default position for journalists unless it can be proven that the rights of the consumers of the information are greater. She provides a checklist that provides some guidance when these dilemmas are encountered.

- Why is this information considered private by the subject of the story?
- Do these reasons make sense?
- Would I want to keep this information private, if it concerned me?
- How important is it to the subject and the subject's life that this information is kept private?
- For what specific life choices does the public need this information?
- Are these relatively trivial or significant choices? How vital is this information to those choices?
- Is similar information available from public sources?[124]

Gauthier also provides a *utilitarian model* of privacy invasion based even more directly on the notion of competing claims. As with all utilitarian judgments, dealing with invasion of privacy requires a weighing of benefits and harms. Because of the requirement of impartiality, the moral claims of the subject of a story carry no more weight than those of the consumers of news. Gauthier warns us, however, that we must not make utilitarian decisions based on sheer numbers. Rather, we must consider the nature and severity of the potential harm. As John Stuart Mill warned, much can be sanctioned in the name of the common good that violates the dictates of justice. As Gauthier points out:

> when individual reporters or editors are attempting to justify a specific invasion of privacy by benefits for the common good, they must be reasonably certain that the information revealed really will promote the common good and that this good is generally recognized, as such, by the community.[125]

Gauthier's third construction is the *transfer of power model* based squarely on the "conception of personal privacy as our control over who has access to us and to information about us."[126] As mentioned at the beginning of this section, information is power. If this is true, then invasion of privacy equates to the theft of that power.[127]

> Privacy protects our thoughts, words, relationships, and activities from being used against us. It protects us from the judgments and repressive or punitive reactions of institutions, groups, and individuals. Privacy, understood in this way, serves as a valuable counterweight to the power of others.[128]

As with the other models, a journalistic decision to invade a subject's privacy must involve a recognition of the reason for the act. Reporters must question their motives for disclosing as well as the motives of their audience in knowing information about someone that is clearly private. Simple curiosity isn't enough. It must be shown to be of vital importance to the public, which is especially relevant in cases concerning political candidates or office holders. It may be that private information about people who have more power over others than most of us do deserve more scrutiny, even into their private lives or the aspects of their jobs that might otherwise remain private.

This brings up the important distinction between private and public individuals. Louis Day notes that the private–public distinction has developed into a situation in which private individuals are privileged by the courts when it comes to privacy. This has resulted in a near elimination of protection for public officials and public figures. Loosely defined, public figures include celebrities and others who, for whatever reason, find themselves in the limelight. Public officials are those who work within the various levels of government, from the lowly file clerk in the hall of records to the president of the United States. The courts, and common sense, seem to conclude that, because public figures and officials *choose* to do whatever they do within the glare of public scrutiny, they have asked to be scrutinized more closely. This may have some merit legally, but ethically it is suspect. Even if the "zone of privacy" accorded public figures and officials is necessarily smaller, should it be non-existent? Day argues that even these individuals deserve some modicum of privacy, and some level of control over their private affairs.

Of course, the level of privacy an individual *deserves* is also determined, in part, by his or her position. Logically, then, those with less power to affect the lives of others should be accorded more consideration than those who have more power. For example, it may be more ethically appropriate to investigate the private life of the President of the United States than the clerk in the hall of records in your hometown. However, even those subjects who may be classified as public figures (especially those not holding power themselves that directly affect the well-being of others) deserve a modicum of privacy, and it would be wrong to assume that the possession of power automatically allows for invasion of privacy.

Finally, Day sums up by proposing three moral values that should provide the foundation for an ethic of privacy for media practitioners.[129]

Respect for persons.

- As autonomous individuals we are all entitled to a certain amount of dignity, which should not be arbitrarily compromised for the sake of some slogan such as "the people's right to know."
- When invasions of privacy are inevitable, as when someone involuntarily becomes a subject of public interest, the goal should be to minimize the harm.

Social utility.

- The moral agent must decide what information is essential or at least useful to the audience in understanding the message being communicated.

    This principle eliminates appeals to sensationalism, morbid curiosity, ridicule, and voyeurism as a justification for invasion of privacy.

Justice.

- Moral agents are obliged to render judgments based on how much privacy their subjects really deserve under the circumstances.
- Public officials who are accused of violating their oath of office would, under most circumstances, deserve less privacy than victims of human tragedy.
- Certainly, the degree of "voluntariness," or purposeful behavior, is a consideration in deciding what kind of treatment an actor really deserves.

The bottom line is that we must protect the privacy of individuals when at all possible. Even in an era in which, by choice or circumstance, the concept of privacy is under attack, we need to remember the reasons we require and desire it. To imagine a world without it is becoming, sadly, easier to do. Jeffrey Rosen, law professor and legal affairs writer for the *New Republic*, laments the erosion of privacy when he says:

> Privacy is a form of opacity, and opacity has its values. We need more shades and more blinds and more virtual curtains. Someday, perhaps, we will look back with nostalgia on a society that still believed opacity was possible and was shocked to discover what happens when it is not.[30]

Ethics and the "New" Media

Journalism is changing, and the most visible manifestation of that evolution has come in the form of new media, specifically the internet. In this section we will take a look at its most recent transition from a profession privileging the few working in the traditional mainstream media (newspapers, television, radio) to the many who are now practicing what has been termed "participatory" or "citizen" journalism. As part of this investigation, we will also narrow the focus somewhat to blogging, or, as many have called it, "the democratization of media."

The State of the News Media 2008 Report suggests that "citizen media" have become a "true competitor to traditional media."[131] A key element in the rise of new media has been the advent of Web 2.0, which the report defines as

> online media that operates as partnership, or interactively, with the consumer. Anything that involves users posting video, writing a blog, reviewing products or connecting with friends on a social network site is a Web 2.0 activity.[132]

Examples of new media abound, including YouTube, the video-sharing site, Facebook and MySpace, the social networking giants, and Wikipedia, the citizen encyclopedia site. The report estimates that, as of spring 2006, 37 percent of all Americans who go online are engaged with user-generated content. In other words, they had actively "uploaded video or photos, blogged, posted comments to an online news group or Web site, remixed a song, or created some other form of media."[133]

However, the question of whether any of this activity constitutes "news" is a large one. Because the information generated is generally done by "citizens," it is often done without the interference, or aid, of editors. In addition, the content served on most of these sites doesn't always meet the traditional criteria for news. Nonetheless, the growth in popularity of such sites as Twitter, launched in 2006, has led to a change in content. Both Twitter and the social networking site Facebook are now being extensively used as news distribution platforms, according to the report, rivaling news sites for breaking news. As savvy newsmakers begin to place content on social networking sites, the all-important journalistic notion of the "scoop" may be shifting away from the mainstream media.

Participatory/Citizen Journalism

Mark Glaser says that:

> The idea behind citizen journalism is that people without professional journalism training can use the tools of modern technology and the global distribution of the Internet to create, augment or fact-check media on their own or in collaboration with others.[134]

Glaser draws the following distinction between this new form of journalism and traditional practices:

> When a traditional media outlet covers a story, the editor usually assigns the story to a reporter, the reporter does the work and turns in a story that gets edited and published. But in the case of ad hoc citizen journalism, a blogger or observer might see something happening that's newsworthy and bring it to the attention of the blogosphere or the online public. As more people uncover facts and work together, the story can snowball without a guiding editor and produce interesting results—leading to the mainstream media finally covering it and giving it wider exposure.[135]

He also points out that the term "citizen journalist" is a bit misleading. After all, aren't mainstream journalists also citizens? J. D. Lasica, senior editor for *Online Journalism Review*, notes that "Participatory journalism is a slippery creature. Everyone knows what audience participation means, but when does that translate into journalism?"[136] He enumerates several models that help define the distinction. First, when online publications and collaborative news sites engage in original reporting based on their own newsgathering, few would dispute that it's journalism. Even if citizens contribute photos, video, and tips to news sites, most would still consider it journalism. However, the definition frays a bit when bloggers merely comment on or link to news sites. Nevertheless, if we mix in *informed* personal commentary, especially if it relies on original research or is provided by an "expert," then it leans more toward journalism—as do the addition of such things as phone interviews with newsworthy subjects posted to a blog site.

Lasica argues that a strict definition of what constitutes journalism in a narrow sense must involve original reporting and an editorial filter, but in a broader sense may also consider travelogues, op-ed commentary and analysis. In either event, "it's certain that audience participation in the news equation is on the upswing."[137]

DETRACTORS AND SUPPORTERS

Obviously, not everyone agrees that citizen journalism is necessarily a good thing. Most of the criticism of the new form of journalism is based largely on questions such as: What constitutes a journalist? How do we tell the difference between news and opinion? How is it obtained and from whom? What is the level of quality control? and What is the level of transparency? On the first two questions, Wikipedia's founder, Jimmy Wales, notes that, "because citizen journalists are motivated to write mostly on stories they care about personally, their output is typically commentary or analysis." And, although he admits that some forms of citizen news tend toward objectivity, it probably won't replace the traditional model "with its mechanisms to ensure reporters are not just pushing an agenda."[138] The New York Times education columnist, Samuel Freedman, agrees when he says "Citizen journalism doesn't merely challenge the notion of professionalism in journalism but completely circumvents it."[139]

> It is journalism according to the ethos of indie rock 'n' roll: Do It Yourself. For precisely such reasons, I despair over the movement's current cachet. However wrapped in idealism, citizen journalism forms part of a larger attempt to degrade, even to disenfranchise journalism as practiced by trained professionals.[140]

Jay Rosen, a staunch *supporter* of citizen journalism, notes that traditional journalists have editors; however the new journalists (specifically bloggers) have "(writerly) readers, and the readers represent an editor." Depending on which side you're on in this debate, this can be viewed as either a positive or negative attribute. For example, the State of the News Media 2008 report cites recent research that seems to show that citizen journalism sites are not as open and interactive as the term implies, noting that in a recent survey,

> the majority of sites analyzed tended to demonstrate the instincts of "strong gatekeepers" who control the content and are somewhat more difficult to interact with than the ideals of citizen journalism suggest. Now, instead of professionals, those gatekeepers were the bloggers or citizens who ran the sites.[141]

Although this is a basically neutral statement, it does allude to a potential dilemma. Does this mean that, as the writer Alissa Quart puts it, "It's amateur hour in America," or does it presage a new way of looking at what we have traditionally defined as news journalism?[142]

Obviously, not everyone is a critic. Jay Rosen believes that citizen journalism, specifically in the form of blogs, are "an extremely democratic form of journalism."[143] He cites the educator and online blogger Jeff Jarvis as saying "the weblog gives people in the audience a printing press, and thus access to their own audience. There's something extremely democratic about that development."[144] The strength of blogging, as Rosen sees it, is that it creates a "sphere of debate" that includes millions of people, not just as listeners (as in traditional journalism), but as participants.

> The form favors individual voices and self-publishers, most of whom will have no media institution behind them, and no hope of profit. What they are after is free speech and the enhancement of public life.[145]

The online opinion author and pioneer blogger Tim Dunlop suggests that the act of blogging revives the "lost art of argument."[146] He cites the historian Christopher Lasch's observation that democracy requires argument among ordinary citizens—a forum that has been "usurped by an elite group of insiders" who have access to the media and who, because of that access, dominate public discourse. Dunlop argues that opinions need to be tested in public. Or, in Lasch's words:

> It is the act of articulating and defending our views that lifts them out of the category of "opinions," gives them shape and definition, and makes it possible for others to recognize them as a description of their own experience as well. In short, we come to know our own minds only by explaining ourselves to others.[147]

Dunlop proposes that blogging has taken up the idea of public debate and, although it is undoubtedly still short of realizing its full potential, it represents an unprecedented move toward a more realized public voice. He sees the democratization of news as a remedy to

> an age where politicians increasingly hide behind media experts and image consultants, where media people themselves have been co-opted by business and political machines and by a star system, where key journalists are spoon-fed press releases and background material by faceless partisans, where almost the ultimate affront is for a journalist to ask a probing question, and, worst of all, where so much decision-making takes place behind closed doors.[148]

And Poynter's Media Business Analyst, Rick Edmonds, predicts:

> Citizen journalism and blogs remain something big, even if that something isn't a news medium. At a minimum, they compete for time and attention, and influence an expectation by readers to be talked *with* conversationally rather than talked *at*, a development that would be imprudent for MSM [mainstream media] to ignore.[149]

Dealing with the Ethics of New Media

As has been said before in this book, many of the moral issues surrounding the new media, whether they are used by public relations, advertising, or journalism, are much the same as those associated with their more traditional forms. There are differences, of course. Although bias is expected in the persuasive media, it is a problem for anyone claiming to be a journalist. In order for a news source to be accepted as legitimate, a distinct line needs to be drawn between opinion and information, and that line must be clear to consumers of the information. Trust is a vital component in the relationship between media professionals and those they serve. For journalists, this trust is best engendered through credibility. Credibility, the quality of being trusted and believed in, is thus essential for anyone hoping to participate in the journalistic process.

One way to look at how the new media can develop credibility and, subsequently, trust is by imagining what a typical visitor to a web site would want if she were looking for a credible new source. The ethicists Arthur Hayes, Jane Singer, and Jerry Ceppos tackle this question by noting that because consumers of online media are faced with a barrage of information, much of it containing biased points of view or actual spin, they must decide what content to trust and from whom.[150] They propose a set of questions that, although they are aimed at the site visitor, also guide the site host seeking to provide a valid journalistic experience. Several of these questions are elaborated below. The first three go to the desire of the consumer to obtain legitimate news.

- Do I want news and opinion that exclusively agree with my views?
- Do I want news mixed with opinion?
- Do I care whether news and opinion are clearly distinguished from one another?

They suggest that true credibility and trust can be obtained only if your answer is "no" to the first two and "yes" to the last.

Probably the most important concept the authors deal with is *authenticity*. Authenticity has to do with how people view purveyors of news as being credible or not. Until recently, most consumers of news simply assumed the authenticity of mainstream media, supposing that real journalism was naturally being practiced by such bastions of the press as the *New York Times* or the *Washington Post*. This probably has more than anything to do with the "aggregated credibility of hundreds of journalists who, as individuals . . . become part of a 'brand' that has, over time, succeeded in gaining public trust as a source of credible information."[151] Authenticity can be extremely useful for building a sort of immediate credibility for an individual journalist who goes to work for an "authentic" media outlet. This is rapidly changing, however. In today's world of online journalism, individuals must build a sense of authenticity other ways. Recent research shows that most people looking for online news gravitate to "aggregators," sites such as Google News or Yahoo that typically don't produce their own news stories. Rather, they help users navigate to work produced by others.[152] One of the problems with aggregation is that it lacks the personalization and credibility of primary news sources organized in actual newsrooms because it relies on computer-generated algorithms to determine which news gets top billing. The priority of stories on Google News, for instance, is determined by how often and on what sites individual news stories appear, causing them to constantly be rearranged in an order that is practically preordained since they are usually selected by being the most often cited by others. This could result in breaking news stories receiving a very low billing because not enough people or web sites have picked up on them yet. Hayes, Singer, and Ceppos point out, rightly, that relegating the responsibility of gatekeeping to a computer program "removes it from the ethical realm, which rests on human choice. The role, in other words, is stripped of the values that, within an actual newsroom, inform it."[153]

Increasingly, however, blog sites are offering a mix of commentary, passed-along or repackaged news stories (often citizen-contributed), and links to other news sites—what the State of the News Media 2008 report calls "news and opinion as social dialogue."[154] For those seeking authenticity in a news source, a note of caution should be sounded over aggregators and re-packagers of news, prompting two more questions:

- Does this source break news itself or merely aggregate?
- Are some articles based on first-hand observation rather than secondary sourcing?

Even though commentary on what other's have said is valuable, "a diet of nothing but commentary increases the volume of discourse without necessarily adding to its quality."[155]

Because information providers in the new media cannot automatically achieve authenticity by association with an established news organization, there is an increased need to provide accountability. Hayes, Singer, and Ceppos suggest that related concepts of accountability and transparency are one avenue for achieving authenticity—which equals credibility and trust. As with the other uses of new media in public relations and advertising, transparency is a key factor in determining the validity of information. By exposing the source of information, we are able to judge not only level of expertise, but also motivation—a key to recognizing potential bias. Today's internet environment both exacerbates the problem of lack of transparency and, at the same time, allows for a greater transparency than ever before. Ideally, consumers should be able to identify the sources of information easily and determine the authenticity, thus the credibility, of those sources for themselves. These proposed questions speak to the issue of transparency.

- Is my source of news transparent? Can I easily find out about the news organization and its staff members? Does my news provider publicize its principles and adhere to them?
- Are the sources used in articles clearly identified? Are unnamed sources used sparingly if at all? If unnamed sources are used, is it clear why?

Transparency is more easily accomplished by news aggregators because they typically link directly to stories produced by established news organizations. For bloggers, however, the transparency requirement is harder to handle, because it deals not only with the validity of cited sources but also with the authenticity of the individual blogger. In other words, personal disclosure becomes the primary element of transparency. What are the blogger's biases, expertise, financial considerations?—all of which lead to understanding motivation. Ultimately, it's up to the information providers, whether aggregators or bloggers, to provide the ethical impetus needed to create authenticity.

> The people using these media forms can choose to use them in a way that enhances the transparency of communication and thus builds trust in the communicators, journalists included, over time. The medium provides the capability; it's up to humans to provide the credibility.[156]

In a 2005 working paper produced for a conference on blogging and journalism by Bill Michell and Bob Steele of the Poynter Institute, many of these issues were taken up, and suggestions were made to ensure that the future of new media will include a healthy dose of commitment to ethics.[157] They note that, "Like the Internet itself, blogging is a publishing tool invented by non-journalists that holds enormous opportunities, risks, and consequences for journalism and society."[158]

Their central premise was a recognition that publishing of any kind generally holds consequences for stakeholders beyond the writer. Thus, the major ethical issue is to determine what exactly are the writer's obligations to those stakeholders. They cite the journalist and new media pioneer Dan Gillmor, who says, "No matter which tools and technologies we embrace, we must maintain core principles, including fairness, accuracy, and thoroughness. These are not afterthoughts. They are essential if professional journalism expects to survive."[159]

Bloggers, if they are to be considered as engaged in journalistic practices, need to be open about the principles they subscribe to (fairness, accuracy, etc.). However, whatever standards they adopt, they cannot be imposed from outside. Rather, they must evolve in the same way that other media have traditionally set their own standards—generally through a recognition of their obligations to society as a whole and to the consumers of their product specifically.

As already noted, credibility and trust are essential to the practice of good journalism. Ethical standards help to generate those qualities by providing guidelines for practitioners and a way for the public to measure the success of the profession in living up to their own standards. Likewise, bloggers and other new media purveyors of information need to set their own standards with a recognition of their obligations to their interactive public. In other words, in forming standards and guidelines for new media, it is vitally important that those ideals and aspirations be jointly arrived at through open and honest discourse. There does seem to be a general recognition among purveyors of new media that the most important of these ideals is transparency. As the paper's authors note:

> Transparency can alert the audience to important information. It addresses the critical question of *how* the work is created. Transparency by itself rarely reveals much of the *why*, though, and that's a critical dimension for any audience. That's why we urge bloggers—as we urge journalists—to be transparent about the principles they stand for and the processes they follow in the course of upholding them.[160]

Ultimately, the paper recommends setting standards, especially in the area of transparency and accountability, that will move online journalists/bloggers toward credibility.

Blogging Codes

Like their counterparts on the mainstream media, bloggers hesitate to construct codes that would seem absolute standards for everyone (the Kantian approach). Or, as the former journalist and blogging expert Jeff Jarvis puts it:

> What I have a problem with is the idea that one person presumes to come up with an ethical code for an entire culture . . . This is complex and can't be handled in a single code. It's as complex as human character: It's all about the integrity of the individual.[161]

Instead, bloggers spend a good deal of time "suggesting" elements they think are important to consider, if they actually were to ever need a code. This is, of course, an excellent way to think about ethics, and an important first step in the process of building credibility. Here are a few of their thoughts.

The Web guru Rebecca Blood believes that the "uncensored, unmediated, uncontrolled voice"of the weblog is both its greatest asset and its greatest weakness.[162] Thus, she proposes several standards that she says share the common characteristic of transparency.

- Publish as fact only that which you believe to be true.
- If material exists online, link to it when you reference it.
- Publicly correct any misinformation.
- Write each entry as if it could not be changed; add to, but do not rewrite or delete, any entry.

- Disclose any conflict of interest.
- Note questionable and biased sources.

Writing in the *Journal of Mass Media Ethics*, Martin Kuhn proposes a code that expands on the idea of the journalistic function of blogging and moves into the realm of blogging-unique values—the form of blogging itself.[163]

- Promote Interactivity

  - Post to your blog on a regular basis.
  - Visit and post on other blogs.
  - Respect blog etiquette.
  - Attempt to be entertaining, interesting, and/or relevant.

- Promote Free Expression

  - Do not restrict access to your blog by specific individuals or groups.
  - Do not self-censor by removing posts or comments once they are published.
  - Allow and encourage comments on your blog.

- Strive for Factual Truth

  - Never intentionally deceive others.
  - Be accountable for what you post.

- Be as Transparent as Possible

  - Reveal your identity as much as possible (name, photo, background info, etc.).
  - Reveal your personal affiliations and conflicts of interest.
  - Cite and link to all sources referenced in each post.

- Promote the "Human" Element in Blogging

  - Minimize harm to others when posting information.
  - Promote community by linking to other blogs and keeping a blogroll.
  - Build relationships by responding to e-mails and comments regularly

What Now for New Media?

As Jimmy Wales puts it, "This community will continue to live and breathe and grow only so long as those of us who participate in it continue to Do The Right Thing."[164] As with all of the media discussed in this book, doing the right thing isn't always easy—mostly because the "right thing" is a slippery concept. What is certain is that both the audience and the providers of news are changing and, in the sense of new media, becoming the same thing. Wikipedia's own entry for citizen journalism says it "usually involves empowering ordinary citizens—including traditionally marginalized members of society—to engage in activities that were previously the domain of professional reporters."[165]

The question of credibility has become the driving concern among journalists of all denominations, whether in the mainstream media or the new media. And credibility implies a journalism that is reliable and trustworthy. If we are to maintain any sense of what journalism contributes to a democratic society, the purveyors of news must be able to construct the clearest version of reality that they can, based on accuracy and fact, and tempered by human involvement and interaction. The American philosopher John Dewey imagined a community of communicators who, together, would define their reality and then live it in common purpose. Perhaps that's where the new media will take us. Only time will tell.

What Does It All Mean?

Journalism has come a long way in the 60 years since the Hutchins Commission issued its statement on press responsibility. Journalism's report card hasn't always been filled with straight As, but it has generally received at least a passing score. The obligations listed by the Commission in 1947 are still valid today.

- To provide a truthful, comprehensive, and intelligent account of the day's events in a context that gives them meaning.
- To serve as a forum for the exchange of comment and criticism.
- To develop a representative picture of the constituent groups in society.
- To be responsible for the presentation and clarification of the goals and values of society.
- To provide full access to the day's intelligence.

Within the myriad manifestations of modern journalism, we can still find people striving to fulfill these charges every day. They may work for the mainstream media. They may work in the new media. They are probably all struggling to do the right thing. As journalism feels its way into the twenty-first century, there will surely be times when we will despair of the changes that both technology and the human beings who use it have wrought on journalism. If the proponents of "new" journalism are right, it will be only through open and public participation and debate that we will be able to elucidate clearly what we expect of the press, however defined. And that debate will most certainly center around ethics.

Notes

I What is Media Ethics?

1 Richard L. Johannesen, *Ethics in Human Communication*, 5th ed. (Prospect Heights: Waveland Press, 2002), 3.
2 Robert Entman, *Democracy Without Citizens: Media and the Decay of American Politics* (New York: Oxford University Press, 1989), 17–18.
3 Bernard Gert, *Morality: A New Justification of the Moral Rules* (New York: Oxford University Press, 1988), 214–215. Gert prefers to use *credit* instead of *praise*, as some others hold, since it is the proper opposite of *blame* as a "responsibility standard"; whereas *praise* and its opposite, *condemnation*, are considered to be moral standards.
4 James Grunig and Todd Hunt, *Managing Public Relations* (New York: Holt, Rinehart, and Winston, 1984), 100.
5 Johannesen, *Ethics in Human Communication*, 4.
6 I. F. Stone, *The Trial of Socrates* (Boston: Little Brown & Company, 1988), 207.
7 Clifford G. Christians, Kim B. Rotzoll, and Mark Fackler, *Media Ethics*, 5th ed. (New York: Longman, 1997), 2.
8 Vincent Ryan Ruggiero, *Beyond Feelings: A Guide to Critical Thinking* (Port Washington, NY: Alfred Pub. Co., 1975), 147.
9 James Fieser, *The Internet Encyclopedia of Philosophy*, http://www.iep.utm.edu/e/ethics.htm.
10 Henry Rosemont, Jr., "Whose Democracy? Which Rights?: A Confucian Critique of Modern Western Liberalism," unpublished paper (St. Mary's College of Maryland).

2 Moral Claimants, Obligation, and Social Responsibility

1 Clifford G. Christians, Kim B. Rotzoll, Mark Fackler, Kathy Brittain Mckee, and Robert Woods, Jr., *Media Ethics: Cases and Moral Reasoning* (New York: Pearson, 2005), 22–23.
2 George Borden, *Human Communication Systems* (Boston: American Press, 1985), 35.
3 James Rachels, *The Elements of Moral Philosophy* (New York: McGraw Hill, 1993), 76.
4 Louis Day, *Ethics in Media Communications: Cases and Controversies*, 2nd ed. (Belmont: Wadsworth Publishing Company, 1997), 29.
5 T. M. Scanlon, *What We Owe to Each Other* (Cambridge: The Belknap Press of Harvard University Press, 1998), 360–361.
6 Bernard Gert, *Morality: A New Justification of the Moral Rules* (Oxford: Oxford University Press, 1966), 154.

7 Ibid., 156.
8 William David Ross, *The Right and the Good* (Oxford: Clarendon Press, 1930).
9 Milton Friedman, "Social Responsibility and Compensatory Justice," in Joan Callahan (ed.), *Ethical Issues in Professional Life* (New York: Oxford University Press, 1988), 349–354.
10 Keith Davis and Robert L. Blomstrom, *Business and Society*, 3rd ed. (New York: McGraw Hill, 1975), cited in Grunig and Hunt, *Managing Public Relations*, 54–56.
11 Christopher Lasch, "Journalism, Publicity and the Lost Art of Argument," *Gannett Center Journal*, Spring 1990, 1–11.
12 Jay Rosen, "Beyond Objectivity," *Nieman Reports*, Winter 1993, 48–53.

3 The Media and Professionalism

1 Michael D. Bayles, *Professional Ethics*, 2nd ed. (Belmont: Wadsworth Publishing Company, 1989), 7–10.
2 Ibid., 10.
3 Ibid.
4 Ibid.,10.
5 John Kultgen, *Ethics and Professionalism* (Philadelphia: University of Pennsylvania Press, 1988), 114.
6 Bayles, 112.
7 Kultgen, 62.
8 Lasch, "Journalism, Publicity and the Lost Art of Argument."
9 Bayles, 117.
10 As quoted by Joann Byrd, "Let's Stop Abusing the First Amendment" (Seventeenth Annual Ruhl Lecture, University of Oregon School of Journalism and Communication, 1993).
11 For a thorough discussion of the professional–client relationship, see Bayles, *Professional Ethics*, 70–100.
12 Bayles, 74.
13 *American Bar Association Code of Professional Responsibility*, Canon 7, EC 7–3.
14 W. H. Simon, "The Ideology of Advocacy: Procedural Justice and Professional Ethics," *Wisconsin Law Review*, 1978, 29–144, cited in Bayles, *Professional Ethics*, 71–72.
15 Bayles, 72.
16 Byrd, "Let's Stop Abusing the First Amendment."
17 Bayles, 79–100.
18 Richard L. Johannesen, *Ethics in Human Communication*, 4th ed. (Prospect Heights: Waveland Press, 1996), 197.
19 Philip Meyer, *Ethical Journalism* (New York: Longman, 1987), 17–18.
20 Richard L. Johannesen, "What Should we Teach about Formal Codes of Communication Ethics," *Journal of Mass Media Ethics*, 3 (1), 59–64.
21 Ibid.
22 Ibid.
23 Ibid.
24 Karen Lebacqz, *Professional Ethics: Power and Paradox* (Nashville: Abington, 1985), 63–91, as cited in Johannesen, *Ethics in Human Communication*, 202–203.
25 Andrew Olsen, "Authoring a Code of Ethics: Observations on Process and Organization," Center for the Study of Ethics in the Professions at IIT (Illinois Institute

of Technology), http://www.iit.edu/departments/csep/codes/Writing_A_Code.
html.

26 Chris MacDonald, Ph.D.—Chris MacDonald teaches philosophy at Saint Mary's
University in Halifax, Nova Scotia, Canada. He has published on a wide range of
topics in ethics, ranging from business ethics and professional ethics through health-
care ethics and ethical issues in new technologies. He also runs the world's largest
ethics bookstore, which can be found online at http://www.ethicsweb.ca/books, as
well as a popular webpage on Codes of Ethics, at http://www.ethicsweb.ca/codes.

4 Theoretical Approaches to Ethics

1 James Rachels, *The Elements of Moral Philosophy* (New York: McGraw-Hill, 1993),
15–23.

2 Ibid., 40.

3 See especially Matt Ridley, *The Origins of Virtue* (New York: Penguin Books, 1998).

4 See especially James Q. Wilson, *The Moral Sense* (New York: The Free Press, 1993);
and Mary Midgley, *The Ethical Primate: Humans, Freedom and Morality* (London:
Routledge,1994), and *Beast and Man: The Roots of Human Nature* (London: Routledge, 1995).

5 Walter Lippmann, *Public Opinion* (New York: Macmillan, 1922), 29–38.

6 John C. Merrill, *Journalism Ethics: Philosophical Foundations for News Media* (New York:
St. Martin's Press, 1997), 36–37.

7 Rachels, 147–148.

8 David J. Fritzsche, "A Model of Decision-Making Incorporating Ethical Values,"
Journal of Business Ethics, 10, 841–852.

9 For an excellent discussion of the political component of Kant's philosophy as well
as a clear explanation of his ethics as a whole, see Roger J. Sullivan, *An Introduction
to Kant's Ethics* (Cambridge: Cambridge University Press, 1994).

10 Joann Byrd, "Let's Stop Abusing the First Amendment" (Seventeenth Annual Ruhl
Lecture, University of Oregon School of Journalism and Communication, 1993).

11 Stephen Carter, *Integrity* (New York: HarperCollins, 1996).

12 Harriet Taylor's first husband requested that her name not appear on works jointly
or almost wholly written by her and Mill, with whom she had been carrying on a
very close relationship. Following her husband's death and her subsequent marriage to Mill, she was, according to Mill, still reluctant to have her name appear on
their works. After her death from tuberculosis in 1858, *The Subjection of Women* was
finished by Mill and Helen Taylor, Harriet's daughter. Mill credited both of them
with the bulk of this work, even though only his name appeared on it.

13 Alexis de Tocqueville, *Democracy in America* (New York: Barnes & Noble, 2003), 233.

14 Richard L. Johannesen, *Ethics in Human Communication*, 4th ed. (Prospect Heights:
Waveland Press, 1996), 12.

15 Rachels, 163.

16 Aristotle, *Nichomachean Ethics*, Book II, section 9, translated by James Weldon (New
York: Macmillan, 1906).

17 Stanley Cunningham, "Getting it Right: Aristotle's 'Golden Mean' as Theory Deterioration," *Journal of Mass Media Ethics*, 14 (1), 11.

18 Weldon, Aristotle, *Nichomachean Ethics*, Book II, section 6.

19 Ibid., Book X, section 9.

20 Carol Gilligan, In a Different Voice: Psychological Theory and Women's Development (Cambridge: Harvard University Press, 1982), 19, 73-74, 127, 143, 156-165, 174.

21 Joan Tronto, Moral Boundaries: A Political Argument for an Ethics of Care (New York: Routledge, 1993), 102-160.

22 Rita C. Manning, Speaking from the Heart: A Feminist Perspective on Ethics (Lanham, MD: Rowman & Littlefield, 1992), 49, 56, 65-69, 139, 152.

23 Julia T. Wood, Who Cares? Women, Care, and Culture (Carbondale: Southern Illinois University Press, 1994), 41-49, 106-110.

24 Henry Rosemont, Jr., "Whose Democracy? Which Rights?"

25 Linda Steiner, "Feminist Theorizing and Communication Ethics," Communication, 12 (1989), 157-173, cited in Johannesen, Ethics in Human Communication, 236.

26 Louis Day, Ethics in Media Communications: Cases and Controversies, 2nd ed. (Belmont: Wadsworth Publishing Company, 1997), 218.

27 James Grunig and Todd Hunt, Managing Public Relations (New York: Holt, Rinehart and Winston, 1984), 21-25.

28 Carter, Integrity, 92.

29 J. S. Mill, On Liberty and Other Essays, ed. John Gray (New York: Oxford University Press, 1991).

30 Frederick Schauer in his introduction to Sissela Bok, Violence, Children, and the Press: Eight Rationales Inhibiting Public Policy Debates, Discussion Paper D-16 (The Joan Shorenstein Barone Center for Press, Politics and Public Policy, Harvard University, John F. Kennedy School of Government, 1994).

31 Neil Postman, Technopoly: The Surrender of Culture to Technology (New York: Alfred K. Knopf, 1992), 42.

32 Ibid., 87.

33 For an exhaustive discussion of the failings of the marketplace theory and a recommended alternative, see C. Edwin Baker, Human Liberty and Freedom of Speech (New York: Oxford University Press, 1989), 47-69.

34 Ibid., 56-66.

35 Ibid., 69.

36 Jean Hampton, Political Philosophy (New York: Westview Press, 1997), 169-185.

37 Huston Smith, World's Religions: A Guide to Our Wisdom Traditions (San Francisco: Harper San Francisco, 1994), 107.

38 John C. Merrill, Journalism Ethics: Philosophical Foundations for News Media (New York: St. Martin's Press, 1997), 34.

39 J. S. Mill, On Liberty and Other Essays, 10.

40 Henry David Thoreau, Walden (Thomas Y. Crowell & Co.: New York, 1910), 430.

41 Alasdair MacIntyre, After Virtue (Notre Dame: University of Notre Dame Press, 1981), 187.

42 Michael J. Sandel, Liberalism and the Limits of Justice (Cambridge: Cambridge University Press, 1982), 179.

43 J. S. Mill, On Liberty and Other Essays, 32.

44 Sissela Bok, Mayhem: Violence as Public Entertainment (Reading, MA: Addison-Wesley, 1998).

45 Carter, Integrity, 96.

5 A Checklist for Ethical Decision Making

1 Vincent Ryan Ruggiero, *The Moral Imperative* (Port Washington: Alfred Publishers, 1973).

2 D. J. Fritzsche, "A Model of Decision-Making Incorporating Ethical Values," *Journal of Business Ethics*, 10, 841–852.

6 Meta-issues Across the Media

1 Mary Midgley, *Can't We Make Moral Judgements?* (Bristol: Bristol Press, 1991), 135.

2 Ivan Preston, *The Great American Blow-Up: Puffery in Advertising and Selling* (Madison: University of Wisconsin Press, 1975), 6–8.

3 Carl P. Wrighter, "Weasel Words: God's Little Helpers," *I Can Sell You Anything* (New York: Ballantine Books, 1972).

4 Richard L. Johannesen, *Ethics in Human Communication*, 4th ed. (Prospect Heights, IL: Waveland Press, 1996), 138–139.

5 Tom Wheeler and Tim Gleason, "Digital Photography and the Ethics of Photofiction: Four Tests for Assessing the Reader's Qualified Expectation of Reality," paper presented to AEJMC Magazine Division, August 1994.

6 Stephen Carter, *Integrity* (New York: Basic Books , 1996), 94.

7 Stephen Klaidman and Stephen L. Beauchamp, *The Virtuous Journalist* (Oxford: Oxford University Press, 1987), 93.

8 Ibid., 94.

9 Joel Feinberg, *Harm to Others* (New York: Oxford University Press, 1984), 34–35.

10 Klaidman and Beauchamp, *The Virtuous Journalist*, 99.

11 Ibid.

12 Mike Price, "Out There: Hardball with a Heart," *Brill's Content*, November 1998, 83–85.

13 Steven Brill, "Curiosity vs. Privacy," *Brill's Content*, October 1999, 98–129.

14 Eric Effron, "Letter From the Editor," *Brill's Content*, October 1999, 7.

15 Carter, *Integrity*, 85, 94.

16 Ibid., 92, 95.

17 Brill, "Curiosity vs. Privacy," 129.

18 Klaidman and Beauchamp, *The Virtuous Journalist*, 105.

19 Brill, "Curiosity vs. Privacy," 129.

20 Michael J. Sandel, *Democracy's Discontent: America in Search of a Public Philosophy* (Cambridge, MA: Belknap Press of Harvard University Press, 1996), 70.

7 Meta-issues in Public Relations and Advertising

1 Based loosely on Apryl Duncan, "10 Differences Between Advertising and Public Relations," *Your Guide to Advertising*, http://advertising.about.com/od/careersource/a/10advpr.htm.

2 *Chrestensen v. Valentine*, 122 F.2d 511 (2nd Cir., 1941) (2–1 ruling); *Chrestensen v. Valentine*, 34 F.Supp. 596 (F. Dist. Ct., 1941).

3 *Central Hudson Gas & Electric Corp. v. Public Service Com.*, 447 U.S. 557, 563, 65 L. Ed. 2d 341, 100 S. Ct. 2343 (1980), and Ohralik, 436 U.S. at 456.

4 *Edenfield v. Fane*, 123 L. Ed. 2d 543, 113 S. Ct. 1792, 1798 (1993), cited in "Advertis-

ing is Protected by the First Amendment," http://www.lawpublish.com/amend1.
html.

5 "First Amendment, Religion and Expression, Freedom of Expression—Speech and
Press," extracted from *Analysis and Interpretation: Annotations of Cases Decided by the
Supreme Court of the United States*, 1992 edition, pp. 1113-1118, with 1996 updates
added, http://www.abuse.net/commercial.html.

6 Wayne Overbeck, "Unmuzzling America's Corporations: Corporate Speech and the
First Amendment," paper presented at the Annual Meeting of the Association for
Education in Journalism, East Lansing, Michigan, August 8-11, 1981, 1.

7 *Kasky v. Nike*, 02 C.D.O.S. 3790 (California Supreme Court) and *Nike, Inc. v. Kasky*,
539 U.S. 654 (2003).

8 Robert Sprague, "Business Blogs and Commercial Speech: A New Analytical Framework for the 21st Century," *American Business Law Journal*, 44 (1), 127-159.

9 Ibid., 147.

10 Karla K. Gower, *Legal and Ethical Considerations for Public Relations*, 2nd ed. (Long
Grove, IL: Waveland Press, 2008), 40.

11 Minette E. Drumwright and Patrick E. Murphy, "How Advertising Practitioners
View Ethics: Moral Muteness, Moral Myopia, and Moral Imagination," *Journal of
Advertising*, 33 (2), 12-13.

12 Ibid.

13 Richard M. Perloff, *The Dynamics of Persuasion: Communication and Attitudes in the 21st
Century*, 2nd ed. (Mahwah, NJ: Lawrence Erlbaum Associates, 2003).

14 Ibid., 12.

15 C. Edwin Baker, *Human Liberty and Freedom of Speech* (New York: Oxford University
Press, 1992), 57-60.

16 Ibid., 59.

17 Sally Miller Gearhart, "The Womanization of Rhetoric," *Women's Studies International Quarterly*, 2, 195-201.

18 Sonja K. Foss and Cindy L. Griffin, "Beyond Persuasion: A Proposal for an Invitational Rhetoric," *Communication Monographs*, 2, 2-18.

19 James E. Grunig and Todd Hunt, *Managing Public Relations* (New York: Holt, Rinehart and Winston, 1984), 21.

20 Benton Danner and Spiro Kiousis, "Persuasion and Ethics in Public Relations:
Towards a Taxonomy of Means and Ends," paper presented at the Association for
Education in Journalism and Mass Communication conference, San Francisco,
California, 2006.

21 J. Michael Sproule, *Argument: Language and Its Influence* (New York: McGraw-Hill,
1980), ch. 8.

22 J. Vernon Jensen, *Argumentation: Reasoning in Communication*, (New York: Van Nostrand, 1981), ch. 2.

23 Ted J. Smith, III (ed.), *Propaganda: A Pluralistic Perspective* (New York: Praeger, 1989),
80.

24 Austin Cline, "Propaganda and Persuasion: Misuse of Language and Meaning,"
About.com, http://atheism.about.com/od/criticalthinking/a/propaganda.htm.

25 Cline, "Propaganda."

26 Jay Black "Semantics and Ethics of Propaganda," *Journal of Mass Media Ethics*, 16
(2-3), 132-133.

27 Ibid., 133.
28 Ibid., 134–135.
29 Ibid., 135.

8 Ethics and Public Relations

1 Seol Kang and Hanna E. Norton, "Nonprofit Organizations' Use of the World Wide Web: Are They Sufficiently Fulfilling Organizational Goals?," *Public Relations Review*, 30, 279.

2 James Upshaw, Gennadiy Chernov, and David Koranda, "Telling More Than News: Commercial Influence in Local Television Stations," *Electronic News Journal*, 1 (2), 67–87.

3 Al Ries and Laura Ries, *The Fall of Advertising and the Rise of PR* (New York: Harper-Collins, 2004).

4 "Telling More Than News: Commercial Influence in Local Television Stations," *The Daily Dog*, 8 January 2008, *Bulldog Reporter/TEKgroup International 2008 Journalist Survey on Media Relations Practices*: Survey conducted September 11–23, 2008. Downloaded report from http://www.tekgroup.com/marketing/mediarelationspractices_bulldog/.

5 Alex Kuczynski, "Media Talk: In Public Relations, 25% Admit Lying," *New York Times*, 8 May 2000.

6 "Poll results show support for Iraq pullout, flag-burning amendment," *USA Today*, 26 June 2006. See also Michael Muller, "The Polls—a Review: American Public Opinion and the Gulf War: Some Polling Issues," *Public Opinion Quarterly*, 57, 80–91.

7 Arthur E. Rowse, "How to Build Support for a War," *Columbia Journalism Review* (CJR), September/October 1992, http://backissues.cjrarchives.org/year/92/5/war.asp.

8 Ted Rowse, "Kuwaitgate—Killing of Kuwaiti Babies by Iraqi Soldiers Exaggerated," *Washington Monthly*, September 1992, http://findarticles.com/p/articles/mi_m1316/is_/ai_12529902?tag=artBody;col1.

9 Sherry Baker, "Five Baselines for Justification in Persuasion," *Journal of Mass Media Ethics*, 14 (2), 69–81.

10 Kathy Fitzpatrick and Candace Gauthier, "Toward a Professional Responsibility Theory of Public Relations Ethics," *Journal of Mass Media Ethics*, 16 (2–3), 194.

11 Amanda Holt, the PR Ethics Resource Center, http://iml.jou.ufl.edu/projects/Spring02/Holt/.

12 James E. Grunig, "Collectivism, Collaboration and Societal Corporatism as Core Professional Values of Public Relations," *Journal of Public Relations Research*, 12 (1), 23–48.

13 Shannon A. Bowen, "A State of Neglect: Public Relations as 'Corporate Conscience' or Ethics Counsel," *Journal of Public Relations Research*, 20 (3), 271–296.

14 Ibid., 290.
15 Ibid.
16 Ibid., 284–285.
17 Ibid., 289.
18 Ibid., 292.
19 Ibid.

20 Sherry Baker and David L. Martinson, "The TARES Test: Five Principles for Ethical Persuasion," *Journal of Mass Media Ethics*, 16 (2–3), 148–175.

21 Ibid., 158.

22 Ibid., 159.

23 Ibid., 160.

24 Ibid., 163.

25 Shannon A. Bowen, "Expansion of Ethics as the Tenth Generic Principle of Public Relations Excellence: A Kantian Theory and Model for Managing Ethical Issues," *Journal of Mass Media Ethics*, 16 (1), 65–92.

26 Ibid., 81.

27 Ibid., 82.

28 Ibid., 83.

29 Ibid.

30 Ron L. Pearson, "Business Ethics as Communication Ethics: Public Relations Practice and the Idea of Dialogue," in C. Botan and V. Hazleton (eds.), *Public Relations Theory* (Hillsdale, NJ: Lawrence Erlbaum, 1989), 185.

31 Pearson, "Business Ethics as Communication Ethics," 125.

32 Carl Botan, "Introduction to the Paradigm Struggle in Public Relations," *Public Relations Review*, 19 (2), 197–210.

33 Ibid., 196.

34 Ron Pearson, "Beyond Ethical Relativism in Public Relations: Coordination, Roles and the Idea of Communication Symmetry," *Public Relations Research Annual*, 1, 67–86.

35 Larissa A. Grunig, James E. Grunig, David M. Dozier, *Excellent Public Relations and Effective Organizations: A Study of Communication Management in Three Countries* (Mahwah, NJ: Lawrence Erlbaum Associates, 2002).

36 Karey Harrison and Chris Galloway, "Public Relations Ethics: A Simpler (but Not Simplistic) Approach to the Complexities," Public Relations Resource Center, http://praxis.massey.ac.nz/fileadmin/Praxis/Files/Journal_Files/Issue3/Harrison_Galloway.pdf.

37 Ibid., 6.

38 Alisdair MacIntyre, *After Virtue*, 2nd ed. (Notre Dame, IN: University of Notre Dame Press, 1984), cited in Harrison and Galloway, "Public Relations Ethics," 8.

39 Harrison and Galloway, "Public Relations Ethics," 12.

40 Ibid., 13.

41 Fitzpatrick and Gauthier, "Toward a Professional Responsibility Theory," 209.

42 Michael D. Bayles, *Professional Ethics*, 2nd ed. (Belmont, CA: Wadsworth Publishing Company, 1989), 97.

43 Ibid., 98.

44 Ibid., 111–129.

45 csrnetwork, "What is CSR," http://csrnetwork.com/csr.asp.

46 Sir Geoffrey Chandler, "Defining Corporate Social Responsibility," *Ethical Performance Best Practice*, Fall 2002, cited in "What is Corporate Social Responsibility?" Catalyst Corporation and U.S. Agency for International Development (USAID), http://www.rhcatalyst.org/site/DocServer/CSRQ_A.pdf?docID=103.

47 Michael Hatcliffe, Executive Vice President, US Corporate Practice, Ogilvy Pub-

lic Relations Worldwide, "Expertise: Corporate Public Relations," http://www. ogilvypr.com/expertise/corporate-social-responsibility.cfm.

48 Jane Nelson, "The Public Role of Private Enterprise: Risks, Opportunities, and New Models of Engagement," working paper of the Corporate Social Responsibility Initiative, John F. Kennedy School of Government, Harvard University, February 2004, 6, http://www.hks.harvard.edu/m-rcbg/CSRI/publications/ workingpaper_1_nelson.pdf.

49 Ralph Waldo Emerson, "Letters and Social Aims: Progress of Culture," Phi Beta Kappa Address, July 18, 1876.

50 Deborah Doane, "The Myth of CSR: The Problem with Assuming that Companies Can Do Well while Also Doing Good is that Markets Don't Really Work That Way," *Stanford Social Innovation Review*, Fall 2005.

51 Ibid., 26.

52 Ibid.

53 Sharon Beder, "Greenwash," in John Barry and E. Gene Frankland (eds.), *International Encyclopedia of Environmental Politics* (London: Routledge, 2001). Excerpted online at http://homepage.mac.com/herinst/sbeder/greenwash.html.

54 Sheldon Rampton, "This Earth Day, Let's Scrape off the Greenwash," prwatch.com, April 2008, http://www.prwatch.org/node/7226.

55 Ibid.

56 Greenwashing Index, http://www.greenwashingindex.com/.

57 Zena James, "The impact of good CSR practice on corporate reputation," February 19, 2002, http://www.ethicalcorp.com/content.asp?ContentID=43.

58 Gerry McGovern "Blogs and Blogging: Advantages and Disadvantages," http:// www.gerrymcgovern.com/nt/2004/nt_2004_08_23_blogging.htm.

59 Ibid.

60 *McIntyre* v. *Ohio Elections Commission*, 514 U.S. 334 (1995). Cited in the Electronic Frontier Foundation, http://www.eff.org/Privacy/Anonymity/.

61 Patrick Lee Plaisance, "Transparency: An Assessment of the Kantian Roots of a Key Element in Media Ethics Practice," *Journal of Mass Media Ethics*, 22 (2–3), 187–207.

62 Ibid., 191.

63 Ibid., 188.

64 Shanti Atkins, "Online Deception Creates Ethics Scandal for Whole Foods," ELT Specialists in Ethics and Legal Compliance Training, http://www.elt-inc.com/ blog/2007/07/online-deception-creates-ethic.html.

65 Most of this information comes from Robert Pear, "U.S. Videos for TV News Come Under Scrutiny," *New York Times*, March 17, 2004, http://www.nytimes. com/2004/03/15/politics.

66 "Telling the Truth: PR Ethicist Tchividjian on the Edelman Fake Blog Scandal, Transparency and Why Current Ethics Codes Lack Bite," *Bulldog Reporter's Daily Dog*, October 26, 2006, archived at http://www.bulldogreporter.com/.

9 Ethics and Advertising

1 Richard F. Beltramini, "Advertising Ethics: The Ultimate Oxymoron?," *Journal of Business Ethics*, 48, 215–216.

2 John M. Phelan, "Advertising and Commercial Rhetoric," in Paul A. B. Clarke and Andrew Linzey (eds.), *Dictionary of Theology and Society* (London: Routledge, 1995),

"Essay on the moral and ethical implications of commercial rhetoric and their adaptations for political, religious, public order and public service purposes" http://www.religion-online.org/showarticle.asp?title=156.

3 Minette E. Drumwright and Patrick E. Murphy, "How Advertising Practitioners View Ethics: Moral Muteness, Moral Myopia, and Moral Imagination," *Journal of Advertising*, 33 (2), 7–24.

4 Frederick B. Bird, *The Muted Conscience: Moral Silence and the Practice of Business Ethics* (Westport, CN: Quorum Books, 1996), 27, cited in Drumwright and Murphy, 11.

5 Bird, 31, cited in Drumwright and Murphy, 15.

6 Drumwright and Murphy, 15.

7 Ibid.

8 Ibid., 16.

9 James R. Rest, "Theory and Research," in James R. Rest and Darcia Narvaez (eds.), *Moral Development in the Professions: Psychology and Applied Ethics* (Hillsdale, NJ: Lawrence Erlbaum, 1994), 23, cited in Drumwright and Murphy, 17.

10 Christopher E. Hackley and Phillip J. Kitchen, "Ethical Perspectives on the Postmodern Communications Leviathan," *Journal of Business Ethics*, 20 (1), 15–26.

11 Ibid., 15.

12 Ibid., 16.

13 Ibid., 19.

14 Ibid., 20.

15 Ibid., 22.

16 Ibid.

17 Ibid.

18 Ibid., 23.

19 Ibid., 23.

20 Ibid., 24–25.

21 Johannes Brinkmann, "Business Marketing Ethics as Professional Ethics. Concepts, Approaches and Typologies," *Journal of Business Ethics*, 41, 159–177.

22 Ibid., 161–162.

23 Ibid., 162.

24 Ibid., 163.

25 Ibid.

26 J. C. Wimbush and J. M. Shepard, "Toward an Understanding of Ethical Climate: Its Relationsip to Ethical Behavior and Supervisory Influence," *Journal of Business Ethics*, 13, 637–647, cited in Brinkman, 165.

27 Brinkman, 166.

28 John Alan Cohan, "Towards a New Paradigm in the Ethics of Women's Advertising," *Journal of Business Ethics*, 33, 324.

29 John P. Foley, President, and Pierfranco Pastore, Secretary, Pontifical Council for Social Communications, "Ethics in Advertising," Vatican City, February 22, 1998, http://www.vatican.va/roman_curia/pontifical_councils/pccs/documents/rc_pc_pccs_doc_22021997_ethics-in-ad_en.html, par. 3. This online document contains numbered paragraphs, which will be used in subsequent citations.

30 Cohan, "Towards a New Paradigm," 324.

31 Michael Schudson, "An Anthropology of Goods," in *Advertising, the Uneasy Persua-*

sion (New York: Basic Books, 1984), 129–146. Reprinted in *Advertising & Society Review*, 7 (1), 11.

32 Carl P. Wrighter, *I Can Sell You Anything* (New York: Ballantine Books, 1979).

33 There have been various other names for this, including Roland Marchand's *social tableau*; however, I have chosen to use the term *ambience* because it speaks more directly to what is being created in these types of advertisements.

34 David S. Waller, "Attitudes towards Offensive Advertising: An Australian Study," *Journal of Consumer Marketing*, 16 (3), 288. See also "What Factors Make Controversial Advertising Offensive?: A Preliminary Study," paper presented at the Australia and New Zealand Communication Association Conference, Sydney, July 2004.

35 Rosalinde Rago, "Finding the Magic: Cognitive Aspects of Mood and Emotion in Advertising," *Review of Business*, 11, 9–10.

36 Ibid.

37 Ibid.

38 Jill Stark, "Coke in the Firing Line as Caffeine Flunks the Taste Test," *theage.com.au*, January 9, 2007, http://www.theage.com.au/news/national/coke-in-the-firing-line-as-caffeine-flunks-the-taste-test/2007/01/08/1168104922295.html.

39 Quoted ibid.

40 Brad VanAuken, "Advertising: Emotional vs. Rational," http://www.brandingstrategyinsider.com/2008/01/slowly-ive-watc.html.

41 Ibid.

42 Bob Garfield, "Not Really Granola in a Bucket: New KFC Fried Chicken Claims are a Bit Slippery," *Advertising Age* online, http://adage.com/garfield/post?article_id=38718.

43 Donald J. Boudreaux, " 'Puffery' in Advertising," *Free Market*, 13 (9) (September 1995). This is a monthly publication of the Ludwig von Mises Institute and can be found online at http://mises.org/freemarket_detail.aspx?control=228.

44 Ivan L. Preston, *The Great American Blow-Up: Puffery in Advertising and Selling* (Madison: University of Wisconsin Press, 1996), 113.

45 Ibid., 113–114.

46 Ibid., 152.

47 Ibid., 151.

48 Ibid., 152.

49 Ibid., 7.

50 Meghan O'Rourke, "Diamonds Are a Girl's Worst Friend," Slate.com, June 11, 2007, http://www.slate.com/id/2167870/.

51 Foley and Pastore, "Ethics in Advertising," par. 3.

52 Kim Bartel Sheehan, *Controversies in Contemporary Advertising* (Thousand Oaks, CA:Sage Publications, 2003), 118–119.

53 Robert E. Wilkes and Humberto Valencia, "Hispanics and Blacks in Television Commercials," *Journal of Advertising*, 18 (1), 36–41, http://www.allbusiness.com/marketing-advertising/advertising-television-advertising/105172-1.html.

54 Walter Lippmann, *Public Opinion* (New York: Harcourt, Brace and Company, 1922), 79.

55 Ibid., 59.

56 Jean Kilbourne, "Beauty . . . and the Beast of Advertising," *Media & Values*, 49

(Winter 1990). Online at the Center for Media Literacy, http://www.medialit.org/reading_room/article40.html.

57 Media Awareness Network, "Media Stereotyping—Introduction," http://www.media-awareness.ca/english/issues/stereotyping/index.cfm.

58 Kim Sheehan, *Controversies in Contemporary Advertising* (Thousand Oaks, CA: Sage Publications, 2003), 82.

59 Ibid., 81.

60 Kilbourne, "Beauty . . . and the Beast of Advertising."

61 Media Awareness Network, "Media Stereotyping—Beauty and Body Image in the Media," http://www.media-awareness.ca/english/issues/stereotyping/women_and_girls/women_beauty.cfm.

62 Ibid.

63 Media Awareness Network, "Media Stereotyping—Media and Girls," http://www.media-awareness.ca/english/issues/stereotyping/women_and_girls/women_girls.cfm.

64 Duane Hargreaves, "Adolescent Body Image Suffers from Media Images of the Impossibly Thin," *Flinders University Journal*, 13 (9), 10–23.

65 National Institute on Media and the Family, "Media's Effect on Girls: Body Image and Gender Identity," http://www.mediafamily.org/facts/facts_mediaeffect.shtml.

66 J. J. Brumberg, *The Body Project: An Intimate History of American Girls* (New York: Random House, 1997), cited ibid.

67 Shawn Doherty and Nadine Joseph, "From Sidekick to Superwomen: TV's Feminine Mystique," reproduced from a report on the 1995 conference on *Children and the Media*, sponsored by Children Now, cosponsored by Stanford University and the UCLA Center for Communication Policy, 1997, http://www.cfc-efc.ca/docs/mnet/00001186.htm.

68 Media Awareness Network, "Media and Girls."

69 Sarah Sobieraj, "Beauty and the Beast: Toy Commercials and the Social Construction of Gender," American Sociological Association, *Sociological Abstracts*, 044, 1996, cited in "Media's Effect on Girls."

70 Nancy Signorielli, "Reflections of Girls in the Media: A Two-Part Study on Gender and Media," Kaiser Family foundation and Children NOW, 1997, cited in "Media's Effect on Girls."

71 For an exhaustive list of articles from various sources on buzz marketing, see http://www.commercialalert.org/issues/culture/buzz-marketing.

72 "What's the Buzz about Buzz Marketing?," Wharton School of Business, University of Pennsylvania, January 12, 2005, http://knowledge.wharton.upenn.edu/article.cfm?articleid=1105.

73 Ibid., 4.

74 Cited ibid., 1.

75 "Stealth Marketing: To Disclose or Not to Disclose—That is the (Legal) Question," *Advertising and Marketing Bulletin*, August 2006, http://www.mcmillan.ca/upload/publication/stealthmarketing_0806.pdf.

76 Ibid.

77 Commercial Alert, "Request for Investigation of Companies that Engage in 'Buzz Marketing,'" October 18, 2005, http://www.commercialalert.org/buzzmarketing.pdf.

78 Annys Shin, "FTC Moves to Unmask Word-of-Mouth Marketing," *Washington Post*, December, 12, 2006. See also Rob Walker, "The Hidden (In Plain Sight) Persuaders," *New York Times*, December 5, 2004, 68.

79 Suzanne Vranica, "Getting Buzz Marketers to Fess Up," *Wall Street Journal*, February 9, 2005.

80 Sourcewatch, A project of the Center for Media and Democracy, http://www.sourcewatch.org/index.php?title=Procter_%26_Gamble.

81 "I Sold It through the Grapevine: Not Even Small Talk Is Sacred Anymore. P&G has Enlisted a Stealth Army of 600,000 Moms who Chat Up Its Products," *Business-Week*, May 29, 2006.

82 Ibid.

83 Commercial Alert, "FTC Gives 'Giant Christmas Present' to P&G, Word of Mouth Marketing Industry," news release, December 11, 2006.

84 Federal Trade Commission, letter to Commercial Alert, December 7, 2006, http://www.ftc.gov/os/closings/staff/061211staffopiniontocommercialalert.pdf.

85 Stefanie Olson, "MySpace Blurs Line between Friends and Flaks," CNET News.com, July 31, 2006, http://news.cnet.com/MySpace-blurs-line-between-friends-and-flacks/2009-1025_3-6100176.html.

86 Ibid.

87 Ibid.

88 Gerry Khermouch and Jeff Green, "Buzz Marketing: Suddenly This Stealth Strategy Is Hot–but It's Still Fraught with Risk," *Business Week Online*, July 30, 2001, http://www.businessweek.com/magazine/content/01_31/b3743001.htm.

89 Ibid.

90 Andrew M. Kaikati and Jack Kaikati, "Stealth Marketing: How to Reach Consumers Surreptitiously," *California Management Review*, 46 (4), 20.

91 Ibid., 19.

92 Ibid., 20.

93 "The WOMMA Ethics Code," http://www.womma.com/ethics/code/read/.

94 "WOMMA's Practical Ethics Toolkit," http://www.womma.com/20questions/read/.

95 Patrick Lee Plaisance, "Transparency: An Assessment of the Kantian Roots of a Key Element in Media Ethics Practice," *Journal of Mass Media Ethics*, 22 (2–3), 187–207.

96 American Advertising Federation, "Advertising Ethics and Principles," http://www.aaf.org/default.asp?id=37.

97 James H. Barnes, Jr. and Michael J. Dotson, "An Exploratory Investigation into the Nature of Offensive Television Advertising," *Journal of Advertising*, 19 (3), 61–69.

98 David Waller, "What Factors Make Controversial Advertising Offensive?: A Preliminary Study," paper presented at the Australian New Zealand American Studies Association Conference, Sydney, Australia, July 2004.

99 Ibid., 6.

100 Timothy P. Christy, "Females' Perceptions of Offensive Advertising: The Importance of Values, Expectations, and Control," *Journal of Current Research in Advertising* 28 (2), 15–32.

101 Ibid., 31.

102 Advertising Standards Authority, "Summary Research Report: Serious Offence in Non-Broadcast Advertising," July 2002, http://www.asab.org.uk/NR/

rdonlyres/2A49A84C-C88B-4499-815B-5C092F67375C/0/ASA_Serious_
Offence_in_NonBroadcast_Advertising_July_2002.pdf.
103 Ibid., 4.
104 Sheehan, *Controversies in Contemporary Advertising*, 85.
105 Stephen Carter, *Civility* (New York: Harpers, 1999). Note that Carter is not specifically talking about advertising, but is concerned with the general lack of civility in
modern American society, which is manifested in many forms, including the media.
106 Sandra O'Loughlin, "Dolce & Gabana Pulls Controversial Ad," *Brandweek*, February 20, 2007.
107 Ibid.
108 Wally Snyder, "Advertising Ethics: An Introduction," American Advertising Federation: Advertising Ethics (online blog), http://www.aafblog.org/blog/?p=1.
109 Darren W. Dahl, Kristina D. Frankenberger, and Rajesh V. Manchanda, "Does It
Pay to Shock? Reactions to Shocking and Nonshocking Advertising Content among
University Students," *Journal of Advertising Research*, 43, 268–280.
110 Ibid., 68.
111 Media Awareness Network, "Calvin Klein: A Case Study," http://www.media-
awareness.ca/english/resources/educational/handouts/ethics/calvin_klein_case_
study.cfm?.
112 Ibid.
113 Waller, "Attitudes towards Offensive Advertising," 7.
114 Foley and Pastore, "Ethics in Advertising," par. 16.
115 Ibid., par. 23.
116 Ibid., par. 14.
117 Ibid., par. 18.

10 Ethics in News Journalism

1 Bob Kovach and Tom Rosenstiel, *The Elements of Journalism* (New York: Three Rivers
Press, 2001), 17.
2 USC Center for Digital Future, "Annual Internet Survey by the Center for the
Digital Future Finds Shifting Trends Among Adults About the Benefits and Consequences of Children Going Online," January 17, 2008, cited in Project for Excellence in Journalism, "Report on the State of the News Media, 2008," http://www.
stateofthenewsmedia.org/2008/.
3 Ibid.
4 Mark Glasser, "Your Guide to Citizen Journalism," *Mediashift*, September 27, 2006,
http://www.pbs.org/mediashift/2006/09/digging_deeperyour_guide_to_ci.html.
5 Richard Wightman Fox and James T. Kloppenberg, *A Companion to American
Thought* (Oxford: Blackwell Publishers, 1998), 501.
6 Ibid.
7 Ibid.
8 Julia R. Fox, "The 'I' of Embedded Reporting: An Analysis of CNN Coverage of
the 'Shock and Awe' Campaign," *Journal of Broadcasting & Electronic Media*, 50 (1),
36–51.
9 Michael Schudson, "The Objectivity Norm in American Journalism," *Journalism*, 2
(2), http://jou.sagepub.com/cgi/content/abstract/2/2/149, 160–161.

10   Walter Lippmann, *Liberty and the News* (New York: Atlantic Monthly, 1919), 79.

11   Michael Schudson, "Lippmann and the News," *The Nation*, December 31, 2007, http://www.thenation.com/doc/20071231/schudson/.

12   Lippmann, *Liberty and the News*, 82.

13   Project for Excellence in Journalism, "Principles of Journalism," 3, September 2006, http://journalism.org/node/1951.

14   Project for Excellence in Journalism, "The Lost Meaning of Objectivity," cited by the Committee of Concerned Journalists, http://www.concernedjournalists.org/lost-meaning-objectivity.

15   Project for Excellence in Journalism, "Principles of Journalism."

16   Schudson, "The Objectivity Norm," 163.

17   Rick Iedema, Susan Feez, and Peter White, "Appraisal and Journalistic Discourse," *Media Literacy* (Sydney: Disadvantaged Schools Program, New South Wales Department of School Education, 1994). Excerpted online at http://www.grammatics.com/Appraisal/MediaLit-Appraise.pdf.

18   Ibid.

19   Evan Thomas and Suzanne Smalley, "The Myth of Objectivity," *Newsweek*, November 3, 2008, 36–38.

20   Project for Excellence in Journalism, "The Lost Meaning of Objectivity."

21   Stephen Ward, "The Invention of Journalism Ethics: The Path to Objectivity and Beyond," *UBC Reports*, 50 (10), http://www.publicaffairs.ubc.ca/ubcreports/2004/04nov04/journalism.html/.

22   Stephen J. Ward, *The Invention of Journalism Ethics: The Path to Objectivity and Beyond* (Montreal: McGill-Queen's University Press, 2004), 306.

23   Philip Meyer, "Public Journalism and the Problem of Objectivity," http://www.unc.edu/~pmeyer/ire95pj.htm. This article is based on a talk given to the IRE conference on computer-assisted reporting in Cleveland in September 1995.

24   Ibid.

25   Ibid.

26   Ibid.

27   Ibid.

28   Iedema, Feez, and White, "Appraisal and Journalistic Discourse."

29   Howard A. Myrick, "The Search for Objectivity in Journalism," *USA Today* (Society for the Advancement of Education), online at http://findarticles.com/p/articles/mi_m1272/is_2690_131/ai_94384327.

30   Andrew R. Cline, "Media/Political Bias," *Rhetorica: A Rhetoric Primer*, http://rhetorica.net/textbook/. Portions cited here are from http://rhetorica.net/bias.htm.

31   Ibid.

32   Ibid.

33   Project for Excellence in Journalism, "State of the News Media 2008," http://www.stateofthenewsmedia.org/2008/narrative_networktv_audience.php?cat=2&media=6.

34   Ibid.

35   Ibid., http://www.stateofthenewsmedia.org/2008/narrative_cabletv_contentanalysis.php?cat=1&media=7.

36   Cline, "Media/Political Bias."

37   Lori Dorfman and Vincent Schiraldi, "Off Balance: Youth, Race & Crime in the News," Berkeley Media Studies Group, Public Health Institute and the Justice Policy Institute, 2001, 7–9. PDF of report downloaded online at http://www.buildingblocksforyouth.org/.

38   Ibid.

39   Ibid.

40   Ibid., 10–11.

41   Cline, "Media/Political Bias."

42   Ibid.

43   Jay Rosen, "PressThink Basics: The Master Narrative in Journalism," *Pressthink*, September 8, 2003, http://journalism.nyu.edu/pubzone/weblogs/pressthink/2003/09/08/basics_master_p.html.

44   Ibid.

45   Shanto Iyengar, "Natural Disasters in Black and White: How Racial Cues Influenced Public Response to Hurricane Katrina," draft of paper, June 10, 2007, http://pcl.stanford.edu/research/2007/iyengar-katrina-cues.pdf.

46   Cline, "Media/Political Bias."

47   Eric Boehlert, *Lapdogs: How the Press Rolled Over for Bush* (New York: Free Press, 2006), 41.

48   See an exhaustive chronological listing of the results of opinion polls at Religious Tolerance.org, "Euthanasia and Terri Schiavo," http://www.religioustolerance.org/schiavo7.htm.

49   Eric Boehlert, "A Tale Told by an Idiot," Salon.com, http://dir.salon.com/story/news/feature/2005/03/31/schiavo_media/.

50   Ibid.

51   David Carr, "A Nation at War: Coverage; Pentagon Says Geraldo Rivera will be Removed from Iraq," *New York Times*, April 1, 2003.

52   Project for Excellence in Journalism, "State of the News Media 2008," http://www.stateofthenewsmedia.org/2008/narrative_networktv_audience.php?cat=2&media=7

53   Cline, "Media/Political Bias."

54   Letter from Thomas Jefferson to John Norvell, 1807, *The Writings of Thomas Jefferson* (Memorial Edition), edited by Andrew Adgate Lipscomb and Albert Ellery Bergh (Washington, DC: The Thomas Jefferson Memorial Association of the United States, 1903–1904), vol. 11, 224.

55   Clifford Christians, "Books in Media Ethics," College of Communications, University of Illinois, http://www.silha.umn.edu/bib1998.pdf.

56   Stephen Ward, "Philosophical Foundations for Global Journalism Ethics," *Journal of Mass Media Ethics*, 20 (1), 8.

57   Deni Elliot, "All Is Not Relative: Essential Shared Values and the Press," *Journal of Mass Media Ethics*, 3 (1), 1.

58   Ibid., 4.

59   Ibid.

60   Ward, "Global Journalism Ethics," 7.

61   Ibid., 8.

62   Ibid., 10.

63   Ibid., 12.

64 Ibid.
65 Ibid.
66 Ibid.
67 Deni Elliot, "Getting Mill Right," *Journal of Mass Media Ethics*, 20 (2–3), 101.
68 Ibid., 102.
69 Ibid., 107.
70 Ibid., 110.
71 Ibid., 110–111.
72 Clifford G. Christians, "Utilitarianism in Media Ethics and Its Discontents," *Journal of Mass Media Ethics*, 20 (2–3), 113.
73 Ibid., 120.
74 Ibid., 122.
75 Ibid.
76 Ibid., 126.
77 Ibid.
78 Christopher Meyers, "Appreciating W. D. Ross: On Duties and Consequences," *Journal of Mass Media Ethics*, 18 (2), 81–97.
79 Ibid., 83.
80 Ibid., 84.
81 Ibid., 93.
82 Ibid., 95.
83 A paraphrase of MacIntyre's position, in Neil Levy, "Good Character: Too Little, Too Late," *Journal of Mass Media Ethics*, 19 (2), 111.
84 Alisdair MacIntyre, *After Virtue*, 2nd ed. (Notre Dame, IN: University of Notre Dame Press, 1984), cited in Karey Harrison and Chris Galloway, "Public Relations Ethics: A Simpler (but Not Simplistic) Approach to the Complexities," The Public Relations Resource Center, http://praxis.massey.ac.nz/fileadmin/Praxis/Files/Journal_Files/Issue3/Harrison_Galloway.pdf.
85 Kevin Gibson, "Contrasting Role Morality and Professional Morality: Implications for Practice," *Journal of Applied Philosophy*, 20 (1), 17.
86 Elliot D. Cohen, "What Would Cronkite Do? Journalistic Virtue, Corporate News, and the Demise of the Fourth Estate," in "Three Essays on Journalism and Virtue," *Journal of Mass Media Ethics*, 19 (3–4), 268.
87 Ibid., 269.
88 Aaron Quinn, "Moral Virtues for Journalists," *Journal of Mass Media Ethics*, 22 (2–3), 168–186.
89 Ibid., 172.
90 Ibid.
91 Deni Elliott and Charles Culver, "Defining and Analyzing Journalistic Deception," *Journal of Mass Media Ethics*, 7 (2), 72.
92 Ibid., 72–73.
93 Steve McClellan, "Controversy over Chung-Gingrich interview," *Broadcasting & Cable*, January 9, 1995.
94 Elliott and Culver, "Defining and Analyzing Journalistic Deception," 79.
95 Cheryl Reid, "A Newspaper Confesses: We Missed the Story," *American Journalism Review*, January/February 1993, http://www.ajr.org/article.asp?id=2101.
96 Jill Rosen, "The Story Behind the Story continued," *American Journalism Review*,

August/September 2004, http://www.ajr.org/Article.asp?id=3708. This not a direct quote from the *Oregonian* editor, but a paraphrase by the author of this *AJR* piece.

97 Joe Saltzman, "A Chill Settles over Investigative Journalism: (Food Lion Markets' Victory over ABC News)," *USA Today* (magazine), July 1, 1997, 29.

98 David Wagner, "Making News, Breaking Ethics," *Insight on the News*, March 17, 1997, 10.

99 Sissela Bok, *Secrets: On the Ethics of Concealment and Revelation* (New York: Pantheon Books, 1982), 249–264.

100 Louis Day, *Ethics in Media Communications: Cases and Controversies* (Belmont, CA: Wadsworth Publishing Company, 1997), 97.

101 Bob Steele, "Deception/Hidden Cameras Checklist," Poynter.org, http://poynter. org/content/content_view.asp?id=866.

102 Brian Stelter, "NBC Settles with Family that Blamed a TV Investigation for a Man's Suicide," *The New York Times*, June 26, 2008, online at http://www.nytimes. com/2008/06/26/business/media/26nbc.html.

103 Aaron Barnhart, "Newsroom-Orchestrated Stings, though Popular with Viewers, Present Concerns for Stations," *IRE Journal*, July/August 2004, 33–34.

104 Ibid., 34.

105 Kenny Irby, "*L.A. Times* Photographer Fired over Altered Image," Poynter.org, April 2, 2003, http://www.poynter.org/content/content_view.asp?id=28082.

106 Ibid.

107 Edwin Martin, "Against Photographic Deception," *Journal of Mass Media Ethics*, 2 (2), 50.

108 Ibid.

109 The following discussion is drawn from: Tom Wheeler and Tim Gleason, "Digital Photography and the Ethics of Photofiction: Four Tests for Assessing the Reader's Qualified Expectation of Reality," paper presented to AEJMC Magazine Division, August 1994; and Tom Wheeler, *Phototruth or Photofiction: Ethics and Media Imagery in the Digital Age* (Mahwah, NJ: Lawrence Erlbaum, 2002).

110 Wheeler, *Phototruth or Photofiction*, 80.

111 Ibid., 141.

112 See the two photos compared at http://www.famouspictures.org/mag/index. php?title=Altered_Images#Kent_State_Pole.

113 Wheeler, *Phototruth or Photofiction*, 81.

114 Thomas M. Cooley, *A Treatise on the Law of Torts, or the Wrongs Which Arise Independent of Contract* (Chicago: Callaghan and Coompany, 1888), 29.

115 Samuel D. Warren and Louis D. Brandeis, "The Right to Privacy," *Harvard Law Review*, 4, 193.

116 Ronald B. Standler, "Privacy Law in the USA," May 24, 1998, http://www.rbs2. com/privacy.htm.

117 The Florida Bar Association, "Reporters Handbook," August 2004, http://www. floridabar.org/DIVCOM/PI/RHandbook01.nsf/1119bd38ae090a748525676f005 3b606/dfc00ac22467b7f5852569cb004cbc2a.

118 Louis Hodges, "The Journalist and Privacy," *Journal of Mass Media Ethics*, 9 (4), 203.

119 Sissela Bok, *Secrets*, 10–11.

120 Hodges, "The Journalist and Privacy," 199.

121 Candice Cummins Gauthier, "Privacy Invasion by the News Media: Three Ethical Models," *Journal of Mass Media Ethics*, 17 (1), 22.

122 Ibid.

123 Ibid., 23.

124 Ibid., 24.

125 Ibid., 26.

126 Ibid.

127 Ibid.

128 Ibid.

129 Day, *Ethics in Media Communications*, 132.

130 Jeffrey Rosen, *The Unwanted Gaze: The Destruction of Privacy in America* (New York: Random House, 2000).

131 Project for Excellence in Journalism, "State of the News Media 2008," http://www.stateofthenewsmedia.org/2008/narrative_online_citizen_media.php?cat=6&media=5.

132 Ibid.

133 Amanda Lenhart, Mary Madden, Alexandra Rankin Macgill, and Aaron Smith, "Teens and Social Media," Pew Internet & American Life Project, December 19, 2007, http://www.pewinternet.org/pdfs/PIP_Teens_Social_Media_Final.pdf. Cf. Mary Madden and Susannah Fox, "Riding the Waves of 'Web 2.0'," Pew Internet & American Life Project, Reports: Internet Evolution, October 5, 2006, http://www.pewinternet.org/PPF/r/189/report_display.asp.

134 Mark Glaser, "Your Guide to Citizen Journalism," *Mediashift*, pbs.org. http://www.pbs.org/mediashift/2006/09/digging_deeperyour_guide_to_ci.html.

135 Ibid.

136 J. D. Lasica, "What is Participatory Journalism?," USC Annenberg *Online Journalism Review*, July 8, 2003, http://www.pbs.org/mediashift/2006/09/digging_deepery-our_guide_to_ci.html.

137 Ibid.

138 A. Adam Glenn, "Wikipedia Founder Lukewarm on Citizen Journalism?," Poynter.org, November 16, 2006, http://poynter.org/column.asp?id=31&aid=114062.

139 "Outside Voices: Samuel Freedman on the Difference between the Amateur and the Pro," CBS News *Public Eye*, March 31, 2006, http://www.cbsnews.com/blogs/2006/03/30/publiceye/entry1458655.shtml.

140 Ibid.

141 Project for Excellence in Journalism, "State of the News Media 2008."

142 Alissa Quart, "The Amateur Revolution," *Mother Jones*, January 8, 2007.

143 Jay Rosen, "The Weblog: An Extremely Democratic Form in Journalism," excerpted from his chapter in Jon Lebkowsky and Mitch Ratcliffe (eds.), *Extreme Democracy: The Book* (n.p.: Lulu.com, 2005). The draft can be found online at *Pressthink*, http://journalism.nyu.edu/pubzone/weblogs/pressthink/2004/03/08/weblog_demos.html.

144 Cited ibid.

145 Ibid.

146 Tim Dunlop, "If You Build It They Will Come: Blogging and the New Citizenship," Evatt Foundation, *Publications*, June 17, 2003, http://evatt.labor.net.au/publications/papers/91.html.

147 Christopher Lasch, *The Revolt of the Elites: And the Betrayal of Democracy* (New York: W. W. Norton & Company, 1995), 170, cited in Dunlop, "If You Build It."

148 Dunlop, "If You Build It."

149 Rick Edmonds, "As Blogs and Citizen Journalism Grow, Where's the News?," Poynter.org, http://poynter.org/content/content_view.asp?id=91391s.

150 Arthur S. Hayes, Jane B. Singer, and Jerry Ceppos, "Shifting Roles, Enduring Values: The Credible Journalist in a Digital Age," *Journal of Mass Media Ethics*, 22 (4), 262–279.

151 Ibid.

152 Project for Excellence in Journalism, "State of the News Media 2008," http://www.stateofthenewsmedia.org/2008/narrative_online_audience.php?cat=2&media=5.

153 Ibid., 270.

154 Ibid.

155 Ibid., 269.

156 Ibid., 273.

157 Bill Mitchell and Bob Steele, "Earn Your Own Trust, Roll Your Own Ethics: Transparency and Beyond," paper presented at the conference on Blogging, Journalism and Credibility: Battleground and Common Ground, sponsored by the Berkman Center for Internet and Society at the Harvard Law School, the American Library Association's Office of Information Technology, and the Shorenstein Center on the Press, Politics and Public Policy at Harvard's Kennedy School of Government, January 15, 2005.

158 Ibid.

159 Dan Gillmor, *We the Media* (Sebastopol, CA: O'Reilly Media, 2004), 134., cited in Mitchell and Steele, "Earn Your Own Trust."

160 Mitchell and Steele, "Earn Your Own Trust."

161 J. Jarvis, "Blogging, Ethics, & Credibility" [comment on post], January 13, 2005, cited in Martin Kuhn, "Interactivity and Prioritizing the Human: A Code of Blogging Ethics," *Journal of Mass Media Ethics*, 22 (1), 34.

162 Rebecca Blood, *The Weblog Handbook: Practical Advice on Creating and Maintaining Your Blog* (Cambridge, MA: Perseus Publishing, 2002), 114–121. Excerpted online as "Weblog Ethics," on the online blog, *rebecca's pocket*, http://www.rebeccablood.net/handbook/excerpts/weblog_ethics.html.

163 Kuhn, "Interactivity and Prioritizing the Human," 23–24.

164 Jimmy Wales, "Jimbo Wales/Statement of Principles," Wikipedia, http://en.wikipedia.org/wiki/User:Jimbo_Wales/Statement_of_principles.

165 http://en.wikipedia.org/wiki/Citizen_journalism.

Bibliography

Alter, J. (1996, May 27). Beneath the waves. *Newsweek, 127.*

Baker, C. E. (1992). *Human liberty and freedom of speech.* New York: Oxford University Press.

Baker, S. (1999). Five baselines for justification in persuasion. *Journal of Mass Media Ethics, 14*(2), 69–81.

Baker, S. and Martinson, D. L. (2001). The TARES test: Five principles for ethical persuasion. *Journal of Mass Media Ethics, 16*(2–3), 148–175

Bayles, M. D. (1989). *Professional ethics* (2nd ed.). Belmont: Wadsworth Publishing Company.

Barnes, J. H., Jr., and Dotson, M. J. (1990). An exploratory investigation into the nature of offensive television advertising. *Journal of Advertising, 19*(3), 61–69.

Beder, S. (2001). Greenwash. In *International Encyclopedia of Environmental Politics.* London: Routledge. http://homepage.mac.com/herinst/sbeder/greenwash.html.

Beltramini, R. F. (2003). Advertising ethics: The ultimate oxymoron? *Journal of Business Ethics, 48,* 215–216.

Black, J. (2002). Semantics and ethics of propaganda. *Journal of Mass Media Ethics, 16*(2–3), 121–137.

Bok, S. (1982). *Secrets: On the ethics of concealment and revelation.* New York: Pantheon Books.

Bok, S. (1994). *Violence, children, and the press: Eight rationales inhibiting public policy debates* (Discussion Paper D-16). Cambridge, MA: The Joan Shorenstein Barone Center for Press, Politics and Public Policy, Harvard University, John F. Kennedy School of Government.

Bok, S. (1998). *Mayhem: Violence as public entertainment.* Reading, MA: Addison-Wesley.

Botan, C. (1993). Introduction to the paradigm struggle in public relations. *Public Relations Review, 19*(2), 197–210.

Bowen, S. A. (2004). Expansion of ethics as the tenth generic principle of public relations excellence: A Kantian theory and model for managing ethical issues. *Journal of Mass Media Ethics, 16*(1), 65–92.

Bowen, S. A. (2008). A state of neglect: Public relations as 'corporate conscience' or ethics counsel. *Journal of Public Relations Research, 20*(3), 271–296.

Brill, S. (1999, October). Curiosity vs. privacy. *Brill's Content, 2,* 98–129.

Brinkmann, J. (2002). Business marketing ethics as professional ethics: Concepts, approaches and typologies. *Journal of Business Ethics, 41,* 159–177.

Bruning, F. (1992, May 4). How a private citizen lost his privacy rights. *Maclean's, 105,* 13.

Byrd, J. (1993). *Let's stop abusing the First Amendment*. Ruhl Lecture. Eugene: University of Oregon School of Journalism and Communication.

Carter, S. (1996). *Integrity*. New York: Basic Books (HarperCollins).

Carter, S. (1999). *Civility*. Basic Books (HarperCollins).

Christians, C. G. (2007). Utilitarianism in media ethics and its discontents. *Journal of Mass Media Ethics, 20*(2–3), 113.

Christians, C. G., Rotzoll, K. B., and Fackler, M. (1997). *Media ethics* (5th ed.). New York: Longman.

Christy, T. P. (2006). Females' perceptions of offensive advertising: The importance of values, expectations, and control. *Journal of Current Research in Advertising, 28*(2), 15–32.

Chua-Eoan, H. G. (1992, April 20). The burden of truth. *People Weekly*, 50–51.

Cohen, E. D. (2004). What would Cronkite do? Journalistic virtue, corporate news, and the demise of the fourth estate. In: Three essays on journalism and virtue. *Journal of Mass Media Ethics, 19*(3–4), 266–275.

Cohan, J. A. (2001). Towards a new paradigm in the ethics of women's advertising. *Journal of Business Ethics, 33*, 323–337.

Cooley, T. M. (1888). *A treatise on the law of torts, or the wrongs which arise independent of contract*. Chicago: Callaghan and Company.

Cunningham, S. (1999). Getting it right: Aristotle's 'golden mean' as theory deterioration. *Journal of Mass Media Ethics, 14*(1), 110–112.

Dahl, D. W., Frankenburger, K. D., and Manchanda, R. V. (2003). Does it pay to shock? Reactions to shocking and nonshocking advertising content among university students. *Journal of Advertising Research, 43*, 268–280.

Danner, B. and Kiousis, S. (2006). *Persuasion and ethics in public relations: Towards a taxonomy of means and ends*. Unpublished paper presented at the Association for Education in Journalism and Mass Communication conference, San Francisco, California.

Davis, K. and Blomstrom, R. L. (1975). *Business and society* (3rd ed.). New York: McGraw Hill.

Day, L. (1997). *Ethics in media communications: cases and controversies* (2nd ed.). Belmont, CA: Wadsworth Pubishing Company.

De Nesnera, A. (2002). *Payne Awards nomination letter*. University of Oregon School of Journalism and Communication, Eugene, OR.

Doane, D. (2005, Fall). The myth of CSR: The problem with assuming that companies can do well while also doing good is that markets don't really work that way. *Stanford Social Innovation Review*, 23–28.

Drumwright, M. E. and Murphy, P. E. (2004). How advertising practitioners view ethics: moral muteness, moral myopia, and moral imagination. *Journal of Advertising, 33*(2), 8–24.

Effron, E. (1999, October). Letter from the editor. *Brill's Content, 2*, 7.

Elliot, D. (2007). Getting Mill right. *Journal of Mass Media Ethics, 20*(2–3), 100–112.

Elliott, D. and Culver, C. (1992). Defining and analyzing journalistic deception. *Journal of Mass Media Ethics, 7*(2), 60–84.

Emerson, R. W. (1876, July 18). *Letters and social aims: Progress of culture*. Phi Beta Kappa Address.

Entman, R. (1989). *Democracy without citizens: Media and the decay of American politics*. New York: Oxford University Press.

Feinberg, J. (1984). *Harm to others*. New York: Oxford University Press.

Fitzpatrick, K. and Gauthier, C. (2001). Toward a professional responsibility theory of public relations ethics. *Journal of Mass Media Ethics, 16*(2–3), 194.

Foley, J. P. and Pastore, P. (1998, February 22). *Ethics in advertising*. Vatican City: Pontifical Council for Social Communications.

Foss, S. K. and Griffin, C. L. (1995). Beyond persuasion: A proposal for an invitational rhetoric. *Communication Monographs, 2*, 2–18.

Fox, J. R. (2006). The 'I' of embedded reporting: An analysis of CNN coverage of the 'Shock and Awe' campaign. *Journal of Broadcasting & Electronic Media, 50*(1), 36–51.

Fox, R. W. and Kloppenberg, J. T. (1998). *A companion to American thought*. Oxford: Blackwell Publishers.

Freedman, M. (1988). Social responsibility and compensatory justice. In J. Callahan (ed.), *Ethical issues in professional life* (pp. 349–354). New York: Oxford University Press.

Fritzsche, D. J. (1991). A model of decision-making incorporating ethical values. *Journal of Business Ethics, 10*, 841–852.

Gauthier, C. C. (2002). Privacy invasion by the news media: Three ethical models. *Journal of Mass Media Ethics, 17*(1), 20–34.

Gearhart, S. M. (1979). The womanization of rhetoric. *Women's Studies International Quarterly, 2*, 195–201.

Gersh, D. (1992, April 18). Unclear boundaries: Was it news that former tennis pro Arthur Ashe has AIDS? *Editor and Publisher*, 7–10.

Gert, B. (1988). *Morality: A new justification for the moral rules*. New York: Oxford University Press.

Gibson, K. (2003). Contrasting role morality and professional morality: Implications for practice. *Journal of Applied Philosophy, 20*(1), 17–29.

Gilligan, C. (1982). *In a different voice*. Cambridge, MA: Harvard University Press.

Gower, K. K. (2008). *Legal and ethical considerations for public relations* (2nd ed.). Long Grove, IL: Waveland Press.

Grunig, J. E. (2000). Collectivism, collaboration and societal corporatism as core professional values of public relations. *Journal of Public Relations Research, 12*(1), 23–48.

Grunig, J. and Hunt, T. (1984). *Managing public relations*. New York: Holt, Rinehart, and Winston.

Grunig, L. A., Grunig, J. E., and Dozier, D. M. (2002). *Excellent public relations and effective organizations: A study of communication management in three countries*. Mahwah, NJ: Lawrence Erlbaum.

Hackley, C. E. and Kitchen, P. J. (1999). Ethical perspectives on the postmodern communications Leviathan. *Journal of Business Ethics, 20*(1), 15–26.

Hampton, J. (1997). *Political philosophy*. New York: Westview Press.

Hargreaves, D. (2002). Adolescent body image suffers from media images of the impossibly thin. *Flinders University Journal, 13*(9), 10–23.

Hayes, A. S., Singer, J. B., and Ceppos, J. (2007). Shifting roles, enduring values: The credible journalist in a digital age. *Journal of Mass Media Ethics, 22*(4), 262–279.

Hodges, L. (1994). The journalist and privacy. *Journal of Mass Media Ethics, 9*(4), 197–212.

Iedema, R., Feez, S., and White, P. (1994). Appraisal and journalistic discourse. In *Media literacy*. Sydney: Disadvantaged Schools Program, New South Wales Department of School Education. Excerpted at http://www.grammatics.com/Appraisal/.

Jefferson, T. (1823). *Letter to M. Corey*. Archived at Monticello: Jefferson Digital Archive. http://etext.virginia.edu/jefferson/.

Jensen, J. V. (1981). Argumentation: Reasoning in communication. New York: Van Nostrand.

Johannesen, R. L. (1989). What should we teach about formal codes of communication ethics. Journal of Mass Media Ethics, 3(1), 59–64.

Johannesen, R. L. (2002). Ethics in human communication (5th ed.). Prospect Heights, IL: Waveland Press.

Kaikati, A. M. and Kaikati, J. (2004). Stealth marketing: How to reach consumers surreptitiously. California Management Review, 46(4), 6–22

Kang, S. and Norton, H. E. (2004). Nonprofit organizations' use of the World Wide Web: Are they sufficiently fulfilling organizational goals? Public Relations Review, 30, 279–284.

Kennedy, G. A. (1991). Aristotle on rhetoric: A theory of civic discourse. New York: Oxford University Press.

Kilbourne, J. (1990). Beauty . . . and the beast of advertising. Media & Value, 49, http://www.medialit.org/reading_room/article40.html.

Klaidman, S. and Beauchamp, T. (1987). The virtuous journalist. Oxford: Oxford University Press.

Kovach, B. and Rosenstiel, T. (2001). The elements of journalism. New York: Three Rivers Press.

Kuhn, M. (2007). Interactivity and prioritizing the human: A code of blogging ethics. Journal of Mass Media Ethics, 22(1), 34.

Kultgen, J. (1988). Ethics and professionalism. Philadelphia: University of Pennsylvania Press.

Lasch, C. (1990). Publicity and the lost art of argument. Gannett Center Journal, 4(2), 1–11.

Lasch, C. (1995). The revolt of the elites: And the betrayal of democracy. New York: W. W. Norton & Company.

Lebacqz, K. (1985). Professional ethics: Power and paradox. Nashville, TN: Abington.

Lippmann, W. (1919). Liberty and the news. New York: Atlantic Monthly.

Lippmann, W. (1922). Public opinion. New York: Harcourt, Brace and Company.

MacIntyre, A. (1984). After virtue (2nd ed.). Notre Dame, IN: University of Notre Dame Press.

Manning, R. C. (1992). Speaking from the heart: A feminist perspective on ethics. Lanham, MD: Rowman & Littlefield.

McMannus, J. (2002). Does Wall Street have to trump Main Street? http://www.gradethenews.org.

Merrill, J. C. (1997). Journalism ethics: Philosophical foundations for news media. New York: St. Martin's Press.

Meyer, P. (1987). Ethical journalism. New York: Longman.

Midgley, M. (1991). Can't we make moral judgments? Bristol: Bristol Press.

Midgley, M. (1994). The ethical primate: Humans, freedom and morality. London: Routledge.

Midgley, M. (1995). Beast and man: The roots of human natures. London: Routledge.

Mill, J. S. (1991). On liberty. In J. Gray (ed.), On liberty and other essays. New York: Oxford University Press.

Morrow, L. (1992, April 20). Fair game? Time, 139, 74.

Overbeck, W. (1981). Unmuzzling America's corporations: Corporate speech and the First Amendment. Paper presented at the Annual Meeting of the Association for Education in Journalism, East Lansing, Michigan, August 8–11, 1981.

Pearson, R. L. (1989). Business ethics as communication ethics: Public relations practice and the idea of dialogue. In C. Botan and V. Hazleton (eds.), *Public relations theory*. Hillsdale, NJ: Lawrence Erlbaum.

Pearson, R. (1989). Beyond ethical relativism in public relations: Coordination, roles and the idea of communication symmetry. *Public Relations Research Annual*, 1, 67–86.

Perloff, R. M. *The dynamics of persuasion: Communication and attitudes in the 21st century* (2nd ed.). Mahwah, NJ: Lawrence Erlbaum Associates.

Phelan, J. M. (1995). Advertising and commercial rhetoric. In, Paul A. B. Clarke and Andrew Linzey (eds.), *Dictionary of Theology and Society*. London: Routledge.

Plaisance, P. L. (2007). Transparency: An assessment of the Kantian roots of a key element in media ethics practice. *Journal of Mass Media Ethics*, 22(2–3), 187–207.

Postman, N. (1992). *Technopoly: The surrender of culture to technology*. New York: Alfred K. Knopf.

Preston, I. L. (1996). *The great American blow-up: Puffery in advertising and selling*. Madison: University of Wisconsin Press.

Price, M. (1998, November). Out there: Hardball with a heart. *Brill's Content*, 1, 83–85.

Rachels, J. (1993). *The elements of moral philosophy*. New York: McGraw Hill.

Rago, R. (1989). Finding the magic: Cognitive aspects of mood and emotion in advertising. *Review of Business*, 11, 9–10.

Ridley, M. (1998). *The origins of virtue*. New York: Penguin Books.

Ries, A. and Ries, L. (2004). *The fall of advertising and the rise of PR*. New York: HarperCollins.

Rosemont, H. J. *Whose democracy? Which rights?: A Confucian critique of modern western liberalism*. Unpublished paper, St. Mary's College of Maryland.

Rosen, J. (1993). Beyond objectivity. *Nieman Reports*, December 22, 1993, Harvard University, Nieman Foundation.

Rosen, J. (2000). *The unwanted gaze: The destruction of privacy in America*. New York: Random House.

Ross, W. D. (1930). *The right and the good*. Oxford: Calrendon Press.

Rowse, A. E. (1992, September 1). How to build support for a war. *Columbia Journalism Review*, 31(23), 28–29.

Ruggiero, V. R. (1973). *The moral imperative*. Port Washington, NY: Alfred Publishers.

Ruggiero, V. R. (1975). *Beyond feelings: A guide to critical thinking*. Port Washington, NY: Alfred Publishing Company.

Saltzman, J. (1997). A chill settles over investigative journalism: Food Lion markets' victory over ABC News. *USA Today (magazine)*, 125, 29.

Sandel, M. (1982). *Liberalism and the limits of justice*. Cambridge: Cambridge University Press.

Sandel, M. (1996). *Democracy's discontent: America in search of a public philosophy*. Cambridge, MA: Belknap Press of Harvard University Press.

Scanlon, T. M. (1998). *What we owe each other*. Cambridge, MA: Belknap Press of Harvard University Press.

Sheehan, K. B. (2003). *Controversies in contemporary advertising*. Thousand Oaks, CA: Sage Publications.

Schudson, M. (2001). The objectivity norm in American journalism. *Journalism*, 2(2), 149–170.

Simon, W. H. (1978). The ideology of advocacy: Procedural justice and professional ethics. *Wisconsin Law Review*, 1, 29–144.

Smith, H. (1994). *World's religions: A guide to our wisdom traditions*. San Francisco: Harper.

Sproule, J. M. (1980). *Argument: Language and its influence*. New York: McGraw-Hill.

Steiner, L. (1989). Feminist theorizing and communication ethics. *Communication Monographs, 12*, 157–173.

Stone, I. F. (1988). *The trial of Socrates*. Boston: Little Brown & Company.

Sullivan, R. J. (1994). *An introduction to Kant's ethics*. Cambridge: Cambridge University Press.

Sprague, R. (2007) Business blogs and commercial speech: A new analytical framework for the 21st century. *American Business Law Journal, 44*(1), 127–159.

Tronto, J. (1993). *Moral boundaries*. New York: Routledge.

Upshaw, J., Chernov, G., and Koranda, D. (2007). Telling more than news: Commercial influence in local television stations. *Electronic News Journal, 1*(2), 67–87.

Wagner, D. (1997). Making news, breaking ethics. *Insight on the News, 13*(10), 10.

Waller, David S. (1999). Attitudes towards offensive advertising: An Australian study. *Journal of Consumer Marketing, 16*(3), 288–302.

Waller, D. S. (2004). *What factors make controversial advertising offensive?: A preliminary study*. Australian New Zealand American Studies Association Conference, Sydney, Australia.

Ward, S. J. (2004). *The invention of journalism ethics: The path to objectivity and beyond*. Montreal: McGill-Queen's University Press.

Warren, S. D. and Brandeis, L. D. (1890). The right to privacy. *Harvard Law Review, 4*, 193–220.

Wheeler, T. (2002). *Phototruth or photofiction: Ethics and media imagery in the digital age*. Mahwah, NJ: Lawrence Erlbaum.

Wheeler, T. and Gleason, T. (1994, August). *Digital photography and the ethics of photofiction: Four tests for assessing the reader's qualified expectation of reality*. Paper presented at the Association for Education in Journalism and Mass Communication, Atlanta, GA.

Wilkes, R. E. and Valencia, H. (1989). Hispanics and blacks in television commercials. *Journal of Advertising, 18*(1), 36–41.

Wilson, J. Q. (1993). *The moral sense*. New York: Free Press.

Wood, J. T. (1994). *Who cares? Women, care, and culture*. Carbondale, IL: Southern Illinois University Press.

Wrighter, C. P. (1972). *I can sell you anything*. New York: Ballantine Books.

Index